For

Fola and George

my dearly beloved,

brethren in-and-out-of

Cooperation

H. M. Kallen

3 November 1936

THE DECLINE AND RISE OF THE CONSUMER

By H. M. KALLEN

PHILOSOPHY

WILLIAM JAMES AND HENRI BERGSON
CREATIVE INTELLIGENCE (WITH JOHN DEWEY AND OTHERS)
WHY RELIGION
INDECENCY AND THE SEVEN ARTS
CULTURE AND DEMOCRACY IN THE UNITED STATES
EDUCATION, THE MACHINE AND THE WORKER
INDIVIDUALISM, AN AMERICAN WAY OF LIFE
A FREE SOCIETY

BELLES LETTRES

THE BOOK OF JOB AS A GREEK TRAGEDY

POLITICAL AND SOCIAL PHILOSOPHY

THE DECLINE AND RISE OF THE CONSUMER
THE STRUCTURE OF LASTING PEACE
THE LEAGUE OF NATIONS TODAY AND TOMORROW
ZIONISM AND WORLD POLITICS
FRONTIERS OF HOPE
JUDAISM AT BAY

PAMPHLETS

COLLEGE PROLONGS INFANCY
EDUCATION VERSUS INDOCTRINATION IN THE SCHOOL

EDITOR

SOME PROBLEMS OF PHILOSOPHY (BY WILLIAM JAMES)
PLURIVERSE (BY BENJAMIN PAUL BLOOD)
FREEDOM IN THE MODERN WORLD
THE PHILOSOPHY OF WILLIAM JAMES (DRAWN FROM HIS OWN WORKS)
AMERICAN PHILOSOPHY TODAY AND TOMORROW (WITH SIDNEY HOOK)

THE DECLINE AND RISE OF THE CONSUMER

A PHILOSOPHY OF CONSUMER COÖPERATION

BY

HORACE M. KALLEN

Author of "Individualism, an American Way of Life," "A Free Society," "Culture and Democracy in the United States," etc.

D. APPLETON-CENTURY COMPANY
INCORPORATED
NEW YORK 1936 LONDON

PRINTED IN THE UNITED STATES OF AMERICA

TO

RACHEL

HARRIET

AND

DAVID

PREFACE

SHORTLY after I published *A Free Society,* the Editor of the *Christian Century,* Mr. Charles Clayton Morrison, invited me to discuss consumer coöperation in that bravest and most forthright of religious periodicals. "What is needed," he wrote, "is that consumer collectivism should get itself stated in terms of a fundamental philosophy. . . . Your distinction between consumer and producer, which derives from the fact that consumption is a natural function involving values and ends, whereas production is an acquired function derived from necessity . . . together with your proposal to organize this consumption function into the structure of the social order . . . will come nearer to satisfying the religious mind, which is seeking social expression, than the orthodox socialistic conception."

Out of the articles composed for the *Christian Century* grew this survey of the principles and practice of consumer coöperation and exposition of the philosophy of life which underlies them, nurtured by the interest of Mr. Morrison and the urging of Mr. E. R. Bowen, Secretary of the Coöperative League of the United States of America.

Fundamentally, the philosophy is as simple and obvious as Columbus' egg, and as surprising.

Its point of departure is the fact that first and last human beings are not employers and employees, capitalists and laborers, carpenters or clerks or undertakers or farmers or physicians or miners or machinists, but human beings, simply living men of flesh and blood. As living men of flesh and blood we are organic individuals; we are persons. In our feeling of ourselves, in our living, we do not split off into vocations or professions. We do not define ourselves by special functions or by this or that separate and distinct set of social or institutional relationships, each tending to overrule and exclude the others. To one neighbor we may count as carpenter, to another as patient, to another as customer, to another as Elk, to another as Christian, to another as husband and father, or son and brother, and so on, indefinitely. Husband, father, son, brother, Christian, carpenter, patient, customer, Elk—these are different and often conflicting ways of associating the same individuals. They are many, he is one. They are relations his personality takes on or drops; they do not define it and they cannot exhaust it. It coincides with them all and exceeds them all. It is numerically quite another thing than their sum and qualitatively quite different from their mutual compenetration. To any person himself, he is the center in which these associations meet and through which they pass—uniquely one, and not by him to be mistaken for any other one in the universe.

The idea of this self-feeling of all persons is implicit in the concept of democracy and in the gospels of religion. The democratic rule that all men are equal is sometimes confused with the quite opposite idea that all men are the same and that any man can be substituted for any other so that his differences make no difference. The two are not at all the same. The democratic rule that all men are equal means that men's being different cannot be made a basis for special privilege or for the invidious advantage of one man over another; equality, under the democratic rule, is the freedom and opportunity of each individual to be fully and completely his different self. Democracy means the right to be different. The gospels of religion propound the same notion when they say that all men are equal before God and that salvation is open to all alike. The discoveries of science confirm the positions of democracy and religion. To the Nature which the scientist studies, each of her multitudinous components, as it is in itself, apart from everything else, endeavors on its own power to sustain its identity, to live and to grow. If it perishes it is not because Nature has taken sides against it; if it survives it is not because Nature has preferred and chosen it. Each succeeds or fails in its own right and by its own energies. Its world was not made for it; but yet is made by it, as its activities combine or conflict with the activities of other beings, that environ it.

And so it is with man in Nature. His existence and his action are one. But civilization turns chance association into permanent division. It develops institution and status. It distinguishes men not in themselves but by their associative relationships: it establishes them, apparently forever, as patrician and plebeian, lord and serf, priest and layman, soldier, artizan or merchant, and so on, endlessly. To these apparently permanent associative divisions, these classes, an indefinite number of transitory ones get added. All the while, the living man of flesh and blood identifies himself now with this or separates himself now from that. Each is appropriated or alienated by the passion that rules him, and his selfhood remains at once the center in which they meet and the point through which they only pass.

The real division of labor, which is one of the pillars of the industrial economy, has become tantamount to a false division of men, distinguishing them from one another by their vocations rather than their persons, splitting the persons into producers and consumers and giving primacy to the producers. This schizophrenia of the industrial economy dominates our world. Alike the masters and the servants conduct their lives in its shadow. They affirm and impose the dogma of the primacy of the producer. The masters employ this dogma to rationalize their supremacy, to justify their rule and advantage. The servants employ it to rationalize their rebellion, to justify their claims, their defiance and their sabotage. From the image of man as intrinsically producer flow streams of consequences among which the chief have been the imposition of a servile conception of human nature, the reduction of human values to labor energies, and the persistent effort to make and to keep consumption a tool of production.

Yet there is no science of man but reveals or implies that this effort is based on a myth. We are consumers by nature and producers by necessity. We are born consumers, and remain consumers all our lives. But we are not born producers. We become producers under coercion, contingently, and we stay producers also under coercion, in response to the police-power in the hands of our "betters"; we are compelled to live to work instead of living to live. And the secret hope of all of us is that we may, by living to work today, be enabled to live without working tomorrow. That is, the intrinsic or natural end of life is not labor but leisure; its intrinsic values are not instrumental but consummatory; human nature is freely, spontaneously, itself when it is engaged in consumption: in not only using, but in using up, in consuming, its materials and energies via activities which, regarded as means or instruments, have themselves as ends; regarded as ends or goals, have themselves as means. We can not, for example, live to eat without eating to live. If we pursue any of the liberal arts or the learned professions such as literature, or the law, the stage or the church, the army or the government, a science, a fine art, or music, in it we do not merely earn our livelihood but live our life. These arts and professions are as sport and play; in them labor is indistinguishable from leisure, life from a living; they are means to themselves as ends, and we do not call those who take them as their life-work laborers or working-men. We call them artists, scholars, sportsmen, gentlemen. We reserve the other classification for the great multitudes of men and women to whom earning their livings and living their lives are two disparate and contrasted activities, who are compelled to accept the living of their lives as secondary and incidental to the earning of their livings, although what they work at is to them sheerly a means, employed with hardship and pain, to ends they do not share in and usually are not aware of. The activities of these multitudes are what we mean by labor; they are servile, not free; unpleasant, not pleasurable; means to alien ends, not their own ends.

To vindicate the primacy of the consumers they are at heart, to liberate themselves from the yoke of their necessity, has been, as recorded history shows, automatically the unconscious but ineluctable desire and effort of the multitudes. Consumers by birth and nature and producers by nurture and untoward necessity, they have striven blindly but unremittingly to win back the natural freedom of their nativity. The sects and churches of religion, the parties and wars of government, the fantazies of letters and the arts—all the great movements and mutations which history records—may be regarded as moments of this striving. As I read the record, its resolution begins—so far as anything can ever come to resolution, short of death, in this world of ours—at the point where, at last, men hit upon, in some ways as unaware of the import of their discovery as

Columbus, a method by which the primacy of the consumer and the rule of the consumer function may be so built into any people's economy as ultimately to characterize it, and to replace servility with freedom. This is the method of consumer coöperation developed in Rochdale, England, in 1844.

The birth, the fortunes and the meaning of this coöperation of men as consumers in a world where production is master are the theme of this book. It begins by surveying the changes in the consumer-producer relation from primitive man to the days of early capitalism; taking note in passing, of the rôle of the female as producer and the male as consumer; of the master-slave relation in antiquity, of what influence Christianity exercised on this relation; how it was changed and accented in the economy of monastery and manor, and how this feudal economy of scarcity was replaced by the early capitalist economy of abundance.

That economy, consisting in a redirection of the minds and energies of men to the materials of nature and their reshaping to human desire, set free our abilities and shifted the meaning of abundance from an increase in the quantity only of one thing to an increase also in quality and variety. But it suffered perversion before it could get well started. The very existence of plenty made it possible to deal with the consumer not as living man of flesh and blood, but as an abstract impersonal profit-provider for the producer; to impose the producer as ideal and to turn consumption into a servant of production. With the formation of the image of the producer as the ideal of human excellence, even the rebellion of our intrinsic consummatory nature came to be formulated in producer terms. These terms govern the prevailing programs for "industrial democracy," from the trades-union, or the "self-governing workshop" to the "classless society." The ideal of the natural man with his natural rights was abandoned for the idol of the economic man with his economic pretensions. Human beings were classified as capitalists and proletarians; labor was lifted up from a menial necessity into a free man's dignity, made into a "right" as well as an obligation, and its inherent indignities and unrighteousness and servility were attributed to the exploitations automatically resulting from the institutions of private property, the profit motive, and inherent in the price system.

But these institutions, declared to be the differentiæ of capitalism, turn out, on examination, to be far from engines of malice invented for the purpose by greedy sadists eager to exploit their fellows. They are ways of thinking and working which express drives intrinsic in our nature and whose first intention is consummatory. Economic reformers can change their incidence and employment and call them by other names. But they cannot eliminate them and pretend to maintain the economy of abundance of which they are the ground. It is their perversion and abuse, not their existence which does violence to the consumer in us, and the organization of the consumer and the establishment of his primacy must rest on them.

The record shows that this organization to be successful must be autonomous and inward. The consumer has received little protection or help from government with its pure food and drug laws, its blue sky laws, its inspections and policings; services of private institutes to examine and report on consumer goods have resembled the endeavor to bail out the sea with a pail. Consumer emulation of the collective bargaining of trades-unions has been abortive. All these efforts are based on accepting, without endeavoring to alter, the conditions and mentality of a producer's world. The effective enterprise, establishing the working-man as a free man and a consumer in personal thought and action and in economic organization and philosophy, has been on a record of fifty years, the consumer's coöperative movement which began with twenty-eight men in Rochdale and now counts twenty-eight millions all over the world.

This movement too, had to shed the skin of the producer way of thinking and feeling and doing; had to find its own different philosophy of value and program of life. Growing slowly and without ballyhoo, it has become a molding, shaping force of contemporary society. It embodies more nearly than anything else, the economic pattern of that "American dream" which the Declaration of Independence defines and which American history has been a struggle to make real. Its principles and method would keep money and credit the servants and not the masters of men. By recognizing and reverencing the personality of the laborer they transmute the idea of the dignity and inward worth of labor from a slogan of rebellion and a war-cry into a positive reordering of employer-employee relationship. For the same reason they make it possible to break down in education the invidious distinctions between vocation and culture, labor and leisure, work and life. They make possible an education which can reintegrate the split personality of industrial society and maintain this unity as a way of life.

Today's chief rivals of the consumer economy—Communism, Fascism, Nazism—exclude all this; they nullify human individuality and compel people to subject their lives to the hope of a false security in the place of the half-freedoms of producer-capitalism and the true freedom of consumer coöperation, which is but the economic organization of liberty.

Such is the argument of this book. Its method has been determined by its material. In this the dynamic agents have been and are persons, ideas, institutions and movements sometimes blocking and frustrating, sometimes strengthening, sometimes distracting one another; weakening certain traits, enhancing others, manifesting new and unexpected ones that shape and change old forms into novel and surprising patterns with their own lasting quality and goal. The record of this ever creative ferment is to be found in the life-stories of personalities, in official reports of institutions, in periodical literature, in books, in the memories of living men and women who have shared in or witnessed the formation and growth of the new pattern; and finally, in the existing structures and organizations themselves as going concerns, the British being the oldest and most powerful.

Upon all those I have drawn for the making of this book. I have interviewed whom I could; those with whom I could not speak directly I have addressed by letters, and I have consulted as many of the earlier studies of the coöperative movement as I could lay my hands on.

Living with the material so assembled for a long time, I have found it to fall into a pattern with certain accents and rhythms; a flow of events some fruitful, some barren; some definitive, some confusing; some blind, some directive; but all entering into and composing the evolving pattern of the consumer economy. I have endeavored to present this pattern as clearly and distinctly as I am able.

It remains to make especial acknowledgment of the help I have had not only from many books, periodicals and documents, but from experts in the field and from coöperative and trades-union officials both at home and abroad, especially in England, Denmark, Sweden, Finland and Russia. To these, among whom I count especially, Mr. Louis Blachly, of Consumers' Coöperative Services; Mr. Howard A. Cowden, President of Consumers Coöperative Association, North Kansas City, Missouri; Mr. Hyman Cohn, pioneer of the coöperative movement in New York City; Miss Gladys Dickason, Director of the Research Department of the Amalgamated Clothing Workers of America; Miss Margaret Digby of the Horace Plunkett Foundation in London, England; Mr. E. J. Lever of Coöperative Distributors, Incorporated; Professor Karl Llewellyn of the Law School of Columbia University; Mrs. Julia N. Perkins, Financial Secretary of the Coöperative League of the United States of America; Mr. J. J. Schalet of the United States Department of Agriculture; Dr. James P. Warbasse, President of the Coöperative League of the United States of America, my best thanks. If I mention certain of them by name, it is not because I have profited any less from the information and judgment of the others, but because my communications with those named have been nearer and more direct, because my feeling of dependence on their instruction and advice has been more intimate and personal.

For help with the manuscript I am indebted to Robert O. Ballou, publisher, author and critic; and especially to Gladys Dickason; and Elsie Glück, Director of Education for the New York Women's Trade Union League; to Constance Stungo, my secretary; to Dr. Warbasse; to the excellent novelist, Leane Zugsmith. For their alert and careful reading of the script, their acute criticisms and wise suggestions I owe them thanks I hardly have words to express.

HORACE M. KALLEN

CONTENTS

BOOK I
THE PRODUCER'S WORLD

CHAPTER I
CAPITALISM AS THE ECONOMY OF ABUNDANCE

CHAPTER II
THE PERVERSION OF CAPITALISM

CHAPTER III

PROPERTY, PROFIT, THE PRICE SYSTEM AND THE PRIMACY OF THE CONSUMER

CHAPTER IV

PRODUCER CONFLICT IN THE PRODUCER WORLD

CHAPTER V

CONSUMER DEFENSE IN THE PRODUCER WORLD

BOOK II

THE ECONOMICS OF FREEDOM

CHAPTER VI

THE CONSUMER EMERGES, I

CHAPTER VII

THE CONSUMER EMERGES, II

CHAPTER VIII

THE CONSUMER IN AMERICA: I, THE FARMER

CHAPTER IX

THE CONSUMER IN AMERICA: II, THE INDUSTRIAL WORKER

CHAPTER X

THE CONSUMER IN AMERICA: III, COÖPERATION IN THE DEPRESSION

BOOK III

THE CONSUMER'S FUTURE

CHAPTER XI

MONEY, CREDIT, AND THE CONSUMER

CHAPTER XII

THE ORGANIZED CONSUMER AS EMPLOYER

CHAPTER XIII

EDUCATION IN THE COOPERATIVE MOVEMENT

CHAPTER XIV

THE CONSUMER ECONOMY AND ITS RIVALS

THE DECLINE AND RISE OF THE CONSUMER

THE DECLINE AND RISE OF THE CONSUMER

PROLOGUE

HUMAN IDEALS AND HUMAN DESTINY

MAN of the machine age is inclined to disbelieve that ideals can be forces in men's lives, that they can affect character or guide destiny. He has learned from the sciences to think in matter, and to treat the conduct of men as an illustration of the behavior of matter. If he is of the sect of Karl Marx he believes that this matter follows dialectic laws; if his faith rests upon the works and ways of the natural sciences, he holds matter to be governed by mechanical principles.

But whether he be a naturalistic or a Marxian materialist, he identifies material causes with economic motives and assigns every aspect of man's struggle to live to a central greed, a pecuniary hunger and thirst. He regards humanity as made up of "economic men." He accounts for all behavior as economic behavior. He talks assuredly about "historical materialism" and "the economic interpretation of history." With Marx he declares, "the mode of production conditions the social, political, and spiritual life process." With Veblen he ascribes the qualities of men to "the state of the industrial arts." He magnifies production. He ignores and suppresses the living fact that human beings desire to love and hate and fight and think and play at least no less than they desire to eat and drink and work and save. He defines and interprets their paramount interest as production, and their rôles as employers and employees, intent upon the everlasting making and selling and making of products. Ideals, like everything else which is not production, tend, consequently, to figure in his mind as no more than parasites upon production, flourishing as it prospers and failing as it fails, and impotent to alter it whether for good or ill.

But students of the life-history of ideals know that the dogma of the impotency of ideals is itself an ideal which influences the conduct of those who profess it. Such students know that the definition of men as producers, as "capital" and "labor," employer and employee, are to the people so defined what parts in a play are to players—rôles to enact, alternatives to other rôles in which men and women might play out their lives. Such students know that the definition does not describe men as they are, in their feeling and doing; that it only adds to the figures of life already existing one more standard or pattern for men to live up to.

The existence, the influence and the value of these figures make the fundamental distinction between our human nature and its animal or material ground. All of us, even Marxists and scientific materialists, live out our lives in these two dimensions, one animal, the other human. As animals, we follow a more or less predetermined course. We are born, we grow up, we grow old, we die. Eating, drinking, lusting, the animal generations repeat each other with hardly more variation than the phases of the moon or the cycles of the seasons. Alike they live, alike they die, and the worm covereth them. As humans, on the other hand, our lives are history; they diversify; their courses pursue no foregone conclusion. As humans we do not repeat a past, we differentiate a future; what we become is far more important than what we are born as.

Now the shape of what we seek to become is prefigured by our ideals. So far as a future can be envisioned, ideals are its envisioning. As a man, no individual merely is; he is always changing, always struggling against weakening and diminution, and toward fulfilment and abundance. The form he gives to this fulfilment and abundance is his ideal. As a rule, his life's efforts are not directed to one such form only. In the course of a lifetime, he pursues many, now this one and now that, and sometimes two or more antagonistic ones simultaneously. His animal nature does not predispose him to any particular ideal. He finds many in the fabric of the society into which he is born; images of action and passion which invest his animal energies, give them direction and shape and thus humanize his animality.

At different phases of a man's life-cycle, this process is called by different names. In infant and child it is "play." In all play there is a component of make-believe, of simulation and pretence. The player assumes a rôle he does not live; his playmates and playthings receive characteristics they do not have. Men and things are for the moment deprived of the qualities they possess and endowed with qualities they do not possess. The qualities of which they are deprived are those which obstruct or suppress or irk or hurt the individual, though others may find them good; the qualities with which they are endowed are those which liberate, interest, gratify and fulfil the individual, though others may find them bad. The terms and forms of the make-believe are based upon that in the environment which has been heard of or felt or seen as powerful and free and desirable. For small children, the models are adults. They play at being mothers and fathers, and treat their dolls as their parents treat themselves; they play at being firemen, policemen, teachers, Indians, pirates, fighters, robbers, soldiers, aviators, inventors, kings, explorers and other embodiments of force and freedom they encounter as powers over the day's routine or as figures in tales they hear or read. From these themes of the heart's desire the child-mind draws, as it grows older, the stuff which it shapes unconsciously into the image of its own personality as it desires this to be. Its play consists of the endeavor to incarnate this image in its person, its dress, its speech, its posture and its behavior. The image is its ideal; its play, the effort to realize the ideal.

The process repeats itself in the different setting of school and college. The figures of force and freedom are now made of a different stuff, provided by the school and college scene, of the stuff of "the undergraduate tradition" with its ordinances of dress, manners, ceremonials, obligations to rivalry or service which, enacted in a boy's person, make up the "typical" Groton or Harrow lad, the "typical" Princeton or Oxford man. Apart from the disagreeable realities of the classroom, school and college "life" are in essence a continuation of the play of childhood, the enactment of a rôle assumed consciously, perhaps, and often under felt coercion. The model for imitation is compounded of the traditional and current school heroes; to conform to it may be a schoolboy's necessity no less than desire. Playing out that rôle, realizing that ideal, however unsuccessfully, may be the price of freedom and fulfilment rather than their attainment. In the vacation, away from school, the youth drops the rôle of schoolboy or college man and becomes once more a spontaneous human being.

Should he long continue in the scene calling for his rôle, what begins as simulative play becomes personal habit and acquired character, as sometimes happens in actors who have long played a single rôle. When the rôle is uncongenial to their temperaments and ways, it works on them distortingly. Their behavior suggests an inner conflict, an artificiality, and we call it "mannered." This happens even when an actor is a master of his craft. Directors, therefore, in casting parts, incline to seek "types," that is, not excellent mimes but persons who naturally "fit" the part and in acting, play themselves rather than a rôle.

But types of the stage are not chosen primarily because of their social or human qualities, but because of their animal traits. They are "constitutional types," tall or short, fat or thin, with posture, temperaments, rhythm of speech and disposition corresponding. They may play indifferently doctor, lawyer or Indian chief, rich man, poor man, beggar man, thief. These social rôles men are not born to, they do not depend upon a native bent or inward preference; men fall into them as they find their way in a crowded street. They are the paths open and easiest to follow at the moment. Imitation, rivalry, opportunity, accident, or the pressure of family and community all share in the definition and selection of a life goal to be attained as a career or vocation. The specific form of this goal, the personality-image, is compounded of many items both material and psychological. Perhaps the most important, because the most subtle and pervasive, is the bent and rhythm of the age—its dominant pattern, its activity, direction and interest. Those are chiefly projected and communicated by its "spiritual" implements—the press, the stage, the novel, the church, the school, the graphic and plastic arts. They compound, out of images and words, a psychological type, an ideal personality which variously reproduces, idealizes and represents the characters who achieve and embody force and freedom in the social life of the age, the age's dominant personalities, its known actual or alleged masters. To be as one of those, to equal them, to beat them down and surpass them, becomes the secret dream in every man's heart: *aut Caesar aut divus.* From them he derives the basic anatomy of the personality-image which he identifies with his own selfhood and which his biography becomes a struggle to embody and enact. Although we no longer call his effort *play*—the name it now goes by is *ambition*—it remains the playing of a rôle which gives a figure and a name to a self that no man ever fully is but is always striving to become. This self is his own definition of his destiny, his inwardly chosen line and form of growth and program of action—his ideal. Consciously or unconsciously, it is his actual soul, the theme song of his life, whose execution and fulfilment in and through his body is his deepest concern. His biography with all it contains of frustration and failure, inadequacy and incoherence and defeat, draws whatever unity and singleness it can have from the constancy of this personality-image, this ideal of himself.

As its route is to an airplane or its course to a ship, so this image is to the man living his life. It is nourished, of course, upon the *Zeitgeist,* upon the particular tempo and temper, the specific moral atmosphere and æsthetic tone in which it lives and moves and has its being. It assimilates from and is assimilated to the temper, the spirit, the tempo of its age. A child's growth into humanity consists largely in his assimilation into his physical traits and psychological personality of the ways of being and doing constituting the *Zeitgeist.* It begins as an imitation of others and ends as a personal habit, so that he eats and drinks and talks and sleeps and loves and fights, he lives his whole life, according to patterns which item for item and whole for whole he might replace by others in other places, at other times, and even in his own place and time. The more "civilized" his bringing up, the less the natural environment affects him and the more sensitive he is to the nuances of images and patterns in the man-made world. These are the shaping forces of his personality, these mold him, these free him, these educate him. They compose dramatic models of the "success" he desires to impersonate and repeat in his own life. Chosen because they appear at the time the most vivid, the most potent and alluring, of the forms in which men find power, freedom and fulfilment, they yet cannot help—originating as they do—being abstract and vague. For they are only selections from the multitude of images actual and potential, any of which might be established as a dominant ideal; they strip their contexts away and offer themselves as the true and clear and distinct configuration of the good life for the man of the age. The generations see in these images the current answers to the questions: *What is man? What is his destiny?* But they also see that each answer has its alternatives and that neither any one of them nor all together completely define and exhaust the nature of man. If not in fact, then in fantasy, a personality coincides with them all and exceeds them all.

Hence, that any are current and prevail must not be taken to mean that their competitors are destroyed and their rivals exterminated. On the contrary, the older a civilization is, the longer its recorded history and social memory, the more likely are alternatives to survive from the past and variants to develop in the present. Rivals and competitors have simply been overruled, suppressed and forced into the underground of the social mind; variants have simply not yet found their place in the sun of social preference and personal simulation.

They do not stay overruled and suppressed. The ruling "type" continuously defends its rule by all forms of doctrine and discipline, force and persuasion. Social life is impatterned in a warfare of moral ideals, each embodied in a characteristic symbol, a composite personality-image, drawn from living persons, which churches, schools, the press, the pictures and the police are conscribed to safeguard.

Such an image was the ascetic saint of the church, nourishing his immortal soul upon the mortification of his mortal body; the knight of chivalry, *sans peur et sans reproche;* the renaissance gentleman, as apt at loving as fighting, at learning as loving; the eighteenth-century wit, with his formal suave grace, his spacious reason and hard commonsense; the nineteenth century romantic, imaged in the living Byron and imaginary Faust; and the Victorian "economic man." Each of these expressions stands for a complex of sentiments, dispositions, ideas and behavior combined into a typical figure—which serves as the counterfeit presentment of the villain or hero or both of the current drama of life. Each is a frame of reference for all the persons and all the personality-images of the age it dominates, a projection of the heart's hopes and the heart's fears, the leading rôle of man the histrion. Each is an ideal derived from many originals: new inventions, cultural survivals, present fashions, and above all actual figures of force and freedom. But none can be described as a consequence merely of "the method of production" or "the state of the industrial arts." Each is compatible with either a low or a developed state of these arts, a personal or mechanical method of production. The methods of production and the state of the industrial arts, at whatever level of modern history, can maintain what is essential in any and all of these personality-images—the force, the freedom or both. The Victorian "economic man" can arrange to live like a church ascetic, the twentieth century efficiency engineer like a renaissance gentleman. The personality-images enchannel and give form to the energies of aspiration; if they depend on the industrial arts they depend on them as a lily on its soil, as consummations depend on instrumentalities. The industrial arts are not of themselves answers to the questions *What is man? What is his destiny?* The personality-images are.

During the past hundred years and longer, one image has come to overrule all others depicting man and his destiny. This is the figure of "the economic man," man as a producer of goods to sell. He is defined and approved in Hogarth's cartoons of the "Good and Idle Apprentice"; in the works of Samuel Smiles and Oliver Optic, and in the great procession of plastic and graphic and literary works, from *John Halifax, Gentleman* to the last success story in a popular magazine. He is the orthodox theme of the new "science" of political economy, from Adam Smith to the latest statistician. He is also the figure of rebellion imagined in this "science," from Karl Marx to the last hatched fledgling of literary communism by whom "worker" is used with the same unction as his opponents say "manufacturer," "banker" or "gentleman." His attributes have been elevated to the paramount moral qualities of the age; and "thrift," "service," "efficiency," "100 per cent," "rating," "the dignity of labor" and similar terms are spoken of as the Greeks used to speak of wisdom, courage, temperance and justice. The image of the economic man suffuses and transforms also the older images of religion: missionaries and ministers are engaged not in preaching Jesus Christ and him crucified, but in "selling Jesus"; while rebellious writers like Upton Sinclair transform him into a carpenter and conformist ones like Bruce Barton make him over into a captain of industry and major-general of advertising.

These are all items of the event that our age draws its dominant personality-image from the industrial scene; that its core is "the producer" whether as employer or employee. Marx and Veblen to the contrary notwithstanding, the state of the industrial arts had little influence upon the selection and embellishment of this figure. No state of civilization can exist without industrial arts. Production was as indispensable before the evolution of machine-industry as after, and the producer as instrumentally important. But heretofore his status was that of a means, not an end, and in countries like Nazi Germany or Japan or Italy, industrialized as they are, or desire to be, it remains such. The "social, political and spiritual life process" can harness the mode of production to its purpose, and does. Not a single one of the aristocracies of land or arms or learning lost caste because of the rise of industry in England or Germany, and the title-hunting of American parvenus is notorious. If the Producer and production are magnified it is from another cause—from the more or less successful endeavor, conceived and organized by scions of these same aristocrats, to exalt the lowly, to liberate the enslaved and to bring happiness to the unhappy which has come to be known as democracy. A classical expression of this endeavor survives in the American Declaration of Independence. The affirmation that all men are equal, that their rights are inalienable, that governments are made for them and not they for governments gave new courage and new hope to the laborious multitudes who are the most of mankind. It took men as men, not as workers merely; men in the naturalness of their personalities, not the artificialities of their vocations. But since the distinction between lord and vassal and master and servant turns upon a difference of vocation and not of person, the democratic spirit has tended from its beginnings in the early renaissance to glorify men's vocations rather than their persons. To uplift the laborer it "dignified" labor, and proclaimed it the source of value.

But this transvaluation of labor is a philosophical device by which the democratic spirit could make the manual worker at least the peer of the man of leisure, and could confirm its claim that all men are created equal. By exalting the vocations of production, it was in a better moral position to combat the resistance of landlord, soldier and clerk to democratic equality; it could fight the more vigorously to liberate the laborious multitudes from their subjection. In effect, capitalists were individual producers who succeeded in accomplishing this liberation in and for themselves, employer-producers; workers were the multitudes of producers who didn't. Much of the story of the nineteenth century is the story of the struggle to free the multitudes. Their image of the state of freedom was drawn, naturally, from captains of industry, employer-producers like, say, Henry Ford, whom the opinion of industrial mankind appreciated as patterns of force, freedom and fulfilment. First a figure of defiance and rebellion, then of sovereign law and order, the Industrialist, go-getter, master of efficiency, engineer of humanity, was projected, in the course of time, in an image of the archetypal Producer, the ideal of self for employer and employee alike. As this took form and grew to dominance it reshaped men's ideas and speech, altered their interests, shifted their attitudes, and disposed their lives to move with an increasing momentum upon exclusively economic ways and to live passionately economic lives.

But in entering with a conscious and ardent will upon the rôle of Producer, men disposed themselves to play a part in too many respects out of harmony with their spontaneous nature and fundamental dispositions. Acting out this part gave rise to divisions, distortions and conflicts which are among the persistent causes of the malady of our time. Especially consumption and production—which naturally pass into one another like the tones of a melody, or the meanings of words in a sentence, with consumption always the completion and last term of the sequence—were artificially separated, and the separation enforced by all the devices of marketing and exchange. The consumers we are by nature were thrown into an artificial subjection to the producers we are compelled to become by nurture.

The Decline and Rise of the Consumer is a study of the character and consequences of this separation and this subjection in the life of the modern world, and a research of remedies. Asking, what has the playing of the rôle of Producer Paramount done to the quality and method of human life, it analyzes and interprets the struggle of our spontaneous nature against the subjection and constraint which acting out the Producer rôle imposes; it traces the resurgence of the consumer in us, the slow formation of the consumer ideal and the progressive embodiment of this ideal in the forms of coöperative association and the techniques of the coöperative arts, which are singular among the arts of economic organization, management and control in that the means employed are of an identical nature and form as the ends sought.

The argument begins with a review of the consumer-producer relation from primitive times to the days of early capitalism. It shows how capitalism, by its own inward logic developing as an economy of abundance, was perverted into a technique of scarcity which degraded consumption from an end into a means. Since we are consumers by nature, this was but a reorganization of the more ancient subjection of the many into a modern form. Its implements were the mechanics of capitalism. In themselves as unmoral as a tree or a truck, they were put to evil uses. The price-system, the "profit-motive" and private property, described as the pillars of capitalism, are not less fundamental to any other organization of a going industrial society; only their names and employments can be changed, not their characters. They are bound to be abused wherever the Producer and production—and not the Consumer and consumption—determine the mode of industrial association. All attempts at amelioration by reform or revolution within a frame of reference which has production for its governing concept are automatically self-condemned. They do not abolish, they merely shift the geography of the evils they fight against.

To conquer the evils, men must make the Consumer their paramount rôle, and the Producer secondary, accessory. They must learn to appreciate each other as consumers, to regard production as a means and consumption as an end. They did learn this to a measurable extent in England, mother of factory systems as well as parliaments, model of capitalist perversion as well as democratic idealism. In the year 1844, a handful of unemployed Rochdale weavers formed a consumers' coöperative society according to the plan of Charles Howarth. During the near to hundred years since this event there has grown up, along the lines then defined, a free self-governing association of consumers—six million British heads of families—whose fields and factories, stores, transport, banks, schools, playgrounds, clinics, are organized into a mighty consumer economy, producing ever more and more of every possible thing which need might demand or desire seek. The establishment of this ever-growing economy was marked by many struggles over techniques, program and ideal. Its very progenitors had taken for granted the primacy of the Producer rôle, and had aimed at a company of self-governing Producers rather than a community of self-governing Consumers. Christian Socialists, socialists, churchmen and politicians, trades-unionists, philanthropic aristocrats, humanitarian intellectuals, all dominated by the personality-image of the Producer, labored and argued to direct the movement to a Producer goal. But as the consumer's experience of coöperation grew richer, more varied, more integrated, the coöperators drew from it, with ever greater clearness and distinctness, the principle and the method of the primacy of the consumer. Under the leadership of J. T. W. Mitchell this idea developed the lineaments of an ideal; there accrued to it the qualities, the allure and the force of a personality-image incarnating the ideal of man as consumer, and defining his nature and destiny in consumer terms.

England being the first to adventure upon the coöperative organization of consumers, is naturally looked to as the measure of all such organization. Other countries, most signally and successfully the Scandinavian countries and Finland, followed the English model. Opportunity, disposition, need and circumstance gave rise to variations and made possible new modes, but the Rochdale plan remains basic. And so the case is in the United States. The American philosophy of life uttered in the Declaration of Independence rests upon the paramountcy of the consumer: life, liberty, the pursuit of happiness are, unlike "the right to work," consummatory, not servile, rights. The Declaration vindicates the equality of the consumers we are born as. In spite of the overweening shapes of Producers and Politicians which the American scene has generated and endowed and which American aspiration perversely takes as models, Americans are coming to realize that their individual lives can best come to force and freedom and fulfilment in the rôle of the consumer. Americans need a new personality-image to embody and to define this rôle and to oppose to the Producer-image that both the rulers and rebels of the land aspire to incarnate. And in the United States too, such an image is shaping itself. As the institutions of the consumer economy take form among farmers and workers and intellectuals, as the coöperative methods of finance spread, coöperative organization of employer-employee relationships establishes itself, and coöperative education advances, variant philosophies of consumption and consumer education emerge, confront each other and move toward a consensus. The image is still rudimentary, much philosophical illumination and practical development will have to precede the shaping of a perfected image, particularly respecting the nature of value. For first and last values are consummatory. Their ground is not labor expended but impulse gratified, and they must necessarily so figure in the faith and knowledge of the multitudes. Finally, the differentiæ of the Consumer personality must needs become more precise, more numerously and widely perceptible in the leadership of the coöperative movement. Their cultural spirit, their personal disposition, their social attack, their economic method must oppose themselves in unmistakable contrast to those of the *duces, Führers* and *commissars* of the Fascist, Nazi and Communist cults as well as those of the captains of industry and finance of the capitalist economy.

The conclusion of this book is that the thing is happening, that the Consumer rises, that men have found a way at last to an image of force, freedom and fulfilment which they can embody and enact in their own persons without doing them violence, without conflict and without distortion—the image of man as Consumer, realized by means of the free association of free individuals in a consumer-economy, with all that this involves for our faiths, our allegiances, our techniques, our ideas of what is useful or right or good or true or beautiful. To the everlasting questions *What is man? What is his destiny?* this image contains an answer in which our minds can be finally at rest; for the ideal it depicts, with the tools supplied by the sciences and the industry of our day, reconciles us to accepting ourselves; to regarding the fulness of our own nature as our destiny, and the achievement of this destiny as our nature.

In the development of my own social philosophy, I may be permitted to add, this book counts as the high place of a way of thinking which I first set down explicitly in my *Individualism—An American Way of Life* and continued in *A Free Society*. Those essays express a reasoned faith in individualism and democracy as the governing principles of the industrial and financial as well as the religious and political establishments of the world; an individualism and democracy based upon experiment, validated by experience and to be still further validated experimentally by the scientific will to believe which has the courage to act on its faith at its own risk.

In *Individualism* I pointed out that institutions of society justify themselves only in the degree that the candid student finds in them affirmative answers to the following questions:

Does it work in such a way as to set free and to enhance the powers of individuality, enabling it to change and to grow in self-knowledge and self-mastery?

Is it unimposed by authority and unrationalized by dogmas? Is it tentative and experimental, to be freely abandoned if it fails and as freely strengthened if it works?

Does it require and facilitate that coöperative unity of purpose and that competitive diversity of effort which is characteristic of the sciences?

Is its cohesion the consequence of the strength and freedom of its members?

Can it live and work together with other associative units without sacrificing its functional pattern to the exigencies of this association?

Does it operate and coöperate with a minimum of coercion and a maximum of consent?

To date, I have not been able to discover, among the capitalisms, Fascisms, Nazisms, Communisms, and other *isms* which rival consumer coöperation as social facts and as social ideals, one which can with greater right answer an honest *Yes* to these questions.

BOOK I

THE PRODUCER'S WORLD

CHAPTER I

CAPITALISM AS THE ECONOMY OF ABUNDANCE

§ 1. THE CONSUMERS' WORLD OF ADAM SMITH

THE PHILOSOPHY of American democracy and the *laissez-faire* philosophy of business enterprise received their classic formulations in the same year.

The philosophy of American democracy was stated in the American Declaration of Independence, which tells briefly, in very simple, straightforward language, on what principles, for what purposes and by what methods governments are established among men. It declares that all men are born equal and that they have the same rights to life, liberty and the pursuit of happiness, and that these rights cannot be taken away from them.

The *laissez-faire* philosophy of business enterprise was stated in a book entitled *An Inquiry into the Nature and Causes of the Wealth of Nations.* Its author was Adam Smith, who is called the father of political economy. At the time he wrote merchants and manufacturers were struggling hard to free themselves from the restrictions and tyrannies of obsolete laws and arbitrary interferences of government with business. These were serving only to keep up old privileges and create new ones. Instead of guaranteeing to merchants and manufacturers a fair field and no favor, governments imposed legal or political handicaps which gave a few unjustifiable advantages over all others. Adam Smith expressed the progressive spirit of his time when he urged that there should be an end to all that, that the individuals engaged in making and buying and selling, should be able to do so without fear or favor. He proposed that they should be let alone, that each should be free to succeed or fail on merit and no other ground. He urged, that is, what came later to be called the principle of *laissez-faire.* His book is a justification of this principle. It explains why men behave as they do in the fields of business and industry. His explanation is very simple, clear and direct, but it has been confused by the ideas and constructions of others, who came after him and who called themselves his disciples. It is Adam Smith's notion that each man by nature seeks his own interest, and that he struggles to live and to grow in liberty and happiness, in a world where perhaps air and sunshine may be enough for everybody and to spare; but where there is not enough of any of the other necessities of life to go round. The economic behavior of men follows from this condition. They try to turn the "scarcity" of nature into the abundance of civilization. The effort results in their doing many blind and foolish things. Some, deluded by the magical new uses to which gold can be put as a medium of exchange, mistake the accumulation of gold for the increase of wealth; they endeavor by every means to export goods and import gold. Others believe that persons or peoples can grow richer alone as they increase their natural resources—their fisheries, their mines, their land. To them manufacture is only a transformation not an increase of resources; and therefore it can only affect the distribution of wealth but not the amount of wealth. The illusion that wealth is money was rationalized as Mercantilism. The error that wealth consists solely in natural resources was expounded as Physiocracy.[1]

Adam Smith laid bare the fallacy of each. The riches of a country, he demonstrated, consist in the plenty and cheapness of its provisions. These are not found in nature ready-made; nature provides only the raw material of them; men must work them up and work them over, altering not merely their form but their very substance, so as to fit them for human use. If human economy began by each man's making everything he needed for his own use, it could not grow until a division of labor took place. Then a man ceased to be jack of all trades, making the little bit of the many things he needed. He learned to be master of one trade; he made a great quantity of one thing many people needed; and he exchanged what he made for goods which others made. The instrument of this exchange is gold or silver formed into Money. Money is but the name for a way of using gold and silver. They are commodities employed as media of exchange and only so. They are not provisions; they can neither be eaten nor drunk. Ultimately all exchange is exchange of goods contrived for the satisfaction of wants; with a value determined by the labor required for their contrivance, according to Adam Smith, and measured by the price in money which they bring. The greater the number, the variety and the competency of men's skills, the freer and surer men are to exercise their skills and to exchange the product of their labor, the more abundant the wealth of the nations.

For the well-being of any is the interest of all.[2] From the standpoint of national wealth or international trade, it is not true that one person's loss is another's gain. Poverty and prosperity are equally reciprocal and contagious. Since under the division of labor, each is the customer of all, it is to everybody's interest that each should be prosperous enough to be

[1] Both error and illusion are hardy, protean annuals and crop up in different forms with every crisis; they are not inconsiderable components of the New Deal.

[2] Marx makes this conception of the classic *laissez-faire* economics the principle of his classless society, which he described as "an association in which the free development of each is the condition for the free development of all" (*The Communist Manifesto*).

able to buy from all. The rule also governs the behavior of nations. If war and revolution so break down the Russian economy that Russia cannot buy China's tea, then China must buy fewer British guns and less British oil and textiles, and England must buy less Australian beef, and Australia must buy fewer American fords and radios and other gadgets, and Americans must buy less French wine and French perfume, and France has less money to pay interest and war debts with, and therefore makes stricter and bitterer demands of Germany, and Germany gets unbalanced and goes Nazi and becomes a menace of war to all the world. Unless the things we each make can be used, and indeed used up, by others, our labor is in vain; our well-being as producers depends on the capacity of our customers to consume; and equally their security as producers depends on our ability as consumers. In the nature of things, the world is a consumer's world, the civilized world even more than the savage one. The entire driving energy of civilization lies in the number, intensity, variety and extent of the wants it serves. This is what Adam Smith discovered in the course of his inquiry into the nature and causes of the wealth of nations. "Consumption," he declared, "is the sole end and purpose of all production; . . . the interest of the producer ought to be attended to only so far as it may be necessary for promoting that of the consumer."

§ 2. THE DISTINCTION BETWEEN CONSUMER AND PRODUCER

IN PRACTICE, this view of the paramountcy of the consumer had come to its maturity at the time Adam Smith pronounced it, but a new view, the idolatry of the producer and of production, came into being with the economy of the modern industrial world, and it is this latter view which we now know as the tradition of our economy. Although much was made of the "law of supply and demand," the practice and the theory of political economy from Adam Smith on were more concerned with the processes and forms of supplying than with the nature and action of demands. Consumption was taken for granted; its reality was assumed, and ignored, by the producer and the theoretician of political economy until such a time as the consumer failed to yield the profits of the projected exploitation. Then he became an object of concern, and, as an impersonal "market," not a living personality, was sought through foreign trade rather than domestic. The idea that one's fellow-countryman is the greatest consumer of the producer's output has come to significant notice rather recently, as the advertiser's last stand before the problems raised by quantity-production under machine conditions in a world where jealous nationalism and tariff barriers impede foreign trade: it has been christened "consumptionism."

The distinction between producer and consumer is like those between *supply* and *demand, labor* and *capital, competition* and *coöperation.* The terms stand for contrasting and complementary activities of day-to-day life and labor. The expansion and elaboration of modern business have caused people to believe that, somehow, consumer and producer are independent and autonomous beings struggling for mastery over one another. The belief is an illusion. The distinctions and duplexities which the words point to and emphasize did not exist at all times. They are results of the division of labor, elaborated by capitalism. Although the producer and consumer activities of the economist were patent enough in antiquity, neither the Greeks nor the Romans had a name for them; nor for that matter, had the mediævals. The definition and discrimination of these activities are themselves a product of capitalism and a part of the "science" of political economy which is a cultural expression of this capitalism.

§ 3. THE DISTINCTION IN PRIMITIVE SOCIETY

IT IS WORTH WHILE to have in mind a little the pattern of this development.

At its foundation is the life-cycle of all life on earth, from conception to death. Living creatures begin their careers as consumers, and their biographies are records of their unceasing efforts to so live all their lives. Their first economies are, by and large, economies of abundance. Normally, the non-mammalian egg and the mammalian uterus provide as perfect shelter, as adequate protection from disease and enemies as the world can find; the flow of nourishment is so continuous and ample that the interval between desire and satisfaction is for practical purposes nil; desire obtains without want, merely as the activity of self-nourishment; satisfaction takes place without effort, purely as the feeling of the self-nourishing action.

Birth is a catastrophic passage from the intra-uterine economy of abundance toward the scarcity economy of life in the world. The new-born, whether human or animal, is still a sheer consumer. It neither can produce anything nor is expected to. Its existence is all consumption and leisure. Its elders provide it so far as they are able with the food, the warmth, the clothing, the shelter, the protection against enemies and disease, which it needs to continue living in this way. But its abundance is a much modified abundance. Between desire and satisfaction considerable intervals must at best obtain. The most assiduously cared-for infant knows hunger and pain, cold and heat. To supply its needs it must exert itself with cries, strains and movements. These exertions compose the interval between its desires and their satisfaction. They might be described as its labor, and they lead directly, without a break, from desire to satisfaction. They are themselves consummation, for they begin and end in the experience and sensibilities of the individual child. The mother who stills the child's cries, quiets its movements and otherwise tends it, is only an event accompanying its satisfactions, a means and sign of them in childhood, and remains their symbol ever after, the "Great Mother" of classical religion, the Madonna of Catholic Christianism, the Oedipus Complex of contemporary sophistication.

Something of the same sort, could we but know it, must obtain among the birds and beasts and insects. On all levels of zoölogical existence, the state of nature in infancy is the state of the consumer, served, defended and sustained by the female of the species. Child-bearer, milk-giver, food-bringer, she is the producer in nature, and hence the first to be degraded into the worker of nurture. Among social insects, such as ants, wasps and bees, the workers are females whose whole life consists in producing the goods which others use and enjoy. Among men, all through historic times and perhaps from the formation of the patriarchal order, the situation has been analogous: the pattern of human sexual congress—wherein alone male and female are face to face, yet the male is above and the female beneath—together with the natural relationships of infancy and motherhood are prolonged into the nurtural relationships of family, tribal and community life. Men and children remain, so far as the situation permits, sheer consumers. Their activities are free activities having the character of play and sport: hunting, fighting, herding, communing with ghosts and gods—finally, those phases of agriculture requiring prowess. The productive responsibilities of women are coercively prolonged from child-bearing, nursing, tending or mothering, to all the drudgeries of the household economy. Much of what the men do they need not do in order to live; most of what the women do is indispensable not only to their own survival, but to that of the men and the children. It is the women of primitive societies who are the practitioners of the industrial arts; who till the soil, weave the baskets, mold the pots, prepare and sew the skins, cook the flesh and serve the men and the children.

All this remains to a very great degree "the custom of the country" in even the most enfranchised land, such as Soviet Russia. Woman, no less than man is born a consumer, equally entitled to gratify her passions and satisfy her desires. She also becomes a producer under compulsion. Her relation to the male becomes that of slave to master; her function in life that of a tool without an existence, without a goal and purpose of its own. Custom and law sustain the prolongation of the male infancy as the privileged consumer. Even after the male slave supplants and replaces the woman drudge, the distinction holds; the female of the species is kept more servile than the male. As compared with his woman, even the male slave enjoyed what Sombart calls "the lordly way of life": both were chattels, but the woman in addition was enslaved to her man, the subject of his exploitation; her service was free income for him, rendering his life more abundant than hers, and enabling him to consume more than he himself produced. In his eyes she is a tool to keep in repair, while he is a person to prosper and shine. The rule in all these relationships, tended to be: like master, like man. German Nazism makes of this double enslavement of the woman a paramount national ideal.

§ 4. THE DISTINCTION IN THE SLAVE ECONOMY OF ANTIQUITY

In the course of time, the slave came to supplement the woman of a family or a community, and to a considerable extent, displaced her. Probably, in the beginning, the appropriation of women and children and the extermination of men was the conventional outcome of victory in battle, for whatever cause. Then some great anonymous benefactor of the race, victorious, discovered that a servant alive was a richer fruit of victory than an enemy killed or even eaten; no doubt most of the vanquished felt that it was better to be a living slave than a dead hero. Slavery was the domestication—that is, the feminization—of the human male; like the ox, he willy-nilly passed under the yoke. No longer, for him, were the free activities of shrine and chase, of tillage and council. He was compelled to assume the woman's tasks: to do whatever was dull and mean and dirty and hard.

And so as we pass to classical antiquity we find its economy to be a slave economy, in which slaves embody and thus may be said to be the owners and carriers of the tradition of the useful arts. Slaves are the producers, freemen are the consumers. The independent farmer, working his farm, has become an absentee landowner, living lordlike on the work of others. In the theory and practice of life developed by the ancient world, handicrafts and the useful arts are too mean for a free spirit to practise. Aristotle avers that no citizen of a perfect state could work at any mechanical art. He sets forth the standards and expresses the judgment of all the ancient world: the arts proper to the worth and dignity of a free man are the liberal arts, the arts of consumption. They are war and worship; politics and æsthetic and philosophical contemplation; and recessively, agriculture perhaps. At least, agriculture is not *dis*honorable. By the time of Augustus, however, the dominant rule of life among the Romans has joined agriculture to the servile arts. No freeman may soil his hands with work and save his face; no freedman can afford to labor like the slave he was without corrupting the liberty he has. All citizens, the poor equally with the rich, must live as free consumers, their worth undiminished by the practice of the useful arts. Rome becomes a city of proletarians and slaves, the proletarians living without working, on income created by the labor of the slaves.

At first the proletarians had been a selected group of citizens whose distinguished services a grateful country rewarded with free and sure maintenance, and whose children it desired and cherished. In the end the proletarians were all the Romans who, landless and penniless, but half-military, were yet too worthy to work and too poor to live. Not slaves, and as jealous for their status as a southern "poor white" is for white supremacy in Dixie; idle, and with no means of their own to support their idleness, the proletarians were moved by custom and tradition as well as by inclination to demand for themselves the same life of sheer consumption as their propertied fellow-citizens enjoyed. With their aspirations and desires directed by the practices and precedents of the rich, they called upon the Imperial government to provide for them. And the government did provide for them. It drew upon Egypt and all the provinces of the empire for their nourishment and entertainment. By means of its slave-economy, it was able to maintain them as a leisure mass of sheer consumers of a free income of "bread and the games of the circus."

Essentially the ancient world had no "middle class." It was divided into slaves who produced without consuming and citizens who consumed without producing. The former were simply the living tools of the latter. As Aristotle had said, "A slave is a tool with life in it; a tool is a lifeless slave." For all that, the slave was still a living man of flesh and blood, often of the same breed as his master, with the same passions in his heart and driven by the same desires and aspirations. As a person he was frequently his master's superior, stronger, wiser, kinder, and, moreover, possessed of all the skills and knowledge upon which the continuity and structure of the master's household depended. His slave status was an artificial thing rationalized and sanctioned by custom and the force behind the law. The last, in the history of the Roman Empire, tended from Nero's day on, to become more and more careful of the security and well-being of slaves.

§ 5. CAVEAT EMPTOR AND THE CONSUMER-PRODUCER RELATION

As a rule, masters were aware that one man's being slave and another man free was largely accident of fortune and not, Aristotle to the contrary notwithstanding, a consequence of the nature of things. They knew their dependence on the wisdom and skill of their slaves, and were heedful of the slaves' selfhood. But inasmuch as the slave like his master, was born and by nature remained, a consumer; inasmuch as he was a producer only by the accident of fate, the condition of bondage was automatically intolerable to him and in his heart he persistently sought his freedom. He too aspired to the way of life of the master; he too desired the freedom to consume what he needed and to produce only what he considered reasonable in the light of his strength and impulses. He could win this freedom at least by fraud if not by force. Brain and muscle of the economy of antiquity, the slaves could draw from their skill and knowledge a hidden profit which they need not turn over to the master; some of what they produced they could secretly sell and keep the price to buy their freedom with. They could collect secret perquisites and commissions and they could get a larger price than they turned over to their owners for what they disposed of publicly. The customers with whom they dealt, being as involved in the fraud as they, bought at their own risk, whether they were slave or free. Every such customer, in his dealings with the seller was knowingly taking a chance in a game forbidden by law and custom to both. It was, I do not doubt, out of some such situation, that the rule of *caveat emptor* arose.

This maxim, warning the buyer to beware, expresses a relationship in which the advantage goes, not to the consumer but to the producer. It is a relationship occurring in a consumers' world; obviously illicit, obviously tangent to the powers and aspirations of the consumer-masters of Roman civilization. It stands for what might be called an underworld technique in the consumer-dominated economy of antiquity. Also the

Greeks deprecated it, and Plato decried trading as degeneration. *Caveat emptor* signalizes the war of the unprivileged producer against the privileged consumer. Significantly, investigation to date has failed to discover the expression in Latin literature. A maxim defining an ignoble practice of ignoble people, *caveat emptor* looks perhaps toward the kind of trading which is done with smugglers, thieves and fences. It has all the ear-marks of a proverb of the under-privileged, of the type which never or hardly ever pass over into the written language of the privileged. Literature fails to record it until the second quarter of the sixteenth century, when Fitzherbert, discussing in his "Boke of Husbandrie" the amenities of horse-trading, writes, "If he [the horse] be tame and have been rydden upon, then *caveat emptor*."

§ 6. PRODUCTION, CONSUMPTION AND THE CHRISTIAN DISPENSATION

IF *caveat emptor* represents the defensive behavior of a producing majority in an inequitable world dominated by a consumer-minority, it does not long remain so. The slave's attitude toward his position could not help being like the prostitute's. He might make no effort to change from the thing he was, but he accepted the judgment of society upon it, and hated both his state and the force that kept him in it. In his heart he was always aspiring to revenge and freedom. But for only a few did this aspiration take form in facing the danger of overt rebellion. For the great multitude of slaves it had to be revenge without risk and freedom without hazard. Such revenge and freedom the salvational religions of antiquity were able to offer; especially Christianity, with its evangel of a God dying to expiate the sins of man, promising a last judgment soon to come, in which the whole existing order should be turned upside down and the mighty lowered from their seat and those of low degree exalted. This gospel exercised a powerful influence on the slaves of the Roman world. It offered the double satisfactions of revenge for wrongs suffered in this world and the leisure life of consuming without producing in eternity.

Not that the Christian system of ideals or the transformations of the pagan way of life which they effected, inverted the values of production and consumption. The values remained what they always had been: consumption was blessedness and production damnation, but those who enjoyed and those who suffered exchanged rôles. Work does not come off any better in Christianism than it does in paganism. In the scheme of salvation it is a curse due to disobeying God's commandment. Jehovah had created the first man and the first woman to be consumers, not producers. Adam and Eve began their careers in the Garden of Eden under a divinely ordained economy of abundance. They might, if they had not chosen to break the rule of their Maker, have enjoyed forever the abundance of Ganaiden and their lives would have been an everlasting Sabbath of leisure and plenty. But they broke the rule, with a little help from Lucifer, whereupon God expelled them from the Garden of Eden, damned forever; Adam was "to till the ground whence he was taken"; Eve to be subject to Adam and to suffer the pangs of childbirth. God cursed Adam with the curse of labor: "With the sweat of thy face shalt thou eat bread, until thou return unto the ground." Such then is production according to the Word of God: a curse, a punishment for sin and a prelude to death.

This legend of Genesis, which loomed so large in the dogmatic formulation of Christian otherworldliness, was without particular significance in the Hebrew one. The Jews employed it as a device to account for certain social and historical phenomena. In addition, their sacred literature included a record, incorporated into a tradition, of indignant resistance toward slavery and a passionate defense of the non-consuming producer against exploitation by non-productive consumer, in effect, therefore, a championing of the slaves against their owners. Passionate and practical in the prophets, it is transformed into an otherworldly liberation by the Gospels with the beatitudes' exaltation of the poor, the humble, the meek, the lowly, and their promise of a heavenly after-life which shall be one eternal Sabbath.

The church, largely recruited at first from among slaves, retained, when it came to power, its initial antagonism to slavery. This attitude was reinforced by the disintegration of the Roman Empire and the destruction of its economy. In no small degree it received its characteristic tone and accent from the bondsmen's flight from the civilization which was their bondage. All of its amenities, being the amenities of the masters, were identified as sin, all of its hardships as the indispensable preliminaries to salvation. Labor and privation on earth became necessary precedents to leisure and plenty in heaven: if they were earthly penance, they were at the same time a laying-up of heavenly treasure, an otherworldly thrift. The ideal of life on earth became completely expiatory. Asceticism set in on a large scale. Men and women went to the wilderness to live alone, or in communities, as nuns and monks. The monastic way of life was identified as the Christian way.

The monks came mostly from the servile castes. They continued to live and to labor as was their wont only with ceremonial and prayer added; but their attitude toward their way of life was transformed; it now had a new meaning. They no longer planted that another might reap, nor prepared the feast that another might eat. Their labor was all for their own salvation. Their poverty and their work were not imposed on their weakness by alien strength but chosen by their own desire and borne for their own satisfaction. The duties of their monkish vows were not a slave's tasks, they were a free soul's penance, the savings for salvation. If they did not consume what they produced, it was because they were saving it up for the more glorious and abundant feast which was heaven.

§ 7. CONSUMERS AND PRODUCERS UNDER MONASTERY AND MANOR

IN THE COURSE of time the formal master-slave relation disappeared from the Western world. The slave was replaced by the serf and the serf became any one who, in the disorder of Roman decay and mediæval formation, was willing to barter his land for protection and his freedom for security. If many free peasants chose to make themselves bond-servants of armed bandit chiefs, rather than suffer from the uncertainty of their banditry, many more preferred the greater security of monastic protection. It was not long till the monks vowed individually to poverty and the penance of labor for subsistence only, figured collectively among the richest folk in Europe —owners of immense lands, lords of considerable towns and villages, masters of multitudes of serfs. Naturally, collective wealth bred personal idleness. Serfs replaced monks in the performance of productive labor. In the monkish orders themselves the liberal arts became more important than the useful ones, and the amenities of consumption, instead of being postponed till heaven, began to be enjoyed on earth. In a few generations they replaced production. The invidious classical distinction between producer and consumer reasserted itself.

With, however, a difference. Monk and lord, separated though they were by caste, by status and by power from serf and peasant, were joined to them in the quality of their living. Serf and peasant might need more than they consumed; what they ate and drank and wore and spent might go, with never a sufficiency, to restore energies burnt up in production; their lives might be built on scarcity, their existence be a mere subsistence. But the goods they consumed for repair were in substance and form not different from the goods their master consumed as enjoyment. The difference lay in the quantity and not in the quality; masters consumed more than they needed. Status was measurable by dearth and satiety; the standard of living was defined by *how much,* not by *what kinds:* the number and diversity of goods were not components of it. Qualitatively, castle and cottage were more nearly on a par than villa and hutch of antiquity.

This contraction and levelling down of the standards of those who consumed much without producing anything to the standards of those who produced much while consuming little followed directly from the demoralization of civil government and the disintegration of the institutional structure of the Roman Empire. As these advanced, the repair of highways and aqueducts and canals and sewers diminished and finally stopped; soon they returned to the wild. Soldiers made a living as bandits, and joined other marauders who infested the roads. The movements of men and goods whose circulation was the life of the empire slowed up till they were almost imperceptible; communications broke down; the services required to keep up the complicated functional organization of the ancient cities were cut off; this meant the breaking down of the division of labor necessary for such services. The cities crumbled into smaller, simpler, far less interdependent units. Most of the arts on which the upkeep of the great ancient municipalities depended, fell into disuse. Living declined from the cultural to the subsistence level. For safety's sake the people cut themselves off from their associations in space; for salvation's sake the church cut them off from their associations in time. The heritage of the past ceased to be a living memory implementing present knowledge and present skill. It became a dead manuscript lying forgotten and despised in some monkish keep. The organic economy of the Roman Empire had dissociated into a collection of self-contained and self-sufficient manorial communities, practising an agricultural economy for little else than a subsistence.

§ 8. FROM THE MANORIAL VILLAGE TO THE MEDIÆVAL TOWN

IN ITS ECONOMICS, the manorial village was what would today be called an agricultural autarchy. The serfs farmed the land to which the law fastened them as nature fastens the grass, according to an immemorial tradition. The cobblers, the weavers, the potters similarly did their parts. All furnished and fed and clothed the lord of their land and its priest whose sacred vocation constituted his title. They produced what he required and they needed, and no more. Surpluses could not long be stored without corrupting; they could not be carried to a market more needful of them, because roads were practically impassable. Thus rich harvests could not mean wealth; poor harvests, rain or drought often meant famine, disease and death.[3]

Essentially, their economy, like that of every autarchy, large or small, was a scarcity economy. Its material staples were sour black bread, porridge of the same stuff, occasional salt or

[3] China and India still provide adequate examples of this agricultural village autarchy.

smoked meat, as a rule half rotten, one single garment worn day and night till it rotted on the unwashed body; a stone or earthen cottage with a roof of thatch, one door, no windows, often no hearth, and likely as not housing hens and pigs as well as people. Its spiritual and intellectual staples were the instructions of the church and the tradition of ceremonial and ritual carried over from pre-Christian cults in the forms of game and dance and chanty. Its tempo was that of the vegetating soil, with whose seasons it was in tune. The life of the manor was hardly more extended in scope, but a little more diversified in kind by the military arts. With so many non-producing consumers to provide for—priests, men-at-arms, pages, minstrels—it operated to separate the many tasks performed in the village by one person into single tasks separately performed by many persons.

This division of labor tended to develop specialized craftsmanship, it led to the recovery of the industrial arts, and to a diminution of scarcity. Law and custom prevented it, however, from generating plenty. They ordained what the different castes of men should eat, what they should wear, in what dwellings they should live, what they should know and how they should comport themselves. It was of the essence of feudalism that every man should have his betters, and that none should aspire to be as good as his betters, but live content in the station of life to which his God assigned him. The minority of freemen were somewhat anomalous; the "masterless man" was a man in danger, and therefore dangerous; serving nobody, nobody owed him protection; he was without place and without status, and so a wanderer like Cain. Consequently, agriculture was not for him; he had to be either outlaw or craftsman, and often he was both. The wandering tinker, the journeyman printer and the peddler, now so near to extinction, stem from him. With the freeman, defending himself against the oppression of manor and monastery, the masterless man is the vital force in the growth of the mediæval town.

The town is the creation of the producer, in a primitive consumer's world. Apart from military deviations, its topography, the layout of its streets, and the organization of its citizens for civil government and for defense derive from the divisions of labor into special arts and crafts. The practitioners of these joined together, each according to his kind, to form guilds or unions, and the street where they took up their collective habitations became accordingly the Street of the Cobblers, or the Chandlers, or the Saddlers, or the Cloth-merchants, and the like. Workshop and household were one; master and apprentices were a family. The trade was a "misterie" transmitted by precept and practice from the expert to the learner. With growing towns came better roads; proprietor and peasant could bring their materials to the craftsman to be made into shoes or swords or candles or saddles, or woven into woolen or linen cloth and cut into garments. Nothing could be provided "ready-made." The "market" was personal; the relation between the maker, who was also the seller, and the buyer, who was also the user, was a personal face-to-face relation. All goods were "custom-made," few in number, of negligible variety, and of known quality. The one possible variable was workmanship, and the chief field of competition between cobbler and cobbler or tailor and tailor was the quality of workmanship. Regarding this, the customer was in a position to be as good a judge as the seller. His position was further reënforced by the rules of the guild, which were designed to regulate the competition between different members of the same craft for the advantage of all its members.

§ 9. COMMERCE, CREDIT, AND CAVEAT EMPTOR AGAIN

In this situation the rule of *caveat emptor* got a new meaning. Still the maxim of oppressed producers in a world dominated by sheer consumers whose advantage was further safeguarded by laws of church and state, still the device of the producers in a struggle toward freedom and equality, it was now operative in situations where the two were more nearly on a par. The buyer bought at his own risk, but he was practically as aware as the seller of the character and conditions of his risk; his buying, called "cheapening" of goods, was to a considerable extent a sport, the exercise of the liberal art of bargaining, whose limits were the rule of the "just price." In essence, he did not buy more economically, nor did the seller sell more dearly: both had more fun, and their consumption was enriched by that addition. Within the limits of the vegetative cycle, those who produced much while consuming little consumed a little more and came, as consumers, somewhat closer to those who consumed without producing. Surpluses, when they happened, were a little more widely distributed; and their transportation from places where nobody desired them to places where many did became easier and more frequent.

This was commerce, that grows by what it feeds on, in a subsistence economy whose mark was scarcity for the many and a narrow abundance for the few. Better roads, more specialized craftsmanship were agents tending to move this scarcity toward abundance; the narrowness toward variety. They transformed insufficiency into surplus, waste into wealth; they gratified desire by satisfaction. They multiplied choices for the consumer; they gave to gold and silver and copper as media of exchange an importance which they had lacked under the simple manorial autarchy. The dangers which continued to beset the use of gold and silver led to their replacement by bills of exchange; and by credit—first for the consuming nobles, then for the producing commoners. Crops were grown, hides tanned, cloth woven, vessels shaped, not alone to use and use up on the spot, but also to convey distances to where people needing them were eager to exchange for them their own goods and such gold and silver as they had. To the distant market as distinct from the home market, the craftsman took not only his workmanship but its materials; his wares now had the character of the "ready-made." His customers were no longer only near neighbors, old friends; they were strangers come to buy or denizens of a foreign town where he had gone to sell what the homefolk did not need or would not pay for. His success lay in carrying his goods from a low-priced market to a dearer one, where "cheapening" would still result in the "just price," but nevertheless, a more advantageous one. For obvious reasons, he preferred his price in good coin instead of good wares, and his journeymen preferred wages to subsistence. This preference led to the standardization of money values and the control of the medium of exchange by the political government, steps which enormously enhanced and spread the use of money.

§ 10. CAPITALISM TRANSFORMS SCARCITY INTO ABUNDANCE

THE CRAFTSMAN was now the germinal capitalist and the economic arrangements which he animated were elemental capitalism. Wherever it made a good start it raised the general standard of living. It transformed scarcity into abundance, awakening wants where none had been before, multiplying few into many, bringing more and more varied goods to more people at lower prices, so that what had been formerly, if at all, available only to a few who were free to consume without producing, was now in reach of many of those who had produced much and consumed little. As it could function best only if roads were safe, markets secure, money sound and merchants and merchandise trustworthy, and as these depended on the continuous exercise of authority by a single centralized power, every organization and individual engaged in the practice of making goods for an unknown buyer instead of a known customer sided with city against country, with kings against nobles, with the secular power against the ecclesiastical.

In all this the traders were reënforced first by the thin bright stream of Moorish culture slowly diffusing through the marches of the west and the north, then by the torrent of the Crusades, which brought thousands upon thousands into contact with the ways and valuables of a civilization which had taken up the industrial and intellectual tradition of antiquity, had been enriched by it and had enriched it. Men came back with memories of good things consumed that would not let them rest. They wanted spices for their rotten strong meats instead of salt and smoke; cotton and muslin and damask for their garments instead of itchy wool and scratchy linen, the compactness and speed of money to buy with instead of the bulk and delay of produce to trade with. They told their neighbors of wonders and could not rest until some one or other of these delights were attainable at home. In the words of a song popular after the World War: "How ya gonna keep 'em down on the Farm, after they've seen Paree"? They wanted to bring "Paree" home.

§ 11. "USURY" AND PLENTY VERSUS SCARCITY AND THE CHURCH

THE CHIEF BARRIER to the satisfaction of this desire was inward and psychological. It was the acquiescence of the people in the attitude of the church toward the labor and trade which are the tools of satisfaction. The attitude toward labor has already been described. Its formula was reached by assimilating the prevailing master-slave relation of the pre-Christian economies to the legend of evil in Eden, thereby establishing as a religious dogma the notion that work is a curse laid by God upon man as punishment for disobedience. The attitude toward trade was similarly established. Aristotle's rationalization [4] of the practice and prejudice of the leisure classes of antiquity was joined to the laws and ordinations of the Hebrew Scriptures; [5]

[4] . . . The business of nature is to furnish food to that which is born, and the food of the offspring always remains over in the parents. Wherefore the art of making money out of fruits and animals is always natural . . . a part of household management . . . necessary and honorable; [Another art of money-making is] retail trade . . . a kind of exchange which is justly censured; for it is unnatural, and a mode by which men gain from one another. The most hated sort, . . . is usury, which makes a gain out of money itself, and not from the natural use of it. For money was intended to be used in exchange and not to increase at interest. And this term usury (Tokos), which means the birth of money from money, is applied to the breeding of money because the offspring resembles the parent. Wherefore of all modes of making money, this is the most unnatural. (Aristotle, *The Politics,* I, 10.)

[5] Thou shalt not lend upon usury to thy brother; usury of money, usury of victuals, usury of anything that is lent upon usury. Unto a stranger mayest thou lend upon usury; but unto thy brother thou shalt not lend upon usury, that the Lord thy God may bless thee in all that thou settest thine hand to in the land whither thou goest to possess it. (Deuteronomy XXIII: 19, 20.)

And if thy brother be waxen poor, and fallen in decay with thee; then thou shalt relieve him; yea, though he be a stranger or a sojourner, that he may live with thee. Take thou no usury of him, or increase; but fear thy God that thy brother may live with thee. Thou shalt not give him thy money upon usury, nor lend him thy victuals for increase. (Leviticus XXV: 35, 36, 37.)

Give to him that asketh thee, and from him that would borrow of thee turn thou not away. (Matt. V: 42.)

And if ye lend to them of whom ye hope to receive, what thank have ye? for sinners also lend to sinners to receive as much again. (Luke VI: 34.)

and lending money at interest became, under the name of usury, a sin prohibited by God and forbidden by canon law. Aristotle's disapproval and the Biblical prohibitions embodied a common observation but were due to contrasting interests and motives. As Aristotle saw it, money was an artifice. Unlike earth and plants and animals which are fertile and yield increase and profit by nature, money is barren; it cannot breed. The breeding attributed to it, the usury that is the premium or interest, whatever the rate, paid for the use of money lent, is really an exploitation of man by man, whereas the money-profit gained from selling the produce of the land and its growth is an honorable record for productive service.

The fallacy in Aristotle's distinction—which was not exploded until John Calvin's *De Usuris Responsum* (Jeremy Bentham's *Letters on Usury* elaborate Calvin's analysis) eighteen hundred years later—has a deeper source than the confusion of material and function which it embodies. The fallacy derives from the prejudices of power and station among the Greeks. It projects the scorn of a leisure class of landowning lordly consumers. They, holding "a position above toil," and tending to borrow greatly, despised the laborious servile multitudes, with their menial knowledge and menial arts. For these multitudes, money was the surrogate of land; interest or usury played the rôle of rent; possessions they could conceal and reserve for themselves against their masters: a gate toward freedom, a step on the ladder toward equality.

The Biblical prohibition of usury contains no trace of this misprison, and probably fear, in a higher caste, of the goods and values of a lower. It appears to arise directly out of the bitter experience of the exploitation of equal by equal. Its standpoint is that of consumer over against consumer, not consumer against producer. Usury is forbidden, not only on the loan of money, but on everything men borrow because they lack the wherewithal to live, not because they desire profit or display beyond their needs.

When the church combined the aristocratic prejudice of Hellas with the humanitarian passion of Judea, the rule laid down by the latter became a major instrument in the protection and entrenchment of the former. The landed aristocracy, among whom churchmen bulked large, were, first and last, sheer consumers. They could marry, conquer, or steal wealth, but they could not in decency produce it. Like all goods, money was to them not a capital to invest but an income to expend. When they got any they squandered it quickly in ways that have come to be called "conspicuous consumption." They were always short of it, always borrowers in a world where lending at interest was to risk one's life, and where mere lending was to waste one's living. Thus, artizans and freemen who got any money hoarded it. The demand always immensely exceeded the supply and the supply, when available, had to be bootlegged at great risk not alone of property, but even of life. The price of money, expressed by the interest rate, was a measure of the demand and the risk; the rate was staggering. Much later, after the loan of money at interest had become an inconspicuous routine of everyday economics, *usury* which had meant simply any premium or increase paid for the use of money, came to mean only the conspicuously high interest paid for such use. The usurer or money lender was a social outlaw from the beginning, and money lending was practically the only vocation which the mediæval economy left for the Jew. The ancient opprobrium still attaches to *usury,* but the function it gives a name to is held in high respect when it is called *banking* or *finance.*

The breakdown of the taboos and fears against usury came slowly, with the increasing division of labor and the corresponding expansions of towns and town life. The taboos themselves, discouraging as they were to the accumulations of surpluses, and retarding as they were to investment, were major forces in the slow tempo of mediæval enterprise and recovery. By the twelfth century, however, the thing was done. The Italian city republics had reached a state of economic organization and enterprise where money for investment became as necessary as the farmer's material and the craftsman's skill. To the things, such as leather, wool, silk, or iron now sought in the market, money was joined as another commodity, and similarly bought and sold. Usury was seen to function as an instrument in the transformation of scarcity into plenty, of bringing more goods of more different kinds to more people at lesser costs. It lost its terrors. It spread wherever men endeavored to make living fuller, more diversified and healthier. Catholics were soon trading in money more numerously than Jews, in the cities of the Hansa no less than in those of Italy. Capitalism was now definitely on the way. It was on the way because at the time and under the circumstances, it was an economy of abundance displacing a scarcity economy.

That the church resisted this movement goes without saying: As late as the middle of the eighteenth century Pope Benedict XIV described usury as a mortal sin. But it was a sin which seemed to bring general good. By providing the sinews of enterprise it facilitated and sped the division of labor, and thus the spread and enrichment of leisure. Under this new economy a new freedom of living came, breaking down the invidious distinctions of diet and clothing, dwelling and duty. Periodic fairs are slowly ousted by itinerant peddlers and permanent "stores." Farmers and smiths and cobblers are able to pack a more varied lunch than can be produced at home; they are able to wear better clothes and live in better houses. Throughout the fifteenth century the folk who had produced much and consumed little came to use many things which had been distinguishing privilege of the gentry who consumed without producing. The latter are aroused. First state and church alike denounce the sin of luxury into which the people are fallen: then sumptuary laws are decreed to hold back the expansion of life set in motion by capitalism.

But to no effect. Although the division of labor, with its specialized craftsmanships, made men more interdependent, it also set them free. It detached them from the soil of folkway and status in the ancestral village; it gave them mobility, in which the substitution of a money-wage for goods was a potent factor. Wages, in the morning of capitalism, were liberty, not slavery; they marked the free man as against the serf; they enabled a richer self-fulfilment of man as consumer, even as specialization opened the road to initiative and invention in the producer.

§ 12. MERCANTILISM—BASTARD CHILD OF SPANISH NOBILITY AND AMERICAN GOLD

THIS INWARD TRANSVALUATION of European social relationships was tremendously speeded and strengthened by the development of new trade routes and the discovery of unknown lands, especially the Americas. These added untold resources to the available wealth of Europe. They diversified the diet and the amenities of the common life with potatoes, rum, molasses and sugar, chocolate, tea, coffee and tobacco. At the dinner table of the gentry the fork becomes an accessory to the knife and spoon. The hot drinks—"the cup that cheers but not inebriates"—took the place of the fire-waters of Europe; they helped the European to the comfort and escape of alcohol and diminished its intoxication. Europe became gayer, brighter and not so drunken. But especially gold and silver became plentiful as they had never before been in European history. Brought into Europe from the mines of Mexico and Peru by the adventuring grandees of ruthless Spain, the noble consumers of that country found themselves all at once possessed of a mobile wealth beyond their pre-Columbian dreams. Never had wealth been so free, and its taking so irresponsible; the wide-spread piracy of other nations against Spanish shipping modified it not a tittle. The leisure classes entered upon an orgy of sheer splendid expenditure, of conspicuous consumption unprecedented in their record. The money which enabled them to do this became in their eyes the supreme economic force. To have and to hold minted coin became far more important than to make and have the goods for which, first and last, coins are counters. The Spanish practice, coincident with the brief upthrust of Spain as the dominant world power, blinded Europe. Formulated as mercantilism, it defined an economic program seeking at all costs to accumulate bullion rather than to make and move goods; therefore to export without importing, and to have a "favorable balance of trade." To increase the cash reserves, the American mines were worked through Indians enslaved for the purpose. As the slavery killed them too numerously and too quickly, they were replaced by Negroes bought or kidnapped in Africa.

Thus slavery, which had died out among Europeans was, not with the disapproval of the church, resurrected in Spanish America. In a short time traffic in human beings became a profitable undertaking in which all the peoples of Europe competed.

Mercantilism reënforced by the revival of slavery ruined the economy of Spain and brought trouble to all of those countries that tried it. Its basic illusion was the transfer of the attitude and practices of the leisure class of sheer consumers to the ways and works of the producers on the fruits of whose labor they lived. Joined to the Catholic taboo of usury, it weakened the power of the Catholic economy. Superiority in commerce and industry passed to the Protestant communities. The decay of the Italian city states, Catholic though they were, had another cause. They were not deluded by mercantilism, and they practised usury as fully and freely as the Protestants, and more so. But the stream of trade had shifted from the Mediterranean to the Atlantic, from the Southeast to the Northwest, and internal dissension and foreign foes made impossible any united effort by those cities to hold their advantage or to recover it.

§ 13. PROTESTANTISM AS THE RELIGION OF THE PRODUCER AS CONSUMER

CERTAIN SCHOOLS of economic philosophy practise the deprecation of Protestantism by identifying it with the spirit of capitalism. The identification rests simply on the fact that the peoples among whom Protestantism prevailed did better than their Catholic competitors in commerce and industry. They did better for the same reasons that they became Protestants —because they were freer and braver; because they resisted with greater success the oppression of their hereditary nobilities of sheer consumers, lay and ecclesiastical; because the implements of their resistance were the industrial arts practised, within the limitations of custom and statutes, freely instead of servilely; because, in their practise, the interest of the producer *as consumer* figured in juster proportion to the interest of the sheer consumer. Especially they did better because they were the agents through whom the common man was able to live a better life; because they not only brought within his reach more and better things to consume, but because their religion raised him in feeling to the same level as his betters.

By transvaluing labor from a penance for sin into a service of God, Puritanism, without intending it, lifted somewhat the curse from work, and wiped away the dishonor of being a producer. In the place of the monastic vow, the Protestant set the personal conscience; in the place of faith and *works* as the due observance of ceremony and rite, he set faith and *work,* faith and labor performed not as a penitential rite but as productive effort in obedience to God's word. Because it denied the monastery and the monastic life, while it at the same time renewed the monastic intensities of faith and devotion, Protestantism deprived the individual Protestant dignitary of the device of corporate ownership by which he could, in keeping with his vow of poverty, own nothing himself yet hold great wealth. As Puritan, the Protestant became a monk without an order under the duress of joining his personal wealth to otherworldliness. To the Puritan productive labor was, as to his first monkish predecessors, not only a method of salvation, a means of laying up treasure in heaven, but the way of life on earth commanded by God. If he is to enjoy heaven, he must like the monk refrain from enjoying the produce of his work on earth, and unlike the monk he has no community which may claim this produce and to which he can surrender it. What then, after he has rendered unto the poor their due, is he to do with the residue? Leave it to rot and waste? That would be even more sinful than to consume it. What then remains? Only to invest it, so that the service of God by work may go on till the earthly end. Did not the Lord command: Be fruitful and multiply? If the increase of one's labor is money, then it is money that must be reinvested and not spent; the usury it brings is also produce of labor in the service of God. John Calvin both justified investment at interest and forbade oppression and luxury.

Thus, against the tradition which identified power with free income, superiority with the manners and amenities of the leisurely life of the lordly consumer, lay and ecclesiastical, nobility with war and sport and play and extravagances of pageantry and ceremony and patronage of the "liberal arts," there set itself growing a power identifying itself with income from productive labor; with, not so much thrift (which is usually attributed to Puritanism), as a disinclination to extravagances and conspicuous waste. These puritans in Holland and Geneva and England did not deprive themselves of anything, necessity or comfort. Compared with their fathers and grandfathers and with their Catholic peers, they lived richly and well. But they made no show. For the first time, perhaps, in civilized history, work is, in social esteem, organically and inwardly joined to wealth. Wealth had been blessing, freedom, enjoyment; work had been curse, servility, suffering. Now the valuations of wealth suffused and transformed those of work. In the end they tended to become identical. Dignity accrued to labor, dishonor to leisure. It felt strong enough to teach:

When Adam delved and Eva span
Who was then the Gentleman?
When Adam delved and Eva span
The Devil was the Gentleman.

§ 14. CAVEAT EMPTOR BECOMES THE MERCHANT'S LAW OF WAR AGAINST THE LORDLY WAY OF LIFE

THE DEVIL had been in the beginning of his career the father of labor; he was now the menace of leisure, who "finds work for idle hands to do." But, growing wealth and power of the plebeian producer notwithstanding, the handicap was still on the side of the gentleman-consumer. The landlord of agriculture remained more honorable than the captain of industry. The unearned income from rent remained more noble than earned income from manufacture; but interest on investment held a middle ground between the two, and on that ground country squire and city tradesman came together.

The attitude of the latter to the former is ambivalent. The prestige and privilege of the landed gentry worked as a suction pump upon the property and power of the townsmen; trade and industry might be dishonorable for the lord of a manor to practise, but gave his honor a new life if he married into it: also for the pre-industrial ancestor of the industrial townsman loving a lord had its satisfactions equal with serving the Lord. The kindly light of the sheer consumer and his lordly way of life led capitalism on. His will got done. Beside aspiring, not knowingly, not purposely, but spontaneously and inexorably, to identify himself with the lord and his way of life, the plebeian holder of the new power knowingly and of purpose endeavored to overcome him. The world has begun to be the world of the producer with a vengeance, and *caveat emptor* has a new meaning. It has risen from the underworld of slavish practise; from the face-to-face matching of equal skill and knowledge of mediæval "cheapening." It is now the law of war of the merchant-craftsman feeling his power, against his stronger, deeply entrenched, more respected and emulated superior opponent, who buys but does not pay, borrows but does not pay back, and treats the tradesman whose goods he consumes with scorn and laughter, ridiculing his person, despising his vocation and seducing his women. The tradesman's attack automatically extends from the lord to all his underlings; and its intentions, wherever its practitioner has power enough, are enacted into law.

By interest and disposition the laws of both state and church were designed to keep the producer in the subjection appropriate to his accursed state. Trade being sin to the mediæval mind, let the seller beware. On him rests the whole responsibility for the quantity, the quality and price of his goods. And the law of the land endeavored, not consistently or effectively, to enforce the view of the church, inspecting weights and measures, prohibiting adulteration, keeping spoiled goods from the market, and so on. But as crafts divided and by division multiplied, as specialization grew, as the craftsmen became mobile and production increased beyond local needs, the weight of the law tended to shift toward the interest of the producers. Their organization had changed with their markets. The family-like union of the workshop was displaced by a rudimentary factory system, supplemented by the form of household industry or domestic production now known as sweating. By the seventeenth century in England six different economic types were engaged in making and in selling what only one craftsman was enough for, three hundred years earlier. These different people were of different degrees of power, vocation, influence and station: large master, small master, journeyman, apprentice; merchant-master, large merchant, shopkeeper. If this multiplication of producers indicated a higher standard of living in the community at large, it indicated also the destruction of the suppositious parity on which guild membership was based. Industry was undergoing the dichotomy of agriculture into fixed castes of masters and servants. Guild history, between the fifteenth and eighteenth century was the story of a warfare between the big men and the little men. In the course of time the small masters were made too small to remain in the guilds and the apprentices were not permitted to grow big enough to get in. Guilds were replaced by monopolistic companies where the greatly rich held all the offices and determined all the rules. It was in these times that *caveat emptor* begins to figure favorably in the laws.

Nevertheless, the producing consciousness has not yet reached the state of regarding production as an end in itself and consumption as its means. Production was still an instrumentality of consumption. Countlessly many more people, formerly mere producing tools, were now counted among the consumers, for whose sake production was a means of living, not life's end. The capitalist producer was bound to the service, as against the exploitation, of the general consumer, first: by the protestant-puritan religious outlook and spirit; second: by the tradition of guild law regarding quality and fair dealing; and third: by the statutes of states and cities which first supplemented and later replaced the guild law.

§ 15. PROTESTANTISM AND CAPITALIST ABUNDANCE

THE NEW THING was the secular piety of the puritanic sects of Protestantism, their religious democracy, their social rebelliousness and their moral courage. These penetrated the dry-rot and bureaucratism of the guilds, and enabled journeyman, apprentice and small master whom the vested interests of the entrenched guildsmen excluded, competitively to set up on their own. Since all men are equal in the congregation of the Lord, in the affairs of the church, one man could hardly be less than another in the vocations by which they make their livings. Each is the peer of the other in the equal excellencies of their diverse callings. All alike are, as in the Psalm, instruments to praise the Lord who commanded "as ye work so shall ye eat," who accepts the servant on the same level with the master, and whose Providence provides the servant the wherewithal to buy his freedom from the master. This Puritanism combated the extension of the traditional sharp practices of the producer with at least no less vigor than the mediæval church. If, unwillingly, it condoned usury for investment, it warred powerfully against usury as exploitation; it revitalized the Biblical attitude toward price, and during two centuries opposed an almost impassable barrier to establishing the modern rule of "all that the traffic will bear" in the place of the rule of "just price" which is the price measured not by the buyer's need and desire but by the seller's labor and skill. It opposed the agricultural capitalism rising in the "enclosures" of the common land. In every direction the Puritan spirit strengthened the activity of capitalism as an economy of abundance and acted as a brake upon its perversion toward a new exploitative scarcity imposed by masters on servants, in many respects worse than the mediæval.

For these reasons, it held upright the failing guild ideal of work and worth, even while it furthered the disintegration of guild domination of industry. The craftsmen of the guilds, desirous of maintaining equal competition, protecting the repute of their craft and extending its power, enforced certain standards of material and workmanship. The upkeep of these standards they effected by requiring long apprenticeship, prohibiting night work (candlelight does not make for good work), prescribing the measure of materials, forbidding mixing them together, and so on. Width and weight of cloth, for example, were fixed by rule; silk and woolens, since the customer could not know the amount of each, might not be woven together; colored glass might not be put in bone ornaments lest the customer, unskilled in jewelry, might mistake a jewelled bone for ivory. The rules were formulated with not merely profit but the customer in mind. The work under the rules was personal work, on which the pride and integrity of the worker were staked. As the guild was driven out by the factory and the domestic system, its attitude and ideals became a charge upon the religion of the worker-on-his-own; they passed from the policing of the guild into the keeping of his conscience. And this, even with all the immemorial and unforgotten tricks of the trades was, until well into the eighteenth century and beyond, enough. Manufacturer and merchant desired profit and freedom, but profit as a consequence of use, and freedom as a postulate of mutual service. Their employees, now no longer members of their households, but workers at a wage, were nevertheless persons, not hands, to them. Many an early capitalist refused to adopt a labor-saving device because it would throw men out of work; and where such a device was adopted, either the industry had no tradition—as in cotton-spinning in England—or competition had so endangered the undertaking, that the alternative to mechanization was bankruptcy.

§ 16. THE EXALTATION OF THE PRODUCER AND THE NEW SOCIETY

THE FINAL CHECK upon the perversion of capitalism was public law. From the beginning, municipality and king supervised, with a difference, the regulation of the conduct of merchants and manufacturers toward one another and toward the consumer. As their own prohibitory statutes and their police system indicate, guildsmen were far from the upright merchants anti-capitalist legend has painted them. Every trade, it is worth repeating, had its tricks. Cheating the consumer antedated defending him. The code of Hammurabi testifies to this with the same clarity as the statutes of Florence or Leeds. Theft, short measure, disguised defects, unfair prices were always implicit in the guild structure; they happened when they could, and the law punished them. It policed shops and markets, it checked weights and measures, it limited the number of apprentices any master might take. If government liberated the capitalist from the burdens of feudal obstruction and exaction, it also laid upon him duties toward itself and the community. Laws were added forbidding corners and monopolies, restraining the unnecessary multiplication of middlemen, regulating prices and the like, constantly endeavoring to protect the consumer.

In the end, none of these checks was sufficient. As the network of commerce spread from Europe to the Americas, Asia, and the rest of the world, and a loose external linkage of exchange between men and places became a self-integrating system of inward market-relationships growing with time and spreading through space, the force of religion became tangent, the tradition of the guilds died away, the state, possession and tool though it still was of the anti-industrial consumer nobility, became suffused with the techniques and passions of the capitalist on its own behalf. And the capitalist became powerful enough to demand that the state shall take its hands off him, let him go and let him do as what he held to be his interests required. The early underworld intent of *caveat emptor* now became its respectable publicly avowed purpose. It became a rule of law that the buyer who has failed to protect himself against fraud and deception when buying, deserves to take the consequences. Oliver Goldsmith sets forth the consummation in his *Vicar of Wakefield*. The Vicar's son, Moses, trading at the fair, brings home some razors that cannot cut butter, to say nothing of shaving beards. When the seller is reproached for cheating, he disclaims all such intention. He had never said that the razors could be used for shaving. What, then, were they made for, he is asked. His reply, which every user of the modern safety razor can appreciate, is that the razors were made to sell.

The view exhibited by this reply indicates a final mutation in the economic common sense of Europe. Adam Smith, when describing the positive attributes of capitalism as a growth of abundance achieving itself via the mechanism of the competition of equals seeking each his own good through free trade, marks not the beginning but the end of an era. The father of political economy is the philosopher of the old capitalism, not the prophet of the new. In the old capitalism consumption was the end, production the means. Producer and consumer were equally human beings of flesh and blood serving each other's needs. Neither was a sub-species of the "economic man" engaged in a deadly conflict with the other, selling dearly, buying cheaply. But by the time Adam Smith was writing this specialization and polarity of producer and consumer was becoming a part of the commonsense of Europe. Antagonism of suppliers to demanders was accepted as the law of economic behavior. For the continuity of movement from production to consumption had been broken: "the consumer" was now to the producer an unknown alien, an abstract, impersonal profit-provider existing only for the producer's advantage. Selling changed from a means of distributing goods for people to consume to a device for assembling profits for the producer to possess. "Political economy" emerges as a "science." Its professors and their works multiply geometrically in a hundred years. The farther they are from Adam Smith, the more dominantly is their theme the producer, his interest, his works and his ways. And Marx, the revolutionist, is even more deeply absorbed in him than John Mill, the traditionalist. In the course of time the producer's activity is denuded of even its political implication. Political Economy breaks up into Political Science and Economics. The producer alike as master and as man, stands supreme, alone, the maker and lord of all the tangible values of civilization, the sole support of its intangible values. This transvaluation of the producer is the fundamental fact in the perversion of capitalism which now sets in.

CHAPTER II

THE PERVERSION OF CAPITALISM

§ 1. CONFUSION OF CAPITALIST IDEAL WITH CAPITALIST FACT

CAPITALISM is neither the beneficent providence its defenders proclaim it, nor the power of evil its opponents make of it. Means, method and plan of dealing with one another happened upon by the peoples of Europe in the course of their long uneven endeavor to improve upon their poverty of life, this capitalism is not merely a present pattern of structures and functions composing an economy. It is a historic life, growing and changing in time and space as an individual's does, with its past alive and active in its present, laying down the inward lines of development for its future, providing the continuity without which there can be no identity. This is why capitalism remains willy-nilly an economy of abundance. This is why, among the depersonalized captains and go-getters of the cartel, the trust, the financial corporation, we still find countless master-workmen and merchants to whom their employees are not merely labor, but people; and to whom the customer is not merely an instrument of profit, but a human being with wants to be served. Nor can it be said that capitalist society is a worse exploiter, so far as the values of human life are concerned, than its predecessors and rivals. Only a faith uncontaminated by the facts could assert that the owner's concern for his property which tempered the lot of the slave in imperial Rome or republican Dixie, or the Christian charity and feudal rule which tempered the lot of the serf in mediæval Europe, were any more beneficent than the democratism, the humanitarianism, and the feeling for progress which temper the exploitations of the capitalist. It is open to doubt whether the anarchic small-scale wars of the military piracy of earlier times were more desirable than today's periodic great wars of financial imperialism. Except that the ills we know not of seem more preferable than the ills we have, except that we always tend to reject what is and desire what is not, it is a Hobson's choice between the predations of a modern banker, or those of a mediæval suzerain or an ancient monarch.

The fallacy both of the champions of capitalism and of its foes is due to confusing the capitalist ideal with the capitalist fact. The champions purport to vindicate the facts by the ideal. The foes purport to damn the ideal by the facts. The ideal is established as a logical movement from selected premises to desired conclusions, set down as a unitary well-ordered system. The facts are events outside of logic, and very refractory to its control. Among these events, the logical system, pretending to mastery over them, counts as one. The story is made by the action of the illogic of events upon the logic of the ideal. Falsify the ideal as it may, it does not cause men to abandon it or to speak as if it were not true. Could the logic of capitalism have worked itself out with dialectical purity in the mind and blood of events, capitalism would have set up in actuality the utopia that Communism aspires to, and Communism would never have arisen. Could the facts of Communism conform to its logic, the communist practice would be innocent of the evils which so sharply contradict its principles. Capitalism is wicked because it is older, not because it is worse than Communism. In these matters, too, only the young die good. Now the principles of capitalism are simple and the practice of capitalism contradicts them even more than Communist practice contradicts Communist principles. In essence they endeavor to account for the political economy of man by applying to it the Newtonian mechanics of nature. The resulting philosophy may be summed up as follows.

§ 2. THE PRICE SYSTEM AS THE MECHANICS OF PLENTY AND INSTRUMENT OF FREEDOM

MEN are born into a world which was not made for them; they have wants which it does not supply and which therefore they must supply for themselves. The act of supplying wants is labor, and such labor is the source of wealth. Since no man can supply all his own wants, a division of labor ensues: each man labors to supply one want of all and all men labor to supply every want of each. But men are distributed widely in space; work requires time; much of what is produced cannot be consumed on the spot where it is produced; it must be carried from where it is made and not needed to where it is needed and not made. Thus the supply of wants depends not only on the production but on the exchange of goods.

To render exchange smooth and swift, a medium of exchange is required, easy to handle and to transport and to measure the relative value of goods with. This medium is a given measure of a metal, gold or silver or copper, and is called money. The cost of goods in money is price. The price of each thing is connected in a great many different ways with the price of every other thing. Some of the connections are immediate and direct, others are remote and indirect. Together they form a web, a network, of which the prices are the intersections or nodes. Into this web weave all the relations which prices can possibly have with one another. Logically, the web should be a firm, stable, self-sustained and self-sustaining pattern. Actually, it is nothing of the sort. A strain, a tension at any one connection or node sets all the others in vibration. A modification in any starts a process of change affecting all.

Not many changes are simultaneous; the process takes time, the changes occur piecemeal, going item by item from next to next. The lapse of time makes a complicating addition to the process. Now increase or decrease in the demand for certain goods, or an alteration of the quantity available, will alter the price. Alterations of this sort result in profit or loss in exchange.

Realizing this, some men endeavor by conscious intervention to prevent or diminish loss and to hold or increase gain; others attempt to "fix prices" and "keep the market stable." Efforts of this kind, if successful, may crystallize into customs or into monopolies. Like any other mechanical system, the price-system as a whole will, when not interfered with, automatically take on the form required for maximum stability; its direction is always toward the position of greatest equilibrium. On the other hand, each separate and distinct price composing the system is at all times a point of departure for variation and change. The price system is thus a whole which tends toward stability, composed of parts each and every one of which tends toward change.

The forces making for change are lumped under the term *competition*. Economic competition is described "as the effort of two or more parties, acting independently, to secure the custom of another party by the offer of the most favorable terms." This offer is in terms of price. Accepting one offer is automatically rejecting the other, and competition is a somewhat obscure way of naming the fact that the same person cannot accept two offers at the same time for the same thing. "Free competition" between producers should diminish the price for the consumer to the lowest possible figure. This is what is presumed to happen under conditions of "competitive bidding." For the price which any producer sets has to be adjusted to the price which every competing producer of the same commodity sets; the price which any consumer is willing to pay has to be adjusted to the price which every competing consumer is willing to pay. Hence, the wage at which a worker can sell his labor is determined by the wage that all other workers applying for the job are willing to take; the price which a worker pays for his victuals is determined by the price which every other worker is willing to pay for the same victuals. In a word, the competition of workers with one another in selling their labor brings wages down to the lowest possible price; the competition of workers with one another in buying victuals brings victuals up to the highest possible price. The competition makes work cheap and living dear.

But it is not the only competition. Its effects are wiped out by the competition of employer with employer and merchant with merchant. The wage which any employer of labor is willing to pay is raised by the competition of other employers of labor; the price for which any merchant is willing to sell his goods is levelled down to the lowest price any other merchant will take. Similarly, the price of one kind of goods, say cotton stockings, will be modified by the price at which rayon stockings are offered; through its price, fowl will compete with beef, beef with lamb, lamb with fish, linen dresses will compete with cotton, cotton with woolen. The competition will be vertical as well as horizontal. The sellers of raw materials will compete with its fabricators; the fabricators with the wholesalers and jobbers, the jobbers with the retailers; the retailers with the ultimate consumer.

Into the price of the clothes we wear and the food we eat there enter all competitive differentials, from the farm, through the factory and store to the table or closet. It will involve the price of land, the price of seed or feed, the price of ores and finished tools, the price of railroad cars and engines, the price of paper and twine, the price of advertising and delivery; and each of these prices will have been fixed competitively. The price of any commodity is the lowest price possible, i. e., the most stable and inert price, in the immediate circumstances and the general state of the industrial arts. The law which "controls" prices is the law of supply and demand. Under it the price-system works automatically and inexorably to the advantage of the consumer. So, the mechanics of nature spontaneously serve the ends of man. The satisfaction of the consumer's wants is the whole purpose of production; the price system is its means and measure. Wealth is only another name for its vehicles, at once the security and the liberty of men.

For by assuring them their subsistence it sets them free from need; it lifts up their struggle for mere life to a high endeavor after the good life.

The good life is distinguished from mere life through the greater number, variety, range and intensity of the wants it satisfies, of the pleasures it contrives and the pains it excludes or reduces. Socially, it is definable as the greatest happiness of the greatest number. Each person is the best judge of his own happiness; each, if he only knows, can make his own unique calculus of his pleasures and his pains. When correctly informed, his self-interest is his best guide, and in pursuing it he automatically contributes to the interests of all others. But he must pursue it knowingly, not darkly, not blindly. His self-interest must be an "enlightened self-interest." Thus its first and foremost call is for education, for that equalization of men which only the "diffusion of knowledge" can encompass. Unless the individual knows the nature of his interest, knows its background, causes, conditions and connections, unless he is aware how the forces act which favor it and how forces act which hinder it, he cannot truly know himself nor truly pursue his interest. Knowing, however, what his interest is, freedom to pursue it is indispensable. The freedom and enlightenment of each is the condition of the greatest good of the greatest number.

§ 3. CAPITALISTS, BY EMULATING HEREDITARY ARISTOCRACY, PERVERT CAPITALISM

OBVIOUSLY, at no time in its history did capitalism attain in fact the organizational pattern and Utopian results defining its ideal. Its paramount and unique consequence is its steady increase in the number, the variety and availability of goods for consumption by the masses of men. Right up to 1929, in whatever portions of the world capitalism reached, more things were added to the daily economy of the common man, and in the more industrialized countries, such as England, Germany, the United States, the addition ranges over a considerable diversity of spiritual as well as material values. Between the tea which became available to "the poor and humble" from 1742, to the motor cars and radios which became available from 1920, there is a variety drawn from the whole world. The extension of personal service is even more significant. Teachers, doctors, dentists, oculists, nurses and the like, today bring to the masses of the people a quality of service more intimate and competent than kings and noblemen could get one hundred years ago.

A consequence second only in importance to the creation of plenty is the reënforcement of political freedom. As the serf was replaced by the wage-worker, and the operative relationships in the daily economy changed "from status to contract," the capitalist claim that each man should count as one and not as more than one in a contract to work was reënforced by the claim of the subject and tributary that all should be equally citizens, that each man should count as one and not as more than one in the political contract. The positive intent of the capitalist system, as expounded by the early philosophers of capitalism such as Adam Smith and Jeremy Bentham was to effect a positive change from scarcity to abundance and from subservience to freedom.

Need it be repeated that the conflict between capitalist fact and capitalist ideal is not to be attributed to an innate hypocrisy of the capitalist soul? Capitalism was not a creation *ex nihilo*. It arose as a variant upon a prevailing economy. It struggled to survive and to grow within the environment of that economy, and as it conspicuously modified its environment, the modifications which the environment worked on the original nature of capitalism have been passed by without the notice they deserve.

The ruling powers of the world in which the capitalists were themselves growing to power remained, and in some small degree remain, the hereditary nobility. Their lordly way of life retained the prestige of ancient authority and deferential habit. It is not altogether true that they became capitalists. It is rather true that all capitalists wanted to become aristocrats and if they were unable or unwilling themselves to live life in the lordly way, they desired that their children should, and for the most part, their children do. Nor is there anything perverse or unnatural in the contamination of capitalist habits by the standards and values of the hereditary aristocracy. Those habits are not, and for the most part cannot be, spontaneously acquired. They are laborious and servile. Those who live by them do so not because they are a source of enjoyment but for the sake of the power and wealth they bring. Formed as means to an external end they finish by dislodging the end they were to serve and become ends in themselves.

But never happily, never easily. The original nature of man, which is all set for consumption, not production, may be suppressed, but is not abolished. It persists and manifests itself in many new and often perverse forms and receives new names. In the Puritan it is *the old Adam;* in the modern it is *the unconscious,* but whatever be the name it is called by, it remains the consummative appetite of each and every one of the impulses that compose us. The aristocracy used to incarnate this appetite, gave it a form and a name. Capitalism, struggling for freedom, for power, began by denouncing it and repressing it. But the merchants and manufacturers, the bankers and brokers, ended invariably by imitating and adopting it. They entered for themselves into the utter abundance of life which is possible only to one who can consume without producing because many produce more than they consume. So the ideals of dignity and worth characteristic of the hereditary aristocracy were taken over by the self-made plutocracy. They came to be called "new rich," "parvenu" and their persons were as despised as their wealth was appreciated. The daughters they dower continue to be sought in marriage by the nobles needing dowry, thus ennobling wealth and enriching blood. Their sons, though not sought in marriage by the nobility with the same verve and in the same numbers as their daughters, are permitted to pay themselves into the aristocratic clubs, and initiated in the aristocratic ways. As this happens, the parity of enterprisers and workers, characteristic of early capitalism, is dislodged by the master-servant relation which it had superseded and the exploitative habit of the military aristocracy is translated into terms of industry.

§ 4. WITH THE AID OF THE FACTORY SYSTEM AND OF MACHINERY

THIS TRANSLATION has been facilitated by two other forces. Both these forces were directly correlated with the coming of abundance.

The first was the factory system. The factory system arises wherever more goods are required than can be provided by a single craftsman producing them alone; a division of labor is called for coördinating the different steps in production in an ordered sequence such that one worker performs one operation and one only. Instances of it occur sporadically throughout the Middle Ages. There were factories in Flanders as early as the fourteenth century which employed no less than one hundred workers. When numbers are so great, the relations between employer and employee are depersonalized. They cannot be direct; they must be indirect, represented by symbols and the subject of bookkeeping, rather than the face-to-face relation of living people. Moreover the scale of operations exceeds a certain natural limit only where the customers or consumers are as remote as the employees are numerous. The distant market is not seen and felt as living people who buy. The mind regards it as a locus of exchange and as a price received for goods delivered. These goods are conceived not as a material of such and such a quality made in such and such a way for such and such persons; the goods are conceived as a cost; stuff so much, labor so much. Cost is set against price and a balance struck.

The activity, beginning as a natural endeavor to know what one is about, develops into bookkeeping, and bookkeeping has since been built up into the tremendously complicated puzzle-box of modern accountancy, which functions more often to cover what one is about than to disclose it. In the bookkeeping process, the living men and women, whose personal wants and works are the one and only foundation for living for this impersonal superstructure, are forgotten under the superstructure. They become defined in abstractions. Their names are replaced by numbers and their personal vitalities by depersonalized, quantified concepts—labor, market: Labor, so much; market, so much. People fall out of view. The Flanders merchants who ran factories also sent out homework to peasant cottages on a piece-rate basis. They combined to fix the rate of pay and got laws passed forbidding workers to combine in their turn for the purpose of changing it to a better rate. These workers were producing for export; the production for the local consumer was based on quite different relationship between employer and employee.

The difference tells the tale. . . .

Machinery and the mechanization of industry, which started what is known as the industrial revolution, accelerated this process of depersonalization. Today it stands out as a dominant feature of industrial society. Machine production radically alters the relation of the worker to his tool. It makes of him an extension of the tool, an animated and detachable machine-part, interchangeable with any similar part. His individuality, his personal life, is irrelevant to his working value. In contemporary production any man can be taught the simple execution of each of half a dozen jobs and can perform them with complete competence in as many hours. Only certain trades-unions and the learned professions now require long apprenticeships, and there is good reason to believe that they do so not because art is long, but because long apprenticeships are good devices for keeping down competition. Professional schools which shorten the time of study are declassé and their graduates start their careers with a handicap.

With the factory came the modern city. But it is not the factory which makes urban society, it is the progressive abundance of the means of living that the city assembles and concentrates within its environs. Abundance was in England accompanied by an unprecedented increase of the population. Increase had been noticed already in the fifteenth century and by the time the industrial system was under way, the number of persons competing for each job was such as, in spite of abundance, to push down wages to a level below that of mediæval subsistence. The country-side had been blackened and poisoned by the muck and dirt and smoke of mine and the factory; "London fog" acquired its present-day meaning. Infants, as well as their mothers, were sucked into the vortex of production. Between the cities stertorous rail-trains smoked and flamed setting a new tempo in a new rhythm. Ships carried English textiles, tools and minerals to the far countries of the earth. The nation was prosperous and the people were dying of malnutrition and exposure. . . .

§ 5. THE OPPRESSION OF PRODUCER BY PRODUCER

THE PRODUCER has come to power. He has compelled the consumer living upon inherited income to make place for him, place in the seats of government, place in the ritual and ceremony of church and state, place in the liberal arts. In the sciences, hitherto ignored by the aristocrat, the producer has long ago taken place for himself; his power is closely bound with their prosperity. Now he has entered into the liberal life of the hereditary leisure class, and on the same conditions as the founding fathers of this class had established it for themselves—the misery and degradation of the multitudes of employee-producers. In other systems, ancient and contemporary, producers are slaves to military and clerical castes. In the industrial system, they were made subject to members of their own caste. The master-slave relation was restored. In a world whose increasing plenty was being interpreted as the gate to liberty, workers were forbidden to move from one locality to another; law designated a breach of contract by an employer as only a civil offence; a breach by a worker, as a crime. The notorious Combination Laws forbade the formation of unions. Wrote Adam Smith, "We have no acts of Parliament against combining to lower the price of work, but many against combining to raise it." "Strikes," he said elsewhere, "end in nothing but the punishment and ruin of the ring-leaders."

The cunning and force employed to create and maintain a state of peonage among industrial workers during the early years of English industry are but extensions and the methods but elaborations, of the devices used in fourteenth-century Flanders. To these innovations in oppression the people responded at last as any living thing responds to hurts from which it cannot flee. It turns and writhes, it snaps and bites and strikes out until it falls exhausted. Many people behaving in the same way for the same reason are said to riot. Like the slaves of antiquity and the mediæval peasants, when they could endure no more, the factory workers of early industrial England rioted. Their blind rioting struck terror into the hearts of Englishmen of wealth and position whose first reaction was an equally blind heightening of cruelty and harshness.

To many it seemed as if the misery of the many which came together with the prosperity of the few was something inherent in the nature of things that wanted accounting for; the classical conceptions of Smith and Bentham which pointed to the precise opposite seemed to need supplementation. This supplementation was supplied by Thomas Malthus and the Malthusian theory became a permanent item in the armory of apologetics which the new economy of the marriage of capitalism to machine-industry provided for itself. It was Malthus' idea that abundance can never overtake population, that scarcity must be the permanent state of man. People, he thought, increase by multiplication; supplies only by addition. Since 3×2 are 6 and $3 + 2$ are only 5, population must outdistance sustenance, there never can be supplies enough to go round. Always there must be more hungry mouths than food to fill them with, more backs than clothing to cover them, more hands than jobs. Always, hence, there will be unemployed, and their numbers will grow more, not less. Unless the people could be taught that continence which would reduce numbers until they balanced supplies.

§ 6. THE NEW SCARCITY OF THE "CRISE PLÉTHORIQUE"

AT THE VERY TIME Malthus was writing, the now historic "paradox of plenty," which is one of the major stigmata of the financial industrial economy, was manifest in its full irony. The business cycle was not only noticed but studied and described, its causes were analyzed and its cures proposed. Fourier, discussing it in 1825, when Marx was seven years old, called it *crise pléthorique*—the undernourishment in the body-politic due to overstuffing. The multitudes were starving at home for want of the goods they had made but could not buy, and because those goods had not been moved to other multitudes abroad, who could not pay the price which their own needs lifted above their own ability to pay.

Notwithstanding, the producer as consumer was more plentifully supplied, crisis or no crisis, than his grandfather and great-grandfather. "It is now the fashion," Macaulay writes, in the year of the *Communist Manifesto,* 1848, in his *History of England,* "to place the Golden Age of England in times when noblemen were destitute of comforts the want of which would be intolerable to a modern footman, when farmers and shopkeepers breakfasted on loaves, the very sight of which would raise a riot in a modern workhouse, when to have a clean shirt once a week was a privilege reserved for the higher class of gentry, when men died faster in the purest country air than they now die in the most pestilential lanes of our towns, and when men died faster in the lanes of our towns than they now die on the coast of Guiana. We, too, shall, in our turn, be outstripped, and in our turn be envied." But, because of one thing, of this same plenty, the worker suffered more acutely than ever before. Because of this same plenty, more than ever before the caste-like boundary between producer and consumer has become the overruling convention of the business mentality. The unnatural distinction is employed as if it were a biological difference, like that between species or the sexes.

Since at best the worker can consume very little of what he under industrial conditions produces, he ceases to figure as a consumer at all in the mind of his employer. The consumer is always somebody else far away able to pay a profit; he cannot be the anonymous laborer who receives a wage. Consequently, for this laborer a scarcity obtains which is of an altogether different character from the scarcity confronting the pagan slave and the Christian serf. If those went hungry or naked it was on account of a disorder of nature—drought or plague. The industrial worker goes hungry or naked because of the stupidity of the lordly men who are moved by self-interest, but not of the enlightened variety. They rationalize the misery of the multitudes as the condition of progress. They ascribe it to the arrangements of the Providence which gave into their hands the possession and rule over the good things of the earth. They possess and rule by divine right, which has descended from the kings to them. It cannot be otherwise than that God is with them, that he is their Lord and they are his people. For behold: Their personal fortunes do not suffer in the business cycle, even though their businesses do. They themselves do not go hungry or naked but enjoy the plenty which is the free gift of capitalism to them alike in depression and in prosperity. In depression, indeed, the newly established difference in kind between consumer and producer asserts itself most sharply. During a depression, the multitude of those who produce more than they consume go down; many go under; the small aggregation of those who consume without producing shine with living fat more brightly than ever.

§ 7. THE REBELLION OF THE PRODUCER

THE PROCESS just described is by no means uniform nor does it everywhere take the same shape. Not all the beneficiaries of the financial-industrial arrangements acquiesce in its evils, not all are willing to accept its good without sharing. The spirit of independence and rebellion which was first enchannelled in Protestantism and found its high place in Puritanism, now manifested itself in a new incarnation among the descendants of the Puritans. The sentiment which embraced all souls as equals before God found a new language. It allowed that of religion to lapse. It was speaking now the language of politics with only overtones from religion. The spirit of democracy, now entirely secularized, animated movements for both political and social revolution. Religion came in for its own revival, but this revival threw the authority of the church on the side of the authority of the ruling minorities. The Wesleys produced for the multitudes a religious method which, like some new theological thrift, should lay them up treasure in heaven more successfully than any competitor ever. Methodism turned out a by-way and cul-de-sac as far as the economic scene was concerned. The real force in early capitalism first passed over into and took form as the socialist sects and then the Chartist movement. The priority of the socialisms which came to be stigmatized by their successful competitor as "Utopian" is a sign of how completely the perversion of man into a mere producer has ousted the actuality of man as a consumer.

Ideas magnifying the dignity of labor, the duty to work, labor the source of all values, became a part of the battle-cry of freedom against the new perverted capitalism. Already in those days St. Simon, apostle of one of the Utopian socialist sects, added a new right to those enumerated in the political bill of rights which had become the faith and the backbone of the libertarian struggles of Europe—*le droit du travail,* Saint-Simon called it; the right to work. Since the depression of 1929, this right has been newly affirmed even by tory social philosophers and their overlords. Most of the leaders and prophets of these struggles were not then, as they are not now, disinherited workers but prosperous heirs of the older capitalists. John Ruskin is as typical of them as anybody. He saw as clearly as any that labor is justified by its uses; that no other justification serves; that wealth was made for men and not men for wealth; that the only values which are self-sustaining and inalterable are the values intrinsic to people living their lives abundantly and joyously. "That country," he said, "is richest which nourishes the greatest number of noble and happy human beings; that man is richest who, having perfected the function of his own life to the utmost, has also the widest helpful influence both personal and by means of his possessions over the lives of others."

The degradation of citizen into servant because he must work to live revolted Ruskin. "You must," he said, "either make a tool of a creature or a man of him. You cannot make both." His personal life exemplified his doctrine; and he had many companions. If his program was more imaginative than practical, so was that of most of his contemporaries. Tory mediævalists like Carlyle, the Christian Socialists, the French communists, William Morris,—they were all concerned far more about escape than control. In this respect the Marxists, who have superseded them and have established the orthodoxy of dogma and program regarding the socialist society to come, were not different from their competitors. Marxist self-styled

Scientific Socialism is no less Utopian and compensatory than other socialisms. The cause of its influence is not its pretension to being scientific. The cause of its influence is the fact that it provided a formula which rationalized and gave direction to the indignation and hatred of the employee-producers toward their oppressors. In the great tradition of Europe emotions of this sort are not respectable, especially if they are entertained toward one's betters. The Marxist teaching rendered them not only respectable but righteous. It set "class war" in a cosmic frame and in their hearts transformed the people who lived and felt like the dregs of society into the hope of the world.

§ 8. COMBINATIONS—TRADES-UNIONS, EMPLOYER ASSOCIATIONS, TRUSTS—AND THE CONSUMER

THE COMPETITION of each with all on which the price system depends for its unity and stability is a logical limit, not an observable fact. In fact the competitors group themselves, and the groups are at least as remarkable for coöperation as for competition. Men learn very early that in some fields association and harmony with certain other men are more advantageous than conflict. Groups learn that competition against some groups can be effective only on condition of coöperation with others. The advantageous associations are those with persons or groups pursuing similar ends. Plato demonstrated the principle and established its mechanism in the early books of his *Republic:* in any group, war and conflict without can be successful only in the degree that peace and harmony obtain within. Plato calls this peace and harmony, *justice,* and he shows how it is the honor among thieves as well as the good order in States.

The associative relations of all members of economic groups exemplify this Platonic justice. If each producer wants high prices and each consumer low ones, if each employer wants wages to be low, and each employee wants them to be high, the resultant sums will only be the lowest possible. Let, however, the employees be moved by their hunger and privation beyond the reflex of rioting to a more reflective organization of coercion, and they will combine, all endeavoring to secure for each the wage none could secure for himself. By combination thc individual producer saves himself from the consequences of his competition with his fellow-producers for the wage one employer will pay. The strength nullified by the competition of each against all is now more than multiplied by the coöperation of all with each. So, in collective bargaining with any one employer, the competitive advantage shifts to the employee. To hold this advantage, the employees will attempt to establish a monopoly of the labor in their industries. This aim determines the policy of trades-unions toward all possible competitors in their fields. They not only endeavor to unionize the un-unionized, and to render the status of the scab and the blackleg that of a social pariah; they often try to create a scarcity of skilled workers, by making admission to their union difficult and expensive, and apprenticeship arduous and long. Like any other association with monopolistic aims, from families to states, in order to establish and maintain its monopoly, the trades-union feels justified in employing all available forms of force and fraud. The governments of trades-unions know that if they are to succeed against the antagonist without, they must eliminate competition within. Among producers, thus, the competition of each with every other for jobs and wages has been changed into a competition of one association of such persons with another; and of all organized groups with the unorganized multitude.

Like man, like master. To hold or gain a bargaining advantage over labor, the employer will combine with other employers, as Adam Smith noticed. To prevent workers from combining with other workers, should strike-breaking activities fail him, he will resort to courts and to legislatures. Should those fail, he will resort to "company unions" so as to exclude independent unions. He will endeavor to bribe his employees by "welfare" arrangements, sales of stock, group insurance and analogous "benefits." He will use the blacklist, industrial spies and strong-arm men.

Bitter and violent as employer and employee may feel about each other, they have a common interest in relation to the consumer. The higher the price the greater the profit; the greater the profit, the better the chance for higher wages. It happens that unions and employers in their common interest as producers may combine against the consumer. Coal miners have so combined with coal operators here and abroad; union employees of the American stove manufacturers with their employers; certain taxicab companies with their drivers. The purpose of the combinations was to maintain prices, at the expense of the consumer.

In the United States there are some twenty thousand employers' associations, more or less. Those most in the public eye are the Chambers of Commerce, the Manufacturers' Associations, and so on. Among their purposes the outstanding are war against trades-unions, by all means from propaganda to strike-breaking; the regulation of trade practices; national advertising and propaganda; and lobbying to prevent undesired laws from being passed and to get desired laws passed. An organization like the National Metal Trades Association may be conspicuous for concerning itself almost exclusively with strike-breaking. An association like the Iron and Steel Institute may concern itself with "codes of fair competition," with endeavors to arbitrate disputes between members; to mitigate "cut-throat" competition and business graft; to eliminate "waste"; to conduct research and vocational training; to correct "trade abuses"; and to provide expert advice to those members who need it. Such producers' associations set the price level of their products on the basis of what the least competent and weakest member of the group can produce for. Thus enterprisers, by the standards of their peers unfit to survive, are kept in business, while all their helpers enjoy a greater profit by virtue thereof.

The stability of all such combinations, their capacity to maintain themselves and to grow, be they manufacturers, merchants, financiers, or employees, is strongest in those periods of high business activity called prosperity, and weakest in periods when activity is depressed. At such times the associations tend to break up into the original competitive units. Among banks, a competition in terms of interest rate changes intensity and tempo; among manufacturers and merchants "price-cutting" ensues, among employees readiness to accept employment at any wage. This tendency toward dissolution is, however, largely confined to those combinations whose members are individual manufacturers or merchants or farmers. During the depression the prices of foodstuffs, clothing, petroleum, leather and farm goods fell very low, while the volume of goods produced fell much less. On the other hand, the production of iron and steel commodities, of building materials, farm machinery, motor cars and their appurtenances fell very much lower than their prices. The latter were produced by trusts. That form of combination has a stability which depression does not much shake. The associational structure is so ordered as to hold price comparatively rigid amid swift changes of every other item in the industrial complex.

This rigidity of prices is a significant component of the perversion of capitalism. Where "free" industries are flexible and adjust prices and production to changing demands, monopolies tend to inflexibility. They fix prices, and if demand diminishes cut down production and disemploy labor. Within the dynamics of the system only the consumer remains to date unorganized. There is no instance in the record of consumer-organization parallel to producers' combinations. Sometimes buying has stopped spontaneously and this stoppage has been called a consumers' strike. Sometimes resistance to the exactions of the producer or merchant has taken an organized form and lived a brief life; among such organized resistances have been tenant strikes, meat strikes and milk strikes. Since the consumer is as important as the amount he is able to consume, the widespread withdrawal of custom sometimes has temporary effects, but so far as the system goes, consumers remain competitive with one another, unorganized, and save for semi-occasional government intervention, at the mercy of the producer.

§ 9. THE ETHICS OF LAISSEZ-FAIRE AND INDUSTRIAL AUTARCHICS

THE COMBINATIONS of employers, and their consequences, had been observed already in the early days of capitalism. How much they keep the postulated automatically self-correcting equilibrium of the price system off balance had been noticed, and their interference with *laissez-faire* reflected upon. To a humanistic libertarian economist like John Stuart Mill *laissez-faire* did not exclude the protection of the consumer, compulsory public education, the regulation and control of societies such as joint-stock companies whose managements, not members, hold the power; implementing the judgment of minorities concerning their own interest; the protection of "incompetent" individuals, like children; charity and welfare work. *Laissez-faire* implied, that is, a certain enforcement of liberty. Individual liberty being the sole sure ground of the soundness and stability of the economic system, government had the right, even the obligation, to protect this liberty. Self-interest is a sufficient guide only where it is properly enlightened. In such issues as education, or child labor, government has the duty to intervene: "freedom of contract in the case of children is but another word for freedom of coercion." [1]

Laissez-faire itself has, from the beginning, recognized that *laissez-faire* without order would be anarchy; without law, tyranny. But its prophets envisaged law and order as tools to render liberty and plenty more bountiful, not to render them scarce. Their distrust of government intervention concerned the end and manner of intervention, not the fact. Hence, the modern intervention of government in business has proceeded from the inspiration of *laissez-faire* or liberalism itself, upon the initiative of liberals, and always to safeguard liberty. To a great extent its tasks remain what they were in Mill's day: the protection and education of children; the enforcement of majority decisions; general welfare; the regulation and control of "delegated agency"; in sum, the vindication and guarantee of equal liberty. The form and character of the action has changed with the mutation of the institutions that called it forth. In the instance of "delegated agency" it has had little success. With the best will, in no country has oppression by great combinations of business or industry been permanently overcome. In none have the trends to combination been arrested, and the liberty of the individual producer preserved. Least of all, in the United States.

[1] John Stuart Mill, *The Principles of Political Economy,* Book V, Ch. XI.

Imposed or adopted in the beginning by producers of one commodity as aggressive or defensive weapons against the consumer or against producers of another commodity, or as a means to monopoly, these combinations developed very quickly into independent and self-sufficient powers, with even those not directed toward monopoly acquiring a characteristic trend thereto. Trade associations, cartels, trusts, were constructed both horizontally and vertically. The vertical structure is today the more significant one. It might be described as a building set up from the top down. The endeavor to control the end-product leads to the absorption of all the precedent materials and mechanisms. The vertical trust is the sort of pyramid we observe when, say, a motor company instead of buying tires, glass, steel, and other materials employed in the production of cars, acquires and owns the industries which manufacture those materials. Then, because it needs rubber for tires it may pass on to growing rubber; because it needs steel for engines, it may pass on to mining and smelting ore; because it needs transport for its raw materials and finished products, it may endeavor to secure control of roads and vehicles. It may build as readily as appropriate or buy. The industry, by establishing complete continuity of movement from the production of the raw material to the finished product, has eliminated all the independent middlemen intervening. As against its competitors, it possesses the differential advantage of this elimination; that, in its drive toward autarchy for itself, it may have acquired worse troubles than those it sought thus to escape is another story. It stands before the consumer who needs or wants a motor vehicle as practically insuperable power, with no alternatives he can turn to. He must take what he is offered, as it is offered; he cannot choose as he prefers.

§ 10. MONEY: THE STRATEGY OF CREDIT

THE TREND toward such autarchy of the industry is noticeable in every type of big business. It was incipient in the dependency of saloons on breweries or distilleries; it is explicit in the "agencies," chain-stores, mail-order houses and their ilk. Once more, the consumer meets the producer face to face. But now it is a Lilliputian consumer confronting a Brobdignagian producer. True, the giant is not all bone and muscle. A good deal of him is water and wind. But water can drown and wind can strangle, and not infrequently they dissolve and blow up the body which incorporates them.

What I am referring to is the financial dimension of the industrial economy. Originating as a device to facilitate the exchange and the production of real goods, an accessory to the division of labor and the enrichment of life, finance soon developed a separate and independent activity, muscled into every large-scale industry, and made itself master and overlord of the economic scene. Demagogues denouncing Wall Street and the "international bankers" as the devil of the piece may be unreasonable but are not without reason. As business enterprises multiply and extend their relationships in space and prolong themselves in time, cash money becomes, for reasons of safety, convenience, and speed, too clumsy a medium of exchange. The Spartans, to discourage money-wealth, coined iron; normally, nobody who is sure that he can exchange a $100 paper note for the same goods as $100 in gold, will want to carry gold. As the quantity increases, the unavailability grows. Where considerable sums are involved cash transactions in coin can be more difficult and inconvenient than the direct barter of goods. So that the general practice is to store coin and to replace it with paper as a medium of exchange. What money had been to barter, paper has become to money.

The paper may take the form of a bank-note, a government treasury note, a corporation bond, a mortgage, a stock certificate, a personal check, a promissory note, and so on. Each one of these papers is a promise to pay for actual or presumable value received and to pay interest, dividends, rentals, principal. Each one of them is presumed to have behind it some tangible "security" for which it can be ultimately exchanged —land, buildings, tools, goods, money, the drawer's integrity and honor. Each one of them can be and is used in its turn as a "security." Each one of them is in a greater or less degree a "negotiable instrument"; the holder can exchange them for cash money or goods. Each has a value of which the rate of interest, the safety of the principal and the future prospects of them both are components. Each has a price which is what the traffic will bear. Each one of them is subject to the pushes and pulls of the rest of the price system and the seesaw of supply and demand; the longer the interval between investment and profit, the greater the risk each presumes. Each links up with the others in such a way that they form a special system of their own, having its special habits and movements. The life of the system and its members is credit. Credit is faith, more or less insured, that a promise to pay will be kept. Credit is faith in the future. The faith may be rationalized or blind. Rationalized faith is faith reënforced by "business forecasts" and analyses from the hands of statistical forecasters or astrological fortune-tellers. Blind faith is faith standing unaided on suggestibility, hunches, intuitions, and the throw of the dice. In actual consequences the difference between the two is moral and æsthetic; the first is more respectable than the second.

Rationalized or blind, credit has been a prime instrument of enterprises whose manufacturing and selling operations take considerable time and involve the linkage of widely separated geographical areas. The larger the enterprise, the larger its credit component. The great corporations, such as railroads, steel companies, traction and power companies, are ostensibly owned by thousands of stockholders and indebted to hundreds of bondholders, distributed possibly in every walk of life and through every part of the world. Such ownership, ownership in the form of negotiable security, was only 16 per cent of the total ownership of the United States in 1880; it was 40 per cent in 1930, and 34 per cent in 1933. One-third of the total wealth of the land, of its private, personally-owned property, is held in the form of credit—a promise to pay by an indebted corporation, whose officers and directors have no obligation to the constantly changing stockholder-owners other than those formally set down in by-laws they themselves have framed, and who often do not feel obliged even to maintain the forms.[2] Such ownership is fluid and ephemeral. The

[2] Wesley C. Mitchell, *Business Cycles* (University of California Press, 1913): "While the corporate form of organization has made a theoretical division of the leadership of business enterprises among several parties

"securities" continually change hands, and the only material event signalizing the change is an entry in a book. The bookkeeping is the keeper of one-third of the personally-owned property of the land.

The promoters and organizers of the first corporations invested their own money and that of their friends. When they needed more, for purposes of expansion or replacement, they issued stock or sold bonds. The later promoters and organizers hardly ever invest anything of their own. They begin by issuing stock or selling bonds, and assign a block to themselves as bonus for their labor. What they take has no base in money or plant. Though it enters into the "capitalization" of the company as if it did, it is an appropriation of credit, a bill against the future, a promise to pay something for nothing.

§ 11. "ALL POWER TO THE FINANCIERS!"

THIS cannot be done unless the stocks and bonds are sold. It is the function of the banks and the stock exchanges to facilitate and to manage these sales. Bankers and brokers traffic in money and credit. They are masters of art in usury. Their basic and enduring function is to keep the channels of lending and borrowing open so that capital may move from where it is useless or not used to where it can be put to work. But like

at interest, it has also been possible to practise a centralization of power. The great captains of finance and industry wield an authority swollen by the capital which their prestige attracts from thousands of investors, and often augmented still further by working alliances among themselves. Among the enterprises of the whole country, this small coterie exercises an influence out of proportion not only to their numbers but also to their wealth. The men at the head of smaller enterprises, though legally free, find their field of initiative limited by the operations of these magnates.

"In large corporations the few individuals in control have an opportunity to make money for themselves at the expense of the enterprise itself, or at the expense of the other parties at interest. By giving lucrative contracts to construction or repair companies in which they are interested, by utilizing their advance information of the corporation's affairs for speculation in the price of its shares, by rigging its accounts for the same purposes, by making loans or granting rebates to other companies in which they are interested, it is possible for an inner ring to make profits out of wrecking the corporation. There are certainly instances enough to invalidate the easy assumption that every business enterprise is managed to make money for the whole body of its owners."

the traffic in other goods, the traffic in credit moves toward monopoly by the characteristic ways of force and fraud. And because it starts with credit the monopoly tends to include the corporate enterprise it lent money to. So comes the banker-owned and banker-directed railroad, power company, manufacturing plant, oil company, and so on. The methods by which direction and control are attained are not only the legitimate ones of direct purchase, but often less direct foreclosing of mortgages or disposing of securities. Railroads are "looted," companies are "wrecked," stockholders are "frozen out," "reorganizations" are arranged, "holding companies" are formed. Advantage is taken of "inside information." False information is spread by all the agencies of rumor and propaganda. Pools and combinations "rig the market." They prepare an appearance of prosperity when an enterprise is failing and "unload their holdings." They manipulate an appearance of failure when an enterprise is prospering, and when such an induced panic-sale of that particular stock has brought its price down, they buy it. By opposing their "inside information" to the desirous ignorance of the outsider, they can "sell short" or "trade on margin" without running any risk. They deal with "futures" which are sure things to them and always objects of faith to the public, and they manipulate this faith. So millions may change hands, hundreds be enriched and hundreds of thousands impoverished without any relation whatever to the actual nature, condition and value of the material ground for this faith, and without anything real changing hands. Bankers and brokers handle only "paper," book-sums, and balances; they deal in symbols of symbols of symbols, and in those signs they have conquered. . . . In their field, until the turn of the century, *caveat emptor* was the absolute rule.

§ 12. TECHNOLOGICAL AND CULTURAL CONSEQUENCES

PRODUCTION by means of machines has radically modified the character, function and status of superintendence. It has demoted the manager from the status of capitalist-employer whose business is his life as well as his living, and all whose relations to it are inward and personal. It has reduced him to the status of the salaried technological expert whose life is separate and distinct from this business, by which he makes his living, and whose relations to it are external and depersonalized. By a similar process, the suffusion of production with finance, the insurgence of the lender as the guide and providence of industry, has brought about something like a mutation in the frame of mind and scheme of values of contemporary industrial society. While discovery and invention have steadily increased production and reduced the number of persons and skills required for production, the financier's necessities of counting, estimating, drawing balances, alloting or withholding rents, interests, dividends, bonuses, have steadily multiplied the number and kinds of clerks, bookkeepers, secretaries, stenographers, sales persons, and other "white collar" employees, until today the latter equal all workers on materials. Thus the mentality of the multitude tends prevailingly away from facts to figures, from events to symbols, from the manual to the lingual, from the actual to the fictional. The preponderance of influence has shifted from the industrial arts to the notational techniques.

The outlook is that this shift of influence is only beginning. The ratio of clerks contributing only to overhead to productive labor contributing to wealth will increase, if not by addition to their ranks (they are also subject to technological displacement) then by the more rapid displacement of genuine industrial and agricultural workers. Tomorrow's prospect is that agriculture may be transformed from an art of tillage into a chemical industry. This will not only invalidate the advantage which good land has over bad, but the distinction between good material and poor, and will drive more and more people from the land. When fodder can be grown "commercially" in trays under chemical control; when cotton waste or any material convertible into cellulose can be remade into textiles of which rayon is only the first, textiles which promise, as they improve, to displace cotton and silk and wool for quality and strength; when dyes and scents can be "commercially" constructed from chemicals instead of being extracted and distilled from vegetables; the likelihood that making agricultural products will displace growing them, becomes convincing.[3] The technological unemployment of farmers, already very conspicuous the world over, is sure to be accelerated; that of industrial workers, even if it slows down relatively, to increase absolutely.

As the multitudes become in fact less important to production than machines, they become assimilated more and more to machines. If "scientific management" pays attention to human psychology, and makes meticulous studies of fatigue and day-dreaming and the mechanics of movement, if it sets up "welfare" or "social service" departments as integral units of a plant, it is not because the employee has been realized as a living personality, but because he has been assimilated to a gadget of the machinery, requiring the same prudent greasing and guarding while attached, and as certainly destined for the scrapheap when detached. The earlier capitalist who exploited his employees without conscience did so on the ground that they were human beings like himself, like himself under the obligation to look out for their own interest and deserving to take the consequences if they failed. His successor looks after their welfare on the ground that to be careless of them is as wasteful and expensive as to be careless of any other item of machinery and plant.

Personal, face-to-face relations now exist only within the frame of reference of one's peers. If it were not for the arts, no half would "know how the other half lives." Each functional association generates its own mentality via its function, in very few things is this mentality coterminous with any others; in most respects the other is realized only as a symbol and a tool.

It is alone on their interests as consumers that all mentalities come together, overlap, and in some respects interpenetrate. The consummative experience of the leisure few remains as ever the consummative dream of the servile multitude. We can understand how these incorporations of the ideal think and feel by examining the tools they use. Except in the extraordinarily narrow circle of their passional lives, their rival-

[3] *Cf.* O. M. Willcox, *Reshaping Agriculture;* W. J. Hale, *The Farm Chemiurgic.*

ries, their amities, their emulative self-love, and their sensual drives and frustrations, they deal in counters only, figures, signs, symbols, and signs of symbols of signs of symbols, as artificial and abstract as a pack of cards or a set of chess. The conduct of business, consequently, like the conduct of war, acquires to its captains the character of a game. Men, materials, workmanship, fall below the threshold of attention in the new setting; they cease to yield the self-satisfaction, the sense of prestige and power which the personality craves. These come from victory over the opponent alone—and the fate of the counters with which the game is played is an irrelevancy.

So costly is the mere maintenance of plants and equipment, that to work them at a loss costs less than to let them stand idle. Nevertheless, at work, they produce so much more than customers can pay for at the price, that always it is needful in order to control the old markets to eliminate the competitor, by destroying him, assimilating him, or combining with him, if he is a fellow-countryman or corporation; by procuring tariffs to shut him out, if he is a foreigner. But still fields and factories produce more and more, and exert themselves less and less; selling is far more problematic and strenuous than producing; workmen grow fewer; salesmen and other white-collar counters multiply. To keep up profits and dividends at home, free markets must be found abroad; foreign trade in money and goods grow terribly important in esteem. Soon the markets in other lands cease to be free. Tariff replies to tariff, impost to impost. The reach for markets becomes the animus in the policies of states; it shapes treaties and alliances, armament and education; continually it threatens war; finally it culminates in war. Here again, explicitly worldwide as are the competitive relationships, competition tends to compel coöperation. National cartels or trusts or open price associations meet, reach understandings about markets, methods, prices. International gentlemen's agreements delimit the production and distribution of sugar, and other items of general consumption. "National interest" is invoked to sponsor and share in financial-industrial agreements. Licenses, quotas, reciprocities and balances are employed to make a national advantage in a supernational economic network in which the ideals of nationality are an irrelevance, and the facts of nationality just another combination, like the steel, oil, aluminum or other trust. The consistent production of "surpluses" in the total economy of the peoples of the earth may bring every major product under agreements of the financiers and industrialists concerned. They are of the type that recover from the breaks and dislocations caused by bad times and wars. Applauded by the patriots of each country, they organize the exploitation of the consumer by the producer on a worldwide scale.

§ 13. PLENTY AS DISASTER

THE AIM and problem of all combinations, whatever their scale, is to limit to themselves the benefits of the plenty produced by the instruments and skills they command. Plenty lowers price and cuts profits: Preservative devices notwithstanding, all goods which are not soon consumed are finally spoiled; to offer them in the market is to lower prices, to keep them is to lose them and more. Most profitable, therefore, is to destroy them. The destruction of plenty is the problem. Although the life of everything has been shortened, and even a house or a church is built to last, not for ages, but for twenty years, nevertheless neither capital goods nor consumers' goods are used up quickly enough. Surpluses accumulate, capital accumulates, and in liquid form,[4] and these must be invested. Even though production decreases the burden of debt, the amount of debt-claims, interest, dividends, rents and royalties, does not and will not decrease. As Malthus said of population, the first debt is fruitful and multiplies to the point where it bankrupts the debtor. If he is a sovereign state, he stops paying; if he is a poor farmer, the state will help the creditor get his own back. Aristotle's argument against usury, ironically enough, may be vindicated by the too great practical success of its refutation. . . .

[4] In 1935 the banks are bursting with useless capital; nevertheless, savings banks report greatly increased deposits.

§ 14. SALVATION BY ADVERTISING

NOW THIS PROBLEM of plenty set the consumer before the producer in another light. As it became more and more pressing, the classical tricks of the trade—adulteration, false measure, *ersatz* instead of real material, etc., etc.—though persisting on a mass scale, and of a technical excellence unprecedented, became somewhat déclassé. Advertising was resorted to on a national—and on occasion, an international—scale. Artificial obsolence was attempted by appeals to the invidious sentiment, the snobist and emulative passions. All the drives comprehended in the expression "keeping up with the Joneses" were energized by suggestion, argument and exalted precedent. The newspapers and the periodical literature were, at increasingly greater sums, brought into the service. Shoes, hats, clothing, furniture, table wares, textiles, funerals, motor cars, voyages, all things and their containers are now *styled,* that this season's style may push last season's goods out when they are hardly used, not to say used up. Sometimes indirect consumption was engendered—as when power companies with a surplus of power, set themselves to procuring devices through which surplus might be absorbed without any reduction of price. The variety of electrical gadgets for household use are the offspring of this procuring. Nobody who is anybody could afford to be "out of style." To absorb the excess of capital, production became even competitively imitative on a grand scale. Production is competitively imitative when it is undertaken not to supply demand, but to offset, invidiously or otherwise, existing supplies. The production of armament, of jewelry, of cosmetics, is competitively imitative; it is not the demand which brings the supply, it is the supply which brings the demand.

§ 15. "CONSUMPTION ENGINEERING"

SO THE EFFORT to maintain high prices and increasing profits in the face of abundance, when taking the form of investment and production, led but to a more diversified abundance. In some countries, in some respects, the growth seemed geometric. Notably in the United States. To the advertising agent and "public-relations counsel," who often took competitors for clients, it was naturally obvious that the established competitive devices were of no help. That type of functionary came into existence—there are now some 25,000 employed in the business in the United States alone—because the devices were of no help. The attention of the publicity agent had naturally to be directed toward the consumer. Still valued as only a means toward the producer's ends, the consumer was to be employed in a new way, to be wooed with honey, smoothed and oiled into service. A sort of Platonic moratorium was declared on *caveat emptor.* New slogans embody the new attitude: "service"; "the customer is always right"; "satisfaction or your money back." Competition for the same limited aggregation of customers was to be replaced by combination to reach untapped ranges of custom; by means of "national" advertising millions of potential consumers were to be gentled and seduced into actual ones. After all, are not wants illimitable and are there not customers more than enough in the population to go round? Isn't one born every minute?

But these potential customers are the producing multitudes, whose lives are their livings only, all whose labor comes but to subsistence, who have little portion in the now so great embarrassment of riches which industry produces and finance manipulates. So the multitudes shine in a new light. There accrues to them a general importance as consumers which they had hitherto not enjoyed. Let them buy! Let them buy! At all costs let them buy. Make the prices low. If they cannot pay cash, let them have credit; let them pay on instalments, bit by bit; but let them buy. If their wages are too low, raise them. High wages, announces Henry Ford, will keep up buying to keep up selling to keep up production. "Advertising mediums" develop into political and social powers. Beginning, some of them, as literary journals with incidental advertising, they become advertisers with incidental literature—for which they pay fabulous prices to the nation's best fabulists. They become *arbitres elegantiæ* and *censores morum.* They set standards and seal with approval. They are the prophets and protectors of consumers and they wax rich from the pockets of the producers. The sages who guide the advertising and sales campaigns of the producers begin to talk about "consumism," "consumptionism," "consumption engineering." One bold spirit, a twentieth-century Mandeville reading an industrial-financial version of the Fable of the Bees, prophesies the magic salvation in "creative waste" and "creative spending." [5]

[5] So the boy tells the Bishop in Patrick Barrington's poem, "I Want to Be a Consumer," in *Punch* of April 25, 1934, which is reprinted here by special permission of the Proprietors:

"And what do you mean to be?"
The kind old Bishop said
As he took the boy on his ample knee
And patted his curly head.
"We should all of us choose a calling
To help Society's plan;
Then what do you mean to be, my boy,
When you grow to be a man?"

"I want to be a Consumer,"
The bright-haired lad replied
As he gazed up into the Bishop's face
In innocence open-eyed.
"I've never had aims of a selfish sort,
For that, as I know is wrong,
I want to be a Consumer, Sir,
And help the world along.

"I want to be a Consumer
And work both night and day,
For that is the thing that's needed most,
I've heard Economists say.
I won't just be a Producer,
Like Bobby and James and John;
I want to be a Consumer, Sir,
And help the nation on."

"But what do you want to be?"
The Bishop said again,
"For we all of us have to work," said he,
"As must, I think, be plain,
Are you thinking of studying medicine
Or taking a Bar exam?"
"Why no!" the bright-haired lad replied
As he helped himself to jam.

"I want to be a Consumer
And live in a useful way;
For that is the thing that's needed most,
I've heard Economists say.

The magnates who direct the policies of power, steel and electrical trusts declare as a matter of course that the days of individualism are over, and that the management of industry is trustee for its employees and the public as well as the stockholders.[6]

§ 16. THE TRADER AS SHEER CONSUMER

IN THIS DEVELOPMENT trading has become what fighting used to be to the well-born free-livers of earlier times—a liberal art practised for its own sake, with its own tourneys, pageantry and system of honor, with its own rules of emulation and invidious difference. A financial-industrial leisure class of sheer consumers has come into being to which the warrior elder brother is now subordinated all over the world except perhaps in Japan. The landed aristocrat is now ennobled by going into trade, not the tradesman by joining the aristocracy. The honor and the glory are the tradesman's. The football star, the trackman, and even the successful scholar not desiring an academic career, is chosen for his prowess and scholarship to join the gentlemen-rankers who are bond salesmen. To sell bonds is the gentleman's profession; to sell beans, the commoner's. If the gentleman wins his spurs selling bonds he becomes secretary to the president, and in the fullness of time president. The social frame of reference is where "creative spending," that is, sheer consumption, reaches magnificent dimensions,

> There are too many people working
>   And too many things are made.
> I want to be a Consumer, Sir,
>   And help to further trade.
>
> "I want to be a Consumer
>   And do my duty well;
> For that is the thing that's needed most,
>   I've heard Economists tell.
> I've made up my mind," the lad was heard,
>   As he lit a cigar, to say;
> "I want to be a Consumer, Sir,
>   And I want to begin today."

[6] *Cf. A Philosophy of Production* (edited by J. G. Frederick), by Owen Young, Henry Ford, Walter Gifford, Myron C. Taylor, Bernard Baruch, Sir Philip Gibbs, Earnest Elmo Calkins, Henry P. Kendall, Charles F. Abbott, Christine Frederick, J. George Frederick.

beyond the scope of even Veblen's mordant vision. The bond salesman moves in "society," in the world of free income, among those who can live without working, whose vocation is leisure, whose industry is consumption. It is his destiny to marry the boss's daughter and succeed the boss.

With this translation upward of the status of trade in the social hierarchy, the disciplines initiatory to the career of business have become as elaborate and ceremonial if not as arduous as the disciplines of war, the church, or the learned professions. During the past quarter of a century much is said about business as a profession, and all over the modern world graduate schools of business administration have been set up which transmit the total wisdom of the business way of life. These schools are the latest in the hierarchic sequence of the higher education. The first formal institution of higher learning might be described as a war college, and men were trained for war when they were trained for nothing else. The war college was supplemented by the theological school; that by the schools of law and of medicine; those by the schools of the liberal arts; and these prevailed, supplementing each other, not competing with each other, till well into the nineteenth century. Then the sciences struggled for place among the established academic disciplines. They not only won it, but have proceeded steadily to overrun the domains of their competitors. Science was followed by civil engineering, which separated off from the military disciplines and elaborated into the great technological disciplines that are transmitted in the schools of engineering and technology which now loom mighty in the educative world. Latest in the order of succession are the schools of business administration.

Graduates of these schools are indoctrinated in the attitudes, and, to some degree, disciplined in the skills which have been refined out of the dross of the financial-industrial establishment. Their fathers are often archaic capitalist entrepreneurs of the ante-banker days. A few are to be found everywhere, like other early life-forms among their more successful successors. To them their employees are people whom they lend money when their wives are ill, send hams at Christmas, cords of wood or sacks of flour when the baby is born, and so on. Such employers have appeared occasionally before the Exceptions' Committees of Codes Authorities who administered the Codes of "Fair Competition" under the defunct N.R.A. Half their workers are over fifty years old; and they pay them an average wage of $17 or $18, while the minimum is $13; they have not reduced wages during the depression; they reëmploy older workers who have been ill, and discharge the new one that replaced them although the new one produced more than the two together—"these two women have been with us a long time, and what would they do if we didn't take them back?"

The sons of these men have been indoctrinated and disciplined in some graduate school of business administration. Business is their profession, and their attack is impersonally professional. They must gain as much and spend in costs of production as little as possible. They must employ the methods of scientific management and scientific financing. So of wages they pay only the minimum; they cut out all loans, all gifts; they employ only efficient workers and sweat those; all their relations to the people are external and impersonal, and their way of life cuts itself off at every point from the way of life of the actual producers. They produce much more than their parents and they employ when they can all the devices developed in the record and recommended by the advertisers to sell their product. But as a group, they never succeed in quite selling it. They are always confronted by a surplus. They suffer from the threat of loss through the embarrassment of riches due to their own efficiency. They are faced by their self-created problem of plenty.

§ 17. THE PREDICAMENT OF CAPITALIST ENTERPRISE

THIS PROBLEM is the predicament of the financial-industrial economy of our day. It confronts the captains of finance and of industry with a dilemma. In the attempt to save themselves from "losses" they must either destroy much of what they produce and so maintain an artificial scarcity, or they must so limit production that overhead exceeds profits. The producers of foodstuffs, raw materials, and consumers' goods, have tended to choose the first boon; the fabricators of capital goods have tended to choose the second. So far as the general economy is concerned, without particular effect. For with a genuine *laissez-faire* prices left to themselves would drop, under a régime of plenty, to the cost of production. They would be price without profit. But such an economic individualism, whether rugged or frail, has ever been a stick to beat a dog with, never a social fact. Actual economic behavior has consisted in various forms of ganging up on *laissez-faire,* from corporation-building to government control. The sacred "law" of supply and demand has been manipulated, not obeyed. And with ironic consequences. In spite of the skill and cunning of finance, under modern conditions of production plenty cannot be reconciled with profit—save in a country like Russia or China or India, where plenty has not yet arrived and scarcity is a natural, not a fabricated, condition. Profit is postulated on scarcity, not plenty, and scarcity cannot be guaranteed except by scrapping the industrial establishment which most peoples are eager to maintain and expand. In spite of constant stoppages of production, of steadily decreasing demand for men and steadily increasing tension in communities, in spite of the constant destruction of goods of every kind to avoid lowering the prices, the establishments continue to produce more than their captains can handle without "loss." Concurrently, millions of men and women and children the world over starve while meats and grains are destroyed; go naked while cotton is ploughed under and sheep are killed; and have nowhere to lay their heads while buildings stand empty and builders go idle. . . .

CHAPTER III

PROPERTY, PROFIT, THE PRICE SYSTEM AND THE PRIMACY OF THE CONSUMER

§ 1. THE CONSUMER IN THE DYNAMICS OF THE BUSINESS CYCLE

THE PRICE SYSTEM moves as a whole in two ways. One is the movement presumed to be self-balancing, by which a disturbance at any one point of the system should bring on compensating adjustments in the rest of the system. The other motion is tidal; the system as a whole is always moving above or below a level of activity arbitrarily or conventionally agreed upon as being "normal"; it floods and it ebbs. This tidal motion has absorbed more and more of the attention of the economists. They call it the business cycle, and they treat the succession of its phases as an event in time. The self-balancing movements are spatial not temporal, and are now regarded as of secondary importance. It is in this appreciation of the tidal movement that contemporary economics distinguishes itself from classical.

Between the publication of the *Wealth of Nations* and the promulgation of the New Deal, stretch approximately one hundred and fifty years. Within this interval economists have counted some twenty to twenty-five floodings and ebbings of activity, calling the high tides, prosperity, and the low tides, depression. Such tides or cycles were observed as early as the sixteenth century before economics or even political economy had been conceived. The observer of record seems to have been an obscure French writer of comedies, whom Clement Marot quotes in a letter to the Duchess Marguerite written from camp in Hainault in October, 1521. "Minfant," he writes, "bears witness in his comedy 'Fatal Destiny,' saying—

> Peace begets Prosperity
> Prosperity breeds Wealth:
> Of Wealth come Pride and Luxury:
> Pride with contention swell'th:
> Contention looks to War for health:
> War begets Poverty:
> Poverty breeds Humility:
> Humility brings Peace again
> So turn our deeds in endless chain.[1]

Minfant's verses do not sum up the essentials of the cycle with the patness of an old morality. His theory of its causes is, of course, most unscientific and the German record since 1919 falsifies it. But then he had not the benefit of the statistical tools and methods and the technical language whose present-day virtue it is to make scientists of economists today. As an economic philosopher Minfant must be classed with the naïvely psychological or moralist school. Nevertheless, his theory so impressed his readers that it is repeatedly paraphrased throughout his century. Then other matters displaced the observations which made it important in the attention of mankind, and they remained so until industry brought them to the fore again.

The tidal movement seems to occur in any economy of which the financial-industrial technique is a measurable component. Hence the closer we come to our own day, the more likely are these tides to be world tides. Exceptions are due to local conditions, often non-economic, which have little in-

[1] *Cf.* H. Morley, *Clement Marot* (1871), Vol. I, p. 131.

fluence on the general trend. Palestine, from 1933 enjoying a "prosperity" not shared by the rest of the world, was such a local result.

Since the Great War all peoples affected with an industrial interest have occupied themselves with the endeavor to smooth and flatten the tidal wave. There is a consensus among authorities that the business cycle expresses a law of nature even more coercive than the "law of supply and demand"–some have correlated its phases with the procession and recession of sun-spots and others with the phases of the planet Venus. But the hope is general that the waves can be drawn off in such a way that high-tide will not be so high nor low-tide so low. Today in America the New Deal is a projection of this hope. Every country has made some such projection. Some have placed their trust in the manipulation of money and credit, in "balancing budgets," inflating or deflating currency, going off and on the gold standard; others have stressed public works; others have endeavored to compel the bankers and brokers to assume responsibility for the right and honest coordination of available capital with opportunities for investment. Inasmuch as such opportunities offer greater profit when they involve the manufacture and marketing of new goods rather than the reproduction of old, one idea has been to regulate the cycle by controlling the introduction of new goods. And all countries pretend to check speculation more or less, and some even aspire to abolish it. All, finally, are exercised over the alleged vagaries of consumption and the disorderly behavior of demand. They want to make it consistent and orderly, holding that a steady and continuous demand will automatically communicate its own characters to supply. Others think that the State should go halfway into business. They want it to function as a compensating economic force and to plan its enterprises in such a way that they will be active when private business is passive and passive when private business is active. Everybody talks about "planning." The theory and practice of "planned economy" ranges from the industrial-financial autocracy of communist Russia and Nazi Germany to the oligarchies of England and the United States.

§ 2. BUSINESS INTEREST, ADAM SMITH TO THE CONTRARY

NEITHER the theoretical nor actual dealing with the business cycle pays any but cursory attention to the consumer. The moving forces of the cycle being the behavior of producers, the efforts to regulate it rest upon the unconscious postulate of the primacy of the producer and develop consciously as an operation in behalf of the producer's interest. The consumer is taken for granted as a part of the setting, but it is assumed that his lot will improve with the lot of the producer. The maxim is to take care of production—and consumption will take care of itself. This attitude testifies how lifeless the principles and program of *laissez-faire* have become. The question in current discussion is not whether there should be planning but who should be the planner. Naturally the captains of industry and finance prefer to plan by themselves without having to make an accounting to the government or the public; publicists argue that government must dominate the planning, either as supervisor or controller.

But nobody any longer believes with Adam Smith that men promote each other's welfare by seeking their own interest. The components of the price system are now so filiated and interlocked that in a depression no businessman dare make a move unless all others move with him. If one should resume business before the others, he would merely multiply his liabilities without adding to his assets. Each industry is supposed to find its market in the others and to earn its profits from the wages paid by the others; should one be active when the others are not, it would only produce what nobody would have the money to buy. Thus it is to the interest of each to do nothing; yet by doing nothing it prolongs the depression for all. It is to the interest of all that each should resume business; yet for each independently to resume business, is only to suffer some loss. Our credit-enterprise economy appears to falsify Adam Smith's very first principle. It is a new economic world that not Smith nor Bentham nor their followers had any inkling of.

§ 3. MONOPOLY, ITS ENEMIES, AND THE PRODUCER MENTALITY

PERHAPS the material novelty of this world would not matter so much if it were not for the emotional and moral components. After all, monoply is something that must be struggled for daily. It can be maintained only by the continuous application of force and fraud. The "administrative control" of our economy is neither omniscient nor omnipotent. Competitors keep menacing it and have continually to be outsmarted. Unpredictable variables in nature and in human behavior keep challenging the ingenuity of the masters of finance and industry to overcome them. Population trends, for example, uninfluenced by neo-Malthusian agitation, proceed naturally to offset the Malthusian formula for the permanent supremacy of the employer over the employee. "Beware of race suicide," "be fertile and multiply," has been the call of capitalists, war-mongers and dictators to the common man from the beginning of industry. The barrenness of human kind apparently depends on laws which the insistence of even Mussolini and Hitler, to say nothing of an early Roosevelt or a current Vicar of Christ on earth, cannot repeal, nor the oracles of Marx cancel out. Both the epics of a "labor reserve army" of unemployed competing with employed workers, and consumer multitudes competing with each other, all arising from the increase in population, and all for the sole advantage of capitalist producers, are no longer the true stories they were. Their status has changed from the facts they were at the time they were noticed to sectarian dogmas dependent on faith. Science and invention are the causes of unemployment in the industrial world of today. The "reserve army" of labor is the by-product of machinery, and since it has needs which must be satisfied, even though it cannot pay for their satisfaction, it ceases to be a source of advantage and becomes a burden to the banker-entrepreneur.[2] The inventive impulse, moreover, is his constant disturber. The play of the behavior complex which Veblen calls the "instinct of workmanship" may be repressed but it cannot be abolished. Invention is al-

[2] Benefactions, taxes, social insurance schemes tap his surplus to pay for its upkeep. Americans have no inkling how far taxation can go into citizens' pockets: let them try England or any other European country.

ways an active menace to the existing financial-industrial establishment. You can never tell when some workman or student on the loose will produce an implement which may scrap a whole plant. The fear of such productions is constant, and not a few great industrial corporations have bought up and shelved patents, whose manufacture might introduce a competitive factor dangerous indeed. In spite of such instances, unforeseen and unforeseeable accidents happen and when they do, the rule of Adam Smith comes into play. Motor-buses are such accidents in the history of railroads. Many American roads have endeavored to monopolize all forms of transportation within the sphere of influence of their rights of way, including buses. Many have added motor-buses to their equipment, and tried to secure legislation equalizing rates. To no avail. Today the railroads of the United States are endeavoring to lure the traveller from the buses by devices of every sort. The buses not only compete for custom; they compete for capital. They are a new field for the investor. Often he gets his surplus from the establishment his new investment threatens. A railroad's very earnings are thus a menace to its security. For the national surplus of liquid capital has tended to increase beyond its possible proximate uses. It is a profit which threatens the whole economy whose profit it is. . . .

So natural chance and human inventiveness serve to save the capitalist from his always looming plethoric paralysis. They would mitigate his predicament much more than they do if it were not for the mentality of the society in which they obtain. The predicament is intrinsic to the mentality. For it, all values inhere in the producer and production; the consumer is an instrument to the producer, a means to his ends. Because so many of us produce more than we consume, the conclusion is drawn that we do not produce in order to consume, but consume in order to produce. All the good of life comes from production; shall production not be king?

§ 4. PRODUCTION, CONSUMPTION AND PERSONALITY

FIRST A CRY of revolution and a program of liberation, this faith now is a habit of mind making servants of us all. It hobbles action, poisons leisure, and embitters consumption. It turns the most liberal art into a servile craft. Its obsessive enchanneling of the stream of life is the indispensable factor in the capitalist predicament.

And though the predicament is relatively recent it cannot long endure. It is a stretch of the winding road upon which mankind is returning to the primacy of the consumer.

This primacy is, as we have seen, a fact of living nature. So long as men survive, the consumer in them, repressed but indestructible, will push toward the open day of plenty and freedom which have been the privilege of a few. To be consumers is our birthright, to be producers is our bad fortune. Now, because we are consumers by nature and producers only by necessity, personal life or individuality sustains itself by what we consume far more than by what we produce. It is significant that as production gains efficacy and extent the producer loses individuality and personal recognizability. Changed, when he enters the factory, from a craftsman to a machine-tender, from a name to a number, from an identity to an anonymity, he recovers his personality only when he leaves it, and enters the beer garden or restaurant, the poolroom or playhouse, the church or his home. He is a person, a man with a name, in those places and to those people to whom he figures as a consumer. He has a personal identity to those who are his friends or his rivals, his tablemates or playmates. To his employer he is a "hand," a detachable living gadget affixed to his machines.

That the good life, the life more abundant consists in consummative activities all the moralists testify. "Happiness," "self-expression," "self-development," "self-realization" are all ideals of personality which obviously rest upon the activities of free consumption. But the consummative premise obtains just as truly when the moralists proclaim the ideal to be "self-sacrifice," "self-abnegation," "duty," "obedience to God," and all the other ideals of subjection and lack. Those but serve as means to the ends of personality. We make sacrifices, we deny ourselves, we carry obligations and we serve God not for His sake but for our own. "God doth not need man's gifts, nor his own works." He is the Arch-Consumer. If, with Gautama, we make our abnegation absolute it is that we may make our Peace everlasting: if, with Kant, we make duty infinite, it is that we may argue that life is eternal. Salvation or happiness, the good life, are treasures we lay up in heaven by obedience and abnegation on earth. They are not the less ends we seek for ourselves, because they are postponed till we are nothing in ourselves. If we declare, "Thy will, not mine be done," it is because with Dante we recognize "in His Will is all our peace." So far as the inner life of any one person is concerned, God's will, the state's rule, all the institutions and establishments of society, are means to his personal ends, his survival, his peace, his salvation, his happiness. Those who say otherwise do so only because they are seeking additional means, in which they include us others, to serve their personal ends. It is the masters and rulers of the State, the Hitlers, the Mussolinis, the Stalins, who demand an absolute surrender to it; it is the heads of the corporations who exalt sacrifice and service for them; it is the school boards and superintendents who demand unthinking loyalty to the school systems; it is the masters of the armies and navies, not the men, who exalt the "services"; it is the church functionaries who demand the upkeep of the churches, and so on to no end. Always it is the beneficiary of an institution who seeks to make others its servants; and equally, but less commonly, it is the victim feeling hurt by an institution, who endeavors to enroll others against it.

And what is the personal end each seeks save the living and growing of the personality itself? Concerning the essence of this personality, not much can be said. Who you are; what you are, is something self-evident and obvious to you if you are in good health; you know that your identity, that which makes you, you, is inexpungeable, "surest of the sure, clearest of the clear," this, and no other, never by you to be confused or shared.

§ 5. PERSONALITY AND ITS KNOWLEDGES

YES, you have features, you have eyes and nose and ears and mouth, a head which thinks and a heart which throbs, blood in your veins, bile in your liver, passions and habits, hopes and hates. So have others. You are born, you grow up, you grow old and you die. So do others. What then is the unique You of your being, since every item you reckon is common, and the same catalogue of traits enumerates each person, and the same end finishes all? How can you vindicate the sure knowledge you have that the common identical parts of our common humanity are the separate and unique components of your unique individuality through having entered into the composition of your unique individuality? Because they come together with each other and together so distinguish themselves from all else, that none else fill the places they fill or hold the relations they hold, in this place at this time composing *this* living man of flesh and blood, and not another.

This is why the works of the economists and the sociologists and the psychologists and physiologists, with all their struggle to put the finger on individual difference, with all their ingenuity and mathematics, can never capture or reveal personality. At best they can point to it, encircle it, suggest it. But they cannot apprehend it and they cannot render it. They can merely name and enumerate its parts, and by taking them out of their dynamic relationships which hold together the living whole, classify and render them in another and different structure, another and different configuration of relationships, which they call "science," and which many regard as a revelation of life. But it is not a revelation, it is a manipulation of life, an abstraction and depersonalization, a symbol and guide post, but not the thing itself, the residue which escapes all analysis and by its separate existence renders all synthesis a little ridiculous. The biography may be intelligent, the record true, the data correct, but they do not render the actuality of the fierce free play of drives and impulses and insights and appetites with and through and against each other, so compenetrated of harmonies and conflicts that no trait or trend stands forth alone, and the whole but maintains itself in this compenetrated mobility and tension of its parts. This is the unique and living personality.[3] This is You—the subject,

[3] *Cf.* Albert Einstein's foreword to the biography of him by Anton Reiser: The facts, he says, are as set down, but "what has perhaps been overlooked is the irrational, the inconsistent, the droll, even the insane,

for which the sciences of man and the judgments of other men are predicates. They cannot distinguish you from another. Should you have an identical twin, so like you that looking in the mirror, each might believe the other's image is his own, you would still not attribute the confusion of the images to an identity of the persons. Others might. Others might everlastingly mistake each twin for the other. But not you. Not your twin. Each, in the life and feel of him, will forever know that he is himself and not another, nor can he ever mistake himself for another, however like. The naked fact that the two of you cannot occupy the same space at the same time becomes both a cause for all kinds of consequent differences and conflicts and a focus for all kinds of associative relationships and harmonies.

§ 6. INDIVIDUALITY AND THE SOCIAL ORDERS

INDIVIDUALITY, then, is unique, and, moreover, from its dark beginning as consumer in the mother's womb, individuality is autonomous. Whatever be the servile habits forced on it, it grows and finds its fulfilment in its own feeling of itself as free. At heart no person is servile: servility in the eyes of others may be freedom in one's own. Let us assume with Aristotle that some men are truly slaves by nature. Then submission and obedience is their good: self-assertion and self-rule their evil. When they make the choices which inexorable life continuously sets before us all, they consent to the submissive as against the self-governing career, and in the slave-relation to their masters find their strength, their growth, their self-expression and happiness. In their own innermost thoughts their masters are means to their personal ends, much as children are to mothers and mothers certainly to children.

Where this feeling obtains, the master rôle is illusion more than reality. In the illusion that he is served, the master is

which nature, inexhaustibly operative, implants in an individual seemingly for her own amusement." Einstein speaks as if this surd in personality were another identifiable and denumerable item, whereas it is the result of the compenetration and symbiosis of the denumerable items, the actuality of the person himself.

only a servant himself; in the activity of his serving the slave is master. Equally with the master, he pursues, and attains, his own fulfilment. His status "slave" does not express what he is; were his status "master," it would not deny that which, to and for himself, he is. A growth of nature, he stands amid her teeming multitudes as his master stands, equally with him impelled according to his nature to maintain himself and to grow. He is another psychological species, and in the differentia of his being not less or lower than his master, but equal. This equality, this parity of the different, is liberty. As Condorcet says, the individual is "the depository of natural liberty, before whom the power of the state halts, and in some way ceases to exist."[4]

And in fact, not only the power of the state halts; also there halts the power of each and every associative configuration of human beings in which a personality lives and moves and has his being, and any number of which he may, between birth and death, enter and leave as pleasure chooses or need compels. This mobility is intrinsic to his individuality, and the ground and premise of free society. Because of it, classes, castes, churches, states, economic systems, all groupings, save perhaps the groupings of parents and children, are external and transitory; and capable of any degree of integration or competition with one another for the individual's allegiance, as they seek to persuade his consent or coerce his submission. This mobility is the foundation of democracy and explains why democratic society, whatever its mode, tends to be a classless society. A classless society is necessarily a voluntary association—i. e., an association based on *consent*—of individuals in which each enjoys equal liberty; where, hence, in the language of the paradoxical enemy of democracy, Marx, "the

[4] It was a feeling for this fact which led Ralph Waldo Emerson to declare: "*Every actual State is corrupt.* Good men must not obey the laws too well. What satire on Government can equal the severity of censure in the word 'politic,' which now for ages has signified 'cunning,' intimating that the State is a trick. I am glad to see that the terror at disunion and anarchy is disappearing. Massachusetts, in its heroic days, had no Government, was an Anarchy. Every man stood on his own feet, was his own governor, and there was no breach of peace from Cape Cod to Mount Hoosac. . . ."

free development of each is the condition for the free development of all." A classless society is a society in which the parity of the different sustains itself without effort; a society whose members are free consumers.

§ 7. THE SOCIAL PAST AND THE PERSONAL FUTURE IN FREE SOCIETY

SUCH A SOCIETY, the world being what it is, is an ideal, a logical limit, not a possible event. Heaven is another name for it. But if ideals are logical limits, they are also plans of actions, programs to transform the possible into the real, and as such a program the classless society is to no small extent one where all the tools and materials and many of the associative forms composing capitalist culture are essentials. The drive and push of some of them may need to be reduced; their energies to be drained from the level of operative present facts to that of illuminating recollection of a past gone but not forgotten. All of them must continue as either memories or facts if the positive achievements of the modern economy are to be retained. For plenty depends on instruments and the methods of their employment—on the state of the industrial arts—and we cannot have plenty without the arts of plenty. The problem of free society turns on the weight to be given to the components of capitalist society, not on their survival or extinction. Among those components, the institutions of private property, the price system and the "profit-motive" have aroused the most passionate enmity and endured the most bitter attacks.

§ 8. PRIVATE PROPERTY: ITS PSYCHOLOGICAL NATURE AND LEGAL FORM

PRIVATE PROPERTY is an institution which has an intrinsic psychological base and a legal form. The psychological base determines the peculiarities of property as a fact in nature. The legal form precipitates certain customary and conventional rules for manipulating this fact in nature in such a way as to "keep the peace." The legal form is ownership. The psychological base establishes property as such.

In most discussions concerning the abuses and exploitations

consequent on property, the legal form is the subject. Psychologically, property, like competition, has its root in the fact that very many people, all different, are trying each to live together with the others, under conditions that, by making it impossible for two to occupy the same place at the same time, make it necessary for two to fight over that place at the same time, even when there are many available places.

Every animal appears to possess an elementary property sense. Its manifestations begin in infancy. Its objects are food and nesting places. Perhaps the earliest is the effort of one member of a litter to resist being expropriated by any other from its position at the maternal nipple. Nutrition and growth depend upon appropriation and absorption of objects outside the skin. These objects, movable and immovable, acquire the significance of property when a struggle arises as to who shall absorb them. Property is a function of the physical impossibility of two infants nursing at the same teat at the same time. So long as the act of feeding or sheltering, alike among young animals or human infants, is not interrupted or obstructed, the sense of property remains unawakened. When an interruption takes place, in the form of withdrawing the nipple or dislocating the suckling, the holding and clinging movements ensue which are the basis of possession. Defensive movements responding to competition and rivalry, they cry "mine" to the expropriation and constitute its first meaning. "Thine" is an analogic extension of "mine." Bodily activities such as clinging, covering, getting the feet in the trough, holding fast to the person, then become secondary extensions, substitutes and symbols for the process of taking in the nourishment. The contiguous object gets to be regarded as part of the self like the absorbed object. That which is beyond the skin is felt as a prolongation of the skin; it belongs; it is proper to the organism or person or group, its qualification and property; that which an individual can have and can hold. Holding with its overtones of resistance and defense, is more important than having.

Essentially then the sense of property is the conscious activity of appropriation and identification occurring as response to explicit or implicit rivalry and competition for things and places. The object of the rivalry acquires the formal status of private property when the rival acknowledges defeat and no longer spontaneously seeks to take that particular place. Many objects called property, hence, never become so in the minds of either the owners or the non-owners. Many objects not called property stand functionally in the property-relation to people who would be shocked to learn it. This holds under Communism as certainly as under capitalism. Property is never abolished; its locus is redefined.

It would be natural that the mother should be the earliest object of the sense of property. Even in a matriarchal order the competition of the male parent with the infant for attention from the mother-wife must have caused antagonistic appropriative sentiments; and among only children the manifestations composing the behavior complex called jealousy are consequences of an initiating proprietary attitude toward the mother. The attitude is an enduring dynamic of social relations and figures importantly in our folk-ways and mores. It may have been the starting point of the male's appropriation of the female to his exclusive and personal uses. From the female as mother and as wife to the non-personal extensions of her personality is an easy and simple step. Anything attached to her person or employed in her labors becomes associated with her being and thus with one's own. The appropriation of things through persons can extend to the whole family or to a tribe of families. So long as the relationship is face-to-face direct, the appropriation and identification with self which establish the proprietary claim is simple and dramatic. They may reach out from nesting or camping places to hunting grounds, and from hunting grounds to range.

But if out of sight is out of mind, conversely in sight is in mind. The sort of combination that competition brings about in energizing the price system it also forwards in confirming the property sense. In the primitive cultures where the institution of private property seems to be absent, the proprietary relation is analogous to that which a stockholder in a joint-stock company has to the company plant. The personality and privacy are functional and consummative: So far as the consciousness of the tribesman goes, the tribe and its possessions are appropriated and identified with the self, not the self with the tribe. He does not feel: *I am that;* he feels: *That is I.* Signs and speech extend this appropriation and identification to objects and persons out of sight, absent in time and in space, and until *mine* becomes largely a habit of distance reference and symbolization. When we talk about "my race," "my country," "my profession," we do so in virtue of this habit. The appropriation and identification of objects which it signalizes are operated by sentiment, enchanneled in verbal formulæ.

As extensions of the personality fundamentally tenuous and illusory, the objects may be dissociated from it with the same readiness that they were associated. Psychologically, all property has a variable status; one item may be ineluctably identified with the personality, and character and habit entirely conditioned by reference to it; another may be loose and transitive. According to the ruling passion of a given time, having and holding may be succeeded by loosing and abandoning, owning by disowning, without any change in legal or material status. Disowned sons, abandoned farms, unused houses, discarded clothes, ideas, wives, are among the items subject to the claim of the "owner" if he chooses to make it.

Thus by contrast with psychological ownership, legal ownership is fixed and rigid; changing ostensibly according to due process of law. As a rule it is indirect, and its effectiveness depends on the consensus of the community. Legal ownership is the basis of absentee ownership, while psychological ownership can rarely be absentee. For example, many people, having a face-to-face relation with the stocks and bonds from which they draw the income on which they live, inwardly appropriate those stocks and bonds, identifying them with their personality, and cherishing them as property. At the same time, these "securities" may represent the indebtedness of a factory which exploits its workers and gouges its customers. Since legal possession is not psychological identification, the owners of the securities may disown the factory and cling to the securities without any conflict. Yet the ownership of the *usufruct* of the factory, of its profit or increase, makes the stockholders legally responsible for its *use*. They are in a certain sense in the position of consumers who are held responsible for the conditions under which what they consume is produced. Psychologically, they have no portion in those conditions; only those persons have whose actions knowingly maintain the conditions. Having a face-to-face relation with them, those persons are identified with the conditions and are held and hold themselves materially responsible for them. They are the managers, the users; the functional, that is, the psychological, owners. Their responsibility is personal.

The tendency to identify ownership with use is innate. If you are lucky enough to have a seat on a street-car and leave it for a moment, the chances are that your successor will render it back to you. The other riders admit a proprietary claim in the fact of use. A sufficiently prolonged interval of disuse abolishes the claim. The later Roman empire based land-tenure on the principle of use; and the tradition carried over to the Ottoman world. Street-car conductors, clerks in stores, functionaries of all sorts and orders, speak of "my job," "my place," "my counter," "my car," "my store," "my company," and so on. Although they hold their places on sufferance at the mercy of an impersonal personnel manager or foreman, in fact their places are psychologically their property. Property here expresses habit and familiarity, generated by the functional relationship of the individual to that which he appropriates. It stands both directly and symbolically as an extension of his personality. The reason why managements in modern society are able to cheat and betray owners is to be found in this ownership of use, in the automatic appropriation of, and an identification with, what one works upon continuously. Hence though legally without rights, managements enjoy all the rights there are. They act on Mr. Dooley's precept: "Don't ask for Rights. Take them. There's something the matter with a right that's handed to you." For they are in functional possession, and if possession be not nine points in the law, it is another thing with the same validity. When Mr. Charles M. Schwab was challenged on the Gargantuan bonuses handed him and Mr. Grace as heads of the Steel Trust, he replied he had forgotten that he didn't own the damn company.

Psychologically property is use: Use gives things whatever social or spiritual meaning they have. Use, as Plato observed millennia ago, is revelation of reality. Not the carpenter, he said, knows the real bed, nor the maker the real flute; only the users truly know the bed as bed and the flute as flute. Since there can be no use which is not use by persons, all property remains basically personal or private property, whether in Russia or in England or the United States.

For this reason, the whole movement against private property, humanitarian and generous as it is, rests upon an error and threatens disaster. What its members are in truth vexed by is the tragic insufficiency, not the excess, of private property. The great need is not for less private property, but for more private property; not to replace privacy with publicity, but to multiply privacy. The great defect of the system of producer domination, is that it keeps private property the artificial privilege of the few, whereas it is the natural right of the many.

The inner meaning of private property is to enable that continuous expansion and growth of the self whose activities make the life of the free consumer. Collective ownership is only a legal form, a heuristic expression. It does not mean the distribution of property among people; it does not mean ownership of direct use. It means only the recognition of a legal fiction—a corporation, a city, a state, a church, a nation with some of the characteristics of personality sketched in—among them the "right" to hold property. But, functionally, collective ownership is absentee ownership. It is subject to the same abuses and injustices that are complained of with respect to corporations and municipalities and governments. The effective owners are the individuals and groups who directly and in fact hold and use the instrument, the capital, the properties, whatever their forms; that is, the managers and their subordinates: As the experience of Russians, no less than of all other peoples, has shown, such ownership requires the same police power, the same criminal courts and punishments, as the prevailing lesser forms of absentee ownership have called for in "capitalist" countries. Ownership to be efficacious must be direct and functional; it must be rooted in activities of participation and identification; that is, it must be private.

§ 9. THE PRICE SYSTEM

THE ASSAULT on the price system needs little discussion. No other effective device has yet been proposed for integrating swiftly the different phases of an economy based upon the minute division of labor and the free movement of credit. Plenty and the price system go together. The system is a part of the mechanics for the production and enhancement of plenty. Even the Russians, who tried to find substitutes for it, have abandoned their efforts, and the system operates in their communist economy with as many contradictions and complexities as in the capitalist.

§ 10. THE "PROFIT-MOTIVE" AND THE BASIS FOR ABUNDANCE

THE SITUATION is different when we turn to the profit-motive. The formula in which profits are attacked is "production for use, not for profit" but moral indignation has prevented the attackers from trying to work out just what their words meant. The abuses of the profit-motive are even more conspicuous than the abuses of the ideal of private property, and for the same causes, in the same way. In fact, the two may be identified as the war for profits, the trend to monopoly, the effort to secure increase unnaturally and to limit natural increase to one's self alone. What applies, therefore, to private property, applies also to the profit-motive.

Literally, profit is that which comes out; it is bringing forth, increase, growth over and above what has gone in. In this literal sense of the term, profit is the basis of abundance. Everybody desires profit; that is, he desires that his labors shall bring forth more than they put in. On the face of it, everything alive desires and tends to increase and multiply. Our whole economy is postulated on this increase. The problem, therefore, is not the morality and reality of the profit-motive but its aim and its methods. What do we wish to increase and how do we wish to increase it? We think most naturally of the increase of the material components of our lives. We mean plenty, and our profit is this plenty appropriated to ourselves, making us "men of substance." The substance does not, however, accrue to us primarily in the form of food, clothing, shelter, diversified and refined. Primarily we seek plenty through profit in the form of money, and profit is counted in pecuniary terms. The current identification of personal greatness with large money incomes, regardless of whether or how they are "tainted," is one way of enlarging and approving personality. It is an attribution of prestige and power which provides the profit-taker with satisfactions not pecuniary at all, since his material increase can have meaning only in so far as it strengthens and enriches his personality to himself. This effect on personality may be called psychic income. The psychic income is that which material profit is supposed to make more abundant.

Psychic income has its material limits. Even in a consumer economy no man can safely gorge himself or wear more than one suit of clothing at a time or sleep in more than one bed, or ride in more than one motor car, or be in more than one country. The residue of his material profit serves only to earn him the regard of his fellows, and it is the regard of his fellows that matters most to him.

Now, this regard is attainable in two not reconcilable ways. One is that which has become conspicuously and exclusively the method of science and of sport. In science and in sport there is a coöperative competition for excellence. Different men pursue an identical goal by a common method. Scientists working in the same field exchange their information, advise each other of progress, check each other's results, in an enterprise to which all the competitors contribute and in which most must lose. In sport the competitors deal with each other in a similar way, and to be a "sportsman" is to carry on competition coöperatively, so that the best man may win.

The other source of psychic income is sought through business enterprise. It works by the establishment of discriminatory distinctions, the pursuit of honor and prestige, the winning of fame and consumer's satisfactions, not with the friendly competition of others, but against their ill-willed resistance. Two factors are then in play. One is the actual competitive achievement of the personality: the victory of businessman over businessman won by the method of radical or "cut-throat" competition. The essence of this type of competition is its technique, even more than its aim. The competitor is concerned not with doing the same job better than the rival, but with destroying the rival; his interest is not in the goods produced, but in the competing producer. To abolish him no holds are barred. The second factor consists in the employment of all the modern devices of publicity which money can buy: it depends, that is, on self-exhibition through planned advertising; ghost-written autobiographies and similar forms of display. The acquisition and possession of material goods brings a sort of glory from income, the fabrication of prestige and honor brings a sort of income from glory. The two provide the kindly light which leads the businessman on. . . .

The degree to which he can accumulate this psychic income varies according to the group that the individual has identified with himself. Even for so canny a planner as Ford, there cannot be any planned general fame. Each seeks his good according to his kind, and these are not commensurable. Age makes a difference, and the psychic income of children is radically different from that of adults. The psychic income of a criminal comes from other sources and looks to other ends than those of a sportsman, a poet, even a businessman or a politician. The point of importance is that in all groups personality lives upon psychic income. The profit-motive ceases to operate where profits can no longer augment the personality; they may then become extremely unprofitable. Profits signify materially so long as an individual's optimum of consumption has not been reached: Beyond this, what they must produce is social esteem. When they fail to produce that, a tendency develops to win social esteem by disposing of them; so, for example, possessors of great incomes behave like Carnegie, the Rockefellers, and others. The Mellon personality-type is the exception, not the rule.

§ 11. PRODUCER SCARCITY INTO CONSUMER ABUNDANCE BY EXTIRPATING ABUSES OF PRIVATE PROPERTY, THE PRICE SYSTEM AND THE PROFIT-MOTIVE

THE CONCLUSION of the whole matter is, that in order to maintain a continuous economy of abundance, the institutions basic to the capitalist structure are indispensable. Private property, the price system, and the profit-motive are organic to the upkeep of an economy of abundance, and to the making and growth of a consumers' world in which production is fully and consciously a means and consumption an end. In themselves property, profit and price are growths of natural human relationships, not malicious inventions; evil or good by their uses, not their characters. Their characters are morally neutral, and time was, not so long ago, when even the profit-motive of each man served all men well. It is their abuses, not their uses, that must be extirpated.

This extirpation delimits the process by which the present producer-dominated economy of scarcity can be modified into a consumer-controlled economy of abundance. Its institutions and techniques will continue to comprise property, price and profits. But property will cease to imply a few privileged owners and a multitude whose only fortune is their force; everybody will have and hold property for himself as right. The price system will continue to operate as heretofore, but it will be a system of price without the monopolization of profits. Profits will come in directer increments of psychic income, rather than pecuniary values; they will consist in psychological satisfactions rather than in sums of money. Possibly, indeed, it is very likely, that they may continue to be counted in pecuniary terms; but they will not be paid in those terms. There will be a moral equivalent for pecuniary profits such as our nature makes indispensable.

CHAPTER IV

PRODUCER CONFLICT IN THE PRODUCER'S WORLD

§ 1. *Masters versus Men versus Gentlemen*
§ 2. *The Five Ways to the Men's Salvation*
§ 3. *The Way of Paternalism and Robert Owen*
§ 4. *Dr. William King Proposes to Make Every Employee his Own Employer*
§ 5. *Self-governing Workshops, Owenite Trades-Unionism*
§ 6. *The Ways of Socialism: French, Christian*
§ 7. *The Way of Political Liberty*
§ 8. *The Way of Marxism*
§ 9. *The Way of Nationalism*

§ 1. MASTERS VERSUS MEN VERSUS GENTLEMEN

IF THE WORLD where producers are masters has dealt harshly with the consumer, it has dealt no less harshly with the diverse multitudes of producers. The alleged common interest of all producers over against the consumer as such rarely modified the bitter exploitation of producer by producer. The struggle against this exploitation was basically different from the historic struggle of men against masters which is one strand of the social history of the western world. In Greece, in Rome, in mediæval Europe—or for that matter, in India or China—masters and men were of different estates. Masters were warriors and priests, and it was of the essence of their vocation that they should live by the work of others and consume what they did not produce. By status these others were slaves or serfs, and it was convenient to rationalize their status by attributing it to their nature.

This attribution was a sophism. But it was accepted as a sound observation also by those against whom it was employed, because it expressed the aversion of every man to the dirty work and drudgery which are so large a part of the industrial arts. While inborn disposition rebelled at pretending that coerced subjection was spontaneous submission and that the servile status was a consequence of personal consent and not of social compulsion, habit gave force to the dogma that a servile status derived from a servile nature. J. T. W. Mitchell, addressing the congress of his fellow coöperators at Rochdale in 1892, put his finger on the psychological situation. "I don't believe," he said, "in the selection of a few to receive the contributions of the many, and watch them enjoy the luxuries I ought to have a share of. Ministers have got the power, if they would use it, in this direction; and they know a text in the Old Testament which is very applicable to the case. The people wanted a god, and they brought their trinkets and made them into a god and fell down and worshipped it. It is very much like that in the present day. Poor people subscribe to make others rich, and then they fall down and worship them."

Mitchell was speaking of the England of 1892. By then the peerage had been considerably assimilated to the beerage and the day's "noble lords" were an indiscriminate mixture of recent cotton counts, coal barons, market marquises, banking baronets, with ancient landlords and clerics. But the landlords and clerics still held the prerogative and precedence of English life and their ways embodied the ideal which the financiers and industrialists endeavored to realize, but never did, quite. For the financiers and industrialists were producers with the mentality of producers. They were still only makers of the god they worshipped, not the god. Far as their wealth might carry them from the men who served them for a wage, it carried them, like the fat of their bellies, horizontally, not vertically. Masters and men were of the same estate. Their relations did not follow from the different station to which they were born; they were consequences of a bargain which they struck in a barter of work and wages conducted by both under the rule of *caveat emptor*. Contrasted though the fortunes of employer and employee were, both felt a certain kinship, a parity they did not feel toward the hereditary nobility. The employer's insistence on the employee's "freedom of contract," his hatred of collective bargaining apart from the discriminatory advantages it brought him rooted directly in the unconscious feeling that he was bargaining with one of his own kind, with one somehow, therefore, an equal.

And this feeling the employer resented. Rich but lowly, his envy of the well-born expressed itself not a little in his vindictiveness toward the lowly but poor. Because he felt like them and desired to make himself as unlike as possible, he was ruthless to them. Was not he, even as you and I, struggling to live and to grow? And if he throve and prospered and we suffered and sank, was not that a sign of his virtue and our wickedness? He owes us nothing for his success and we have no claim on him in our failure. The hand of God deals to both the fortune they deserve.

The argument was sharp and shrill in the early days of modern financial-industrial England. It was a time when "self-made men" were numerous, and the slavery of children, the exploitation of women and the oppression of men were the rules of a game in which the new-rich were stopping at nothing to show themselves as good as their betters the old rich. The latter had possession of the government, and felt secure in it. Drawing their free income from ownership of land, they were in a position to protect it by whatever legislation was judged needful, such as the Corn laws; and if industrial interests became discommoding, to check them as they judged best. After all, "trade" was an upstart without blood or breeding, a nuisance to government like a bloody cur at a gentleman's table, and so to be handled. *Laissez-faire* was, among other things, the industrialists' French retort to this interference, by a government of country squires, for their own benefit, in matters which they greatly despised and little understood. If the squires passed the Combination laws in 1799, it was not because they sympathized with factory owners, but because they feared revolution. If they adopted the Factory Act in 1819, it was not because their hearts were particularly moved by the miseries of the industrial workers, but because there survived among them a vestige of the seignorial responsibility of an older time. True, the agricultural revolution had more than ever brutalized them; true, they were the complacent beneficiaries of laws which had the effect of expropriating and pauperizing the English peasantry; but they were bound by the folk-ways of the older agricultural economy; among them the rule of *noblesse oblige* still applied, although in mean and small ways, to the master-servant relation. Miserable as were the agricultural laborers of England, the industrial workers were far more so. The agricultural workers were the inferiors and therefore still somewhat the responsibilities and wards of their betters; the industrial workers were the equals of their betters and therefore their own responsibilities and their betters' competitors. The lives of both groups were unspeakably barren and bitter, and their multitudes filled the land. Improved medical science circumvented diseases and reduced the death-rate more rapidly than poverty and privation diminished the birth-rate. Population seemed to increase in direct ratio to misery.[1]

§ 2. THE FIVE WAYS TO THE MEN'S SALVATION

AGAINST THIS MISERY of the producing multitudes and its causes five modes of defense took form. Starting at different points, with distinct purposes and programs, they soon converged, met, and developed their own differences and conflicts even more conspicuously than coöperation for the common end.

The first form of defense of the producing multitudes was paternalistic and philanthropic.

It moved swiftly into the second, which endeavored to establish in fact the fictional equality of employee with employer by making the employee his own employer, or by enhancing his bargaining power, or by making him the employer's partner in profit. The means to the first was the self-governing workshop. The means to the second was the trades-union. The means to the third was "co-partnership and profit sharing." For a time the first two overlapped, with paternalism in the dominant rôle; then the situation was reversed and has remained so to this day. The program of making the employee his own employer has developed into a complex philosophy of production which ranged from the proposals of Robert Owen to the Utopias of the communists, anarchists and syndicalists.

The third defense was political. It was animated by the

[1] *Cf.* Clapham, *Economic History of Modern Britain,* Vol. 1.

belief that manhood suffrage, representative government and other political rights might lead to economic freedom.

The fourth defense was the fighting Socialism of Marx and Engels. Its program was based on the dogma that the economic life is in the first instance a struggle between the economic classes, and that the producing multitudes are predestined to become aware of their struggle, to organize it, and finally to win it and to put an end to classes.

The fifth defense was patriotic and nationalist. Its proponents appealed to an actual or invented consciousness of kind based on race or language or culture or all three, by which the multitudes were moved to prefer native exploiters to foreign benefactors, and the employers were moved to be just to their own employees that they might the more effectively practise injustice on the employees of their competitors in other lands. Voltaire had observed the underlying emotion a half century earlier: "Such," he wrote, in the ironic article on "Fatherland" in his *Philosophical Dictionary*, "is the state of mankind that to desire the greatness of one's own country is to wish evil to its neighbors. . . . It is clear that one country can gain only as another loses."

§ 3. THE WAY OF PATERNALISM AND ROBERT OWEN

IN A CERTAIN SENSE, all these modes of defense except nationalism branch from some form of activity entered on by Robert Owen. During his long life of eighty-seven years he was a leader in the philanthropical, communist, trades-unionist, and political defense of the employee producers against the exploitation of their masters. But in his personal quality he was first and last a philanthropist. To this quality were due both the extraordinary attention and good-will he commanded at the height of his influence and the impatience and ridicule that followed him from late middle life till he died. He was a man of genius who lived too long. His times passed by him but did not outdistance him. His rôle as a prophet and builder of the "new social order" was complex, and its pattern is confused. Even during his lifetime Owenites dissociated themselves from Owen. Fundamentally a man of one idea which spread in an ever greater tangle of roots as well as leafage the less solid support it found, Owen had a certain manic, high-pressure quality that overflowed to the hurt of too many vested interests and the violation of too many taboos of church, family and school. His impact may have been greater than his effect; but both need still to be realized, and their source appreciated.

Owen was the most distinguished of self-made men in the new and parvenu world which was British industrial society during the first quarter of the nineteenth century. He had started on his own making at the age of seven, by becoming an "usher" in the village school where he learnt the rudiments of reading and writing. This was in 1778, two years after the American Declaration of Independence and a generation before the French Bill of Rights. At nine he left school for a job and at ten left the job to seek his fortune in London. Until his eighteenth year he was a shop-assistant in one English town or another. That year, he started with a partner manufacturing Crompton mules. From this he passed to managing cotton mills. At twenty-nine he had married the daughter of his last employer and had taken over from his father-in-law one of the biggest and most modern cotton plants in Great Britain. He came to fame and fortune as chief owner and manager of this plant, at New Lanark. His progress is that of the industrious apprentice. He is Samuel Smiles' *Self-Help* incarnate; Oliver Optic's success stories made flesh and walking on earth in a textile mill town; his march to this success is so steady, so direct, so swift and so sure. His abilities aside, what distinguished him from the generality of such marchers was a certain quality of personal warmth, a loving-kindness which irradiated his extraordinary intelligence and compelled him to transform experience into aspiration and observation into insight.

The son of a poor Welsh tradesman whose schooling ended when he was nine, Owen had to pick up his information where and as he could, reading omnivorously and digesting in the same way. He was self-educated as well as self-made, but the warmth and charm of his personality saved him from the pedantry into which the auto-didact usually hardens. His dogmatism was in character, not acquired, and the same qualities which prevented him from turning pedant vivified his dogmatism into prophecy, Once he had made a decision or come to a conclusion nothing could change him. The certainty and swiftness of his rise turned the initial animal self-confidence which he shared with other successful self-made men into a mystic assurance of his rightness, an assurance which flowed from him to others with whom he spoke. Those were among the country's rulers and intellectual leaders; they included the royalty of Great Britain and the continent; the members of the Holy Alliance and the President and Congress of the United States. To all he told the same story and proposed the same plan.

The story is a philosophical analysis and re-interpretation of the experiences and observations of a great innovating manager of an industrial plant. The plan projects implications of those experiences into a scheme to transform what got to be "the old immoral world" into "the new moral world" in no longer time than it took him to change the village of New Lanark from a typical industrial community into the model factory town of the British Kingdom. Modified by the climate of opinion of his youth and early manhood, this was first formulated in a series of essays on the principles of the formation of the human character, which Owen named "A New View of Society." This work was published in 1814, when Owen was forty-three years old. In essentials everything he spoke and wrote afterwards were supplementations and elaborations of its argument.[2]

The New Lanark which Owen took over from his father-in-law was an industrial plant that treated its employees slightly better than its competitors. Life in it, nevertheless, had that taint of English want and ugliness which Dickens has so movingly described. To escape from their miseries the millhands drank to excess; to piece out their starvation wages they stole what and as they could, and sent their children from the age of three or four or upward into the factories. Under Owen's management, no child under ten was permitted to work; theft

[2] Especially, "Observations on the Effects of the Manufacturing System," 1815; "Two Memorials on behalf of the Working Classes," 1818; "Report to the County of Lanark," 1821; "Outlines of a Rational System of Society," 1830; "The Book of the New Moral World," 1836–44; "The Revolution in the Mind and Practice of the Human Race," 1849.

and drunkenness disappeared; a higher wage than average was paid; company stores sold them better goods at lower prices; the employees were united into a well-ordered community with schools for the very smallest children and an opportunity for education for all. The transformation took remarkably little time. At first suspicious, sullen, and evasively submissive, the employees became enthusiastic participators in Owen's plan in 1806, during the American embargo on cotton. The mills had had to stand idle, but Owen continued their wages for four months. That won them and sealed Owen's success as a philanthropist as well as industrialist. If it irritated his partners and angered his competitors, it won him the friendship of the princes of the state and the church and the attentive ear of all the nobs and toffs of the Kingdom.

Owen's message makes an ironical contrast to his nature and record. As a rule, self-made men have abounding faith only in their makers, and their stars. Owen had faith in makers, but not his own. And this, paradoxically enough, assimilated his mentality rather to that of the land-owning consumers than to that of the factory-managing producers. He felt different enough from his fellow-employers as well as his employees to regard them all more paternally than competitively. He was great-souled in Aristotle's sense of the term. His employees were a charge upon his status, rather than his business, and his relations with them came under the rule of *noblesse oblige* animated by enlightened self-interest. Owen had learnt about enlightened self-interest from the Benthamites. "The happiness of self clearly understood," he argued thence, "can only be attained by a direct and conscious service of the community." So the masters of society can accomplish their own happiness. Having the knowledge and the wealth they have the power. The multitudes are nothing in themselves. They are the creatures of their environment, degraded or exalted according to the environmental forces which work on them. The rich and the great have possession of the engines of social power—the school, the church, the government. What a factory manager can accomplish in a factory, the managers of society can accomplish in society. It is not inevitable that industrial conditions shall degrade human beings. Properly ordered, they will elevate them.

Since nurture transforms nature, a wise and benevolent regulation of the agencies of nurture could recreate the distressful and degrading industrial pattern into a thing of order and dignity and well-being.

The first step to such a transformation is to displace "the creed of universal competition" with the coöperative idea. In the pursuit of wealth men tend to forget that its source is labor. Of course there is capital, and there is machinery. But they are no more than embodiments of past labor, working together with living laborers. Under the stress of the war with Napoleon, machinery has been tremendously improved and elaborated. Its improvement and use have brought such disemployment and degradation to the human worker that now the price of a workman's labor is lower than that of the food he needs in order merely to be able to work. Undoubtedly this cheapening of life is one of the consequences of peace. War created a market which peace destroyed; "the day on which the peace was signed the great customer of the producer died." Now with machinery it is easier to produce goods than to find markets for them. At the same time, nations cannot be always at war; the peace which kills the home market must be; and even the foreign markets must be made up of people who need the things which the factories produce and who are able to pay for what they need. And how can they pay, save as they earn? It follows that low wages anywhere means over-production elsewhere. Thus, high wages are necessary to good business, and necessary not only, but just.

For what, after all, do wages represent except the labor that goes into the making of the goods, of the wealth whose sole function is to satisfy wants. As their wants are satisfied, people's labor improves, and all the produce of labor ought to go back into the satisfaction of wants. But if this is true, profits are condemned. For profit is possible only when the buyer's stake in the results of the industrial process is stronger than the seller's and causes demand to outweigh supply. If the producer is to be enabled to live and grow up and grow old, healthily and happily, trading for profit is ruled out; in the new society trading is merely the exchange of commodities for use. Hence the standard of living will be defined scientifically and the instruments for creating the materials of this standard will be owned collectively. The community of ownership is implied by the division of labor and the character of factory production. Could such a community be organized the evils of the *crise pléthorique,* the "business cycle" and all the other misfortunes which plague the industrial scene would be wiped out.

In 1817, Owen proposed to a select committee inquiring into the Poor Law a plan which would be an application of the scientific methods of production to the process of consumption. He suggested that the machines might be subdued to the uses of men by assembling the unemployed into communities partly agricultural partly industrial. These communities were to be laid out in regular form, to have a common kitchen, common mills, a public reading room, schools; children over three were to be kept in separate boarding houses and, particularly, to receive an adequate education. In Owen's philosophy, as can be well understood, education was a matter of paramount importance. Since education was the foundation of character, it must aim at the development of the whole personality. "Minute division of labor and division of interests are only other terms for poverty, ignorance, waste of every kind, universal opposition throughout society, crime, misery and great bitterness and mental imbecility." The right kind of education, he wrote, would result in a "working class full of activity and useful knowledge, with habits, information, manners and dispositions that would place the lowest in the scale many degrees above the best of any class which has yet been formed by the circumstances of past or present society." [3]

The Report to the County of Lanark, which restates Owen's critique of the system of production more adequately than any other of his works, was written in 1820. That year the tension between the landed aristocracy who held the government and the factory owners who increasingly accumulated the eco-

[3] *Cf. The Report to the County of Lanark.*

nomic power had reached a height and the reaction on the masses of British subjects had been the most miserable in their history. To the minds of his readers and hearers, Owen's economics lost their philanthropic color and acquired a certain revolutionary tinge. His public repudiation of religion still further alienated people of all classes and he turned his back for the time being on England and went to America to set up his "village of coöperation" in that, to Europeans, ideal environment of liberty, equality and fraternity.

His views, meanwhile, had spread throughout England. They stirred intellectuals everywhere and they laid before despairing workmen a plan, a leadership and a promise of swift consummation which the Wesleys and their Methodism and their treasure in heaven could not match for salvational value. Many workers, kept only by some stroke of bad fortune from themselves becoming self-made men like Owen, saw in his principles and program the true instrument by which the multitude of producers could defend themselves against the misery and slavery which are the lot of the producers of the world. But the leadership continued to come from the intellectuals. A flood of writing and a gale of talking sped in Owen's wake; journal succeeding journal and agitator agitator. In 1824, the London Coöperative Society was organized to advance the Owenite doctrine. In 1826, it began the publication of *The Coöperative Magazine,* which continued for four years, and published some of the most telling reinterpretations of Owenism, among them contributions by William Thompson, an Irish gentleman educated in Bentham's household, who combined the political ideas of William Godwin with the economic program of Robert Owen.

§ 4. DR. WILLIAM KING PROPOSES TO MAKE EVERY EMPLOYEE HIS OWN EMPLOYER

BY FAR the most important of the Owenites was Dr. William King. Almost a generation younger than Owen, he was born in 1786. He had advantages which Owen lacked. His father, the master of Ipswich Grammar School, was a clergyman who designed his son for the same profession. Like so many of his generation, King could not consent to the paternal design. His schooling confirmed his contrary disposition. A student at Oxford and a graduate of Cambridge, where he took his baccalaureate and master's degree, he went thence in 1812 to St. Bartholomew's in London to study medicine. In the summer he heard lectures at Montpellier, and in the course of time secured his doctorate in medicine and was made a fellow of the Royal College of Physicians. He married in 1821, and in 1823 settled in Brighton. There he became the helpful friend of the great Elizabeth Fry and by her was brought into a direct contact with the misery of "the industrious classes." He helped her to organize district provident societies by which the working people were to alleviate somewhat their own distress. The provident societies were to be backed by the district visiting societies whose members, visiting the homes of the poor, would encourage them to save and to work hard, relieve distress, and prevent "mendacity and imposture."

King, through Miss Fry, one of whose collaborators was Robert Owen's Quaker partner, William Allen, learned of Owen, his works and ideas. He became in the course of time a convinced Owenite. His first steps of visiting the poor and "encouraging them in frugality and industry" led to the later creation in Brighton of one of the innumerable Mechanics' Institutes that were being organized throughout the Kingdom, and then, in 1827, the creation of the Brighton Coöperative Benevolent Fund Association. The Mechanics' Institute had been formed in 1825 and King had been chosen vice-president. Three hundred members hired a house and King lectured to them on a variety of subjects including the Owenite doctrine of "mutual coöperation," until the society petered out.

A man of striking appearance and charm, with a swift and persuasive mind especially apt in conversation, King's loving-kindness, his intelligence, and his enthusiasm made "the poor man's doctor" also a convincing lecturer and an effective teacher.

The project for the Coöperative Benevolent Fund Association came from these lectures. By means of a small weekly contribution the members were to create a fund which should enable poor and indigent people to form coöperative communities and to spread the knowledge of the coöperative system. As an adjunct to the fund association, King in the same year formed a Coöperative Trading Association. This association set up business when the contributed capital amounted to £5. It had forty shareholders, among them workers of all sorts, and in a year the weekly sales amounted to £38, but the association was handicapped by the limitations of its members and it took King a very short time to realize that the coöperative community could be formed only if knowledge reënforced will. For this reason, King projected a monthly magazine, and on May 1, 1828, published the first number of *The Coöperator*. It ran until August, 1830, and when it was discontinued it had become not only an instrument of communication to, but the organ of, some three hundred workmen's producers' coöperative societies. These, and others of all sorts and conditions began in 1831 to come together for mutual consultation and planning as Coöperative Congresses. Between 1831 and 1835, some seven such congresses were held. Several were called by Owen, who had returned from America; in most he was a well-liked, respected and in the course of time, a very tedious figure.

King participated in none. By 1830, King himself had become contaminated with the opprobrium that attached to Owen's rationalism and anti-Christianism. Owen's attack on the Christian establishment mobilized the clergy of all denominations against his causes. His disciples were regarded as enemies of church and state. King himself was a man of deeply religious spirit with a strong sense of the integrity and worth of the individual and a constant affirmation of the identity of "the spirit of the Gospel and the spirit of Coöperation." He spoke of the "Author of Christianity" as a leader who embodied precept in practice and who set the example for the coöperator. Nevertheless, the clerics did not wait to accuse King of infidelity as well as sedition. Unlike Owen, King had not the liberty flowing from an independent income. His practice was his living and his paying patients enabled him to stay throughout his career "the poor man's doctor." The attack of the clerics so cut into King's practice that if he were to make a living for his family and continue his professional services to the poor he had to give up the coöperative propaganda. He suspended publication of *The Coöperator* and dropped out of the movement. In spite of various attempts to get him to reissue the magazine or to continue his labors in behalf of coöperation, he could not bring himself to do so until near the close of his life, when he reëntered a movement that, starting from the same roots and undoubtedly owing much to King's teachings, had nevertheless developed in quite another direction. At King's death, in 1865, the new adventure was not aware of what coöperation owed the Brighton doctor. It remained ignorant of its debt until the secretary of the International Coöperative Alliance, Dr. Hans Müller, found the files of *The Coöperator* in the British Museum and brought to light King's restatement of the Owenite vision.

With Owen, King held that technology, which could be the friend of the average producer, was being used as his enemy; that the industrial economy had brought progressive impoverishment and degradation to the people of England. He parted from Owen in recognizing that there was no hope in the leadership and good-will of the rich and great. To save himself, the producer could depend only on himself. The whole meaning of production was consumption, and if people had no needs to be served they would not work. But he who works as an employee of another is a slave. It is only when a man works for himself that he is free. Since few workers can amass the capital which would enable them to work for themselves, they must do together what they cannot separately. Their means is at hand: It is the store where they buy their necessaries. They must set up stores for themselves. A store can be opened on a small capital. The profits on its sales can be saved and finally used to create the self-governing workshops in which every employee will be his own employer.

Now the worker has only his wages and these wages are as low as the employer dare make them and they tend always to be the lowest possible. With these wages the worker must buy the necessaries of life which will enable him to go on working. He buys them at a store from a storekeeper who is constantly raising prices. Thus the worker labors between the deep sea of low wages always being forced down and the devil of high prices always being forced up. He is too weak at best to force up his wages, but even with his low wages he is strong enough to force prices down; all he needs is "his wages and an honest companion,"

> If they can find a third to join them they may say a threefold cord is not soon broken. They may subscribe weekly towards a common fund to provide against sickness or want of work. They may market for each other. They may buy a large quantity of goods at once, and so get an abatement of price—which abatement they may throw into a common stock. If they are of different trades they may make domestic articles of comfort for each other, and exchange them. They may do this at odd times, or after work hours.
>
> If a number of workmen were to join together upon these principles their capital would be greater and they might do greater things. They might have a shop of their own, where they might deal for every thing they wanted. Their shop would enter into competition with other shops in serving the public. As the business increased, the profits and the capital would increase. As the capital increased, it would employ the members of the society in any way which might be deemed most advantageous. If there was a profitable demand in the public for any particular commodity the members might manufacture it. If the profits of manufactures were not high enough to make it worth producing them, the members might easily raise their own food by hiring or purchasing land and becoming part of them agriculturists instead of manufacturers.

In about fifteen years a store might develop into a full-grown community and the employee become his own employer and serve his own needs.[4]

He has by his own frugality and labor established his own freedom. And he has done it by his natural power of the consumer. In sum, the producer as spender can save the producer as maker. All he needs is knowledge how to employ his power as consumer in the service of his liberation as producer.

§ 5. SELF-GOVERNING WORKSHOPS, OWENITE TRADES-UNIONISM

THE MOVEMENT which had grown out of King's teaching and guidance was in a certain sense the ceremonial incarnation of the Owen-King doctrine. The actual producers' coöperatives

[4] Owen was always more sanguine. He was promising peaceful revolution in five years—if the large sums needed to start his communities could be obtained.

were the channel for a hope which saw the land, the factories, and all else in the possession of a community whose members worked merely to satisfy their own needs. Not many producers who became members of such self-governing workshops understood the vision which animated their philosopher or had the feeling of community necessary for its upkeep. In 1853, Dr. King, commenting on the failure of the movement of which he was the father and Owen the grandfather, attributed it largely to lack of loyalty and greed for profits. But the cause was something deeper. Unless he was "a slave by nature," the unconscious ideal of the industrial employee was the industrial employer. If the latter had a feeling of equality that caused him to keep the former down, the employee by the same token felt that perhaps he could also lift himself to the wealth and independence of his employer. His miserable state, which he joined the self-governing workshop to improve, did not modify this unconscious emulative drive. Fisherman, weaver, shoemaker, carpenter, or what you will, he treated the shop as an instrument of his personal profit.

Moreover the shop-organization was still so amateurish that it lacked all those controls which our day takes for granted. Like Robert Owen's communities, the shops attracted the weak and the ambitious. The former were capable of submission but not of self-help. The latter were very well able to help themselves but not coöperatively. So a few of the hundreds of shops and societies survived as joint-stock companies; some were appropriated and became personal enterprises; the rest broke up, and the hope which animated them died down to resignation or despair.

Involved in these shops were the trades-unions. Of these the beginning was very different from the present state. Some of them were survivors from the degenerate guild system; some of them were spontaneous movements for better wages and conditions, crystallized and acquiring a certain permanence. As trades-unions all were illegal under the Combination laws. Some therefore developed as secret societies with the vows and rites which the insecure employ to protect themselves against betrayal. Others again took on the guise of "friendly" societies with objectives such as sick benefits or savings and loans, to hide their combative intent. All of them compensated their precarious existence with an indefinite variety of salvational doctrines among which the Owen-King theory was one.

Their chief concern was collective bargaining. The coördination of the factory had its projection in the association of factory workers. It made them feel that a contract between an individual worker and his employer was not a contract between equals. The latter had the former at his mercy; getting his agreements by coercion, not consent; and a coerced agreement was not a binding one. In contracts with employers what owning the factory was to the employer, union with his fellow-workers was to be to the employee. Collective bargaining is the equalizer of unequal bargaining powers. Hence the unions learned to want "closed shops" and to be ready to use every available device in obtaining them.

But this came later, after disillusion, when they completely acquiesced in the status of employee-to-an-employer. Their first intention was that liberty and leisure of the individual which the employer himself seemed to embody, and they were thereby amenable to the argument and persuasion of the Kingites. Owen himself, when he returned from his American adventure an impoverished man, at first rejected and then almost literally took over the shop movement and established himself as a leader of this sort of positive trades-unionism, which was, he preached, to conduct strikes without antagonizing those it struck against and was to relieve all classes through the leadership and coöperation of those who made and drew personal benefits from the conditions needing relief.

Owen now hoped to cut under the bitter competitive profit economy by substituting a "labor note" as a medium of exchange. The idea of the labor note followed from Adam Smith's classical doctrine that labor is the source of value. And if the source, why not the unit-measure of value? Owen pointed out that such a unit was mathematically easy to establish, and did establish one. The moment favored the experiment. The national monetary policy was neither clearly defined nor firmly adhered to. Both localities and businesses produced and circulated their own media of exchange for their own uses. The labor note seemed neither unreasonable nor impracticable, especially as it was almost instantly translated into pounds, shillings and pence. This followed from the fact that there was no way of verifying the number of hours a producer claimed it took him to make, say, a leather purse. The simplest way to check his claim was to find its market price elsewhere, and then to transpose the price into work-hours. Which was done.

In 1832, Owen opened the National Equitable Labor Exchange where the produce of the different union shops was brought and bought and sold, and an immense amount of haphazard trading went on unrecorded and unchecked, mostly to the advantage of the shopkeepers from whose exactions the Exchange was to free the workers. Accepting labor notes for their own goods, they used them to purchase staples at the Exchange, so that in short order the Exchange was heaped with the unsalable residue. Meanwhile, others were organized, and a United Trades Association, in which the trades-unions participated, was formed to give work to the unemployed, payable in these labor notes. By 1833, Owen stood as the recognized leader of the trade-union movement, and the doctrine and discipline of trade-unionism called itself Owenite. Organization followed organization. A Great National Moral Union of Productive and Useful Classes was succeeded by a Great National Consolidated Trades-Union that in a few weeks enrolled half a million members. Owen was everywhere, writing, lecturing, calling meetings, as charming, seductive, and voluble as ever, and more than ever tedious. His activity ceased to be communication and became soliloquy, his fellow-workers continued to like him but failed more and more to get on with him. Many recognized that his influence and intentions were a drag on the combative function and war strategy of the trades-unions. Owen, to whom a general strike was but an instrument toward the coöperation of all classes, dropped out of the picture. Industrial warfare in the form of strikes and lock-outs became so intense and widespread that an alarmed government became to unprivileged workers a ruthless one. The Owenite trades-movement became a fiasco. Trades-unionism went into eclipse to emerge on the now more familiar strictly capitalist lines of the producer economy.

§ 6. THE WAYS OF SOCIALISM: FRENCH, CHRISTIAN

BUT OWENISM did not die. It changed from an organizational channel for turbulent feelings into a frame of mind and an attitude, and this frame of mind for the time being found itself a new language. The "village of coöperation" and the "Owenite" were replaced by "socialism" and the "socialist." So far as is known the word "socialist" was first used in 1827, by a writer in *The Coöperative Magazine*. He described the advocates of Owen's villages of coöperation as "communionists and socialists." But the term seems to have been generally applied to French rather than English social philosophers, to the "utopian socialists" of the Marxists. The first of the group was Saint-Simon and the first Frenchman to use the term Socialism was one of his tradition, Pierre Leroux, who claimed to have invented the word as an antithesis to "individualism," in 1834. He had an article in the *Revue Encyclopédique* entitled "De l'Individualisme et du Socialisme."

Saint-Simon was a scion of the *ancien noblesse*. In youth a hellion who quarreled with his father, he crossed the seas to fight for liberty in the American Revolution and returned to live through the French one. Abandoning caste and losing fortune, he sought consolation in science and compensation in speculative dealings in "national property." He got both, and a jail sentence as a counter-revolutionary suspect besides. In jail something happened to him. He came out believing himself a savior of the world. The instrument of his salvation was to be a great bank to finance great public works, and he invited his partners in speculation to establish such a bank. They wouldn't. He got married and quickly divorced, lived orgiastically and painfully, and finally settled down to an insecure existence and the dissemination of his gospel to the world.

Having lived through the Revolution, he knew the hunger which was king in France during 1793, and the misery of his own state was always with him. Not unnaturally, he had no use for the civilization in which this could be. He was sure he had found the way to a new society and a new religion which should accomplish the well-being of mankind. This is a society wherein everybody works. Its government is a supreme council like the Curia of the Church of Rome, but manned by twenty-one savants, and presided over by a mathematician. This council plan the way of life, and the men of business execute the plan: they arrange and manage. They are chosen to these services by the votes of the multitude, and by their mandate direct the peaceful labors which produce the progress of mankind. Society is a classless hierarchy resembling a factory. Its government is economic, not political —an administration of things, not a coercion of men. The political dimension is a superfluous dimension. The nation is a productive society; its purpose is to increase "positive utility" by means of peaceful industry.

The inspiration of Saint-Simon lay behind Fourier's phalansteries and Louis Blanc's state-supported national workshops. Fourier wanted to abolish, not property but wage-working; to transform the wage-earner into a coöperative owner, working for the love of working, enjoying work as a right, not enduring it as duty. The phalanstery was the way of life to accomplish this—a Grand Hotel where one could dine table-d'hôte or alone in one's room as one liked, and whose inhabitants held its stock, built it and supplied it with their labors. Louis Blanc, like Proudhon, became a public figure in the Revolution of 1848. He had the idea that government might finance associations of producers who would establish national workshops, drive private industry out of business, and replace destructive competition with creative coöperation. The revolution gave him his chance, but the opposition sabotaged his efforts.

All three of these so-called Utopians stressed an alternative organization of production rather than a warfare for the profits of production between the producers who employ and the producers who are employed. On the other hand, Proudhon, affirming the principle that property is robbery and that government is the protection of property, wanted to do away with all organization.

In the Christian Socialists the strain of Owen and the strain of Saint-Simon are fused with the supernaturalist humanitarianism of primitive Christianity. The founder of the group was

John Malcolm Ludlow. A lawyer, the son of an army officer born in India, he was educated in Paris, and thence brought the spirit and ideas of the Fourierists and Saint-Simonians to England. When the revolution came in 1848, he went to Paris, a young man of twenty-seven, to watch the course of events. His letters regarding them to his friend Frederick Maurice were followed when he returned by many discussions, and these came to a head with the failure of the Chartist monster petition meeting, April 10, 1848. Ludlow and Maurice witnessed this meeting. Another witness was Charles Kingsley, a country pastor with the Tory ideals of the country. Christian Socialism began in the reaction of the three to this experience, and grew as program which adapted the French forms of self-governing workshop to the English climate of opinion in Christ's name, amen. It used the Bible as a revolutionists' handbook.

John Frederick Denison Maurice was the chaplain of Lincoln's Inn. He won to the enterprise Thomas Hughes, the author of *Tom Brown at Rugby,* who had just been called to the bar and was in residence at the Inn. Later Maurice drew in Edward Van Sittart Neale, and his cousin, Augustus Van Sittart. These drew others, Chartists, like Walter Cooper; Owenites, like Lloyd Jones–until at one time the little company had as many as seventy members. Their spiritual leader was always Maurice, whom Kingsley described as the most beautiful human soul he had known. The group held together for six years, and its leading members continued its program and defended its ideals in other and more significant circles so long as they lived. Especially they stressed the social obligation of the Christian. "I assert," declared Tory Charles Kingsley in a sermon preached in 1851, "that the business for which God sends a Christian priest in a Christian nation is to preach freedom, equality and brotherhood in the fullest, deepest, widest meaning of these great words; that in so far as he so does he is a true priest doing the Lord's work with the Lord's blessing on him; that in so far as he does not he is no priest at all but a traitor to God and man."

"Doing the Lord's work" lay in preaching and teaching, in arguing and organizing and lobbying and writing, and in paying the bills, like Owen before them, mostly out of their own pockets. In eight tracts the group gave an account of themselves to the public. By the beginning of 1851, they were publishing the *Christian Socialist* to record the movement's progress in organizing self-governing workshops, securing labor legislation and developing coöperative distribution for the purpose of facilitating and spreading coöperative production. Like King and Owen, they recognized the paramount necessity of education and established a Workingmen's College which Maurice, who had been forced to resign from his chair in theology at King's College in Oxford, spent his time in promoting. The college was to bring to working-men the same educational opportunities as their betters and to indoctrinate the well-to-do consumer in the gospel of human equality and brotherhood with the poor producer.

In this endeavor the Christian Socialists earned the hatred of their equals and the somewhat ironic regard of their clients. They were a sort of collective Owen, working in Christ's name instead of Nature's, and as they echoed Owen's attitude, so they repeated his fate. Their chief importance lay in the fact that Van Sittart Neale, Thomas Hughes, and Lloyd Jones carried over into the consumers' coöperative movement, which they joined, the idea of the primacy of production, and forced a clear and final decision between an economy where consumers' coöperation is a means to coöperative production, and one in which producers' coöperation is an instrument of coöperative consumption.

Neale, who has the longest record of service, was no Christian, and he persuaded his colleagues to keep the doors of the movement open to others who did not profess Christian principles but believed in "Christian" practices. He himself gave his life and his fortune to the Coöperative Movement. He was the organizing spirit of the Society for Promoting Workingmen's Associations, and the financial bulwark of the associations so promoted. He drew up "Laws for the Government of the Society for the Formation of Coöperative Stores," and got together some $50,000 to finance a Central Coöperative Agency. He helped meet the great lockout of 1852 by buying the Atlas Engineering Works and putting it in the hands of an engineering association he formed for the purpose. After the Christian Socialists disbanded, he gave his time to the consumer movement, pressing their doctrine.

On the continent and in the United States, what is known as Christian Socialism has little affinity in intent with this British economic-humanitarian retranslation of Christianity. In the United States, where it came much later, "Christian Socialism" meant liberal Protestantism refracting the teachings of Marxian Socialism. On the continent it meant the adoption by clericals of certain items of a trades-union or Marxian program as a device for defending the flock against the contamination of secular trades-unionism and anti-clerical Marxism; it added to this anti-Semitism or Jew-hatred as a substitute for class hatred.

§ 7. THE WAY OF POLITICAL LIBERTY

IN ENGLAND, the interval between the subsidence of Owenism and the rise of Christian Socialism had been taken up by political agitation. In the forefront of the producers' effort were now John Bright and Richard Cobden. Political enfranchisement took the place of economic independence as the gate to the greatest happiness of the greatest number. The atmosphere of political revolution and political agitation was the natural air of all the defensive movements of the producing multitudes. In England one assault on the state had been brought to a successful conclusion long before the economic revolution had begun to work harm on the people. But the political revolutions in America and in France came at the same time as the great upswing of the industrial revolution in England and the revolutionary principles of politics were automatically transposed for the liberation of the economically depressed.

In the struggle for political freedom employers made allies of employees only to abandon them when they got what they wanted. The Reform Bill of 1832 enfranchised the property-holding classes and left the rank and file who had fought for it worse off than before. The Bill's adoption coincided with the disintegration of the first union shop movement, and to the disillusion and indignation which followed, independent political action seemed at last attractive as never before. John Bright and Richard Cobden were finally listened to. Free votes and free trade became the battle-cry of security, and for the time being, political self-help was regarded as the indispensable preliminary to economic well-being. The instrument of self-help was the Chartist movement. The Owenites gave themselves to it, as before they had given themselves to Owenite coöperation. In that, little hope was left; perhaps they could win by their votes a better life than they had been able to win by their work.

So they agitated the adoption of a people's charter of English liberty. They demanded manhood suffrage, the Australian ballot, equal electoral districts, the abolition of the property qualification for voting, and the payment of members elected to Parliament. It seems today a modest program but in the light of the fifty years it took to enact the last of its proposals, radical enough. The interlude between its formulation and the dissolution of the movement which projected it was filled with a tense and bitter struggle that came to its end with the bloody scene following the presentation of the Monster Petition to Parliament in 1848. The relation of this scene to the origins of Christian Socialism has already been indicated. But it not only turned the attention of Englishmen again to the pacific socialism of the second self-governing workshop movement, it first pointed up for the English the warrior socialism of Karl Marx.

§ 8. THE WAY OF MARXISM

THE YEAR of the failure of the petition was the year of the promulgation of the *Communist Manifesto*. By this time the idea that political economy is a war of economic classes had already a definite place in public discussion,[5] and the general setback of the multitudes of the producers on practically all

[5] *Cf.* The files of *The Coöperative Magazine* (1826–1830), Thomas Hodgkin, "Labour defended against the Claims of Capital," 1825; William Thompson, "An Inquiry into the Principles of the Distribution of Wealth Most Conducive to Human Happiness," 1824; "Labour Rewarded, or How to Secure to Labour the Whole Product of its Exertion," 1827.

fields had made it poignant. The immediate and specific programs of the Marxists were not in essentials different from the specific programs of the Utopians, the Chartists, and others. They were, however, set in a different frame of mind and enchanneled in a different attitude. Like all the "Utopian" followers of Adam Smith—the Owenites, the St. Simonians, the Fourierites, the communists held labor as the source and substance of all value. But unlike the "Utopians," they agreed with the Manchester school that not coöperation but competition or struggle is the life of the economic establishment; and they departed from the Manchester school by describing the competition between individuals as secondary to a competition between classes. To this primary competition, they gave the name, "the class struggle." They said it was a function of the state of the industrial arts and a part of the nature of things; and that its inevitable outcome is the victory of the worker. "I cannot claim," Marx wrote in 1852, to his friend Weydemeyer, "to have discovered the existence of classes in modern society. . . . I have added as a new contribution the following propositions: 1. That the existence of classes is bound up with certain phases of material production; 2. That the class struggle leads necessarily to the dictatorship of the proletariat; 3. That this dictatorship is but the transition to the abolition of all classes and to the creation of a society of the free and equal." All activities of the proletarian "masses" were to be regarded simply as engagements in the class war and all were to be employed in the winning of the war; all organization was to be the creation and disciplining of an army to win this war.

This way of thinking set the single act of the individual producer in a framework of cosmic forces and cosmic destiny. He was, if not a Christian soldier, a proletarian soldier marching onward as to war and causing crowns and thrones to perish and the church of Jesus to go under.

§ 9. THE WAY OF NATIONALISM

HOWEVER, by 1850, the gains of the English credit-enterprise economy began to seep down to the rank and file of the producers. Real wages rose sharply and continued to rise for a quarter of a century, then fell slightly for a little more than a decade, and rose again; Socialism spread, but in "Utopian" rather than combative mood, by "Fabian" rather than "Bolshevik" tactics. On the continent the spread of plenty to its producers came much later; the Marxist gospel had readier listeners. It became the faith of a movement, with orthodoxies and heresies, fundamentalisms and modernisms. It was crossed, together with all other defensive movements among producers, by the irresistible spread of nationalism.

Beginning as one of the ways of affirming the dignity and worth of the living individual which were a light and a leading to the French Revolution, this nationalism ended by becoming the economic negation of that which it started with.

For in its first form the nationalism was simply the recognition that every man spoke a certain language, had a certain expression, wore a certain type of dress, and followed certain characteristic ways of life which he intimately and permanently identified with his personality, and which was intrinsically noble and precious. Nationality was the collective medium in which individuality lived and moved and had its being. Giuseppe Mazzini, its prophet, argued that human society was a congregation of such nationalities, unique groups which together create and sustain, by each doing its own part and freely exchanging its creations with the others, the international establishment we call civilization. Free trade in ideals and cultures were traditional among the upper classes of Europe; it made the precedent and set the standard for free trade in material goods which liberals built their hopes upon. But such trade could not be free until all ranks of the peoples engaged in it were free and habituated in freedom; free from foreign domination without, self-governing within. The most self-complacent European nation of the nineteenth century, the British, was also that politically freest and most fully committed to free trade.

But the free trade depended on acquiescence in a world-wide economic division of labor analogous to the cultural division. It did not allow for invidious competition; it did not allow for the desire of a group's leaders that the group they lead shall excel its betters and rule its peers. It did not allow for the envious ambition of the customer to fabricate for himself the goods he buys from another, even if thus their price is more and their quality less. When the British adopted free trade as a principle, Great Britain was an industrial country selling to a non-industrial market. But the buyers learned from the sellers, and the very prosperity of the market stimulated it to envy the prosperity-bringer. Instead of being grateful, the buyers became emulative and competitive. They meant to beat the sellers at their own game. The ambition expressed itself first as the competitive arming which is one of the banes of the modern world. The competition finally embraced all the economic enterprises of the country. Its logical limit is autarchy. The record tells how Britain became a power to envy and a model to imitate in the eyes of all other European nations, especially Germany.

Thus, what had first been an accident of growth, without plan and without purpose among the English, became a design of the Germans and a philosophy of all contemporary "great" powers, the most conspicuous being Russia, Italy, and Japan. They all seek to carry on a planned economy. They are all imperialists, imperialism meaning in this connection the monopolization of a non-industrial or unindustrialized market by an industrial state. To win such monopolies an economy must be as fully planned as possible at home so that it may be effectively mobilized to conquer competition abroad. Perhaps the man first to realize this was Bismarck. Under his guidance, the German economy, with its public ownership and control of public utilities, its regulation of finance, became an aspect of bureaucratic government; the care of Owen's "industrious classes," which other countries left to their own self-interest and organizational power, became a responsibility of a government holding itself to be in a permanent state of economic war. So units of a program which socialists proposed for the purpose of setting the producing multitudes free from their servitude were employed to fasten that servitude more firmly upon them. It is Germany that discovered "the rationalization of industry" and it is in Germany that the nationalistic critique of free enterprise reaches its highest and most ironic forms. It is the "third Reich" which struggles suicidally for autarchy. Germany set the pace for the rest of the world in the use by government of devices which protect the producing employees from exploitation by the employer-producer in order to chain them to the ergastulum of production more firmly than ever.

CHAPTER V

CONSUMER DEFENSE IN THE PRODUCER WORLD

§ 1. CAVEAT VENDOR VERSUS CAVEAT EMPTOR

THE INVETERATE endeavor of the consumer to build his natural primacy into a social order has, of course, tended to act as a check on the development of the producer-dominated economy. So that, within the system, a variety of structures and activities appear designed to protect the consumer, and, if possible, to liberate him from subjection to the producer. A tendency in law and custom makes for a sort of rule of *caveat vendor* in antagonism to the prevailing rule of *caveat emptor*.

As a power within the price-system, the consumer has protected his interest against the producer in one or another of three ways. We have seen that the adulteration and counterfeiting of goods, the employment of false weights and measures, and the other "tricks of the trade" are as old as trade itself and early imposed on the buyer wariness and defense. When trade was barter or near it, maker was also seller and buyer was also user; consumer met producer more or less as equal, and "cheapening" was a fair game, without favor, in which the best man won. Each was a member of the same community, guided by the same ideas of honorable dealing. Loss of standing and custom followed swiftly upon any violation of the rules of the game. The transaction was presumably such that each party exchanged what he did not want for what he wanted, and both profited, at least in the fact that each was more satisfied after the bargain was struck than before.

When the use of money became general and trade a commerce between distant markets, an advantage accrued to the producer. The distant buyer lacked the knowledge and the protection of community membership enjoyed by the local one. He had to buy in quantity and quickly, perhaps to sell again before he could make a thorough examination of the goods. And if he were a middleman, his own customer was even twice as far from the source as he, and at a correspondingly greater disadvantage. Although the laws of the guilds purported to equalize this advantage by requiring of their members good material, good workmanship and "just price," they did so not because they loved the producer less, but because they loved his advantage more. In this respect they were not so different from modern "open price associations" or manufacturers of "registered" and nationally-advertised goods. Such improvement of the consumer's position over against the producer as could be actually secured, was secured through the judgment of the church, and the occasional intervention of the state.

In the church, the trader was *persona non grata* anyhow; his vocation being sin, his responsibility for fair dealing was all the greater. Till the seventeenth-century church manuals made the seller responsible to the buyer and laid down the rules of Christian selling. In general the secular power followed the lead of the church, at least formally. But as Pope and Emperor were involved in a prolonged jurisdictional dispute, and as the secular rulers were not so guided by Revelation as the sacred ones, governmental policy vacillated, favoring now the consumer and now producer. For a long time, the issue between *caveat emptor* and *caveat vendor* was undecided. But by the sixteenth century, *caveat emptor* had won. When the monarchical states consolidated their gains and subdued the feudal nobility to obedience and service, the crafts and trades organizations and their communities ceased to be important as allies—in fact became their new opposition, and the consumer gained to that degree. By the seventeenth century the view reappeared that the seller had certain obligations and was liable for fraud, and the vacillation of the state was renewed.

§ 2. DEMOCRACY AND SCIENCE AS ALLIES OF THE CONSUMER

ON THE WHOLE, the advantage remains with the rule of *caveat emptor,* which embodies the primacy of the producer. Its range became wider, more complex and subtler, with the elaboration of the financial-industrial economy. The forces most efficacious in opposing it have not been so much economic, as humanistic. They are political democracy and humanitarian science. Democracy is the political aspect of the consumer economy, and science is automatically humanitarian because its objectivity and impartiality bring to light the natural laws governing human well-being and human excellence. The discoveries of science set the standards and provided the goals, the moral philosophy assumed by *laissez-faire* provided the principles which the operations of democracy endeavored to attain by incorporating them in law.

Laws range from endeavors to enforce free competition by forbidding "conspiracy in restraint of trade," to the ironic piety of the United States Clayton Act which restores the working-man to his humanity by promulgating that "labor is not a commodity." In the "pure food and drug" acts the laws affect the selling of consumer goods; in building laws, the fabrication and sale of housing and shelters; in the "blue sky laws," of securities and credit. Other laws endeavor to police and regulate dairy herds and dairies, the preparation and marketing of milk; the slaughter of cattle and preparation of meats; the price, quality and service of power, gas and transportation, the veracity of brands and labels, the competency of physicians, nurses, and barbers. The laws as adopted have been invariably weaker than the laws as proposed. Usually introduced before legislatures in consequence of some great wave of public indignation following the discovery of some stinking trick of a trade, their introduction draws the concealed fire of all the interests standing to lose by the passage of the bills. Lobbies mobilize, openly and secretly, but mostly secretly. Pressure is applied in all forms, from bribery to flattery, from blackmail to threats of bodily harm, from the fabrication to the purchase of opinion. If the bills cannot be defeated they are emasculated. There is none which does not leave a loophole for any producer desirous of plying the tricks of his trade.[1] At best, policing and enforcement are difficult. At worst, a rivalry obtains like that between the locksmith and the lockpicker, with the locksmith always at a disadvantage.

For their own purchases, governments in the course of time have set up Bureaus of Standards. These Bureaus are scientific institutions. Their work is to carry out the most rigorous and thoroughgoing tests, analyses and experiments; to provide government departments with advice regarding standards of quality, measurement and production, of the goods they desire. The would-be sellers make bids for contracts to produce the goods according to the specifications advised by the Bureau of Standards; the contract is presumed to go to the lowest bidder. The practice is now widespread, wherever large orders are involved. The tendency is to define orders by sample or description. But they are orders from seller to seller in private business. The ultimate consumer has not the advantage of either standard specifications or samples. A Bureau of Standards, supported out of the public funds, is presumed to hold available for public use all of its own results, but those can hardly be of help to any single citizen-consumer. In addition, the Bureau is at the service of producers for testing the product of any one of them. This is at the public expense; but Bureaus do not make their findings available to the public which pays for them and to whom the producer proposes to sell his products. The services of the United States Bureau of Standards, in testing and research, operate consistently in the producer interest. On the whole and in the long run, legislatures, courts, commissions and administrative officers have been more responsive to the steady pressure of the always vigilant and organized producers than to the intermittent indignation of the unorganized and heedless consumers.

[1] *Cf.* Record of testimony at a Canning Industry Hearing, February 8 and 9, 1934, before Department Administrator Walter White. Mr. Charles Mills represented Stokely Bros. and Van Camps, Inc. "There are three well-defined methods by which any of us can escape provisions herewith objected to. They are being freely discussed. I can name them if you wish." On request, he names them.

§ 3. CONSUMER PRESSURE GROUPS: VOLUNTARY AND GOVERNMENTAL

THE CONSUMER's third way to win his safety and liberty in the producer-dominated economy, has been voluntary organization as a pressure group. Consumers have endeavored to turn against their users the devices which the producers employ. The first effort was indirect. It arose from the humanitarian and democratic concern of certain more privileged consumers over the lot of the wage-working producers. It took the form of the Consumers' Leagues. Beginning in England in 1890, the movement spread the following year to the United States, and by 1913, had gained followers in Belgium, France, Holland and Switzerland. Aiming ostensibly to impose decent standards and conditions for the makers of the things their members used, the Leagues attacked sweating, investigated shops, proposed laws, distinguished approved goods (goods made under conditions acceptable to the Leagues) by means of labels, and otherwise endeavored to mobilize consumer pressure in behalf of fair treatment of employees by employers. Their philosophy, more or less explicit, was somewhat as follows. The consumer has a stake in how and where and by whom the goods he consumes are produced. The health and cleanliness of the worker, the sanitation of the shop, the adequacy of the tools are at least as important as the price and quality of the goods. Sweating, insanitary conditions, sick and half-starved producers cannot fail to contaminate with their own evil qualities the homes and persons of the consumers. The protection of the producers is the self-preservation of the consumers. In practice, however, the Consumers' Leagues gathered little strength; their best has been to function as a voluntary industrial police, serving not the employer but the employee.

Long after the Consumers' Leagues, there came, in the United States, a direct counter to producer domination in the form of a voluntary non-profit Bureau of Standards, supported by membership subscriptions for the purpose of testing, analyzing and grading consumers' goods of every sort, and publishing the findings among members and subscribers. In effect it was a volunteer consumer's vigilance committee which, among other things, proposed by its work to offset the complacency of the Bureau of Standards to producers. The type of consumer-defense it represents has not yet found a way of reaching even a substantial proportion of the millions of consumers whom the publishers of women's journals reach, to say nothing of a whole nation. Their effects are limited, but they count just the same. They have caused a state of alarm among hearsting [2] magazine publishers, the advertising agencies, and the advertisers. These have endeavored to restrict the influence of such voluntary Bureaus by setting up bureaus of standards of their own. Within the editorial fanes, they maintain "institutes" which purport to test and recommend advertisers' goods that often are put in the "not recommended" lists of such establishments as Consumers' Research, Inc. In the United States the latter has been a living spring of skepticism regarding claims, pretensions and declarations of hearsters and advertisers, that spreads especially through all groups of "quality" buyers, and which no hearsting, however ingenious and expensive, has as yet overcome. Essentially, corporations like Consumers' Research are pressure groups, employing so far as their limited means permit, pitiless publicity to combat deceptions, false claims, false measures, poor quality and other forms of hearsting. Their power and scope are unfortunately not as great as they can be. Their methods are not the purest. Sometimes their managers appear to be ridden by hobbies which in their turn arouse and spread skepticism; and always their associational form is not the sort that can grow into nation-wide consumer organization.

Following the war and during the depression, such nation-wide organization has been designated as a proper political device under the ægis of the state. Arthur Feiler describes an attempt of this sort in republican Germany.[3] It consisted in a National Economic Council, set up to function as an advisory

[2] The neologism *to hearst, hearsting, hearsted;* and its derivatives, hearster, hearsting, etc., came into use about 1934. They are used as terms of scorn and condemnation. *Hearsting* or *to hearst* are names for actions honorable people do not commit.

[3] "The Consumer in Economic Policy," *Social Research,* Vol. I, No. 3.

body with the power to make recommendations to the authorized political agencies. It had 318 members. Employers chose 144, employees 144. The remaining 30 represented the consumers as such, 12 being assigned to the cities and rural communities, 12 to the consumers' coöperative societies, 2 to the nation's housewives, 2 to the domestic servants, 1 to the employers and 1 to the employees of the nation's hotels and restaurants. The Council operated as it could, from 1920 to 1933. Representatives of the producers-employers and employees alike knew they were speaking for organized bodies; representatives of the consumers, bar the coöperative societies, knew they were not, nor was there at any time during the thirteen-year life of the Council any attempt to effect an organization of "the consumer interest."

Again, an attempt was made to safeguard the consumer interest in industrial self-governing bodies of the Reich such as the Coal and Potash Councils. On the Coal Council workers and owners reached an understanding which raised wages for the miners and prices for the owners, leaving the ultimate consumer to pay the shot. In effect he was not represented. The ostensible representatives of the consumer interest were coal dealers, workers and owners, small craftsmen, and others in concerns using coal in the course of manufacture, and the cooperatives, themselves producers. The mentality and sympathies of these consumer-representatives put them unconsciously on the side of the coal producers. The same was true in the Potash Council where the representatives of the consumers were drawn from agricultural marketing and distributing coöperatives. Also, their psychology allied them to the producers, and limited their concern to the interest of their functional group. All in all, Feiler concludes, in the German republic consumer-representation was illusory; only government can effectively protect the consumer interest and government is amenable to the influence of far better organized pressure groups with an opposing interest.

This conclusion is devastatingly borne out by the American record under the New Deal. A new administration, chosen from a party infrequently successful in elections, came to power at the nadir of the great depression which began in 1929, upon a program of remembering the forgotten man and building a juster and more equitable order by a new deal in agriculture, in industry and finance.[4] And the New Deal demonstrated its newness by officially and explicitly remembering the consumer. A part of the machinery of the Agricultural Adjustment Administration (AAA) was a Consumers' Council; a part of the Industrial Recovery Administration (NIRA) was a Consumers' Advisory Board (CAB), and the National Emergency Council (NEC) set up a Division of the Consumer. This Council had been organized in November, 1933, and has since been merged with the Executive Council and Industrial and Emergency Council. Its function was substantially, under the President to coördinate and plan the recovery program, and to help improve the work of its administrative agencies. The addition of a Division of the Consumer to an authority so high shows how deep was the concern of the New Dealers over the predicament of the consumer.[5]

To the Consumers' Division of the Council the task was assigned to coördinate the work in behalf of the consumer in the A.A.A. and the N.R.A. Among its members were representatives of voluntary consumer organizations, such as The Coöperative League of the U.S.A. and the Consumers' League, economists and sociologists known for their advanced liberalism and their experience on consumer problems. That the understanding of the problem was clear enough, at least among some members of the Council, is indicated by a ten-page pamphlet in mimeograph entitled "The Consumer's Stake."

The pamphlet discusses the consumer's relation to prices and quality not only of consumers' goods but of stocks and bonds. Since the consumer's aim, like the producer's, is security, and since he must find it in income and savings as well as purchase, he has a stake in industrial stabilization, in the banking system, and in social insurance. A recovery program must guarantee those to the consumer. Since he cannot de-

[4] For a discussion of the nature of the New Deal and the reasons of its frustration, see Horace M. Kallen, *A Free Society,* Chapters VII, VIII, IX.

[5] Since this was written the daily press has announced a reorganization of the New Deal agencies dealing with consumers' problems. The entire authority is now vested in an "Advisor on Consumer Problems" serving directly under the President and reporting to him.

pend for any such guarantee on business or competition (business not having as yet shown signs of being wise enough not to overreach itself in grasping for profit), and since the government has done more to aid the producer through the Department of Commerce, the tariff, the interpretation of the Fourteenth Amendment in the courts than it has done for the consumer through its efforts to enforce competition, regulate public utilities, and guard the health and safety of the citizens, the consumer cannot depend on mere government. But "in the machinery of the N.R.A. and the A.A.A. the way to the representation of the consumer interest is open."

What this machinery can accomplish, however, "will depend on the strength of the demand for such action and the availability of personnel equipped to act adequately for the consumer." The need of such personnel is paramount. It must be equipped with knowledge and skill sufficient to meet the representatives of industries on their own terms; it must "know how to ask the pertinent questions with respect to all industries, questions relating to prices, to standard and quality, to watch cost and consumers' security." It must be familiar with accounting. It must know where to turn for information, and how to develop and to utilize the information that it gets. It must be a trained service such as does not yet exist and its creation by educating for its tasks is a large part of the stake of the consumer.

The specific program of the Consumers' Advisory Board, as indicated by official orders and synopses of the functions of the Board, attempted in some degree to incorporate this general view. The Board had a Code Section, a Price Section, an Economic Education Section which was supposed to aid the National Economic Council in organizing local Consumers' Councils, and to furnish them with information and plans of action on consumer problems. It had a special committee to promote better commodity standards, with a membership from the Bureau of Standards, from the Bureau of Home Economics of the Department of Agriculture, from the American Home Economics Association, and the Consumers' Counsel of the A.A.A.

It took the Consumers' Advisory Board some time to find

itself. Beginning with a certain indefiniteness regarding its aims and methods, it deliberated, not briefly, on the nature of the consumer it was to safeguard; the final conclusion reached was that "consumer" stands for an "interest" and not a separate and distinct group of people different from other groups. A measurable interval was required to decide what might be the effective means of implementing the defense of the consumer interest or stake. And when finally the Board got ready to act, it found itself confronted with "Codes of Fair Competition" designating the relations of employers in an industry to one another and to employees, and not only safeguarding, but on all fronts advancing the producer interest to the limit. Face to face with this interest, the representatives of the consumers were the amateurs that the author of "The Consumer's Stake" deprecated. They were amateurs, moreover, guided by the sentiment of producer-primacy which had characterized such volunteer organizations as the Consumers' League. Their concern about the wages of this or that class of employee nullified their obligation to protect the consumption of employees not in that class from the consequences of price-fixing. Their attitude toward high prices was guided by their sentiment about high wages.

To make the protection of the consumer effective locally, Consumers' Councils were provided for. The original plan assented to by the Administrator of the N.R.A. was to organize a Council in every county. The National Emergency Council seemed to feel, however, that this was too much, too dangerous. In matters of consumer-interest they preferred to stop, look and listen rather than to cross the producers' tracks. Wariness was held more important than definitive action, and only two hundred Councils were permitted as experiments. The personnel of these Councils seems to have been recruited without program or plan; nor was any definite plan of action or organization laid out for them.

The amateurishness of the central group was immensely magnified in the local groups. They were doomed to failure from the start. Such things as they were able to accomplish on behalf of the consumer depended on accidents of personality, prestige, or situation, not on a well-conceived, well-executed and effectively administered plan. Since the multitude of consumers had no enduring stake in the Councils, but turned to them—when they did turn to them—only in some emergency of purchase, the Councils did not begin to win the interest and the loyalty of the multitudes nor were they able by action to win them. Advised to send representatives to sessions of Code Authorities dealing with prices, quality, wages and the like, the representatives were given no voice in those sessions. Their lack of expert personnel was obvious. Where they were able to record findings, they had not the wherewithal nor the authority to enforce them. Especially, it is significant that thcy were allowed not even the minimum funds with which they might have advanced their work. The very allowance of the Consumers' Division in Washington was conspicuous for its extreme parsimony. In the local Councils it was conspicuous by its absence.

As the record stands today, the St. Louis Council has succeeded in preventing rises in the price of coal and one or two other commodities; that in Albany, by holding public hearings, has put some of the local Code Authorities on the defensive; that in Youngstown, Ohio, has carried on some valuable educational work. But on the whole and in the long run, the Councils have been abortive mummeries. Although the Consumers' Advisory Board has on several occasions protested price-fixing (as in the oil, lumber and other industries); although it has repeatedly asked for the incorporation of quality standards in codes, nothing happened.

Volunteer efforts to defend the consumer under the New Deal, such as the Emergency Conference of Consumers' Organizations, and the Consumers' National Conference, could protest but had no noticeable effect on the Codes of Fair Competition. The Emergency Conference of Consumers' Organizations had been organized in September, 1933, at the headquarters of The Coöperative League of the U.S.A. Representatives had been sent by the American Standards Association, the National Association of Purchasing Agents, the Consumers' League, and Consumers' Research, Inc. The conference memorialized both the President and the N.R.A. administrator; they asked publicity for the consumer; they asked that the government arrange for and finance effective representation of existing consumers' organizations at all code hearings; they asked that the technical data in the hands of the government be made available to the consumer interest. But as usual, nothing happened.

The representative of the consumers' organizations on the national Consumers' Advisory Board, Dr. James P. Warbasse, president of the Coöperative League, wrote at that time to the conference: "The interests of the consumer have had to stand aside while the Codes were being organized and industry rehabilitated. The time is coming when more attention will have to be given to the consuming public." And the time continues, like the Messiah, to be coming.

As Professor Paul Douglas declared, nearly a year after Consumers' Councils had on his initiative been launched, the chief victim of the recovery administration was the consumer. The pressure of the voluntary organizations may have energized the Consumers' Advisory Board. The Emergency Conference had called for its resignation at the end of 1933; it had been attacked for its failures at various public conferences and meetings; but it was hung up by its own tether; its intentions were as worthy as its performance had to be weak. At one time it was urged to draw and propose a plan for a Department of the Consumer with a place in the presidential cabinet for the Department Chief, but nothing, fortunately, came of that.

The Board's helplessness emphasizes how necessary it is for consumers to organize on another basis than that provided through governmental agencies. It stresses the futility of trying to give the consumer priority over the producer by means of a government technique. The fact is that the mentality of the producer-dominated world directs the disposition of even those deeply concerned about the status and destiny of the consumer and inhibits the will of those charged with the task of protecting his interest. Indeed it might be said that the underlying philosophy of the members of the Consumers' Advisory Board was that of the trust and the trades-union. They seemed to be hoping to transform the consumer from a passive to an active competitive force in the economic struggle.

They would, one guesses, have held their task well done if they could have mobilized the consumer as a third to labor and capital among the pressure groups. Mr. Tugwell, famed among other things for authorship of a pretty good Pure Food and Drug Bill which of course failed to pass, addressing the Consumers' League of Cleveland, declared that the organization of industry into larger producing units has progressively weakened the position of the consumer in the market and therefore imposed upon the consumer the necessity also to become a pressure group, both on the market and to influence governmental policies.

§ 4. WHY SUCH CONSUMER DEFENSES MUST FAIL

A PRESSURE-POLICY can be effective only in the degree that one group either prevents another group from getting something that it desires or takes away from another group something it already possesses. This invidious relationship is impossible as a basis of consumer organization. For everybody is a consumer of many things and a producer of one or at most a few. The discriminatory and competitive technique is applicable only when the groups are limited. It doesn't apply in the form of an organization of all against each. The often invoked analogy of the trades-union with its limited membership breaks down when it is applied to the unlimited multitudes who compose the consumer group. Some of the multitude can be organized to compete against all (this happens whenever an industry endeavors to rule the market); some can be organized to compete against some others (this happens when employers struggle with unions or with one another, and vice versa), but all cannot be organized to compete against some—not in the national economy. The organization of war is another matter: it mobilizes one people against another on a new level of counting; a war between nations is a struggle of some with some.

BOOK II

THE ECONOMICS OF FREEDOM

CHAPTER VI

THE CONSUMER EMERGES, I

§ 1. CONSEQUENCES OF IDOLIZING PRODUCTION

IN ECONOMICS, as in all the affairs of mankind, things that are first in nature are last in thought. The idea of the primacy of the consumer is modernly as recent as the primacy is aboriginal. Since consumption is the end of life and production is but a method of the struggle to live, the attention of economic philosophers was concentrated on production. As compared with its methods and means, the end is enduring, constant, pervasive; the Self which one struggles to preserve stays and continues even while it changes; the tools and the weapons one employs in the struggle—the jobs, the implements and the knowledge required to hold them—come and go with time and place and circumstance. Our Selves we have always with us; our information and skill time antiquates, invention abolishes, discovery displaces; our means and methods tend to elude and leave us even as we are ripest to employ them. The always insecure foundations of our security, we never dare take them for granted as we take ourselves for granted, and we give them our absorbed and solicitous attention.

To Aristotle or to St. Thomas or to John Calvin our preoccupation with the means of life would be unintelligible. Until the industrial revolution, the tempo of the means and the tempo of the ends of western life were commensurable; almost they beat a unison in time. Since the industrial revolution, means and ends, which in the living nature of things are confluent and so interpenetrated that the latter are but the present phases of the former's change, have become separated, externalized one to another, moving with different rhythms and in reversed directions. Tools have become so many, so varied, so complicated, so magnificent, so impersonal and so pervasive, that they lay the road and set the pace of the march of life. Tools are in the saddle and ride mankind.

They are not in the saddle without reason. Men first cherished and endeavored to multiply the engines of the industrial art because by them scarcity was made into abundance, ignorance into knowledge, servility into self-respect and bondage into freedom. It was natural to feel that the instruments by which were created the abundance and knowledge and self-respect and freedom were paramount to the excellences they created. The industrial economy lost its human scale, machinery loomed gigantic over the natural scene, its forms blotted out nature and distorted man. Human ends and industrial means quickly transposed: Since production purposes to enhance life, must not enhanced life mean production? The miser, accumulating his gold, suffers the same illusion. Making himself the servant of his tool, he robs it of the very quality which had rendered it precious to him in the first place. Both he and the gold become sheer waste. Such, today, are the accumulations and the processes of our credit-enterprise economy. The primacy given the producer because production has enhanced life has led to the idolization of production; and this idolization largely deprives production of the function which led to the idolization in the first place. It degrades wealth into waste.

Owen and the Owenites recognized this instinctively, but they could not sufficiently liberate themselves from preoccupation with the tool. The "villages of coöperation," the self-governing workshops, the trades-unions and the stores, were all ruled by the notion that if you took care of production, consumption would take care of itself.

§ 2. CHARLES HOWARTH AND THE ORGANIZATION OF THE ROCHDALE SOCIETY OF EQUITABLE PIONEERS

THE STORY of the Rochdale Pioneers is the Book of Genesis in the growing saga that will make the Bible of the world-wide consumer economy which, bar accidents of fate and fortune, the movement they started is likely to culminate in. First told circumstantially by George Jacob Holyoake in 1857, under the title, *Self-Help for the People: The History of the Rochdale Pioneers,* it has been variously repeated in all the languages and all the countries of Christendom, as poignant, as moving and as triumphant as any parable a Testament ever contained.

The factories of Rochdale wove flannels. In 1843 they prospered. Trade was brisk, and the underpaid and overworked weavers struck for higher pay. They lost the strike. Many were blacklisted; those reëmployed had to accept a cut instead of a rise. At the shops credit came to an end; in the cottages was the beginning of despair. Such was the frame of reference for all discussion of their situation by the workers of Rochdale. Regularly, on Sunday afternoons, a number of these came together in the Temperance or Chartist Reading Room. Regularly they argued, according to their sectarian faiths, "how best to improve the condition of the people."

No doubt all the prevailing sects were represented—Owenites, Chartists, Teetotalers, Christians. No doubt all the doctrines and enterprises current were canvassed. Dr. King's stores, Owen's "villages of coöperation," his workshops and his labor exchanges, the Charter, sobriety, God—the debaters were aware how, in one place or another, each had been tried, and had brought the experimenters little else than the increase of knowledge which is the increase of sorrow. Perhaps discussion centred on the idea of a store—James Smithies, one of the original Rochdale Pioneers, owned a bound volume of Dr. King's *Coöperator* which he later placed in the Society's library. The worker's relation to the shopkeeper was as critical a problem as his relation to the employer. He could buy only a little bit at a time,[1] as often as not he had to buy on credit, with the consequence that he was never out of debt—the provident and thrift societies which the charitable were always urging workers to form testify eloquently to the fact if they as eloquently falsify its causes. The combination of small quantities and long credit meant high prices. And it is still a universal condition that the poorer the customers, the less they get for their money. In terms of actual value received, the poor pay the highest prices in the land. How far they could make their wages go at the shop was a momentous and urgent daily problem. Credit, bad management, the readiness of the member for convenience or other causes to trade with the competitors of their own stores, had destroyed the Kingsite shops. And yet . . . a shop would so obviously help in the day-to-day crisis of sufficient food. How overcome the well-known and apparently insurmountable difficulty?

To Charles Howarth belongs the credit of providing the answer. In 1843, he was twenty-five years old. He already had behind him a record of ten years' thoughtful and persistent effort on behalf of freedom and security for the "industrious classes." By vocation a warper in a cotton mill, an Owenite by faith, opposed to the established religion and its forms, he braved the ill-will of authority in many ways. He agitated for a shorter working day, even going to London to lobby for the Ten Hours' Act. He figured as a strike leader. He played a conspicuous part in Rochdale endeavors to embody the Owenite dream. His mates called him "the lawyer." He had drawn up the rules for an earlier "coöperative shop" in Rochdale's Toad Lane, a shop that had failed in 1835. The difficulties of coöperative shopkeeping were by no means unfamiliar to him, and the tale tells how he spent one long sleepless night racking his brain for a way to overcome them. That the business must be conducted on a strictly cash basis anybody could see. This was obvious. But how overcome the competitive advantage of the credit-giver? How meet the competition of lower prices elsewhere? How keep advantage com-

[1] It is a maxim of contemporary merchandizing that "the smaller the package the greater the profit."

mensurate with use? In the earlier stores, profits, if there were any, were divided in ratio to investment. The increase from use did not accrue to the user but to the owner or producer. Suppose this situation were reversed. Suppose that the investor were to receive interest at a fixed rate, say 5 per cent, and that the profits were turned back to the customers in proportion to their custom? This would provide a defense against all competition and an incentive to the continuous use of the store. The member is held by the fact that the more he spends, the more he gains. "Dividend on purchase" would redress the balance and give the coöperative store its fighting chance.

The device of dividing profits on purchases in proportion to each member's trade was what Charles Howarth brought as a new solution for the old difficulties of coöperative trading. Research has since shown that it had been tried before: it is not, however, its occurrence which makes a device significant, but its consequences. As Howarth's idea the device had consequences at last.

But a store could not be enough. Alcoholism was too prevalent. Housing was abominable. There was always unemployment to deal with and poverty always to overcome. There was always the dream of freedom and security. The twenty-eight workers of Rochdale who organized the Society of Equitable Pioneers meant to realize the dream and to conquer the problems. They meant to establish an Owenite village of coöperation. Here are their objects as finally drawn by Charles Howarth.

Objects of Rochdale Pioneers

The objects and plans of this society are to form arrangements for the pecuniary benefit, and improvement of the society and domestic condition of its members, by raising a sufficient amount of capital in shares of one pound each, to bring into operation the following plans and arrangements.

The establishment of a store for the sale of provisions and clothing, &c.

The building, purchasing or erecting a number of houses, in which those members desiring to assist each other in improving their domestic and social condition may reside.

To commence the manufacture of such articles as the society may determine upon, for the employment of such members as may be without employment, or who may be suffering in consequence of repeated reductions in their wages.

As a further benefit and security to the members of this society, the society shall purchase or rent an estate or estates of land, which shall be cultivated by the members who may be out of employment, or whose labour may be badly remunerated.

That as soon as practicable, this society shall proceed to arrange the powers of production, distribution, education, and government, or in other words to establish a self-supporting home colony of united interests, or assist other societies in establishing such colonies.

That for the promotion of sobriety, a temperance hotel be opened in one of the society's houses, as soon as convenient.

The members are to raise capital in shares of one pound each in order to establish a store, provide themselves with better houses, give work to the unemployed through manufactures and farming, open up a temperance hotel, and magnificently "proceed to arrange the powers of production, distribution, education and government" or, in other words, to "establish a self-supporting home colony of united interests, or assist other societies in establishing such colonies."

Among these objects the store is the first item. But it is first not because it was the most important in the minds of the twenty-eight, but because it met the most immediate need and was the least difficult and most practicable end to bring about. The store was to be only the first step in a wide program of self-help whose other steps embrace the whole Owenite intent and plan. The store was to be the beginning, and for it rules were provided, *viz:*

1. To sell goods at prevailing local prices.
2. Restriction to a fixed rate of the interest upon capital—this interest to have first claim upon the profits.
3. The distribution of profits (after meeting expenses and interest charges) in proportion to purchases.
4. No credit—all purchases and sales to be paid for in cash when the goods were handed over.
5. Both sexes to have equality in membership rights.
6. Each member to have one vote and no more.
7. Regular and frequent meetings to be held for the discussion of

the society's business and of receiving suggestions for improving the society's welfare.

8. Accounts to be properly kept and audited and balance sheets to be regularly presented to the members.

§ 3. THE TREMENDOUS IMPORT OF RULE 3

CHARLES HOWARTH also drew the rules. A cursory reading will show that in the background of his mind was always the failure of the earlier stores, and that failure was to be made impossible this time. Each item—fixed rate of interest on capital, sales at the market price, distribution of profits in proportion to purchases, parity of men and women, one man, one vote, regular and frequent meetings, proper bookkeeping and audit —was determined by a corresponding earlier cause of failure, and devised to overcome it. Neither Howarth nor his twenty-seven fellows of the Equitable Society had any inkling that with Rule 3—the rule prescribing the distribution of profits in proportion to purchases—they had added something which would dissipate their objects and transform their goal. How could any of them see that Rule 3 added just that difference, that Darwinian variation, which would develop, in the struggle for survival, into a new species of social economy, an economy of the consumer with the vitality, the adaptability, and the urge, to displace and atrophy the prevailing producer economy? And how indeed could anybody else see this, in a producers' world, where hearts and minds were bound up in production? What other finality of freedom could any one then have looked to than an Owenite "self-supporting home colony of united interests"? The members of the Society of Equitable Pioneers were as unconscious of the import of their enterprise as Columbus. They made the beginning of a Copernican revolution in the credit-enterprise economy of the world, and they thought that they were only easing and smoothing and freeing the old productive round.

§ 4. THE PIONEERING AND WHAT IT DISCOVERED

AND, burdened as they were, it was enough. They had all they could do to start the store. It took them nearly a year to bring together the £28 or less, collected twopence a week, then threepence, by a committee of volunteers. Ten pounds of the total had to go for a year's rent of the former storeroom of a Pioneer regiment in Toad Lane, £4 more had to go for fixtures and sundries. They had only £14 to spend for the few items of groceries—flour, butter, sugar and oatmeal—with which they began. Able to buy only smaller quantities, they had had to pay higher prices, and therefore to charge higher prices than their competitors. They had had to meet and to live down the ridicule which every innovation, no matter how like an early straw hat perennial and familiar, arouses. Taking down the shutters, that historic evening of December 21, 1844, had been an anxious and dramatic moment; in which Samuel Ashworth acquitted himself like a Pioneer;[2] and he was courtesy and patience itself, when as unpaid, volunteer counterman he regretted to inquiring callers that the store did not yet stock goods which the callers knew it did not stock when they asked. In the face of the convenient nearness of competitors, of their lower prices, their bribes and tips, it was difficult to hold the loyalty of anxious mothers and complaining wives. But their loyalty was held. At the end of three months it was possible to pay Ashworth for his labor. Slowly the counters were filled with goods of different sorts; the two evenings of shopkeeping became three and four and five. The payment of the first dividend on purchases was the turning point. Then the Store was on its way indeed.

But in the eyes of its founders, it figures as a means to coöperative production, ever. In 1850, hoping to improve the quality of the flour they sold their customers, they took shares in a cornmill which a small group had started as a coöperative enterprise; a little later, to save their investment, the Store lent it money. But the tale of the cornmill was from the first the typical tale of producers' coöperation: drunken or lying or treacherous or incompetent managers, inferior grains, bad flour; bad blood among the members, bad goods in the Store; disgruntlement at the consumer's table. Not only did the mill seem likely to go under but to take the Store with it. Rumors

[2] Later research makes "Owd Face" William Taylor the hero. He was killed a few years afterward in an explosion.

spread among the members. Some had left their purchase-dividends to accumulate. Others had lent their savings to the Store at 4 per cent. There was something like a run which competitors did not fail to encourage. In the end the stability of the Store was more than vindicated. The Pioneers took over the cornmill and made it a solvent and profitable enterprise. To do so, they had to change it from a producers' society which the Store was to serve to a producing plant which would serve the Store. (The mill was taken over by the Coöperative Wholesale Society in 1905.) Nevertheless, the Society failed to read the meaning of its own record. In 1853, John T. W. Mitchell, then twenty-four years old, joined the Pioneers. He is listed among the leaders who in 1854 were promoting the Rochdale Coöperative Manufacturing Society. The Society was to manufacture cotton, and the factory was to be a self-governing workshop. But the cotton was to be produced, not for the members of the Society, but for sale in the open market, and the profits were to be equally divided with the rank and file producers. Few among the 300 of these were also among the 1,400 shareholders. As profits came in, discontent with the division grew. The intent of producers' coöperation, precarious at best, was displaced by the intent of the ordinary joint-stock company. Since, to the shareholders, the profit-sharing with the employees seemed preëminently unfair, profit-sharing was, by 1862, abandoned. Early in 1934, the Manufacturing Society, practically a joint-stock company with slightly philanthropic features, was dissolved, a casualty of the post-war depression.

Meanwhile, other issues had arisen. The people were not only men and women. They were Englishmen and Scotchmen, drinkers and teetotallers, radicals and Tories, weavers and smiths, Christians and Owenites, and the Christians were separated into half a dozen sects. Issues over the eligibility to membership could not fail to arise; discriminatory distinctions could not fail to be drawn. Early in its life, the Society was threatened with a certain sectarian exclusiveness. It was not a foregone conclusion that the principle of the parity of the different, implicit in the rule of the equality of the sexes and the ideal of "a colony of united interests," should win an explicit triumph. Indeed, on the continent, once the consumers' coöperative movement was started there, the principle failed, and Christian, that is, Catholic, societies were segregated from the others. Today separatism on a national scale is attempted by the autarchic policies of the Nazis in Germany and the Fascists in Italy. But the early triumph of the democratic rule of the equal right of different interests to enroll in the movement laid down the gradient along which it would develop and established the principle of its growth. It decided that coöperative society should be what Bergson has recently called "open society"; that its membership can be identical with mankind. Years later the Christian Socialist Society for the Promotion of Workingmen's Associations found themselves confronted with the same issue under new conditions, and it is the ultimate testimony to the coöperative idea that it was decided in the same way. For men like Ludlow and Maurice were, first and last, Christians. They were coöperators because they were Christians, and it was natural for Ludlow to propose that membership in the society should be tantamount to a declaration of Christian faith. This would have meant—as Neale pointed out—that coöperators not holding this faith could not be members of the society. The difference seemed irreconcilable; yet it was reconciled, and Ludlow acquiesced in Maurice's famous formula,

1. That human society is a body consisting of many members, not a collection of warring atoms.
2. That true workmen must be fellow-workmen, not rivals.
3. That a principle of justice, not selfishness, must regulate exchanges.

The formula reaffirms that coöperative society is "open society."

The Pioneers were as unaware of the import of their decision, as of the import of Rule 3. Only very slowly, in the course of more than a generation of work and struggle, through day-by-day drudgery and routine, did the meaning of the growing enterprise dawn on any of them. The movement they started won its wisdom out of experience only, line upon line and precept upon precept, against the deep resistance of the

Owenite religion which had been the first faith of them all; against the steady and valiant battle for this faith of the original Owenites and new Christian Socialists who had joined the ranks. The competitive impulse, the push toward discriminatory distinctions, toward exclusiveness and monopoly, were always active and always in force. It took a long time to learn that "united interests" were not exclusive interests, and that harmony within did not have to mean warfare without.

§ 5. SOME CONSEQUENCES: HOLYOAKE'S OBSERVATIONS

THE SUCCESS of the Rochdale store aroused quick imitation. The north of England and the Scottish midlands, where the Owenite enterprises had grown before, saw a new birth of coöperative shops. By 1851, there were about 150 of them each with from 50 to 100 members, and additional ones were being announced continually. Producers' societies were hardy perennials; they claimed the support of the stores and received it, both in share capital and in custom. The original Pioneer store in Toad Lane set up branches in other parts of Rochdale. . . .

Buying was early a vexing problem for all the stores. In the beginning, the principle of cash transactions was a handicap. It was a deviation from custom, and a sort of degradation in a country where the best practice of the best people was to deal entirely on credit, and debt—to tradesmen, of course—was a sign of quality among the well-born and of depravity among the populace. When cash was scarce it was not possible to buy in quantity, and the private shopkeeper buying on credit enjoyed a competitive advantage. In those days goods cost the coöperative stores more. The costs were increased by the fact that coöperative buyers were competitive not only to private buyers, but to one another; that on occasion, sellers or competitors could bribe them, that often they were incompetent. The need for some sort of wholesale organization made itself felt almost at once, and the endeavors to set one up were manifold. The record is neither clear nor consistent, but it signalizes the need, the anxiety and mutual suspicions which delayed meeting the need, and the final adequate action.

Already in 1850, the Pioneers had set up a wholesale department of their own, to supply members requiring large quantities, and hopeful of serving stores, wrote Holyoake in 1857, "whose small capitals do not enable them to buy in the best markets, nor command the services of what is otherwise indispensable to every store—*a good buyer*. . . . The wholesale department guarantees purity, quality, fair prices, standard weight and measure, but all on the never-failing principle, cash payment." By this time the Store had added to the Groceries with which it began five other departments: "Drapery, Butcher, Shoemaking, Clogging, Tailoring." It had remodeled the warehouse at Toad Lane: "Every part has undergone neat refitting and modest decoration. . . . One room is handsomely fitted up as a newsroom. Another is neatly fitted up as a library." The newsroom is free to members, the library to everybody. It contains "2,200 volumes of the best, and among them, many of the most expensive books published. The costs are defrayed out of the Education Fund." . . . Two and a half per cent of all the profits had been segregated for education. From 1850 to 1855, the society had maintained a school for young persons "at the charge of twopence a month."

Since 1855, a room has been granted by the Board, for the use of from twenty to thirty persons from the ages of fourteen to forty, for mutual instruction on Sundays and Tuesdays. . . . Business is now conducted across the street in a new warehouse, bought in 1853, and in rented houses adjoining. . . . Their warehouses are everywhere as bountifully stocked as Noah's Ark, and cheerful customers literally crowd Toad Lane at night, swarming like bees to every counter. The industrial districts have not such another sight as the Rochdale Coöperative Store on Saturday night.

But it is not [Holyoake continues] the brilliancy of commercial activity in which either writer or reader will take the deepest interest; it is in the new and improved spirit animating this intercourse of trade. Buyer and seller meet as friends; there is no overreaching on one side, and no suspicion on the other. . . . These crowds of humble working-men, who never knew before when they put good food in their mouths, whose every dinner was adulterated, whose shoes let in the water a month too soon, whose waistcoats shone with devil's dust, and whose wives wore calico that would not wash, now buy in the markets like millionaires, and as far as pureness of goods goes, live like lords. . . . They are weaving their own stuffs, making their own shoes, sewing their own garments, and grinding their own corn. They buy the purest sugar and the best tea, and grind their own coffee. They slaughter their own cattle, and the finest beasts of the land waddle down the streets of Rochdale for the consumption of flannel-weavers and cobblers. (Last year the Society advertised for a Provision Agent to make purchases in Ireland, and to devote his whole time to that duty.) When did competition give poor men these advantages? And will any man say that the moral character of these people is not improved under these influences? The teetotallers of Rochdale acknowledge that the Store has made more sober men since it commenced than all their efforts have been able to make in the same time. Husbands who never knew what it was to be out of debt, and poor wives who during forty years never had sixpence uncondemned in their pockets, now possess little stores of money sufficient to build them cottages, and to go every week into their own market with money jingling in their pockets; and in that market there is no distrust and no deception; there is no adulteration, and no second prices. The whole atmosphere is honest. Those who serve neither hurry, finesse, nor flatter. *They have no interest in chicanery*. They have but one duty to perform—that of giving fair measure, full weight, and a pure article. In other parts of the town, where competition is the principle of trade, all the preaching in Rochdale cannot produce moral effects like these.

As the Store has made no debts, it has incurred no losses; and during thirteen years, transactions, and receipts amounting to £303,852, it has had no law-suits. The Arbitrators of the Societies, during all their years of office, have never had a case to decide, and are discontented that nobody quarrels.

Holyoake, being partizan, was naturally more sanguine than less interested observers might have been: yet the most critical could little diminish the brightness of his picture. The difference not only among the Pioneers, but in the whole of Rochdale, between 1844 and 1857, was the difference between slavery and freedom, destitution and security. Other forces were doubtless at work beside the Store, but the Store was the Great Divide, and the lapse of time, the succession of depressions and wars and depression has not changed its rôle, anywhere in the world.

§ 6. PROBLEMS OF BUYING AND THE FORMATION OF THE COÖPERATIVE WHOLESALE SOCIETY

BRIGHT as was the local scene in 1857, the general situation was anxious, and the Wholesale Department of the Rochdale store had not alleviated it. In the way were the physical difficulties of meeting as well as the natural jealousies and rivalries of independent similar groups, the dislike of the *primus inter pares*. Societies had met in conference after conference, in answer to call after call. Resolutions were adopted, and nothing happened. Buyers were admonished to work together and that somehow didn't help. Under the law, no plan could be devised by which the local societies could own shares in a wholesale coöperative. Finally, in 1861, it was voted to get the law changed, and it took two years to draft the change, to have it seen through in Parliament. The following year, at a conference in Oldham, after Abraham Greenwood and William Cooper, two of the original Pioneers, had presented a plan and an argument, the establishment of a wholesale was voted. In 1863, Greenwood's plan was published in the *Cooperator* and submitted to public discussion. Soon after representatives of the organizing societies met in Rochdale to decide on the rules. It was agreed that only coöperative societies could be shareholders, that shares should be five shillings and transferable, that the societies should subscribe to as many shares as each had members and that one shilling of the price should be paid in at once.

Among the society delegations participating in this decision were representatives from Dublin and from London. In London a parallel effort to establish a wholesale had been made along contrasting but supplementary lines. London was the headquarters of the Christian Socialists' Society for the Promotion of Workingmen's Associations. Such associations as there were had been competing against each other in the market. A unified sales-agency was obviously indicated. That such an agency might seek a market in the coöperative stores was also obvious, and this meant creating more such stores, which were few in London. That the agency might buy for the latter and sell for the former was a natural conclusion. Van Sittart Neale had seen in Paris what troubles may come from competition between many producers' societies. In 1851, he drew up a memorandum for a general union of Workingmen's Associations and later a scheme for the formation of coöperative stores, and devoted himself in person to establishing a Central Coöperative Agency. He raised the £9,000, and as the law necessitated, set up a trust with himself and Charles Hughes as trustees; inaugurated the Agency under the trade name of Woodin, Jones and Company, and put in Lloyd Jones among the managers.

Lloyd Jones was the contact man between the Christian Socialists of London and the south and the coöperatives of the north. He had attended conferences on the creation of the wholesale at Bury and elsewhere, and it was to be his task to "sell" the agency to the old stores and to organize new ones. Of the profits of the enterprise, if any, one-fourth were to go into a reserve fund, one-fourth to bonuses for employees, the rest for organizing new societies. The Society for the Promotion of Workingmen's Associations dissociated itself from the Agency as outside its promotional purpose. In the six years of its existence it was very active and very expensive. Fifteen societies availed themselves of its services during the first year; during the second it undertook manufacture in order to safeguard purity and quality; and its business grew. But costs increased more rapidly than business, and income could not catch up with overhead. In 1857, Neale felt forced to wind up the enterprise.

Meanwhile, the Christian Socialists, desirous of utilizing the new freedom obtained through the Industrial and Provident Societies Act of 1852, became more tolerant of the coöperative store and united with coöperators of other sects in endorsing the creation of a wholesale society to supply goods and to effect exchanges between producers' societies. Alternative plans of organization were considered, but nothing actually happened until after the Rochdale meeting of 1863. Then the London Association for the Promotion of Coöperation, which had recently come into existence, called a conference to discuss creating for the south a wholesale like that of the north. The North of England Wholesale Industrial and Provident Society, Limited, had been organized in Manchester, on October 10, 1863, by forty-odd societies, who subscribed fourteen thousand shares. Abraham Greenwood had been chosen president, James Smithies, treasurer. The Scottish Wholesale Society followed in 1868.

The organization of the coöperative wholesale societies may be compared to the adoption of the Constitution of the United States. Societies joined it as states added themselves to the Union and many availed themselves of its services before they took on the obligations of membership. By first intention, the Wholesale was to engage only in trade; to buy, not to produce —production was to remain the domain of producers' societies —and it was to be a favoring if not favored customer of such societies. In relation to private business, however, its existence shifted the competitive advantage to the side of the coöperatives. The magnitude of the sums at its disposal made cash more valuable than credit; the more it bought, the less, proportionally, it paid; its services gave the weakest society the same advantage as the strongest: making available to it, and to its members through it, the best quality at the lowest rates, the surest information in the shortest time.

The Wholesale actually implemented the strength of all for the advantage of each, while the reverse was not the case. Its existence compelled the organization of the competitors of the societies into associations of their own. These survive and function to date. Their methods are the conventional ones: misrepresentation of their competitor through the channels of public information, lobbying against him in the legislatures; procuring the discharge of members of coöperative societies by their employers; procuring the boycott of coöperative societies by merchants and manufacturers and the like. Sir William Maxwell, chairman of the Scottish Coöperative Wholesale, testified before a royal commission of inquiry in 1893, that railroads had endeavored to keep their employees from joining coöperatives on the threat of dismissal. The same inquiry heard Mr. R. Walker, the Organizing Agent of the Traders' Defence Association of Scotland, assert that the coöperatives had not done what they claimed they had done: that they in fact charged higher prices for poorer goods than private cash businesses; that they didn't reach the really poor, as private dealers did; that even with the dividend their prices were higher than those of private dealers, and that the dividend was a deception whose abolition he heartily recommended. Let the coöperatives sell goods at cost plus the expenses of distribution, then the nation would see. . . . He did not mention, perhaps he did not know, that the coöperative stores had begun that way and had failed. . . .

§ 7. ENEMIES, FRIENDS, AND THE DEVELOPMENT OF THE COÖPERATIVE UNION

THE SCOTTISH Trade Defence Association was only one in a succession of organizations fighting the coöperative movement. Their organs kept describing it editorially as dead or dying, while their agents were engaged by every business and political device they could imagine, in an endeavor to kill it. Calumny, taxation and the boycott were the favorites, and remain so to this day. The time came when the general press, which earlier favored the movement, was either silent about it, or printed what was unfavorable to it. Efforts to organize boycotts were perennial: in 1872, *The Grocer* listed eighty-four firms that had agreed to have no dealings with the coöperatives. Parliamentary pressure remains a permanent menace: the endeavors to accomplish by legislation what "business-methods" have failed to accomplish are renewed constantly.

Discrimination against the coöperatives was among the influences leading to the creation of the Wholesale Society. It was equally a factor in the creation of the Coöperative Union with its coöperative congresses, and especially and significantly in forcing the Wholesale to enter the field of production. But the problems of clearing up misrepresentation, answering libels, overcoming prejudice, presenting the principles and methods of the coöperators to the public, advancing their interests in the market place and on the forum were problems of defense first and of growth afterwards. There were certain primary problems of growth whose solution could hardly have other forms than deliberative union and productive enterprise. From the publication of Holyoake's book in 1857, the Pioneers had been flooded with inquiries from individuals and groups hopeful of coöperative salvation. Answering them by pen and tongue was at first a grateful volunteer enterprise. The spirit of the earlier Owenite "social missionary"—Holyoake had been one, and used to write S. M. after his name—

was alive and strong in many of the original twenty-eight, and the leaders particularly were delighted to demonstrate the achieved salvation of both faith and works. But the burden was more than any busy soul could carry, even if he gave every waking hour of every day to it. Other societies had similar experiences. . . . In the course of the work itself problems of technique and attitude kept arising: there was need of an interchange and record of experience, of data and observations to be made available to employees in the coöperative services even more than to the members themselves. . . . In addition, the contemporary trades-unions had come up. A form of producers' association somewhat tangent to coöperative thinking and propaganda, the trades-unions had grown to power in the national economy, and it was necessary for the coöperatives to find a general plan and method of living with them in harmony. . . . And there were always the requirements of the law to meet and the restrictions of the law to overcome. Correct legal form was indispensable to legality, and coöperators often needed help with this, and got it, not a little as free service, from Neale, Ludlow, Hughes and other lawyers among the Christian Socialists. Every step forward in the movement required new legislation, and the drafters and engineers of the new legislation were again these Christian Socialists.

Men of wealth, education and sensibility, trained in the learned professions, who had freely chosen a cause which cut them off from their own kind, the Christian Socialists supplied to the coöperative movement an intellectual and spiritual distinction, a social influence and a professional skill which trade-unionism then still lacked. They were the sponsors of the first of the Industrial and Provident Societies Acts which liberated the movement from the paternalist restrictions of the Friendly Societies Acts of 1829, 1834, under which the Rochdale Pioneers had begun their adventure, and of 1850, under which they had started their wholesale department. The Christian Socialists recognized from the beginning the need for concerted study and propaganda among coöperators, and in 1852, the same year that saw the adoption of the Industrial and Provident Societies Act, they organized a Coöperative League with Van Sittart Neale as secretary. It was this League that, after the adoption of the Act, called a conference of societies which was attended by delegates from the north as well as the south. The labors of the executive committee which the conference created, the interchange of information between the societies which it carried on, the annual conferences it organized, all added momentum and *Stimmung* to the trend toward association on a national scale.

The societies recognized the devotion and the generous goodwill of Van Sittart Neale and his fellows, the lawyers, and, in a somewhat tangent sense, the prophets of the movement. But they began to feel that here, too, they ought to be doing these things together and for themselves. Many recalled the Congresses of Owen's days, the social missions and the missionaries. In 1865, the veteran coöperator William Pare began an agitation to revive the Congresses. He was joined in due course by Lloyd Jones, E. T. Graig and by Edward Owen Greening, a Manchester wire manufacturer, who advocated and practised profit-sharing and figured prominently as a member of the Congresses of the Social Science Association, and as a defender of American abolitionism. His connection with the coöperative movement dated from 1856. He became perhaps the most logical and persuasive of the advocates of producers' coöperation, copartnership and profit-sharing. And the Christian Socialists though no longer alive as a body of course were only too pleased to participate in the congress agitation. Conference followed conference, and that of the spring of 1869 elected an arrangements committee which secured the endorsement of the northern societies, set a date, raised a fund and enrolled a committee of sponsors. These included, besides the representatives of all schools of coöperation, representatives of the trades-unions, leaders of the movement abroad, and distinguished national figures like John Ruskin and John Stuart Mill.

In May, 1869, the first Coöperative Congress was held in London. It sat for four days. Pare, Ludlow and Abraham Greenwood read papers. Pare suggested the creation of a British and Foreign Coöperative League. Among its tasks were to be the adoption of model rules for the organization and management of coöperatives, assembling and providing technical information and advice on all matters affecting the character and conduct of coöperatives and the confederation of coöperative societies; holding annual congresses, and the like. The second Congress was held the following year in Manchester. This created a Central Board and laid down a basis of subscription for constituent societies and recommended the appointment of a permanent secretary, but not enough money was raised to make an appointment possible. Union and Congress remained in a somewhat ambiguous and tentative state until 1873, when Edward Van Sittart Neale proposed a reorganization which embodies the present structure of the British Coöperative Union. Neale was chosen permanent secretary and the Union and its Congresses were at last definitely launched.

It was natural that the Union should develop into the great organ of opinion and policy of the British Coöperative Movement. In structure it is a confederation of the coöperative societies of the United Kingdom. It calls an annual Congress which elects a Central Board of seventy members. These members are drawn from nine geographical regions into which Great Britain is divided for purposes of coöperative administration. "An Executive Committee of ten representatives controls the work of the departments and committees of the Coöperative Union. Other committees of the Coöperative Union are the Joint Parliamentary, the Educational Council and Executive, National Committee of the Coöperative Party, the Joint Trade and Propaganda Committee, the Joint Committee on Technical Education, and the Trade Associations." "The Glasgow Congress of 1932 also established a National Coöperative Authority. The Authority comprises the Executive Committee of the Coöperative Union with representatives of National Federations, the C.W.S., the S.C.W.S., the Coöperative Party, the Coöperative Productive Federation, and the National Coöperative Publishing Society. The Authority gives a lead to the whole movement on questions of national policy." [3]

[3] Edward Topham (Editor of Publications, Coöperative Union), *Services of the Coöperative Union, British Coöperation Today* (British Coöperative Union), p. 83.

§ 8. THE WARFARE OF PROGRAMS: CONSUMPTION IN THE INTEREST OF PRODUCTION VERSUS PRODUCTION IN THE INTEREST OF CONSUMPTION

THE FORUM of the Congress is wide open. No problem which concerns coöperators, either as society members or as persons, is alien to it. The Congresses have dealt with free trade, with woman suffrage, with town planning, with foreign relations, with war and peace, with education, with international coöperation, and the like. Apart from the routinal problems which the Congress was created to solve, the paramount issue before it has been the issue between control by consumers and control by producers, and till the turn of the century this issue overshadowed all others at the Congress sessions.

The issue was finally joined because the Wholesale Society found it necessary to go into production. Even the Wholesale, with its extensive, indeed its excessive, cash resources found itself dealing in a prejudiced market. Its own constituency was constantly being lured away from it by competitors who did not hesitate to treat buyers for local stores with a practicality calculated to gain and to hold the appreciative custom of the buyers. In addition to this induced disloyalty there were certain more or less inevitable deficiencies of the Wholesale's own purchasing: More than once the management learned to their disgrace that they had passed on to the stores adulterated or defective goods. Sometimes it was found that the source of such goods was a producers' coöperative.

As already observed, the rank and file of the coöperators depended for their philosophy on the reinterpretations of Owenism by the wealthy intellectuals of the Christian Socialist sect. The dogma that the producer is paramount was a part of the funded mentality of the coöperative movement. It was Carlyle's premise. It governed William Morris and John Ruskin. Even John Stuart Mill, observing the coöperative movement freshly from outside, could infer from it no different prospect for the producing multitude than their organization into producers' coöperatives. Writing in 1865, of the "probable future of the labouring classes," he declares, "the form of association . . . which, if mankind continue to improve, must be expected in the end to predominate, is not that which can exist between a capitalist as chief, and work-people without a voice in the management, but the association of the labourers themselves on terms of equality, collectively owning the capital with which they carry on their operations and working under managers elected and removable by themselves." [4]

When, however, coöperative societies shall have sufficiently multiplied, it is not probable that any but the least valuable work-people will any longer consent to work all their lives for wages merely: and both private capitalists and associations will gradually find it necessary to make the entire body of labourers participants in profits. Eventually, and in perhaps a less remote future, than may be supposed, we may, through the coöperative principle, see our way to a change in society, which would combine the freedom and independence of the individual, with the moral, intellectual, and economical advantages of aggregate production; and which, without violence or spoliation, or even any sudden disturbance of existing habits and expectations, would realize, at least in the industrial department, the best aspirations of the democratic spirit, by putting an end to the division of society into the industrious and the idle, and effacing all social distinctions but those fairly earned by personal services and exertions. Associations like those which we have described, by the very process of their success, are a course of education in those moral and active qualities by which alone success can be either deserved or attained. As associations multiplied, they would tend more and more to absorb all work-people, except those who have too little understanding, or too little virtue, to be capable of learning to act on any other system than that of narrow selfishness. As this change proceeded, owners of capital would gradually find it to their advantage, instead of maintaining the struggle of the old system with work-people of only the worst description, to lend their capital to the associations; to do this at a diminishing rate of interest, and at last, perhaps, even to exchange their capital for terminable annuities. In this or some such mode, the existing accumulations of capital might honestly, and by a kind of spontaneous process, become in the end the joint property of all who participate in their productive employment: a transformation which, thus effected (and assuming of course that both sexes participate equally in the rights and in the government of the association), would be the nearest approach to social justice, and the most beneficial ordering

[4] *Principles of Political Economy*, 6th Edition, Book IV, Chapter VII, Sec. 6.

of industrial affairs for the universal good, which it is possible at present to foresee.[5]

Mill's view of the method by which industrial democracy might come is, for sufficient reasons, prophetic. His conception of its form and end has been repudiated by events, as well outside of the coöperative movement as inside. Inside, the producers' coöperatives themselves falsified it. Their failure has been attributed to incompetency, to greed, to laziness, to disloyalty. But these qualities are no less manifest among consumer societies than among producers. The fatal defect of producers' societies lies in their nature, not their method and intent. Producers' societies are necessarily self-limiting and exclusive. They are necessarily associations of minorities standing in a competitive relation to each other and to the majority. Coöperative societies of tailors or carpenters or shoemakers may compete with each other for customers, and then they are not different from the individuals or joint-stock companies whose competition partly defines the *status quo*. Or they may confederate and amalgamate and then they are not different from the monopolies which determine the rest of the *status quo*. In either case, they are, as Bergson would say, "closed societies," constitutionally unable to do otherwise than to buy as cheaply and sell as dearly as possible. Their associative nature is such that they draw out and accent the very qualities of men to which their failure is attributed. Consumer societies are by contrast "open." They must inevitably lose more than they can gain by shutting any one out; every new addition to their ranks means greater abundance for every one already enrolled. Other things being equal, the association of consumers tends naturally to become an association of all mankind.[6]

The consumers' movement came to the realization of this difference not positively as a deduction from its consciously held underlying assumptions, but negatively in terms of the disillusioning experiences which kept falsifying its underlying

[5] *Ibid.*, Book IV, Chapter VII, Sec. 7.

[6] For another, somewhat more formal, analysis of this difference see *A Free Society*, Chapter VI.

assumptions. In accord with those assumptions the Wholesale was to be an instrument of trading only. It was to give preference to producers' coöperatives wherever that was possible. It was to help them to be fruitful and to multiply, to the end that the whole national economy might ultimately become a producers' economy of self-governing workshops. From its beginnings, it did all these things. As the capital surplus of the whole movement accumulated, local societies and their members individually as well as the Wholesale took shares in the "Working Class Limiteds" which were constantly soliciting investment. When circumstances brought the decision that the Wholesale must go into production, the argument against it was that loyalty to the coöperative ideal necessitated organizing coöperative production autonomously —this in view of the fact that often autonomous producers had dealt with the Wholesale and the societies on the principle of *caveat emptor*. Considerations of the purity, the quality and the measure of the goods sold to the members nevertheless made productive undertakings indispensable. The decision was on all sides recognized as momentous: "I felt," wrote William Pare, "that we had passed the Rubicon." And across the Rubicon the old ideal held. Neale and Greening, among others, warned of the danger of "joint stock capitalism," and pressed, failing "co-partnership," for a regular bonus to the employees of the Wholesale's factories. Learning the manufacture of biscuits, blankets, boots and shoes and sweets—which were the first undertaken—was an adventure in a new dimension, calling for new habits and new techniques with machines and men—and finally, a new vision of coöperation.

CHAPTER VII

THE CONSUMER EMERGES, II

§ 1. JOHN THOMAS WHITEHEAD MITCHELL AND THE WEBBS

THE MAKING of the new vision took some twenty years. Arrayed against it throughout this time were the veteran champions of the old vision—Van Sittart Neale, Charles Hughes, E. O. Greening, Jacob Holyoake, and some new ones, among them Arnold Toynbee and A.O.H. Acland. Leaders to the new vision were John Thomas Whitehead Mitchell—and experience.

Mitchell was a Rochdaler. The only child of an unmarried mother who made a living for him and herself by selling beer and letting lodgings to working-men, he had inward knowledge of both the emptiness and the drudgery of the workaday life. His devotion to his mother amounted to a Freudian passion. It was probably the chief factor in his remaining a bachelor all his life, as her standards and ideals were the prime influences in his developing into a teetotaler and a Sunday school superintendent. Although he was born into a period when child labor was still common—1828—she managed to keep him out of the mills till his tenth year, when he went to work as a piecer in a cotton mill, twelve hours and more a day at eighteen pence a week. His spare time he spent with her, or studying as he could. A flannel manufacturer who persuaded John's mother to let him go to Sunday school gave the boy a job in his warehouse, and in the course of time he grew to be its manager.

In 1867, Mitchell went into business for himself. By that time he had been a member of the Pioneer Society fourteen years and a leader almost as long, and a Sunday school teacher thirteen. He desired, Percy Redfern says, to give himself more fully to his causes and since he could not unless his time were his own, he undertook to sell the product of the "coöperative" cotton factory at Mitchell Hey, which he had helped found. In 1869, he became Rochdale's representative on the C.W.S. Board, and a fortnight later a member of its finance committee. Mitchell had learned from experience with the Rochdale Manufacturing Coöperative Society—which he himself had helped to organize—how much trouble the practice of paying bonuses could make, and as a salesman for a producers' society, so-called, he had learned the advantage which a store, with custom and capital at hand, enjoyed over a shop which "even if it manages to get the capital, had the customer to seek." As a member of the Wholesale's finance committee Mitchell was called upon to face the problem of what to do about a chairman of the C.W.S. who at the same time held the job of manager in a company which was both selling to the C.W.S. and trying to borrow money from it. When, in 1874, Mitchell was elected to succeed this man as chairman—they kept him at this post from then till his death—Mitchell's deviation from coöperative orthodoxy, though unformulated, had already begun. As Beatrice Potter who later became Mrs. Sidney Webb was first to realize, he learned and taught the primacy of the consumer.

A big man with a bull voice, self-educated and self-made, personally as austere, almost ascetic, as he was vital, the coöperative movement became to Mitchell what his order might have been to an early Franciscan. It absorbed all his passion and all his vitality. Unlike most self-made and self-educated men, he remained self-reverent and self-acquiescent; his heart was too simple and his mind too single for invidious distinctions; he never emulated his "betters" because he was as good as his betters, being himself. His homely wit, his experience as operative and as manager, as salesman and as committeeman, his genuine piety turned out to be more than a match for the culture, the suavity, and the logic of the no less devoted gentlemen-consumers who championed coöperative production.

So far as he knew, still of the same coöperative faith as Neale and his comrades, it was Mitchell's duty as chairman of the C.W.S. to protect the interests of the men and women who had entrusted their coöperative fortunes to his leadership. First the producer-cultists had their day in the Wholesale, as they had in the Congresses to the last. But when failure followed failure, and the collieries and the great engine company near Newcastle in which the Wholesale was heavily interested, all crashed and, but for Mitchell's resourcefulness, almost wrecked the Wholesale, autonomous producers' cooperatives were finished so far as the Wholesale was concerned. Neale and his group took their cause to the Congresses and the Congresses voted periodically that producers, if not their own employers, should participate in the profits and management of the employing consumers. Nevertheless, by 1880, there were only about fifteen self-governing workshops left, and these not in fundamental factory trades but in the lighter industries in which some vestiges of craftsmanship remained. Neale and Greening organized them in 1882 into the Cooperative Producers' Federation. "Man," Neale told the Derby Congress of 1884, "is a spiritual being, and it is impossible for him to be enthusiastic about the price of tea and coffee"—but quite possible to be enthusiastic about self-governing workshops.

It was at this Congress that the Federation held a conference on production. They hoped by means of some sort of union to overcome the problems of financing and marketing, the differential advantage of their competitors, and their own competitive relation to the Wholesale both as trader and producer. They set up the Labour Association for Promoting Coöperative Production, dedicated to the propaganda of producer participation in the profits and control of industry both coöperative and ordinary. The Federation and its agencies improved on the past, sufficiently to remain stable and make progress. It has now a membership of about fifty associations, all registered under the Industrial and Provident Societies Act, all paying a fixed interest on loans. The shareholders are the workers. Each has one vote and only one. Each receives a fixed share of the profits over and above his wages, a fixed interest on his investment, and participates in the management. The societies are members of the Coöperative Union. Their central bodies make propaganda for their cause, manage a loan department which finds them capital, etc., etc.

Essentially, producers' organizations are survivals in the coöperative movement, and their ideology is recessive. It was beautifully reformulated by Greening at the seventeenth Annual Congress of the Union in Oldham: "The future of the worker, we believe, will be work in societies which will be practically free states, of which they will be the citizens, owning their share in the common property, voting for the parliaments which will govern, and receiving a due proportion of the common results. These labour associations will be linked together in productive federations as our stores are linked together in distributive federations, and we hope that one common union will bind all to work together in reasonable harmony." Its high point was reached at the Congress of 1887, when five ex-presidents, George Jacob Holyoake, Charles Hughes, Van Sittart Neale, the Marquis of Ripon and Sedley Taylor, urged the reëndorsement of the principle and the readoption of the practice, at least at the minimum of profit-sharing: Nobody ever mentioned sharing losses, then, before or since.

Of course the Congress did what they asked.

And on this matter the Wholesale as consistently disregarded what the Congress did. It held fixedly to the spirit and the letter of its obligation to protect the consumers' interest. That same year new premises were opened in London and Mitchell made a speech. The history of the past, he said, showed very clearly that power followed the possession of capital and property, and when the consumers became possessed of these they would become powerful too. The system of coöperation was not a negation, but an earnest and determined attempt to regulate the commerce of the world for the benefit of the many instead of the few, and it had become a great power in this country. It was the best system for securing the greatest good of the greatest number, and formed the only means of practical reformation of the people. . . . There was another question in which they were very much interested. As coöperators, they had the greatest possible interest in good government and in peace all over the world. He would not trench on politics, for coöperators belonged to no party or sect, but to that great class called humanity, and will strive to do that which will aid the distressed and the unemployed everywhere. He thought the time would soon come when our movement will exert a beneficial influence on our relationship with all other countries. He thought so for this reason. Their business with other countries was large, and growing fast. They wanted their representatives abroad to know that coöperators cannot have their interest in this trade interfered with, and that our diplomatists should be required to cultivate cordial relationships all over the world.

Again and again he struck the same note. Appearing before the Royal Commission on Labor, in August, 1893, he told them that universal coöperation would of itself prevent the unequal distribution of wealth, and invited the rich to join the movement. Not law, but "the ordinary forces of commerce, industry and perseverance" enchanneled in coöperation are the best implements of a just redistribution of wealth. The coöperative movement, he said, in reply to a question by Tom Mann, had already begun to buy up railroads and if another implement could do its work better, such as a municipality, he would favor that. He did favor municipal gas, water and any other supplies that municipalities could provide more effectively than the coöperatives. He was "not bound down to C.W.S. methods."

And this was his word to his comrades in coöperation. Speaking in 1892, as president of the Coöperative Congress, which met that year in Rochdale, he said:

I don't believe in the present distribution of wealth. It is said that the United Kingdom has a capital of something like ten thousand millions sterling, equal to about £300 per head of the population. Now I say, that instead of one man having £200,000 or £300,-

000 and others having nothing, it would be better if they had £300 apiece. I am not opposed to capital; I am not opposed to wealth; I like it, and I want to accumulate it, but I don't want wealth to stand to the credit of the "upper ten," but of those who are sometimes called the "lower five." I want wealth to stand to the credit of the whole population. The joint-stock companies of this country own a thousand millions of money. The National Debt is about nine hundred millions, and the capital of railways as much. Between two and three thousand millions of money are engaged in those three enterprises. Now, what I would like would be for coöperators to allow their profits to be so massed together, that instead of a few persons owning this money, it would belong to the whole people of the United Kingdom. That is the burden of my remarks. My desire is that the profits of all trade, all industry, all distribution, all commerce, all importation, all banking and money dealing, should fall back again into the hands of the whole people. If coöperators will manage their enterprises in such a way as to concentrate all their trade in one channel, I am certain that this can be accomplished. I made a calculation the other day, that if the world would conduct its business on coöperative lines, the population of the world could have amongst them between three and four hundred thousand millions of money; and if the fifteen hundred millions of population divided it amongst them at so much each, it would be much better for the world at large. I am not one of those who would divide other people's property. I am nothing of the kind. I want no laws to be passed to divide anybody's property. What I want is for coöperators, trades-unionists, and all the industrious classes of this and every other country to combine in keeping their own shop, making a good dividend, producing, distributing, and financing, and let all the profits come to those who consume the goods, because they have made them.

It was about this time that Beatrice Potter, later Mrs. Sidney Webb, found Mitchell. The vision of the economy of the future peculiarly identified with the Webbs,[1] begins in her intellectualized restatement of Mitchell's experience, perceptions and vision. *The Coöperative Movement in Great Britain* has been to the movement from its publication what the first edition of Mill's *Principles of Political Economy* was to the order of free capitalist enterprise. After the war, in 1921, Mrs. Webb and her husband reviewed the import of the movement: "Unless we completely misinterpret the irresistible ground swell of British democracy," they wrote, "it is this Con-

[1] *Cf.* especially *The Consumers' Coöperative Movement* (1921), and *A Constitution for a Socialist Commonwealth of Great Britain* (1925).

sumers' Coöperation, in its twofold form of voluntary association of members (in what we now know as the Coöperative society) and obligatory association of citizens (in local government)—in organic connection with an equally ubiquitous organization of the producers by hand or by brain (in Trade-Unions and Professional Associations)—which will constitute the greater part of the new social order that is destined very largely to supersede the present capitalist system." In a recent letter Mr. Webb, now Lord Passfield, wrote me: "Nothing has shaken our view that the distinction between associations of producers and associations of consumers is absolutely *fundamental* in all studies of modern society. When Karl Marx, or the soap-box socialist orator, talks of the government of industry *by the workers,* he usually is unconscious of this distinction. Government will doubtless be 'by the workers'; that is to say to the exclusion of those who do not work. But in my view it will not be by the workers associated *as producers.* Whether in Trade-Unionism or in Syndicalism, or anything between these, I see the workers associated as producers having rights of consultation, criticism, suggestion and so on, *but not rights of management.*" [2]

§ 2. ENTER THE CONSUMER

IN RECENT YEARS the thinking of coöperators has been penetrated with Marxist concepts. The spread of the consumers' coöperative movement from Great Britain to the continent made this inevitable. For, as a rule, it was members of the socialist sects who turned to coöperation most readily. But in theory and in practice, the movement retains the essential articulation of the capitalist structure. A study of the literature of coöperation shows all the conventional concepts, attitudes and practices of the capitalist economy. To some extent this follows inevitably from the capitalist nature of the general environment in which the coöperative movement is struggling for survival, but to a very large degree it is due to the fact that the implements of any kind of credit-enterprise conducted

[2] See Mr. Webb's addendum to this statement, dated July 4, 1936, in Appendix III, page 469.

by means of modern technology must depend on capital. So we read of "fundamental individualism," of "property," of "shares and share holders," of "interest and wages," of "prices" and of "profits." We find the movement's basic assumptions those that are basic also to the much decried capitalist world. Indeed, in the parent movement in Great Britain, the word "consumer" is a neologism. The stores are described as practising distribution, as indeed they do; and the societies which organize them continue to be called "distributive coöperative societies," as indeed they are. The inveterate tendency for the consummation of the economic process to disappear from view is as constant and pressing among the coöperatives as elsewhere.

The expression "consumer" was first used on the continent, and the English movement accepted its implications and learned its application only with difficulty. The interest of the societies was rather in the intermediate activities than on the end those finally served, on the *using* rather than the *using up* of things. Thus, the movement in Britain has sometimes been described by its own friends as the natural successful shopkeeping of a nation of shopkeepers.

This success was so signal and the power which the cooperatives came to wield so great that all the old enmities melted into friendship before it. The lords of the church and the manor came like Balaam to admire and to bless. The movement itself, as it drew more and more of the rank and file of the community into the circle of its influence, demonstrated an acquiescence in the orthodoxies that must make Owen turn in his grave. But once the defense of the consumer organization against the encroachment of producer attitude is begun, the realization of the primacy of the consumer is inevitable.

The history that we have treated shows this. Ineluctably the excellence and abundance of life rather than the external steps thereto come into the foreground. If they have not finally come into the foreground until today, it is because their natural priority made their realization difficult. Nevertheless, in everybody's heart there lives and grows a personal ideal of the consummative life. Sometimes it is expressed by the formula: *What I would do if I had a million dollars;* sometimes it is expressed by serious absorption in rebellious and liberative movements. But whether it be symbolized by some dream-form of conspicuous consumption or some no less illusory form of revolutionary reconstruction, the impulse which animates it arises in our original nature and culminates in our adult action. Always it is a process not merely of using things but of using them up.

It is because of this quality and direction of all personal life that our nature as consumers holds priority over our activities as producers. The right definition of the consummative life provides a channel for all services and implementations. If we take care of consumption, consumption will also take care of production.

§ 3. DIFFUSION AND VARIATION OF COÖPERATIVE SPECIES

THE DIFFUSION of the Consumers' Coöperative Movement in Europe followed soon after the publication of Holyoake's *History of the Rochdale Pioneers.* Holyoake himself had close acquaintances among the political refugees of all of the European states who crowded England after 1848. His story of the Pioneers was early translated into French and in due course the essential principles of their system became part of the intellectual equipment of continental Europe. The idea of coöperation was of course not new. The Fourierist propaganda had reached everywhere and shops and colonies endeavoring to embody the principle of Fourier were to be found in most European countries. The Rochdale plan was grafted on the Fourierist growth. To persons like Lasalle, in Germany, with his grandiose schemes of national organization, it seemed trivial; Lasalle stigmatized it as "shopkeeping," and to Marx and the Marxists it seemed entirely irrelevant.

In a certain sense coöperation may be said to have followed the flag of industry. The Rochdale rule moved as industry grew, and the order of succession in the coöperative movement in Europe follows the sequence of industrialization in the countries of Europe; but prevailingly agricultural countries found it even more a way of salvation.

It is not without significance that the earliest societies were in the order of succession, those of Switzerland, Denmark and France. They there developed between the sixties and the seventies, and in the course of time societies were organized in Italy, Germany, Russia, Finland and the Scandinavian countries, the South Americas, India, Palestine, Japan and China. The United States had had the benefit of visits from Owen and Holyoake—Horace Greeley printed the first foreign edition of Holyoake's book—and societies kept appearing and disappearing from the foundation of Owen's New Harmony, on.

The story of the consumers' coöperative movement in each country follows the same general line as in England. Its turning points are the alertness and devotion of some individual leader, the climate of opinion, the immediate social and economic situation, and a generally favorable attitude of government. Switzerland, Denmark, Finland and Italy were prevailingly agricultural countries and have remained so. The consumers' movement in those countries was primarily a movement of small freeholding peasantry. In France, Germany and Belgium it followed the line of industrialization and its development has, on the whole, been coincident with the growth of industry.

As the movement spread, modifications of the classical Rochdale type arose and established themselves. These modifications are consequences of the intellectual climate, the spiritual attitude, and the social frame of reference of each country. Charles Gide, who has written the standard study of the morphology of coöperatives, distinguishes three types of consumers' coöperatives—the individualist, the socialist, and what he calls the true coöperative type. The individualist type, he says, have no other object than the personal advantage of their individual members. Many of the agricultural coöperative organizations are characterized by this mentality. They allocate profits to capital and divide them in proportion to the number of shares, or, if they do pay a dividend on purchases, only a limited number of the customers can become shareholders; the organizing members keep the control of the societies in their own hands. Others allocate a part of their profits to the executive committees and others may distribute profits but concentrate control. Essentially, these types prevail among producer organizations which have consumer agencies. They are closer in character and intent to the joint-stock company than to the coöperative society.

The socialist types function as a rule in terms of the Marxist conceptions of class and property. To them consumers' coöperation is an instrument in the class war. If they acquiesce in the principle of dividend on purchase, they do so as a matter of tactics and with apologies and explain it away as a means to an end, much as today's Russians explain away their own capitalist and tyrannical methods. They desire and sometimes actually do hold all the earnings of their societies in a common fund which they employ for purposes of sick benefits, unemployment payments, old-age pensions, medical or legal service, loans and the like, propaganda and education. Sometimes they contribute their surpluses to helping struggles in the "class war," whether industrial or political. The Belgian societies have been conspicuous for their socialist principle and practice.

And finally, Gide describes the differentia of the true coöperative type, the type he finds in England and in France, and ascribes it to the school of Nimes with which he himself was identified. He apparently did not regard the ecclesiastic distinction as sufficient to define a type, and the exclusively Catholic societies, which operate in central Europe especially, did not seem to him to have been worth a separate classification. Yet it is not certain that the ecclesiastical limitation upon membership does not constitute a distinct coöperative type, especially as the ecclesiastic differential is designed to rule out collaboration with coöperatives of another label.

Since Gide wrote, a fourth differentiation has appeared which may be described as the nationalist or autarchic. Imposed on the Italian movement by the Fascists, it there in the course of time became simply an overtone. It has since been imposed on the German and the Austrian coöperatives. In all three countries the coöperatives have been regimented, but, according to Karl Walter, the regimentation in Italy has not destroyed the essential coöperative structure. Mussolini offered coöperation in 1922, "moral support and such protection as will insure its exercise in an atmosphere of freedom," but the freedom is limited by the fact that elected officers must have the sanction of the Fascist party and the audit committee is subject to control by the ministry. Opinions other than Fascist are not tolerated. In Germany the movement has been impounded in "the labor front," and is under the control of an appointee of "the leader" of that "front." Although it is claimed that no change in the coöperative structure has been made or is contemplated, the movement is treated entirely as a tool of the Nazi interest. Something analogous has happened in Austria. The coöperatives are at present prohibited from building new societies, carrying on any propaganda outside of their membership, or otherwise giving the private trader cause to complain.

Other differentia turn on the voting structure of federations and wholesales and on the relation to the general market. In Finland, for example, the societies have broken up into two federations. The older is organized like the Senate of the United States, so many representatives for each society regardless of the number of members or the size of the society's business. Its principle is one society, one vote. The younger or "progressive" federation insists on representation for societies in proportion to the membership. In relation to the general market, the Scandinavians, the Finns, the Italians and the Germans have given up the practice of selling at the market price and returning the difference in dividend to the purchaser; they prefer to establish an immediate differential advantage by underselling the competitor and paying back a smaller dividend. Some, English societies among them, do not adhere strictly to the system of cash transactions but give credit. Some of the societies combine several of the variant features. However, none may be regarded as a true coöperative unless it conforms to the fundamental Rochdale principles of democratic organization and dividend on purchases.

Another variation, developed this time by the English, is organization and control by the federal unions. In 1928, a decision was reached to create the Consumers' Wholesale Retail Coöperative Society, Limited. The purpose is to set up societies in areas where none exist. The Wholesale, with the consent of the local society, establishes branches on its own initiative. These branches possess a certain amount of autonomy, and as customers in sufficient numbers accumulate dividends to pay off the cost of shares, the Wholesale organizes them into societies and hands over the stores to their complete control. The method inverts the classical process of independent local growth, followed by federation and unification. It is, so to speak, growth by division rather than by accretion. It marks a very important change in coöperative process.

§ 4. THE CASE OF RUSSIA

FINALLY there is Russia. The coöperative movement in Russia began almost at the same time as the abolition of serfdom in the sixties of the last century. Its leaders were intellectuals and noblemen who, moved by the democratic and socialist ideals of western Europe, struggled to remedy the condition of the peasant multitudes of their own country. At all points the mediæval inertia of the church and the reactionary activity of the state obstructed the full development of the movement. Energies were constantly being diverted into political channels, but after the bloody failure of the Revolution of 1905, many who did not turn to orgiastic living for salvation from political despair turned to coöperation. They came to feel that the movement was a sure and easy way to freedom. By 1914, the movement had grown from 250,000 members counted in 1898, to 1,400,000 members; from a membership mostly urban to a membership three-quarters rural, and controlling 7 per cent of the retail trade of the country.

During the World War the coöperatives were the only structure that maintained any integrity and sustained in an orderly way the economy of a people betrayed by its government during a war whose commanders were selling their armies into the hands of the enemy. In the period of the war the movement more than trebled in size. By 1919, food crises, the breakdown of the markets, the disintegration of the general economy of Russia made the coöperatives the one focus of stability in the shattered ruins of the institutional life of Russia. Russians flocked to the coöperatives. Their membership rose to 17,000,000. The local societies were served by a good many wholesales whose activities came to need coördination. These were reorganized as a national federation, Centrosoyus, into which three-quarters of the wholesales merged. In 1913, a school of coöperation had been established in the Moscow People's University and through this school and otherwise, some fifteen hundred instructors were employed to reenforce the business of Centrosoyus with a "non-trading function." The Tzarist government came to fear the coöperatives, and in 1915, suppressed the Central Coöperative Committee, but the following year the rebellious Duma not only restored its powers but gave it complete autonomy. In 1918, the Provisional Government enacted a coöperative code and delegated to the Coöperative Congress, which was thereupon called together, the task of maintaining the national economy.

Then came the communists. The consumer function was inhibited by the political interest and the producer ideology. Self-governing workshops were literally the rage, and production was paralyzed by "self-government." Centrosoyus became merely an agent of the state executing the plan of the Commissariat of Supply. Under the decree of March, 1920, certain of the essentials of the coöperative structure were abolished; voluntary was replaced by compulsory membership; the movement was nationalized, and the red tape of the Soviet bureaucracy cut off its traditions and destroyed its efficiency. By 1921, however, the government had learned an economic lesson. One item in the much-discussed New Economic Policy was the restoration of the coöperatives to coöperation. By 1930, the coöperatives had been made practically a partner of government as well as a tool. The state trusts, whose autocratic rule has replaced "self-government" in Russian industry, now consulted the coöperative movement before they undertook production, and the function of distribution was largely left to the coöperatives. Nor were they themselves prevented from going into production as that seemed feasible. Later their right to hold property had been somewhat returned to them.

Regardless of sect or party, some seventy-three million Russians once were practising economic democracy through consumer societies while they were suffering from economic tyranny through the state trusts of producers and other producer organizations. For in the movement, all peoples of Russia stood equal, regardless of sect or class or race or party. In the coöperatives alone could it be claimed that a non-communist has the same status, privileges and duties as a communist, and enjoys equal liberty to speak, to work and to vote. The members of the retail societies elected delegates to the meetings of their district unions. These union meetings elected the governing boards of the district, and the delegates to the Areal or Regional Union, the National Union, and the All-Union Congress of the Coöperative Movement. The last elected the Centrosoyus, which is the movement's supreme governing body. If coöperatives were subject to the coercions of the superior force of the government, and the contamination of its ideology, their subjection was not greater than in any other country, and by way of recompense they enjoyed a certain privilege and dignity for which only the Scandinavian countries provide parallels. In a country with so low an actual standard of living and so high a projected one, the coöperatives bore the major responsibility of converting the scarcity under which the average Russian lives into the abundance which he has been promised and which to date he has not yet enjoyed. The consumers' coöperative movement appeared, in the summer of 1935, to function as the citadel of free society and economic and personal democracy in Soviet Russia.

But the winter of 1935 showed that appearances were deceitful as usual. Events made it clear that so far as the government was concerned, the consumer coöperatives were not institutions of Soviet civilization but tools of the dictatorship, to be taken up and dropped at will. With apparent suddenness, some 37,000 urban consumer coöperative societies, with nearly 10,000,000 members, were "liquidated." Their members' assets were handed over, without recompense, to the State Trading Trusts which assumed their functions. City trade was made a monopoly of the state, organized and controlled from above. The destruction of the urban coöperatives appears to be coincident with an increase of consumer goods. So long as there was a significant shortage of essentials, the coöperatives were allowed to live and work. As the shortage lessens, the consumer societies are dissolved. This policy extends to the country-side also. But shortage is still conspicuous there, and accordingly consumer coöperatives continue in the peasant villages. Centrosoyus is now concentrated upon serving these peasant societies. But they too will go with the shortage. The first and last interest of the Russian dictatorship is production, and human beings as producers. It is dominated by the producer mentality, and this, with the best will in the world, perforce subordinates life to labor. Glorifying labor and regimenting life, it willy-nilly commits itself to the institutions of the servile state.

§ 5. WORLD FEDERATION: THE INTERNATIONAL COÖPERATIVE ALLIANCE

THAT THE EXISTENCE of coöperatives in different countries should lead to international organization was of course inevitable. This organization is implied by the coöperative principle itself and is necessitated by the integrative action of the credit-enterprise economy. Every wholesale must have correspondents and agents in other countries, and it is therefore either compelled to move into a sort of imperialism like the capitalist imperialism or toward a federalism of the sort that the national structures of the coöperative movement already exemplify.

This federalism is still in the making. The first steps toward it were, as usual, tentative and cautious. They began as a sort of interchange of fraternal greetings between the coöperatives of one country and the coöperatives of another. Swiss, Italian, French, German, Swedish and Danish coöperators attended the London Congress of 1869. For many years letters reporting the status of the movement were exchanged between one country and another. In 1885, the French fraternal delegates to the British Coöperative Congress invited the Coöperative Union to send delegates to a conference which should consider the formation of an international federation of coöperatives. The function of such a federation was to be to serve as a sort of international board of arbitration for labor disputes and to teach working-men the principles and practice of coöperation.

Here again the Christian Socialists saw their opportunity. Neale and Holyoake, who, together with James Johnston, had been appointed as delegates to the first coöperative congress held in France, once more found in the French theory and practice a strong endorsement of the principle of profit-sharing as an essential coöperative principle. This principle, however, had already been tried and condemned by the English movement, and inasmuch as it was to be one of the objectives of the proposed international alliance, the English Coöperative Union would not participate in creating an international organization. Nevertheless, discussion went on and as a result of conferences between the English and the French profit-sharers at the Rochdale Congress in 1892, there was organized an International Alliance of Friends of Coöperative Production, and there the matter stopped. Until 1895, wider organization was discussed to and fro among all the coöperatives of Europe. By that time Neale was dead. The leaders of the movement gave up profit-sharing as the price of getting an international organization launched, and the British Coöperative Union participated largely in arranging for the First International Coöperative Congress which was called in London in 1896. This Congress created the International Coöperative Alliance.

Consistently with the tradition of such organizations, the membership of the Alliance was mixed, individuals and societies. When Henry W. Wolff, whom Greening had won to the movement, was elected president, he travelled over the continent and secured the enrollment of every type of coöperative organization—farmers, workers, consumers, producers, credit-unions. At the Congress of 1902, held in Manchester, the delegates abolished individual membership. The consumers' organizations naturally predominated, and between 1902 and the World War the work of the Alliance consisted in preparing an international coöperative bibliography, an international directory of the coöperative press, and a monthly bulletin in English, French and German. In 1910, the first Year-Book was published. During the War the activities of the organization were naturally limited, but contacts between the coöperatives of the allied countries and some contacts with those of the central European countries were continually maintained. The first Congress after the War was held in Basle, in August, 1921. It was a new world requiring a readjustment of the international coöperative movement: the Centrosoyus was now representing the new Russia as a member of the Congress, and the constitution was revised.

Under this constitution the membership of the Alliance may be primary coöperative societies, national unions and regional federations, and national auxiliary bodies. Eligibility of consumers' societies for membership depends on their conforming to the Rochdale principles. Societies of consumers must have for their object social and economic benefit of their members and observance of the principles embodied in the rules of the Alliance and the resolutions of International Coöperative Congresses. The Congress, which meets every three years, is the supreme authority. During the intervals between Congresses, this authority is delegated to a Central Committee representing the national organizations. The committee elect the president and two vice-presidents of the Alliance from among their own members immediately after each Congress and they meet regularly once a year. In addition they elect an executive committee which consists of eight members of the Central Committee and the officers. The executive committee meets quarterly. The decisions of the Congress and its agencies are executed by the General Secretary. Members pay minimum dues of about $100 a year if they are national organizations. Primary coöperative societies pay at the rate of $5.00 for 1,000 members to $250 for those with a membership of more than 200,000.

The objects of the Alliance are the obvious ones of unification, information, education and propaganda. It collects statistics, maintains a permanent library and press, helps forward coöperative activities of every sort, maintains friendly relations with other international bodies such as the International Federation of Trade Unions, the League of Nations and the International Labor Office. Since the Basle Congress of 1921, it has instituted International Coöperative Day, established the "rainbow" as the badge of the coöperators of the world, and taken over from the British Coöperative Union the International Coöperative School. The *Bulletin* of the early years is now *The Review of International Coöperation.* The Alliance has been recognized by the international agencies of governments like the International Labor Office and the Council of the League of Nations as the spokesman for the coöperators of the world. It has collaborated with the International Labor Office in the collection of coöperative statistics. It is represented at the International Economic Conference at Geneva.

Of course it has endeavored to develop an international coöperative wholesale society and to facilitate international coöperative trade. The Scandinavian countries, Denmark, Sweden and Norway, had already in 1916, formed the Scandinavian Coöperative Wholesale Society and buy coffee and other materials together. The advantages of this practice led to study of the possibilities of developing it on a wider scale. On the basis of the information accumulated, twenty-five wholesale societies affiliated as the International Coöperative Wholesale Society. At the moment, this society functions as a middleman between its constituencies and to many it is not clear of just what use such a middleman might be apart from acting as a clearing house for information. Others see a development analogous to the national developments. They believe that an autonomous international wholesale, in business on its own account, is a way out of the difficulties that attend trading when one wholesale acts as an agent for others. Certainly the International Wholesale can buy for many others. In addition, the Alliance has been encouraging international collaboration by the coöperatives in banking and is assembling information to facilitate a mutual exchange of services. The hope is to establish an international bank which will serve the interests of international coöperative trade. The same thing holds for insurance.

In the face of the world-wide autarchic trends, the Alliance, representing some forty countries, some hundred and forty-three national unions, ninety-one thousand federations and one hundred million members, at its Congress in London, September, 1934, "refused to accept the moral obligations of political neutrality and cash trading." Several delegations held that neutrality was impossible in the present state of the world and that cash trading is not applicable to the elaborate credit economy of the twentieth century. On the basic Rochdale principles there could be no disagreement—open membership, democratic control, limited interest on capital, dividend on purchase and education. It reaffirmed its adherence to the cause of peace and disarmament, and urged the members to employ the Alliance as their international agency in protecting both producer and consumer against capitalist exploitation, in assisting farmers and small producers, and in building up the International Coöperative Wholesale Society as their instrument to increase the interchange of goods between the countries of the world. The decisions indicate that the international movement remains the carrier of the democratic tradition in which coöperation began. Within it the old issues between sectarianism and non-sectarianism, individualism and collectivism are still active. The influence of the Russian frame of mind, with its dogmatism, its aggressive idealism, is conspicuous, but the dominant note is still the note of freedom which was struck in the expression *laissez-faire* and of which voluntary coöperation is the logical development.

§ 6. A CONSUMER ECONOMY AS A VARIANT FROM THE CAPITALIST-PRODUCER ECONOMY

SINCE THE WORLD WAR the momentum toward coöperative organization has noticeably increased in all free countries, and the setbacks in countries not free like Italy, Germany and Austria are likely to last longer but to be as transitory as the setback in Russia.

International coöperative thought is still colored by the preconceptions and prejudices of producer dominance. Nevertheless, both argument and practice indicate a progressing realization of the primacy of the consumer. A consumer economy is growing up within the context of the producer-dominated world as capitalism grew up within the context of a world of feudal souls living on a subsistence level. Capitalism began and spread as an economy of plenty, and so long as the distance between producer and consumer was little it enriched the lives of all the peoples it reached. The modern world is the beneficiary of this enrichment.

But contemporary capitalism differs from its ancestor in the fact that the distance between producer and consumer has been immeasurably increased. Production for an unknown market has led to producer-dominance and the enslavement of one group of producers by another. The Consumers' Coöperative Movement which was called by its founders a "distributive movement," arose as an endeavor to correct this inequity.

A spontaneous variation among a multitude of others in the changing capitalist environment, it grew, it struggled, and it continues to struggle and to grow. As it grows it displaces the capitalist practice of cultivation and production for an impersonal market with the human practice of cultivation and production for a full personal life.

A variation within the system in which it arose, consumer-coöperation is transforming the system as variations in a given biological species transformed this species into a different one. It is displacing the producer economy by overruling the structure and function of its institutional components. As man displaced the ape, as the civilized man displaced the savage, as the automobile displaced the horse, and any improvement displaces that which it is an improvement upon, so the consumer economy is displacing the producer economy. It is not doing so by warfare with that economy. Unlike Marxism, the personalism and individualism of its ends make it objective in its means. From the beginning it has worked, not by the government of persons, but by the administration of things. Its attention is not upon its enemy, any more than the attention of an automobile is upon a horse; it is displacing the capitalist economy because it is doing the same job better, because it is more excellent. And it is more excellent because every step in its activity and development is directed toward the fulfilment of the original nature of man, the realization of abundance in all the ways of consumption. It is the liberation of man because it is the reaffirmation of the consumer in him. In the Consumers' Coöperative Movement the buried and forgotten consumer emerges.

CHAPTER VIII

THE CONSUMER IN AMERICA: I, THE FARMER

§ 1. THE VISION OF MEN AS CONSUMERS

IN AMERICA, the primacy of the consumer is a postulate of the foundations. "The American dream" is a vision of men as consumers, and the American story is the story of an inveterate struggle to embody this dream in the institutions of American life. In one of its forms, the coöperative movement in the United States antedates that of Europe. Like everything else in the record of the white man on the North American continent, it struggled to survive in that simple not-yet-humanized environment with a logic unconfused by the diversity of institutions and interests which hampered its growth among the peoples of Europe. That, by comparison, it failed in America while it succeeded in Europe, is also a consequence of the scene. The very conditions which, in the eyes of European idealists, rendered the American land the environment most favorable to the strong growth of coöperation, acted centrifugally on the hearts of men, drawing them apart rather than binding them together.

The American scene was a wilderness which colonizing white men meant to remake to their hearts' desire. Now the language of the heart has been first religion, afterward politics. Only in the nineteenth century has it become economics. Until then, salvation and freedom were, everywhere in the world, of the church and the state, and the world's masters were churchmen and landlords, its servants peasants and workers. Churchmen and landlords were men of family and property. They consumed that which they did not produce, and their only interest in production was to hold the multitudes that produced without consuming fast bound to their service and use. Priests, soldiers, sportsmen, connoisseurs of the arts and sciences, practitioners of the liberal arts, they were free and safe because they could live without working upon the services and goods provided by those who work without living.[1] To these latter they incarnated an ideal of excellence,

[1] "The art of living within your income is a gift. The woman who has it, will do it with £1 a week; she who has it not, will be poor with £20. Peter Noakes, tired of finding himself always in debt, wants to get his wife one week in advance with the world. He wants to stand clear on the shopkeepers' books. He knows that the small tradesman cannot pay his way unless his customers pay theirs. He therefore saves, by carefulness and secret thrift, a little money, and one week delights his wife by giving her double wages, that she may pay in advance for her things. What is the result? Next week he finds her running into debt as usual. He complains, and then she tells him the everlasting story of a thousand working-class homes, 'What could she do? Mr. Last's bill for Tommy's boots had never been paid, the account for Billy's jacket had stood over till she was ashamed of it, little Jane's shoes were out at the toes and poor Polly, she was the disgrace of the family for want of a new frock, and as for Mrs. Noakes, herself, her own bonnet was not fit to be seen, she would rather stop in the house for ever than go out in that old fashioned thing any longer.' Poor Peter is overwhelmed—he had never thought of these things. In fact, Mrs. Noakes tells him 'he never does think of anything. He gets up and goes to work, and comes home and goes to bed, and never thinks of anything in the house.' What can Peter do? He does the only thing he ought—he allows that his wife ought to know best, confesses that he is very stupid, kisses her in confirmation of his repentance, and promises to save her another week's wages, and she shall try what can be done the next time. In the course of a few weeks, Peter, by over-work and going without customary half-pints of beer, saves up another week's wages, when, alas! he finds that the shoemaker has sent in another bill, and the tailor another account—that Master Tommy's trousers have grown too short for him,

strength and beauty: they are God, the Ultimate Consumer, made flesh and walking on earth. When the slave imagined himself as master, the serf as freeman, the weak as strong, the poor as rich, the producer as consumer, he thought of himself as one of these. When he considered how he might embody his imaginings, his considerations automatically took the form of religious and political ideas, and his efforts the form of new religious and political associations. In the great tradition of the western world the ideologies of freedom follow this sequence: religion, politics, economics.

§ 2. ITS DEFINITION IN AMERICA THROUGH THE PURITAN RELIGION

AND SO IT WAS in America. The social order which the first settlers on the North American continent aspired to establish was defined in terms of religion. Confused and transformed by the urgencies of the struggle to survive in a wilderness, and from the first held back by the dark passions of intolerance and persecution which strong faith so often lets loose, religion's affirmations nevertheless laid down gradients for positive growth toward freedom. But protest and rebellion, which had been the language of this faith in the European society which had generated it, became in the unhumanized American wil-

young Billy's jacket is out at the elbows, Jane's shoes let in water, Miss Polly (bless her sweet soul!) is still the disgrace of the family, and Mrs. Noakes, although Peter thought she never looked so young nor so pretty as she did last Sunday, declares her bonnet 'perfectly hateful; indeed, there is not such another fright as herself in the whole neighbourhood, and if Peter was like anybody else, he would be ashamed to see his wife go out in such a condition.' And the little book still goes to the shop, Peter eats cheese tough as guttapercha, she buys tea that has been used to boiling before it was sold to her, the coffee tastes grievously of burnt corn, Tommy's boots are a long time being mended, Mrs. Noakes never has sixpence to bless herself with, her money is all condemned before it comes in; Peter, degraded and despairing, thinks he may as well drink a pint as a half-pint—things can't be worse at home. He soon ceases to take interest in public affairs. How can he consistently help the public who cannot help himself? How can he talk of independence, who is the slave of the shoemaker and the tailor? How can he subscribe to a political or social society, who cannot look his grocer in the face? Thus he is doubly destroyed." (George Jacob Holyoake, *The History of the Rochdale Pioneers,* Chapter VIII.)

derness the rule of law and order. In old England, the settlers who held this faith had been either rebels or the children of rebels; King James and King Charles had called their "puritanism" rebellion and faction. But in New England, the force against which it was in rebellion and the totality from which it was faction were lacking; faith was merely an ideology of rebellion without its conditions. Perforce it must needs either die out or change from a program of combat into a principle of inner organization.

In the course of time, this happened. Several generations were born and died before the habit of intolerance and persecution wore away. But it did wear away. And the positive principles of the Independents and Levellers who had made the English Revolution without making over the English rule of life entered into the custom and commonsense of their brethren in America. The Independents were the cousins of the Pilgrim Fathers. They believed that before God all difference of earthly rank and station fell away; all souls were peers and equal; that hence the multitude, called "the church," could not be a hierarchic organism and must be a voluntary organization; and that it is established by a covenant of souls, on the principle, *one soul, one vote*. "It appertains unto the people . . . to rule and govern the church, that is, themselves," wrote John Robinson, the Pilgrim's pastor who led them from Scrooby to Leyden and from Leyden to Plymouth.[2]

Self-government, as we know, is the historic principle of consumers; to be governed by others is the historic burden of producers. The religious aspiration of the producer to make himself even on earth as the consumer finds its logical conclusion in the teaching of the Levellers: "It is the first principle of a people's liberty that they shall not be bound but by their own consent." For liberty, held the Levellers, is men's birthright, and cannot ever be taken from them. It extends to their consciences as well as their persons, their vocations as well as their property. A social order which is built upon the principle of liberty will require mutual toleration, democratic government, the land restored to the people, their equality before the law, their freedom to choose their vocations and

2 John Robinson, *A Just and Necessary Apology* (1625).

careers. These requirements will be guaranteed by "an agreement of the people."

> Seeing all men are by nature the sons of Adam, and from him have legitimately derived a natural property right and freedom, therefore, England and all other nations, and all particular persons in every nation, notwithstanding the difference of laws and governments, ranks and degrees, ought to be alike free and estated in their natural liberties and to enjoy the just rights and prerogative of mankind, whereunto they are heirs apparent, and thus the commoners by right are equal with the lords. For by natural birth all men are equal and alike born to like property, liberty and freedom; and as we are delivered of God by the hand of Nature unto this world every one with a natural innate freedom and property, even so are we to live every one equally and alike to enjoy his birthright and privilege.[3]

Such is the formula of rebellion in Europe which became that of construction on the American continent. The congregations into which Baptists, Presbyterians, Quakers and other sectarians were associated depended on a contract between equals. The members of each congregation conceived it in the manner of a small free republic, sovereign in its own domain. To this view the wilderness imparted strength and assurance. In its all-levelling emptiness all old-world distinctions between patricians and plebeians, noble and vulgar, privileged and unprivileged, tended to shrivel to nothing. Titles continued to be used, but with a different meaning. A hereditary native nobility continuous with the European could not grow up. Nor could the old rules of dependence and subordination or the old ways of treating land and goods retain their force. The wilderness levelled every right to superior strength, every priority and claim to greater skill. Although kings gave away land boundless as kingdoms and chartered rights as absolute as sovereignty, although bondsmen and indentured servants were sent in their thousands to people those estates, no proprietary interest could be well maintained, nor any European subjection long enforced.

As in Europe the human scene was weighted against liberty and self-dependence, so in America the natural wilderness in-

[3] Thomas Edwards, *Gangraena,* Vol. III, p. 16.

vested them with its own strength and urgency. It sustains the doctrine and discipline of Roger Williams in his Providence Plantations, where he taught that all civil power resides in the people and derives from them; that government is the people's instrument, for its powers depend on their consent and for its form on their purposes; that salvation is beyond its scope, and that the interests of religion can be in the keeping only of each man's conscience; and that consequently the religious obligation of each church to every other is toleration. Speaking for the Friends, William Penn could also affirm liberty of conscience as a natural right and triumphantly sustain the affirmation on American soil.

The trend reached its logical culmination in the argument of John Wise, to which John Adams subscribed. Writing in 1717 a vindication of the government of New England churches, Wise declared: "Under Christ the reason of the constitution of these and the primitive churches is really and truly owing to the origin of the state and liberty of mankind and founded peculiarly in the light of nature." The natural man, he urged, is a freeman and owes obedience to God alone. God ordains for him but one law: This is the law of nature; and it establishes in his soul the rule of justice, morality and right reason. Before God all men are equal and if they set up a civil government, they do so from choice and on consent; and they shape it suitably to their temper and inclinations. Rulers of a state so established have no other right or task than to care for the people's peace and welfare. The members of such a community have the duty to obey the rules they themselves have made. For a state so made is a compound moral person. Whatever power it possesses derives from the people who made it as they wished—a monarchy or an oligarchy, or a democracy. That democracy has shown itself to be best both for churches and states is due to its being "very honorable and regular government according to the doctrines of right reason," and to its discharging best the function of all government—viz: "To cultivate humanity and promote the happiness of all and the good of every man in all his rights, his life, his liberty, estate, honor, etc., without injury or abuse to any."

These were Puritans speaking. What they said is the other side, the more enduring side of a way of life and thought that too many have come to regard as mean, tyrannical, fear-ridden, witch-killing and persecutory. No doubt these Europe-born attitudes were manifest at the beginning. No doubt the loneliness and isolation of the wilderness intensified them. No doubt it added abnormal force to normal cruelty, natural fear to theological terror. But it also dissipated what it augmented and intensified; it gave positive direction to negative passions. In the great open spaces of the continent there was room for any number of sovereign self-governing religious communities, each behaving like a sovereign state in relation to the others. Many, especially among the twenty sects that were counted in Pennsylvania, sought to establish an economy of producers' coöperation. By the time John Wise was vindicating the government of New England churches the feel and idea of human personality had undergone a change. Men had ceased to think of themselves as immortal souls first and children of nature afterwards. They had learned to think of themselves simply as children of nature and were defining their strivings and goals in terms of politics and economics, not of religion. By the middle of the eighteenth century, the essential mind of America had been considerably secularized. The ideals of the free theocracy were redrawn into the ideals of the free republic, and the teachings of the Independents, the Levellers and the Brownists were restated in the language of Rousseau.

§ 3. ITS REDEFINITION THROUGH THE POLITICS OF THE PIONEERS

THE MEN who spoke the language of Rousseau were not irreligious. On the contrary. But God had for them a new meaning and a different importance. Obeying His will became translated into fulfilling man's ends; those were now the immediate and necessary goals of life. John Wise's religious formula breathes this secular urgency. The autonomy of the personality was as basic as ever, but it had now another context. Liberty was still unalienable: "To renounce one's liberty," declared Rousseau, "is to denounce the quality of being a man, the right of humanity and even its duties . . . it is a vague and contradictory agreement to stipulate absolute authority on the one hand and boundless obedience on the other. Is it not evident that one has not engaged in anything to any person from whom one has a right to exact anything?" For the starting point of all association is this unalienable liberty that is the inward integrity of the person. When persons come together in an association "which defends and protects with the entire combined force the person and property of each individual associated and by whom each uniting himself to all obeys but himself and remains free as before," they turn their natural liberty into social or civil liberty.

At this point, however, the American tradition originating in the religious premise parts company with Rousseau. For to Rousseau the contract which establishes the sovereign is an utter surrender of all his rights by each to all. The surrendering act creates a new and indefeasible being, an organic unity which Rousseau designates as the General Will: In this unity each member figures "but as an indivisible part of the whole body." The "whole body" has now become "the body politic" or republic, the state, the sovereign power or people, whose members are themselves citizens and subjects. But this sovereign power is the power of anarchy. Its rule is absolute. It can impose obligations but owes none. Rousseau says that its law replaces the physical inequality between its subjects with moral or legitimate equality; inequality by physical strength or intellectual ability with equality by convention and right. But short of revolution there is no way by which its rule can be challenged, its law altered or its judgment revised.

Americans, nurtured in the practice and principles of association on American soil, could not find Rousseau's notion that the sovereign is organic and total justified by their experience. Both the church writers and the secularists like Samuel Adams, James Otis and John Adams, were concerned to defend the autonomy of the person against all sovereignty. The personality, they felt, has rights which are antecedent to all earthly governments and survive them. Governments are only attorneys, agents and trustees for those rights and like all other tools subject to change.

During half a century they argued this view. In the stresses and strains of the conflict with the sovereign power of the British monarchy debaters insisted that no person can alienate or curtail his natural rights except for the purpose of preserving them. Life, liberty and property, their support and defense, asserted James Otis in the "Declaration of the Rights of the Colonists as Men, as Christians and as Subjects," which he read in Faneuil Hall, Boston, on November 20, 1772, express but the laws of self-preservation. Men combine in societies but for the purpose of preserving themselves and such societies exist only by the consent of the combiners. The contract they make with one another to create the society is no surrender of their rights. The rights are retained; the society is only an engine devised to defend them. Fear or fraud or error may deprive people of their liberty of conscience or any other of their liberties. But the very nature of such losses rules them out as claims against the individual's liberty. They are void from the start and from the start to be denied.

Even Alexander Hamilton shared this opinion. Of course he was young, and when he came to power, came to another view. That he did so nearly hold the first opinion shows how fully it had become part of the growing commonsense of the English colonists in America. During the latter half of the eighteenth century it was repeatedly embodied in resolutions by colonial legislatures, from Massachusetts to Virginia. In 1774, the Virginians reformulated it in the Virginia Bill of Rights. Its high point is the Declaration of Independence. In that document the stream of religious and secular thinking comes to its classic summation, and the vindication of Everyman's personality as consumer receives a definitive formulation in political terms. Busy as the American scene has become, the producer interest, being still the servile interest, remains unuttered. Throughout the whole period there is hardly a word about "the dignity of labor" or "the right to work." Rousseau, the scion of Genevese artisans living in Paris, does affirm "the dignity of labor" and gives a characteristic secular twist to the Calvinist doctrine of vocation. "Do not work," he says, "for necessity; work for the glory of working." But this is tantamount to transvaluing work from a servile activity into a liberal art. It places labor on the same level as the arts of the priest, the soldier, the poet, and the scientist. It looks toward a classless society.

§ 4. THE DECLARATION OF INDEPENDENCE

BUT on the North American continent the wilderness tended always to make classlessness a fact. There the religious conception of personality, which is consummatory, carried over direct into secular aspiration and enterprise. Consider the propositions of the Declaration of Independence,

> We hold these truths to be self-evident, that all men are created equal, that they are endowed by their Creator with certain unalienable Rights, that among these are Life, Liberty and the pursuit of Happiness. That to secure these rights, Governments are instituted among Men, deriving their just powers from the consent of the governed. That whenever any Form of Government becomes destructive of these ends, it is the Right of the People to alter or to abolish it, and to institute new Government, laying its foundation on such principles and organizing its powers in such form, as to them shall seem most likely to effect their Safety and Happiness.

Concerning this "self-evident proposition" Abraham Lincoln, the year before his election as President, wrote to a great Republican meeting gathered in Boston to celebrate Jefferson's birthday:

> The principles of Jefferson are the definitions and axioms of free society. And yet they are denied and evaded, with no small show of success. One dashingly calls them "glittering generalities," another bluntly calls them "self-evident lies," and others insidiously argue that they apply to "superior races." These expressions, differing in form, are identical in object and effect—the supplanting the principles of free government, and restoring those of classification, caste and legitimacy. They would delight a convocation of crowned heads plotting against the people. They are the vanguard, the miners and sappers of returning despotism. We must repulse them, or they will subjugate us. This is a world of compensation; and he who would be no slave must consent to have no slave. Those who deny freedom to others deserve it not for themselves, and under a just God cannot long retain it. All honor to Jefferson—to the man who, in the concrete pressure of a struggle for national independence by a single people, had the coolness, forecast and capacity to introduce

into a merely revolutionary document an abstract truth applicable to all men and all times, and so to embalm it there that to-day and in all coming days it shall be a rebuke and a stumbling-block to the very harbingers of reappearing tyranny and oppression.

Why did Lincoln so highly prize the principles of the Declaration? It also is silent regarding "the dignity of labor" or "the right to work." The human nature it speaks of is biological and psychological, not industrial; intrinsically diverse, externally equal. Hence it affirms the equal rights of different individuals. The rights which it describes as unalienable are such because so long as human beings live they will so act as to continue to struggle to live, to be free and to find happiness. This action—the endeavor of each individual to live and to grow in his individuality, to "preserve" himself—is not and cannot be servile; it is of the very essence of freedom. Unless it be consummatory, it is nothing. Before it government—and in fact all other associative forms—are but means, extrinsic, alterable and alienable, and to be preserved or abandoned as they secure or endanger the unalienable and therefore inalterable intrinsic rights: life, liberty, the pursuit of happiness. As formulated in the Declaration of Independence, this vision became a lodestone both to Americans at home and Europeans abroad. If the American Revolution brought aristocratic lovers of liberty from all countries of Europe to fight for liberty in the American armies, the American religion of equal liberty brought the multitudes of liberty-loving Europeans to live and labor in liberty on the empty American continent. America and Americanism became to Europe symbols of the heart's desire attained.

§ 5. AMERICA AS WARFARE FOR "THE AMERICAN DREAM"

THAT THERE is another side to the story of the migrations of the white men from Europe into America is not disputed. Many have dwelt on it. I mention it here and pass on because it added nothing and altered nothing in the conduct of Europeans when they came to live in America. Greed for wealth and power were the same here as there; enslavement and exploitation were no different on the western hemisphere than on the eastern. If the undeveloped and unappropriated natural scene gave them greater scope, it also prevented them from doing so much harm. In the continental expanses of North America meanness could not be so mean, nor avarice quite so avaricious. Undoubtedly, as so many historical authorities have so many times proved, the Constitution of the United States was written in skulduggery and enacted in avarice. Undoubtedly its price was the alienation of much of the national domain from the people and the cheating of the soldiers of the Revolution of their pay and pensions. Had not De Tocqueville already in the early years of the nineteenth century signalized the rise of a race of Simon Legrees in the newly developing industrial scene? "Between the workman and the master there are frequent relations but no real association . . . I am of the opinion, upon the whole, that the manufacturing aristocracy which is growing up under our eyes is one of the harshest which ever existed in the world . . . if ever a permanent inequality of conditions and aristocracy again penetrate into the world, it may be predicted that this is the path by which they will enter."

But not less potent, not less militant and enduring, there was also the vision of America that moved the humble and the great of the earth alike: "the American dream" crystallized in the American Declaration of Independence. De Tocqueville spoke as a not too sympathetic alien observer on a visit, judging the country from outside in the light of ideals fundamentally alien to its people. To the aliens who came to make themselves citizens, America had at its height another meaning. "Shortly before the Civil War," writes Frederick Jackson Turner, "a great German, exiled from his native land for his love of freedom, came from his new home among the pioneers of the Middle West to set forth in Faneuil Hall, the 'cradle of liberty,' in Boston, his vision of the Young America that was forming in the West, 'the last depository of the hopes of all true friends of humanity.' Speaking of the contrast between the migrations to the Mississippi Valley and those of the Old World in other centuries, he said:

'It is now not a barbarous multitude pouncing upon old and decrepit empires, not a violent concussion of tribes accompanied by all the horrors of general destruction, but we see the vigorous elements—peaceably congregating and mingling together on virgin soil—; led together by the irresistible attraction of free and broad principles; undertaking to commence a new era in the history of the world, without first destroying the results of the progress of past periods; undertaking to found a cosmopolitan nation without marching over the dead bodies of slain millions.'

"If Carl Schurz had lived to see the outcome of that Germany from which he was sent as an exile, in the days when Prussian bayonets dispersed the legislatures and stamped out the beginnings of democratic rule in his former country, could he have better pictured the contrasts between the Prussian and the American spirit? He went on to say:

'Thus was founded the great colony of free humanity, which has not old England alone, but the world for its mother country. And in the colony of free humanity, whose mother country is the world, they established the Republic of equal rights where the title of manhood is the title to citizenship. My friends, if I had a thousand tongues, and a voice as strong as the thunder of heaven, they would not be sufficient to impress upon your minds forcibly enough the greatness of this idea, the overshadowing glory of this result. This was the dream of the truest friends of man from the beginning; for this the noblest blood of martyrs has been shed; for this has mankind waded through seas of blood and tears. There it is now; there it stands, the noble fabric in all the splendor of reality.' "

These words of Schurz's, as every sophisticate among us now knows, are rank overstatements, delusions that today could mislead nobody. Nevertheless, they voice a persistent attitude in the American people and an enduring judgment of America by the multitudes of other lands. It was natural for Robert Owen to have believed that the spiritual, even more than the natural, environment of the American scene was a fitter soil for his "villages of coöperation." It was within the character of religious organizations such as the Rappites and the Shakers to believe that they could grow freely and establish themselves on the American scene. It was natural that Fourierist communities such as Brook Farm should spontaneously dot the country. The European distinction between an upper class that consumed without producing and a lower class that produced without consuming did not exist. America was more nearly classless than any other country in the western world. Production had no end save consumption, and consumption was the personal act of a free man who worked to live. The American mentality was basically not economic at all. It was a political mentality. The fundamental aim of these communities was a religio-political aim. Owenite villages, Fourierist self-governing workshops, even Kingsite stores, dotted the country, and all of them, however they originated, were endeavors to realize the American dream. Whatever freedom and equality Europe imagined, fought for and failed to attain, Americans freely and peaceably attempted and also did not succeed in. Idealism was more practicable and less expensive in America and disillusion less hampering and more hopeful.

The fact moved Goethe to write:

Amerika du hast es besser
Als unser Kontinent, das alte,
Hast keine verfallene Schlösser
Und keine Basalte.

§ 6. CONSUMER COÖPERATION IN THE AMERICAN CLIMATE OF OPINION

As WITH RELIGIOUS FREEDOM and political democracy, so with the coöperative movement. The stream of European ideas was continuous and their assimilation to American principles and practice constant. The ideology of Robert Owen not only entered the public life as a fallacious Utopian effort at New Harmony, Indiana, and as addresses to the Congress and President of the United States; it worked continuously through his sons and his disciples [4] and was a not inconsiderable influence in the development of the American public education.

[4] In 1821, New York had a society for promoting communities on Owenite principles. Owen prefaced his settlement at New Harmony, Indiana, with a round of lectures, the first before the House of Representatives and the President in 1825. He explained that he chose America as the scene of his endeavor because America was new, free, untraditional and endowed with the mental liberty so needful to strengthen the political. The address is the first of the *Discourses on a New System of Society*.

The Christian Socialists had their simulacrum in Adin Ballou, the founder of Hopedale, who described his enterprise as practical Christian Socialism; in the Society of Christian Socialists which more than a generation later was organized in Boston by the Rev. W. D. P. Bliss, they had a direct projection. Immigrants brought their ideologies as well as themselves and many of them became founders and officers of coöperative societies, especially in New England. Lecturers were always numerous: And literary lights like Dickens and Matthew Arnold were rarer than prophets of a new social order like Robert Owen and social missionaries like George Jacob Holyoake.

The democratic principle which, regardless of deficient practice, Americans professed and passionately believed in, rendered them hospitable to every variant proposal for its embodiment. If Herbert Spencer, championing *laissez-faire,* had a wider audience in the United States, so did Owen and Holyoake and Marx. Under the editorship of Horace Greeley, the New York *Tribune* was a forum for every new scheme to embody the democratic ideal which Europe produced, from Fourierism to Marxism and Christian Socialism. It was Greeley who arranged for the American publication of Holyoake's *Self-Help for the People* soon after its appearance in England in 1857. It was the Sociological Society of America which followed it with a small manual on coöperation. "This epitome," Holyoake tells in his preface to the 1892 edition of his *History of the Rochdale Pioneers,* "excellently executed by ladies, included some of the following chapters. The Manual was popular, I judge, as a share of the profits from it was sent to me." His book was followed by two personal lecture tours, and in 1883, he reported to the Coöperative Congress the creation in New York of an "American Advisory Coöperative Board" with William Cullen Bryant's son-in-law, Park Godwin, as chairman, and J. J. Percival, late of Manchester, England, as secretary. We read at the same time of figures like the Rev. Heber Newton, Edward Beecher and Felix Adler as advocates of coöperation. Newton, indeed, was something of an authority on it, and in 1882, contributed to the *Princeton Review* an article on "The Progress of Coöperation in the United States."

A dozen years later we hear of a Coöperative Union of America organized on the initiative of the Cambridge Coöperative Association, and led by professors at Harvard College, hopeful of coöperation among working-men of New England.

As idea, both producers' and consumers' coöperation seems to have been widespread and favorably regarded in the United States. As program they were undertaken with no less earnestness than in England and perhaps with more abounding enthusiasm. But they were postulated on a different way of life and on different conditions. The American ideal of a free society had another content and another frame of reference than the British. The workers and farmers of Great Britain who did not emigrate had only their wages to win their freedom with. They were proletarians as Karl Marx meant the term, shut in and cut off by custom and law from all resource but the work of their hands. The farmers and workers of the United States, on the contrary, had, in spite of political piracy and financial corruption, at their disposal all the possibilities of an untamed immense national domain of land and minerals. During a hundred years the young men of America were always going west. Workers or farmers, coöperation could be to them but another, and a subordinate, confirmation of the promise of American life. To the European it was from the first salvation from despair, the last weapon against want and servility, the final form of the personal life. To the American, native and immigrant alike, coöperation was but a way thereto. For he began where Europeans hoped to leave off. America was opportunity, America was freedom. Americans were free citizens acknowledging no superiors and serving no masters. If they hired out, it was from choice and not necessity, for their own purposes and ends, and the hirelings sat at the same table with the hirers and ate the same food. The availability of free land enabled the American a little to be in fact what the American idea led him to believe he was, the master of his destiny and the captain of his soul, sure that God must help him because he helped himself; ready because he chose his own way to follow it at his own risk. As Kipling observed when this American was passing from the scene, and the rule of his modern successor had already begun,

. . . While reproof around him rings,
He turns a keen untroubled face
Home, to the instant need of things.

Enslaved, illogical, elate
He greets th' embarrassed Gods, nor fears
To shake the iron hand of fate
Or match with Destiny for beers.[5]

Every such American knew he was as good as his betters and did not hesitate to let others know it, as Kipling complained in the same poem. There was not a post or station in the national life which was not open to him by right; and which he might not aspire to—and attain—under the law. Whatever his start, for his goal the best was none too good.

§ 7. PUBLIC POLICY AND THE INDEPENDENT FARMER AS THE NATIONAL TYPE

IN A MORAL CLIMATE so mobile and free no status could be accepted as permanent and no state as lasting. The feeling that dependency was guilt and servility desert had a ground in the national economy altogether lacking in Europe. The most dependent immigrant industrial worker had the opportunity to make himself an independent farmer. Indeed, as the British Consul, M. E. Archibald, observed in his report of March, 1872, until within a decade of the twentieth century the Independent Farmer was able to call the political tune. From the Declaration of Independence until the Emancipation Proclamation, from the Emancipation Proclamation until the Sherman anti-Trust Act, the dominant ideal of American economy was that of a nation of independent farmers who owned their own land, cattle and tools, who produced what they consumed and who exchanged their surpluses of goods and services with their neighbors that each might live more abundantly. After the Civil War, the ideal, in fact already recessive, was extended to the emancipated slave. Every American, regardless of color, creed or origin, might embody the virtues of Longfellow's Village Blacksmith whose brow was wet with honest sweat and

[5] "An American" in *The Seven Seas,* quoted by permission of Mrs. Rudyard Kipling, Methuen & Co., and Doubleday, Doran & Co.

who owed not any man. He is the hero who is celebrated above the bankers and city-slickers in the play *Fashion* which had such a vogue in the 1840's.[6]

Let sailors sing of ocean deep,
  Let soldiers praise their armor.
But in my heart this toast I'll keep—
  The Independent Farmer.

He cares not how the world may move,
  No doubts or fears confound him.
His little flock is linked in love
  As household angels round him.

The gray old barn whose doors enfold
  His ample store in measure
More rich than heaps of hoarded gold,
  A precious blessed treasure.

Chorus

He loves his country and his friends,
  His honesty's his armor,
He's Nature's nobleman in life—
  The Independent Farmer.
He is Nature's nobleman in life,
  The Independent Farmer.

Public policy, perhaps all too unaware, endeavored to preserve the national type. Its instrument was the Homestead Acts; its history the drama of the race for land, in which railroads and other corporations figured as powerfully if not so publicly as people. The motion pictures are now celebrating as heroic legend events that used to be commonplace occurrences. The covered wagon took the pioneer and his family to the released land. He staked his claim and registered it at the land office. He built his house and for five years he cultivated it. At the end of that time it was his, a great freehold paid for at the rate of the sweat of his face and a dollar and a quarter an acre. In something under twenty-five years—from 1862 to 1883—nearly three-quarters of a million people received quarter and eighth sections. Hardly a third of them

6 Mrs. Cora Mowatt, *Fashion* (1845); produced first in England and revived by the Provincetown Playhouse in 1924.

took final title. Many sold their sections after cultivating them, and passed on to the next, moving ever westward until brought up by the Pacific Ocean; their grand-children are many of them today pushing northward into western Canada and Alaska. Most others, merely to build their houses, to live, to procure seed and tools, mortgaged their holdings. Every land office bred banks and landsharks. Bankers followed farmers as the flag follows the Bible, and the figure of the village Squire with mortgages on all his neighbors, squeezing them to ruin, has become a commonplace of the American stage and story. Nevertheless, so long as land was to be had for homesteading hope rode high, the ideal of the Independent Farmer persisted. Between 1850 and 1910, the farmers of America increased from one and one-half millions to almost six and a half millions; the value per acre of equipped and cultivated farm land from about $14 to about $75.

§ 8. DEBTS, MARKET COMBINATIONS AND EFFECTS ON THE TYPE

BUT THIS INCREASE meant more to the banker than to the farmer. The Independent Farmer was universally the Indebted Farmer. As the burden of debt grew, he came to feel more and more insecure. The swift upswing from scarcity to abundance which chemical science and inventive ingenuity brought to the whole land did not reach quite to his door. Country life, that had been a standard for the nation, became a symbol of insufficiency; the countryman, who had been the nation's hero, became the nation's butt. In transport, communications, housing, health, education and entertainment, as well as in population, the country began to fall steadily behind the city, and the farmer's obligation to the banker kept him from ever quite catching up. The improved farming methods and the invention of new machinery, which were important in changing the general economy of agriculture from one of scarcity to one of abundance for the nation as a whole, intensified this condition.

As transportation became swifter and surer and the farmer's market more and more remote from his farm, the need to preserve and assemble his produce was met by the construction of grain elevators and the invention of refrigeration. The persons who built the elevators were not the farmers who grew the grain or the consumers who ate it. They were third parties who soon passed from competition to combination. They organized line companies, commanded especially low freight rates, and drove independents out of business. They established cartels which pooled purchases and fixed prices. As grain dealers, their associations dominated the farmer's market. The packing industry, in analogous ways and by similar devices secured hegemony over the cattlemen, the poultry-raisers, the fruit and the vegetable growers. Pasteurization led to the formation of dairy companies which dictated the price of raw milk.

The Independent Farmer found himself in the course of time the essential serf of the banker and the middleman. Neither his acres were his own, nor their fruit. Always he had to think of claims on the work of his hands prior to his own. Before he could consume what he produced, the banker must be paid his interest, and the elevator company, the packer and dairymen their profits. The farmer became deeply disturbed over money. Poignantly, ineluctably, as the burden of debt turned him from a freeholder into a mortgagor, a renter, a share-cropper, his became a pecuniary consciousness. His American mentality of self-reliance, self-help and self-direction, his spirit of free citizen who consumed what he produced and produced, not in servile labor for others, but in free satisfaction of his own wants, was diluted by another mood, the mood common to the laborious multitudes of Europe, who produce without consuming and work without living for the benefit of the minority that consume without producing and live without working. The American farmer felt himself becoming peasantized, and he was afraid. Obscurely but certainly, he felt himself being degraded from a free citizen into a mere producer, and he hated and fought it.

§ 9. CONSEQUENCES: THE GRANGE COÖPERATIVES

THE FARMER organizations of the United States were at once the voices of his fear and the weapons of his defense against its causes.

First in their order comes the Patrons of Husbandry or Grange. Its founders were half a dozen government clerks in Washington, who five years after the adoption of the first Homestead Act, saw that its full intent could not be realized unless farm life could be established as the life more abundant on all levels. Accordingly—as was a practice of the United States, which is a country of gargantuan secret fraternal orders and friendly societies that, from Masons to Moose, combine elaborate mummeries and magniloquent pseudo-sacerdotal elective hierarchies with sickness, death or burial insurance—they organized the Grange as a secret non-sectarian fraternal order which both men and women could join, mutually to enrich their fellowship, perfect the art of agriculture and improve their minds. At first uninterested or suspicious, the farmers all over the country turned to the Grange as their one hope during the depression of the seventies. Between the spring of 1873 and the fall of 1874, the number of local Granges grew from 3,360 to 20,365. The new members displaced the original leaders in the organization and redirected its program.

This program was changed from an enrichment of life for the Independent Farmer to a liberation of the agricultural producer from his burdens of subjection to money-changers and middlemen. In the early years of the decade the National Executive Committee was designated to serve the state and local organizations as an agent for the wholesale purchase of farm implements; resolutions were adopted calling for collective bargaining on freight rates and the breaking of the control of credit and storage by commission merchants. Finding the pressure methods of large-scale bargaining inadequate to reduce prices of farm machinery, both the National Grange and state Granges undertook to produce what their members needed. To bring to their members other goods, they established coöperative stores. Intentionally non-political, and expressing this intention in their charter and by resolutions in conventions, they could not keep from political action or from exerting political influence. They were constantly exercised over monopoly, over railroad rates, over foreign trade, over problems of money and credit.

They were numerous enough—by 1875, they had 762,263

paying members—in the agricultural states to win for their views a proper consideration. They forced the creation, first of a Bureau, then of a Department, of Agriculture presided over by a cabinet officer; they urged laws affecting the rate of interest, patents, bank deposits, railroad regulation, taxation, bimetallism, education. Many "Granger laws" were passed. But the opposition of militant capital-enterprise was too strong: most were in the course of time either repealed or greatly modified. Many were taken by "the interests" as far as the Supreme Court: the Court, it need not be stressed, continued to interpret rules to preserve freedom and equality and security in such a way as to give a free hand to those who employed them with precisely the opposite effect.

And all the time coöperation and education continued to be pressed, eloquently, magniloquently, and, on the whole and in the long run, not effectively. Wrote the committee on coöperation, at the eighteenth annual session of the National Grange, in Nashville, Tennessee, November, 1884:

> The subject of coöperation has been so thoroughly discussed as a fundamental principle in our annual meetings that in theory, the subject, in the judgment of your committee is about exhausted. Yet something remains to be done to bring this subject more practically before the people, not in theory, but the methods of its application to practical life. The State and subordinate granges look, as they have the right to do, anxiously for some well-defined policy on this and kindred subjects. No argument is necessary to prove the necessity of coöperation. Proofs are abundant all around us on this line. We have but to look to the rapid success of corporations fostered by special legislation to see this.
>
> The only answer to the rapidly increasing number of millionaires in our country is traceable to the same cause. The excessive charges made for farm supplies in many cases give the same answer. The want of protection to the American farmer is but the want of properly equalised legislation. Class legislation is but the effect of organised effort as against a disorganised class. The importance of agriculture is not questioned . . . it is the want of the necessary protection to our industry; and this condition exists because of the want of organised coöperative effort on our part. 'Tis true that we are met here with another solution of the question, which is, that the interests of agriculture are too diversified, and the class engaged therein too numerous to unite them. Is this the voice of wisdom, or of the thoughtless and the demagogue? Does such reason apply to

political party organisation? Did it ever apply when the life of our nation was in peril? How then can it be made to apply truthfully when the happiness and the home of more than one-half of the population is threatened, as stated in the able address of our worthy master? Your committee aver that combination can be made a success with the American farmers, and done by the means and advantages the Grange affords, if properly utilised. Socially it has done much in removing sectional animosity and division.

Hundreds of thousands of dollars have been saved to the farmers by coöperative enterprise. While it is also true much has been lost by business adventures, is it not also a truth that this has been the result of experiments sprung by the enthusiasm of an hour rather than true coöperative effort in the full sense of that term? . . . But when we are met by the enormous exactions of other organised classes, wrenching from the wealth producers of the country millions of dollars daily to gratify the avarice of soulless corporations, and the rapidly-increasing number of a class known as drummers or commercial agents, who are, in contravention of our declared purpose, separating more widely yearly the producer and consumer. This organised legion, two hundred and fifty thousand strong, create extraordinary and unnecessary expenses, which must be paid in the end by the consumers, of which the farmers constitute a large majority. Your committee, in searching for a plan of coöperation suited to the condition and present wants of the order, are met by another question of not less importance—viz., the educational one. These two go hand in hand as they apply to successful business enterprise. Indeed they are inseparable. The one carries the other. As a consequence, coöperation cannot be successfully inaugurated until we see the necessity for it and understand the safe method for its application. On the other hand, education, in a business sense, naturally leads to coöperation.

The general principle of coöperation we assume to be accepted by the American farmer as sound in theory. He could not disbelieve it if he would. The members of our organisation have been trained to the belief that a line of policy would be indicated for their guidance by the law-making body of the order suited to the exigencies arising in their councils. . . . We are of the opinion that no general plan of coöperation can be suggested by the National Grange suited to all sections and conditions, until the conception of the possibilities of the Grange is better understood by the American farmer.

The term coöperation, in the Grange sense, is not confined to business enterprises. It means sacrifice on the part of some for the uplifting of others. It means the helping of the fatherless and the widows; it means protection to *our* industry by the use of means known and used by others in the selection of law-makers in sympathy with our interests and the advancement of agriculture regardless of the dictation of party managers or the purses of corporate authorities, who seek to pervert legislation to selfish purposes and party ends. As no general plan can be adopted suited to all, because of diversified conditions and wants, doubtless more supposed than real, in many cases, your committee conclude that in order to infuse new life and energy into our work—to place it upon a firmer basis—more zeal must be infused into the primary departments of our great educational system, provided for in subordinate Granges. Coöperation in some form suited to local wants, should be commenced after matured thought by every subordinate Grange. That which promises pecuniary advantage is most likely to be lasting. It is successfully conducted by some; it may be by all. The protection and elevation of the American farmer; the happiness and contentment of our homes; the education of our children, their safety, their best interests and that of society—all demand it.

Coöperation intelligently begun in every agricultural district, and methodically conducted, will be as the leaven in the meal, extending its influence from section to section, until every right of the farmer is regained and respected. We should not forget that if there is one thought more valuable than another, one principle that rises above the rest, it is the one that has ever been the great safeguard to our industry, to wit, pay as you go. Coöperation in the Grange means equal rights and advantages to all. So that the dollar of the poor man shall buy as much as the dollar of the rich.

The hesitancy, the vagueness and the hortative character of the committee's report have for their background considerable bitter experience. The adventure in producing agricultural machinery had proved disastrous. The coöperative stores which had flourished at the start, were hampered, when not wrecked, by the ignorance and inefficiency of the Grange agents and the unethical methods of the competitors. In point of fact coöperation failed to hold the attention of the Grangers. Their habit of pre-industrial rugged individualism made of them, under the conditions of a rapidly-industrializing agriculture, ragged individuals, but their deepest hope and faith were in political pressure and the passing of laws. Their forum gave rise to many farmer political movements—anti-monopoly, greenback, free silver—which sometimes turned an election. Their enterprises, however, in the long run tended to increase rather than diminish their indebtedness. Toward the late seventies the Grange began to break up. It survives as a social and educational organization and continues to concern itself with taxes. The coöperative idea still survives in a few Grange stores dating from the seventies; in the leadership of Grange members in non-Grange coöperative enterprises.

§ 10. CONSEQUENCES: THE FARMERS' UNION, THE NATIONAL EQUITY UNION AND BIG BUSINESS FARMING

THE VITALITY of the Grange idea is evinced by the fact that it has survived its immediate successors. The first of these was the Farmers' Alliance. This group, developing as the Grange declined, grew powerful in the eighties. During the depression of the early nineties [7] its members opened a considerable number of stores. The money question was, however, too strong for them. They could not concentrate on coöperation, and turned to politics. The Alliance became for practical purposes the equivalent of the Populist Party, R.I.P.

They were replaced by the Farmers' Educational Coöperative Union, better known as the Farmers' Union. The organizers of this group were somewhat more skeptical of political effort than their predecessors. Like the Grange, they recognized the importance of education and coöperation, and though they contributed more, perhaps, to coöperative marketing than to coöperative purchasing, they underlined the importance of buying in the farmer's economy.

The growth of the Union was as remarkable as that of the Grange. The Grange had taught farmers the advantages of coöperative organization. Credit-enterprise, with its money and machinery, its high-pressure methods and ruthless push toward monopoly, beating the farmer down, raising the general standard of living for the country without improving country life, reënforced the lesson. Big business entered farming. It incorporated farms and mechanized farm production. In the place of free men working to live, it set up capital organizations employing wage-earners to produce profits; in the

[7] At this time, Mrs. Webb, then Miss Potter, remarking, in the course of her exposition of the Coöperative Movement in Great Britain: "The American people, intent on personal gain, show neither desire nor capacity for any form of government other than a nominal democracy ruled by a corrupt plutocracy" (*The Coöperative Movement in Great Britain*, p. 231). In view of the record, it is evident that she did not inform herself as carefully as usual.

place of land it put chemicals and machinery, fertilizers and glass and tractors and mowers and reapers and threshers. The multitude of quarter-section owners had been reduced to a horde of renters and farm hands. In a grain state like Iowa renters were 40 per cent of the farming population by 1900. They number 60 per cent today. And this, broadly speaking, holds of the whole nation. The farmer on his farm has for more than half a century confronted singly and alone, insurance companies, banks, industrial corporations. Inevitably he has sought to equalize the handicap.

The Union, like the Grange, was one of his efforts at equalization. No wonder it grew rapidly. It spread from its starting point in the Middle West over the entire nation, but it contracted as rapidly. It encountered both competition and supplementation in the American Society of Equity, now known as the National Equity Union. Both at last set out to meet the economic issue on the economic level.

In 1889, the farmers in the neighborhood of Rockwell, Iowa, established the first coöperative grain elevator. They were lucky in their choice of directors and wise in the drawing of their by-laws. They arranged to meet the costs of management by a small proportional fee on all grain handled. This fee was due even if a member sold his grain to a competitor: It was then a penalty. The service was to be the same for all members. Of course the line company dominating the area with the help of its peers resorted to every known device of cutthroat competition to destroy the coöperative. It failed. But the resistance to coöperative elevators was for a time successful elsewhere. Railroads, grain dealers and line companies organized to prevent coöperative grain elevators from arising and to force those that did arise out of business. By the time the Farmers' Union and the Equity Association began to function there were upward of two hundred such elevators scattered through the country. Both organizations devoted themselves to advancing them. The Union in addition promoted livestock shipping associations, terminal grain and terminal livestock marketing associations, while Equity concerned itself with coöperative creameries. Such associations are all associations of producers. They are true coöperatives when they apply the basic Rochdale principles: democratic control, on the principle one man, one vote; limited ownership of share-capital and a fixed rate of interest; dividends in proportion to the business furnished; cash transactions; careful record and regular audit; efficient management. It is significant that they succeed, while coöperative industrial production does not. . . .[8]

§ 11. CONSEQUENCES: THE COUNTY AGENT AND THE NATIONAL FARM BUREAU

THE FORMATION and activity of the Farmers' Union and National Equity were contemporaneous with a growing concern over "country life" among intellectuals, politicians and administrators. The Grange had from the first advocated that the department of agriculture should send out "qualified agents" to collect information and teach agriculture; it had advocated the importance of adequate agricultural colleges and of general education. When a national commission on country life was created to make a survey of the state of the agricultural section of the nation and to bring in recommendations, its findings confirmed the indictments made by the Grange and proposed again many of its remedies. It laid special stress on the deficiency of the farmer's training and proposed, to overcome it, a system of extension work from land grant colleges to homes and farms, so that agriculture might be made to yield a "reasonable profit" and farm life made permanently satisfying to intelligent and progressive people. It called for a method of education adapted to the actualities of the farmer's daily life and general well-being, and a form of organization which would provide full scope for voluntary association and concerted effort: that is, for coöperation.

Partly as a consequence of these recommendations the states, stimulated by the national government, appointed agricultural experts to serve as the guides, philosophers and friends of the farmers in the field. These experts are known as County Agents, or Farm Advisers, and there is presumably one to

[8] This includes secondary agricultural industries like meat-packing and canning.

each agricultural county. They are responsible for their work to the agricultural colleges. These found before long that it would be easier to deal with groups than with individuals. They considered the existing farmer organizations, but gave them up as "radical." They decided to create an organization for themselves. This organization is the National Farm Bureau. With the prestige of its backing, it had a natural affinity for the capitalist farmer, or American *Kulak,* with his large-scale industrialized farm management and mechanized operation. Where he led, the rank and file of the farmers automatically followed. Of the four nation-wide associations of farmers hence the Farm Bureau soon took and still holds the lead in membership and influence. Educational in purpose, the Farm Bureau found, like other pedagogic institutions, that education without action was empty, and soon tended to become hypocrisy. In the course of time, it too began to foster marketing coöperatives, and later consumers' coöperatives. . . .

Thus by the time the World War was well under way the farmers of the land were associated into four distinct mutually exclusive and sharply competitive farmers' organizations, each with the purpose of defending its members from the exploitations to which they were subject, and each stressing both producers' and consumers' coöperation as instrument of defense. They had a hand, together with organized labor, in securing in 1914 the adoption of the clauses of the Clayton Act which declared that labor was not a commodity and forbade the classification of labor unions, mutual, agricultural and horticultural organizations among the trusts. One or another has facilitated the creation of regional or nation-wide marketing associations,[9] like the American Cranberry Exchange, the Eastern Shore of Virginia Produce Exchange, the coöperative dairies and creameries of the Middle Western states, the Fruit Growers' Exchange of California, and the various coöperative elevators already mentioned. Most of these exchanges have added coöperative purchasing, especially of farm supplies, to their functions. Some manufacture certain articles required by their members. All of them have improved,

[9] These Associations increased from 1,000 in 1900, to nearly 12,000 in 1931, with a membership of some three million.

standardized, and identified with a label, the quality of the goods they supply a nation-wide market. The tendency among them toward price-fixing, restricting production and other characteristic producer-practices is constant. But in recent years they have been moving toward increasing their profits by extending their markets rather than by reducing production and raising prices.

The alteration of the world market has enhanced this trend. The Great War set a scarcity value upon farm-products and farms. Farmers mortgaged their very shoes to expand operations and increase production. Land values increased, and obscured the mounting indebtedness. Coöperative marketing conserved for the farmer much of the profit that might have gone to the middleman, although the middleman's profit did not diminish at that. When peace came, and the nations at war resumed production, American farmers, the grain growers especially, found themselves, as they have so many times since, with an undisposable surplus on their hands. Hereupon the Farm Bureau Federation stepped in. The central organization of about a million farmers, it set up, in 1921, amid a great fanfare and much virtuous ballyhoo, the United States Grain Growers. Members paid $10 to join and contracted to sell their grain to no one else for five years. How the grain so sold was to be paid for, to whom resold, or at what price, was not indicated. The sum of the entrance fees paid by fifty-thousand farmers was soon consumed, together with a quarter of a million dollars borrowed from State Bureau Federations. In 1924, when the Grain Growers gave up the ghost, it had sold not a bushel of grain. Its managers appear not to have understood that grain, being a world commodity, is distributed through international markets at practically the lowest possible cost. It cannot often have a world-wide scarcity-value such as a war may cause. In peace times, other things being equal, the producer may find himself reduced even in his own country to destroying his surpluses—burning them for fuel, for example, or dumping them into the sea. His sole alternative to monopoly and fixed price is a growing market with a falling price. This alternative, however, only the coöperation of consumers can certainly provide.

§ 12. FARM COÖPERATIVES AND THE PRIMACY OF THE CONSUMER

TO REALIZE this is to realize the primacy of the consumer. American farmers, like their fellows everywhere else, including England and Denmark, are still far from this insight. The Grange, the Union, the Equity Union and the Farm Bureau Federation, though they foster coöperation in business, do not yet realize as fully as they will that it could be as well applied to themselves. Their leaders are engaged in jurisdictional disputes and other forms of rivalry which are not generous and emulative, but sheerly sectarian. The true coöperative interest is tangent to all that. Coöperative association is open, and each farm organization and every member of each farm organization reënforces his own strength and enriches his own life with the power and riches of all his fellows when he joins himself to them in a coöperative undertaking.

The leaders in the American coöperative movement are fully aware of this; and the coöperatives are likely to play the leading rôle in freeing the farm organizations from the wastes which their present policy causes through effort duplicated, fixed charges multiplied, ideas confused and actions obstructed. Thus the Consumers' Coöperative Association, when it organized in 1929—then as the Union Oil Company Coöperative—made no alliance with any farmer organization and invited the friendship of all. Men affiliated with each of the groups now serve on the Association's board of directors, and the membership of all are enrolled in the Association's constituent societies. The last annual meeting created by resolution a regional planning committee of representatives of all the major coöperative federations and farm groups in the area. The committee is to work out a plan of unified educational activity to be enacted shortly, and a plan of unifying business activities to be executed gradually as time, circumstance, need and opportunity permit. In view of the competitive record of farm organizations, its members have a life-work. . . .

Where the farm organization leadership has vision, coördinating action develops within the organizations themselves. Thus, the Coöperative Grange League Federation Exchange is a distinct business entity created jointly by leaders of the Grange, the Farm Bureau, and the Dairymen's League. It controls more than 125 local stores of its own, 50 affiliated local coöperatives, and 538 local dealers. The membership and the organizations are in New York, northern Pennsylvania, and New Jersey. The Exchange serves them with feed and furniture, which it manufactures itself, and other matters. The central office is in Ithaca, New York. Its territory is divided into districts of several counties each, each with a resident district manager responsible to the central organization. This organization is itself responsible to the board of directors, who are directly chosen by the thirty thousand members. Both the material and the spiritual possibilities of such organizations are still untapped. The fact that they function even more effectively in depression than in prosperity, is a sign of their basic vitality. But to be saved from the sordidness of the merely producer consciousness, it is necessary for them to learn to think of the coöperative practice in terms of the primacy of the consumer. This is a task still before them.

CHAPTER IX

THE CONSUMER IN AMERICA: II, THE INDUSTRIAL WORKER

§ 1. THE AMERICAN MENTALITY, THE IMMIGRANT, AND INDUSTRIALIZATION

ALTHOUGH the United States is a conspicuously industrial country, the coöperative movement has had a more powerful and characteristic development among American farmers than among American wage-workers. Practically until the turn of the century this land of continental proportions suffered a scarcity of men and man-power. It was a nation of farmers, and the common unit of enterprise was the farm-family strengthened when the season required it by the help of neighbors who were the farmer's peers. The "hired girl" was no servant, and the "hired man" no serf. Their service was often a favor, the collaboration of equals, not the performance of hirelings: the price of their labor was like the fees paid to doctors and lawyers, not like the wages paid to the industrial worker or the present-day agricultural laborer. In domestic service this tradition survives. America, unlike any other western country, has always had a "servant problem." It has had a servant problem because during more than a hundred years its open moral and physical atmosphere remains inimical to the servile state of mind.

The handicap of insufficient man-power, if it was a handicap, was overcome by mass immigration and the multiplication of mechanical inventions. Between 1820, when Owen set out to establish his "villages of coöperation" on American soil, and 1928, when Herbert Hoover, accepting the nomination of the Republican Party to the Presidency of the United States, declared: "We in America today are nearer the final triumph over poverty than ever before in the history of our land. The poorhouse is vanishing from us," thirty-seven million men and women from all regions of the globe, but from Europe mostly, had come to the United States to take up a new life. Whether they sought freedom only, or security only, or both, is indifferent. Whether their coming was moved by inward need and personal choice, or stimulated by shipping agencies, labor-contractors and other servants of men of business eager for cheap labor, is also indifferent. What matters is that their coming meant for them a new life, not so much a break with the past as a transformation of it.

They were in their turn pioneers, with the searching and seeking mentality of the uprooted. Such gospels of freedom and safety as any brought from the old home where, usually, they had been proscribed, could be freely spoken and freely implemented in the American atmosphere. And in the climate of freedom the meaning and intent of those gospels underwent mutation. Marxism in America became another thing than the Marxism of England or Germany or Russia; trade-unionism acquired a different ideal; coöperation a different significance. All were Americanized. And during a hundred years, to be Americanized meant to be imbued with the mentality of free contract, equal liberty, self-help, self-direction, and optimistic futurism. I went west for the first time in my life in 1910. In Chicago, where I had letters, I was entertained at a dinner party of notables. One, across the table to my left, impressed me by his distinguished utterance as well as his distinguished appearance. I inquired about him from my neighbor. "Oh, R——," he said, "he's no great shakes: He only inherited his money."

This characteristic judgment of early America on inherited wealth applied to all inheritances; not what men received from the past but what they created for the future was the general criterion. It has since reverted to the European type. The specifically American judgment on inheritances is finding a new life in Russia. The reversion to pre-American types in the United States is a consequence of its repudiation of the American dream. In following the dream, the open spaces were filled; the tendrils of vested interests got a firm hold of all the institutions of the national life; industry was mechanized; the factory system which goes with machine production generated an industrial, which soon grew into a social, hierarchy; ownership changed from direct possession of the land which one tilled and the tools which one worked with to indirect possession of tokens—stocks, bonds, "securities." And however distributed, it became, on all levels, absentee ownership. . . .

As in old England the transformation began with the textile industry, so in New England. From the factory towns of Massachusetts the process spread in irregular and unsymmetrical waves over the continent. It is now irritating awake the old agricultural South which had lain comatose, enjoying a state of arrested development, since the Civil War. Its essential phases, being molded by the material structures to which they are adaptations, everywhere take on the same formations. Slowly the vertical differences between neighbor and neighbor became subordinated to the horizontal differences between employer and employee. The employer soon ceases to feel the employee an equal and begins to treat him as a dependent. He begins to expect servility. The employee, animated by the American dream, and sharing the employer's mentality and ambitions, appreciates the employer's viewpoint but cannot yield to it. Against the dependence and servility which the employer thrusts on him, he opposes, if he does not seek his fortune in the west, employee association. The automatic turn to collective bargaining, to strikes for higher wages and shorter hours is at first not so significant as the philosophy of life which rationalizes and justifies the action.

§ 2. WORKING-MEN'S ASSOCIATIONS, SELF-GOVERNING WORKSHOPS, CONSUMER STORES

We have seen how the ideologies of Owen, Fourier and Marx were naturalized in the American scene and assimilated to the American dream. During the decade of Owen's first sojourn in the United States some eleven villages of coöperation similar to New Harmony had been organized, four in Indiana, three in New York, two in Ohio, one in Pennsylvania, and one in Tennessee. None of them survived longer than three years. A generation later the same essential ideology expressed itself in an epidemic of Fourierist phalansteries, mostly agricultural. Some thirty of them, with Brook Farm as their head and front, were born and died between 1840 and 1850. They ranged from Massachusetts to Iowa, and the area of greatest concentration was Ohio, where eight saw the light. This was the decade of Robert Owen's return to the United States. Between 1844 and 1847, he was giving innumerable lectures on his scheme of social salvation; in 1845, he held one of his characteristic world conventions in New York. . . .

His activity coincides with the early efforts of wage-workers to organize coöperative stores and self-governing workshops. From the first, societies of handloom weavers, tailors, carpenters, cordwainers and other craftsmen were drawn to his gospel. As in 1835, the depression which reached its nadir in 1837 began to make itself felt, meeting after meeting voted to establish coöperative enterprises. In 1836, the Journeymen Cordwainer's (Ladies' Branch) urged the friends "of those who earn their bread in the sweat of their brow" to organize coöperatives as the only means of helping them. In 1837, the trades-union called a special conference on coöperation, reaffirmed its practicability and urged working-men to undertake it. And from that time on producers' societies were unhardy perennials in different parts of the country. As often as not, their antecedents were unsuccessful strikes. During half a century tailors, textile operatives, stoneworkers, smiths and foundry workers, printers, cabinet makers, cigar makers, all tried their hand at coöperative production. Sometimes trades-unions initiated the enterprises, as in the case of the stove foundry which, in 1867, the Iron Moulders' International set up in Allegheny County, Pennsylvania, or of the Amalgamated Clothes System, set up by the Amalgamated Clothing Workers of New York in 1921. But the area of concentration, in the early days, was Massachusetts, Pennsylvania running second. The record kept true to form. Those that survived ceased to be coöperative; those that remained coöperative did not survive. The manufacturing enterprises of the Patrons of Husbandry introduced no change in the record.

The same thing appears to hold of coöperative stores. Agitation in their favor occurs among the members of the New England Association of Farmers and Mechanics; in the middle years of the third decade labor organizations in textile towns, under the pressure of hard times, did open a few stores which shut down or became private enterprises within three to five years. In 1845, toward the end of the depression caused by debt repudiation, a coöperative buying club, organized the year before by the Boston tailor John G. Kaulback, was changed into a Kingsite consumers' coöperative society. Other societies quickly followed, and in 1847, twelve of them formed a confederation with the name Working-men's Protective Union. The stores sold at cost to members and at the market price to non-members. The dividend on purchases was apparently still unknown, and was paid on shares only; democratic control and the rule of *one man, one vote,* were of course the principles of government. The development of the stores coincided with the boom of the California gold rush. They spread rapidly throughout New England, and into Pennsylvania and New Jersey. In five years the twelve locals had become 403, and their turnover mounted into millions of dollars. By 1853, issues over management led to a split and the formation of a rump organization, The American Protective Union. This organization also flourished. When the post-inflationary panic of 1857 began, it had 370 locals and an annual turnover of $200,000. Neither the New England (changed from "Working-men's" in 1849) Protective Union nor The American

Protective Union survived the panic. Most of the New England locals were able to disband and sell their stock without loss; in other places they were not so fortunate.

§ 3. CONSEQUENCES OF BUSINESS BOOM AND WORKER DEPRESSION

THE DISSOLUTION of the Protective Unions and the publication and spread of Holyoake's account of the rise of the Rochdale idea were coincident. The Civil War, which followed soon after, was a drain upon the energies of the northern multitudes that left little room for anything beyond the idea of somehow winning it. That this idea should, or could, be realized by employing the coöperative technique seems to have occurred to nobody. On the other hand, the first two years were of such hardship that the coöperative way of overcoming it would infallibly have been tried somewhere, and on the now known Rochdale principles. The "somewhere" was Philadelphia; the year, 1862; the organization, the Union Cooperative Association. In 1866, it had three branches, but it was spending so much for advertising and other overhead that it had to fold up.

But by this time the great industrial boom, set going by the necessities of the Civil War and set back for a brief period by the inevitable abandonment of certain war activities which is the perennial requirement of return to peace, was resuming again. The construction of railroads, necessary as a war measure, was resumed as a speculative enterprise in the exploitation of the national wealth through the Homestead Acts. The refinement of oil was added to the smelting of ores as a major national industry. The Vanderbilts, the Goulds, the Drews, the Fisks, the Carnegies, the Armours, the Swifts, the Rockefellers and the Morgans begin to figure as the competitive champions of the industrial warfare constituting the national economy. They made of business a battle royal open to all comers, with no blows barred. Their expropriative techniques stripped the just and the unjust with the same impartiality. They forced bankruptcies or sellouts on their competitors; they lured the general public with stocks and bonds, and then rigged the markets against them and each other. They sought monopoly by means of elimination and by means of combination, and above all they needed credit to save their own cash. The usurer and money-changer was fore-ordained to be the ultimate director of the new American *mise en scène*.

In this hurly-burly of the manipulators and managers, the average American worker had little chance. If, to save his freedom, he fled west, the immigrant took the place he left empty. If he remained at his industrial post, the immigrant was his rival, apparently pulling down his wage and degrading his standards. He developed an abiding anger against the immigrant—even when he himself joined the greater wolves in exploiting him—which he expressed in a variety of forms, religious, political, economic and social. But anger against the immigrant did not meet the worker's problems. He began to feel, as a quarter of a century earlier the industrial workers of England felt, the squeeze of the two grindstones, low wages and high prices; the inadequacy and insecurity of purely combative associations as labor unions perforce are. He saw the enormous accruals to corporations and demanded "the same chartered rights and privileges granted to association of capital" for "voluntary labor associations of workingmen and women." In 1866, the National Labor Union had resolved that they hail "with delight the organization of coöperative stores and workshops" and "would urge their formation in every section of the country and in every branch of business." The International Industrial Assembly of America expressed similar sentiments. But in 1867, the National Labor Union voted that "no system of coöperation can help labor while the credit system lasts." They were sucked into the morass of inflation, fiat money, "greenbackism" that the war had mashed up.

The American industrial worker's preoccupation with money and credit almost equalled the American farmer's. Like the farmer, he was being threatened by proletarianization, and like the farmer, was searching and seeking an associative form that would assure him his liberty as a worker and dignity as a citizen.

Hence, his persistent effort to protect his wages and conditions of labor led to the formation of one association after another, each with the same purpose of raising wages and lowering prices.

For a moment the realization of the relation between individual personality and the consumer economy came to him, but it was lost in the struggle over the profits of production.

§ 4. IRA STEWARD'S CONSUMER PHILOSOPHY AND PRODUCER METHOD

THE VOICE of this realization was Ira Steward. With a little luck Steward might have figured in the philosophy of the American industrial worker as John T. W. Mitchell figured in the philosophy of the British coöperator. But his own practical program as well as the climate of opinion and the organizational pattern of the time were against him, and Steward, who was deeply aware of the primacy of the consumer, had to be only a voice crying in a wilderness.

The record is extraordinarily thin concerning his origin and background. It is known that he was born in 1831. It is inferred that he was self-taught. It is known that he was by occupation a mechanic and that he gave much thought to the personal and social significance of the long hours and low wages of workmen young and old. It is known that in 1850, he was as a machinist's apprentice working twelve hours a day. A member, of course, of the Machinists' Union, he figures in the public prints of 1863 as a delegate to the Machinists' and Blacksmiths' Union in Boston arguing for the adoption of an eight-hour resolution and for an appropriation by the Boston Trades Assembly to pay for work with the Massachusetts Legislature in behalf of an eight-hour law. From that time to 1870, he is now and again recorded as appearing with Wendell Phillips, George McNeill and George Gunton to argue the adoption of such a law. He figures as the founder and inspirer of Eight-Hour Leagues and his influence stretches to the National Congress.

In the light of events, Steward's program was a very small focus for a very profound and richly meaningful economic philosophy. But the logic of his action was simple enough. It is summed up in his declaration: "Wages depend upon the habits and wants of the worker, so that an eight-hour day would increase wages." Behind this conception was a notion of the "political economy of eight hours" as a method of getting civilization shaped into a consumer economy. He realized that thrift implies the constriction of life, and argued that in the world's business actual thrift signified rather an inability to consume a "surplus" of goods and services than a reduction of consumption. He recognized that fundamentally men can only save as they spend and must lose what they do not spend. This is why he insisted that short hours and high wages are conditions and instruments of abundance; that as applied to goods, "necessary and "unnecessary" stand for conventional not basic difference, and that an economy resting upon the division of labor and automatic machinery can be effective and orderly only as consumption expands more rapidly than production. Thus, "every financial crash means a failure to consume and then when the crash comes the small consumers are urged to consume still less."

Machinery enriches life "provided the wealth more rapidly produced is *consumed* as fast as days' works are destroyed. But if this blessing is to continue to bless, wages must continue to rise. If wages stop rising, machinery stops blessing." It stops blessing because its productions cease to be of use to anybody. Already in the industrial economy, "wealth is more rapidly produced than consumed in the leading nations. . . . This fact combined with the poverty and misery of the rest of mankind (outside the charmed circle) is the mainspring of enforced idleness (within it). And enforced idleness is the secret of financial convulsions and bankruptcy which from time to time sweep over the most prosperous countries of the civilized world."

This enforced idleness is tantamount to the waste of underconsumption. To producers of every level it is a contagious disease. For, "when the first laborer is discharged he stops buying." He falls into "the deadly but natural competition existing between those who are employed and those who are not." As he goes down he pulls all standards down with him. "An unemployed man is the most deadly fact that exists outside of a graveyard. He is the source of all that is bad. . . . Without raising his hand he takes far more bread from others than he himself can eat . . . more clothes than he can ever wear . . . more opportunities than he alone can improve. . . . The deadly competition between those who have nothing to do and those who do too much for fear of doing nothing as well as for lower wages sets in." Workers are thrown into a state of anxiety and miserliness; and unemployment, which is the same thing as disabled consumption, operates to infect the whole structure of industry. Thus the reduction of hours would imply the multiplication of jobs and the mutiplication of jobs must go with higher and higher wages and an improved standard of living. "Employment for the unemployed can only come through the higher wages and larger expenditures of those who are already employed." As those go up all their fellow-workers must follow. This is the inevitable implication of the division of labor and the use of machinery in industry. "If all mankind consume sufficient wealth, savages will civilize up to the division of labor; barbarians will civilize up to wage conditions, and wage-laborers will civilize up to coöperation."

But, although through industrialization the production of mankind has been much increased, consumption still lags far behind; so that there is a constant waste of wealth and life. Production has no justification apart from consumption; it is consumption that stimulates, and provides the drive for, the progress of mankind. "If everybody had always economized as much as possible in consuming wealth, there could be no progress." Inventors we have always with us; it is the consumers who are insufficient. "No one person, not even a king, can afford to build a railroad and a locomotive to accommodate himself alone." An invention displaces other instruments producing the same goods or services, not merely because it does the same thing better, but also because "it undersells" and the thing becomes available to multitudes instead of few. Most of the implements of industrial economy depend upon the earnings of millions of human beings. Machinery "*never could undersell itself into existence,* until the day's work of the laboring classes had been made sufficiently expensive." "The natural function of the wealthy is to inspire a desire for goods. The unsolved problem is, however, to reach the lowest laborers with such desires. At this point . . . the whole civilized world is standing still. Everything is waiting for the movement that can penetrate the lowest laborers with the habit of using more wealth."

Steward recognized the bitter irony that the virtue of thrift which the employer required of the employee would serve far less to increase the employee's savings than to decrease his earnings. He urged that labor is carried on for the sake of consumption; that habits and wants constitute standards of living, and that the wage men receive for their labor must be set and measured by their standards of living and not their standard of living by their wage. He conceived of a coöperative commonwealth which would employ machinery purely for consumer ends. He urged that it could be attained by raising wages and shortening hours. His Eight-Hour Leagues were designed as instruments to advance workers to this ultimate end. Unfortunately their actual effect was merely to confirm and intensify a habitual wage-and-hour consciousness, a trade-union consciousness, not to transform the "habits and wants of the worker." Like his more popular and less profound contemporary, Henry George, whose *Progress and Poverty* was in vogue in 1879, Steward missed out on method.

For the primacy of the consumer can be vindicated in the economic structure only through the coöperative organization of the consumer; that is, through the organization of the wants and habits themselves. To raise wages and shorten hours or tax unused land is not enough. It is necessary to focus attention on the activities of consumption, their development and control. To these, wages and hours are means only.

Nevertheless, Steward's vision is perhaps the most significant developed among American working-men. Unfortunately, he never reached the state of writing his book on the "political economy of eight hours." What he had to say is to be found in papers and reports of speeches and in manuscript notes set down between 1865 and 1882.[1] Steward died in 1883, a sick

[1] These notes are preserved at the Library of the University of Wisconsin. For data on Steward's ideas and life see, Dorothy Douglas, "Ira Steward on Consumption and Unemployment," *Journal of Political Econ-*

and disappointed man. His immediate object came close to accomplishment; his vision has not received the attention it deserves. The endeavor to fulfil the American as a consumer was renewed through another movement with a more traditionally American disposition. Its vehicle was the Noble Order of the Knights of Labor.

§ 5. THE KNIGHTS OF LABOR AND THE SOVEREIGNS OF INDUSTRY

THE FOUNDERS of the Knights of Labor were working-men, tailors, whose local union broke up when the National Labor Union was dissociating into its elements. They knew of the principles, objectives and associative form of the Patrons of Husbandry which had been founded two years earlier, and they felt that an analogous form of salvation might also work out for the working-man. Accordingly, nine of them organized in 1869, amid the uncertainties of the early phases of industrial over-expansion, a secret order of industrial workers. The object of this order was social salvation of farmer and worker conceived in the terms of Jefferson and Owen. Among the nine were English and Irish immigrants. Frederick Turner, a gold beater, who drew up the Order's ritual, was an English Owenite; Terence Powderly, who was the head of the Order during the whole period of its direct impact on the national life and guided the strikes and stratagems of militant unionism compelled by the attitude of the buccaneer industrialists of the period, was an Irishman, and throughout his leadership preached the larger ends of the democratic commonwealth. J. L. Wright, his lieutenant, a clothing cutter, was also an Irishman. But the initiating mind, Uriah S. Stephens, was a native. He had been a theological student, a schoolmaster, and a wanderer. He had read history closely, and was aware of both the Owenite ideal and the Rochdale method of realizing it. His vision was concentrated on personality,

omy, 1932, Vol. 40, p. 532; Miss Douglas studied Steward's manuscript notes as well as his printed *Nachlass*. See also John R. Commons, *Documentary History of American Industrial Society;* Selig Perlman, *A History of Trade Unionism in the United States.*

not wages. Like Ira Steward he felt that the habits and wants of the worker, his standard of living, determine the level of wages, and basically define the moral and physical condition of mankind. Accordingly, through the Noble Order, the wage-worker was to raise himself "above the narrow view of his class, trade, or job," and realize himself as a helper in the salvation of humanity. The Order would be his instrument of study and discipline. Its ritual would with its symbols lift his mind and heart to the great vision of a free society; and lead the young initiates to higher and higher levels of brotherhood and power. Its secrecy would make a home for them, giving them confidence, intimacy and freedom. With schools and shops and stores and self-insurance, the producing multitudes would win and safeguard their freedom, security, fraternity and equality for themselves.[2]

Accordingly the founders of the Order proposed educational schemes, the organization of both producer and consumer co-operatives, insurance schemes and the other familiar defenses of the exploited producer against exploitation. Like the Patrons of Husbandry, the Order first met inertia and suspicion. The inflationary activities of railroad, oil, mining and smelting magnates kept wages high, though not as high as prices, and ideals low. But with the six-year-long depression which began with the panic of 1873 the case was altered. In a few years, the Order had an organization in practically every state of the Union. It became the efficacious representative of the wage-earners throughout the country. But the multitudes, which brought power, also brought impatience. They wanted, they needed, immediately visible results. They could not wait for the new growth of stores and workshops. They demanded militancy against the looming powers of monopoly. They wanted strikes led, laws forced through legislatures. Their assent to the original intention of the Order became like their assent to the dogmas of their churches. From 1877, when the Noble Order was a power in the great strikes of the coal

[2] There is a certain parallel between the Noble Order of the Knights of Labor and Owen's Grand National Consolidated Trades-Union of Great Britain and Ireland, both of intent and structure and of relationship to the general economy.

miners and railroad workers, the order of the day was one of lobbying, strikes, boycotts. The leadership was often undermined or frustrated by politicians and others who had joined the Order for purposes of their own. Nevertheless, during a decade, the Order dominated the labor movement in America. It held the enthusiastic allegiance of the wage-earners through both the better times that followed the resumption of "specie-payments" and the depression of 1884. Then they began to drop out. Neither the strikes and boycotts of the struggle against the employer, nor the coöperative and educational enterprises of self-help had brought the promised uplift. The secret ritual ceased to exercise fascination or to hold interest; the secrecy had relaxed. When the American Federation of Labor was formed, the Order had lost its drive. In a few years it petered out.

The depression which imparted momentum to the growth of the Knights of Labor brought on a parallel movement which concentrated on coöperation to the exclusion of everything else. This was the organization known as the Sovereigns of Industry. A Massachusetts society founded in 1874 by William H. Earle, the Sovereigns of Industry, like the Knights of Labor and the Patrons of Husbandry, were an endeavor to arrest and offset the de-Americanization of the equities of American life which they felt resulted from the works of the piratical entrepreneurs of the time. But while the Knights addressed themselves to wage-workers, and the Patrons to farmers, the Sovereigns addressed themselves "without regard to race, sex, color, nationality or occupation" to all conditions and callings, except lawyers. Abjuring "the class-struggle," they aimed at "mutual assistance in self-improvement and self-protection" through consumer coöperation. Like so many of the American adventures in coöperation, they labored first and most hardily in New England. In 1874, buying clubs were formed in Springfield and Worcester. These clubs were financed by loans from their members, according to their abilities. The funds were then put in the hands of purchasing agents who took each member's orders weekly and bought for all together. In each community the clubs formed councils and the councils pooled their funds for the purpose of opening a store. Representation in the direction of the store was based on the sum invested, in the ratio of one representative for every $100 put in. Interest on capital was fixed at 7 per cent. Goods were sold below the market price, to members only, and at a profit of 2½ per cent to be divided equally between the "sinking-fund" of the store and the treasury of the councils. The change from this technique to that of Rochdale came quickly, with the growth of the movement. Within a year there were 40 local councils in New England and 170 in the middle and central states. The Sovereigns planned to pass from distribution to production. They had a foundry in Kingston, Massachusetts, and other workshops elsewhere. But their possibilities were frustrated by poor management and nepotism. They did not even survive the depression which started them off. By 1879 they broke up. Private dealers, some of them members, bought them out, and the membership in general turned to other gospels or to the exploitation of foreign labor.[3]

§ 6. BUILDING AND LOAN ASSOCIATIONS

THE ONE TYPE of coöperative association which has had a continuous development and flourishes in the United States has been the Building and Loan Association. Building and Loan societies are fundamentally credit unions whose members pool their resources and lend and borrow money from one another for the purpose of building homes. The first to date recorded was organized in Philadelphia in 1831. The record as we know it is silent about its development or the creation of other societies until 1852. Then the Suffolk Mutual Loan and Accumulating Fund Association was organized in Boston, and by 1854, such associations had become numerous and powerful enough in the State of Massachusetts to secure a special statute determining the conditions of their incorporation.

[3] *Cf.* James Ford, *Coöperation in New England* (1913), "The native American in industrial communities ceased to found coöperative movements because with equal effort he could earn much more by the exploitation of foreign labor than he could by coöperative effort." It is proper to add that each migration of foreign labor endeavored to profit by the example of its predecessors.

From 1857 on, the state insurance commissioners reported on them. But the Civil War was too much for them. In 1866, only three had survived. But that year a second growth began in Philadelphia, and they increased and multiplied by the hundreds. The movement renewed itself in Massachusetts where, under a new act of the legislature, adopted in 1877, the Pioneer Coöperative Savings Fund and Loan Association was incorporated. Other states followed the example of Pennsylvania and Massachusetts. In 1880, according to figures of the Bureau of Statistics of Labor and Industries of the State of New Jersey, there were in the country some 3,000 such associations, with a membership involving the interests of two and a quarter million people. The authorities then had no doubt of their value. As the Secretary for Internal Affairs of the State of Pennsylvania said in his report for 1879–1880: "From their inception up to the present it is estimated that under their operations 60,000 comfortable houses have been erected in Philadelphia alone, and that they have enabled 25,000 householders to pay off mortgages that probably would have otherwise been foreclosed. Through the economical habits they were instrumental in forming, it is estimated that $100,000,000 have been invested within the city limits, which, were it not for them, might possibly have been squandered in dissipation and improvidence. They have been the means of making 80,000 owners of real estate and 80,000 taxpayers; thus giving Philadelphia the preëminent title of being the 'city of homes.' "[4]

The Building and Loan Association has become an institutional component of the economy of the United States. But neither the moral nor social implications of its principle and method have been developed by its leaders or conceived and pressed by its members. Many of the associations are now sheerly mortgage security companies, lending money at interest. All are more concerned primarily with the security and cost of housing than with the expansion of the house of life. For this reason, they have hardly figured in the record of coöperation in the United States. Yet they have a store of continuous ex-

[4] Report of Secretary of Internal Affairs (Pennsylvania, 1879–80), pp. 266, 269.

perience, and resources which, under a practical leadership with adequate vision might become a mighty force in the extension of Americanism from the political to the economic establishment.

§ 7. THE PRODUCER MENTALITY COMES TO POWER

FOR AS THE COUNTRY entered its gilded age, the political and the economic establishment had become definitely distinguishable. Land was being industrialized. The trusts were establishing themselves. Immigrant workers were being rapidly absorbed by the quicksands of certain primary industries like mining and steel-making. And as a result the basic American mentality, the Jeffersonian individualism of the Declaration of Independence and of the frontier, which turn upon the primacy of the consumer, was undergoing suppression by a producer-consciousness emanating from the industrial establishment. "Employer" and "employee" tended to be used as terms of status rather than contract. Immigrants becoming the hirelings of industry took longer and longer to throw off the invidious European feeling of class. The more intellectual among them, mostly Germans and Russian Jews, brought intellectual reënforcement to this feeling in the form of the Marxist philosophy of life. The small proportion of organized workmen who associated as the American Federation of Labor gave no indication that the labor movement had ever thought of workers in terms of habits and wants; they thought only in terms of wages. Their aspirations summed themselves up in the maxim: "A fair day's work for a fair day's pay." At the same time, partly to create a discrimination which the still fluid social life of America did not sustain, partly to compensate themselves for the defeat of their ambitions, certain groups among the descendants of the makers of the American Revolution, which had organized to reverence its memory, began to work to defeat its ideals. They call themselves "patriotic societies"; they are now nativist and authoritarian and militaristic; they oppose the Bill of Rights, and deny that the philosophy of the Declaration of Independence or the preamble to the Constitution is Americanism.

In the circumstances, the idea of coöperation as the method of the national economy fell into the doldrums. There ceased to be a movement in the sense of the Patrons of Husbandry, the Knights of Labor and Sovereigns of Industry. The labor unions fought their blood-stained, bitter way inch by inch toward union recognition, a union wage-scale, and union standards and conditions. Nevertheless, the great majority of the workers of America remain unorganized to this day, the organized trades find themselves forced by the menace of displacement by the unorganized and by new machines to push toward monopoly of jobs.

In the more thinly populated, western section of the country, especially among the native miners, lumberjacks and agricultural workers, another type of labor-union took form. Although ultimately identified with syndicalism, and proscribed by law in several states as "criminal syndicalism," it was nothing of the sort. It was the primary associative reply of frontiersmen, who felt themselves the equals of their bosses, to the violence of the bosses. They simply gave a name and a reason of their own for doing what their employers had done secretly or in the name of law and order. For industrial warfare had been growing in scope and intensity from the Homestead Strike on; and the masters had hired armed gangs—they were called "Pinkertons," "coal and iron police," etc.—and waged a genuine war upon workers on strike. The workers learned to reply in kind, and the interpretation of their reply was the ideology of the Industrial Workers of the World. Growing up at the turn of the century, this organization attained its height in 1912, when it counted 18,000 members. But it aroused a hatred and bitterness which are now a part of the employer-mentality on the West Coast.

Yet it is the purpose and method of this employer-mentality which the I.W.W. chiefly expressed. It presumed a condition of perpetual competition and warfare. It presumed that the method of this competition is not workmanship, but force and fraud. Although the larger, more orthodox labor organization sharply dissociated itself from this militancy, and at times disputed the jurisdiction of the Industrial Workers, it had perforce to accept its mood. However much labor leaders might struggle like molluscs to hold fast to the privileges and emoluments of their offices, it was impossible to hold fast without moving. And the logical limit of this motion, determined for it by the passions of the captains of industry, was a balance of power of mutually antagonistic economic forces, each seeking the limit of domination, and each kept decent only by the counter pressure of its opponents.

Although such a balance is ever a goal and never an event, it was the unmoved mover of the financial-industrial forces in America, with the greater emphasis on finance than on industry. A country of debtors was more excited by the theory of money and the manipulation of securities than by the developing technologies on which the real wealth of the country depended. The turn of the century saw the country finally launched on the "gold standard," the Sherman Act adopted, "trust-busting" developed as a new bait for votes, and the basic monopolies consolidating their control of the nation, nevertheless. Coöperation persisted among the native population in the form of unrelated survivals, scattered over the land, from the earlier movements. Stores maintained a torpid existence, without fertility and without vision, and were justified when they saved their members a few pennies.

§ 8. NEW EFFORTS TOWARD COÖPERATIVE ORGANIZATION

AROUND the brief panic of 1907, something like a movement reared its head among the California fruit farmers, but it receded before it could even begin to cut a channel for itself in the Californian way of life. Before the local stores could confederate effectively, interest and energy were absorbed by the projected "coöperative" fruit-selling, and this drained all the managerial ability and organizing power that might otherwise have been at the disposal of a true consumer movement. What survived of it was reorganized as the Pacific Coöperative League. A similar record was made by the Right Relationship League. This began as a propaganda society in Minneapolis, Minnesota. Its members appear to have had a definite sense of the primacy of the consumer. They sent missionaries to the smaller communities of Minnesota and other Middle Western states, to organize consumer societies. These had reached two hundred before the movement began to recede. The League published a journal, *Coöperation,* which was to serve as a medium of communication and an educational instrument. But the leaders of the League grew tired. The costs were proportionally heavy, the support small. The successful societies were without vision, penny-pinching; and there were too many being destroyed by the usual onuses of coöperative organization: bad management, lack of loyalty, abandonment of one or another of the Rochdale principles. At one time the leaders had conceived the idea of organizing a chain of coöperative stores, centrally initiated and centrally controlled, but the League was disbanded before the enterprise could be launched. The remnants reorganized as the American Rochdale League and soon merged into the general scene. There were also an American Coöperative Organization Bureau and a Northwestern Coöperative League with slightly different methods.

One man attempted by himself what the Right Relationship League could not do as a group. This was N. O. Nelson. Born in Norway in 1844, and at the age of two brought to the United States in a group of seventy Norwegian colonists, who came to seek fortune and freedom on the American continent, Nelson grew up on a Missouri farm, enlisted as soon as the Civil War broke out, served to the end, and returned to build his fortune as a manufacturer and jobber of plumbing supplies in St. Louis. The bitter industrial conflict of the seventies turned his attention to the problems of peace between employer and employee. This was the starting-point of his interest in economic democracy. Nelson is the first among prosperous American men of business to devote themselves to the cause of consumer coöperation with the single-hearted loyalty of the Christian Socialists of England, giving the larger part of his life and all of his fortune to the coöperative ideal. He was the one American at the Second Congress of the International Coöperative Alliance in 1896, and was elected to its Executive Committee. His first step toward industrial peace in his own plant was to institute profit-sharing. This was followed in 1890 by the establishment of the manufacturing village of Leclare, Illinois, and the organization there of a very successful store. Believing the bayou region around New Orleans, Louisiana, to be one of the most impoverished and backward of areas of the United States, he undertook to establish there, with his own money, a chain of stores, which should ultimately pass into the control of the customers. The enterprise, incorporated as the Nelson Coöperative Association, finally included sixty-one stores, four butcher shops, a bakery, a milk-pasteurizing plant, a coffee house, a condiment factory, and a fifteen-hundred acre farm. The chain store structure was designed to secure the largest economies in management and the conduct of business, and for a time seemed to do so. In 1917, the volume was increasing 15 per cent per store, and the total business came to three million dollars more or less. "Consumers' coöperation," Nelson wrote to Emerson Harris in September, 1917,

> depends entirely on the consumer. There is nothing in the wide world so perfectly open to people to act for themselves and save 15 per cent to 25 per cent on their cost of living.
>
> All the European countries are doing it on an enormous scale, running into millions of members and hundreds of millions of sales, now over a billion in Great Britain alone, and it has grown more during the war than ever before, in Russia more than anywhere.
>
> It is mere indifference and carelessness that has kept it from developing in the United States; we shall come to it, but Americans are adverse to anything so commonplace and commonsense as a coöperative store or a coöperative factory.[5]

But in the organization of the Nelson Coöperative Association, Incorporated, he omitted the one technique which establishes consumer coöperation as consumer coöperation. For some occult reason, Nelson did away with the dividend on purchase, and sold goods nearly at cost or at cost. Customer control consequently could only come about through the investment of share-capital in the company's stock. But the dividend on purchase was the only way in which the farmers and workers, especially of the bayous, could ever secure any capital to invest. He established some sixty stores and they bankrupted him.

[5] *Cf.* Emerson P. Harris, *Coöperation, the Hope of the Consumer,* Appendix I, p. 292.

It is the continental immigrants, in whom the coöperative idea was a part of the habit of life, who established it anew in the new land of their choice; and among them it acquired a fresh and different vigor. Finns, Jews, Belgians, and Scandinavians set up coöperatives in their different enclaves, and on the whole, these coöperatives have flourished.

The Finns, especially, have a record of continuity and growth looking back to the early years of the twentieth century. Their organizations possess all the positive and constructive features which the Rochdale pioneers made standard. They have reached out from foodstuffs to banking, recreation, education, housing and printing. But coöperation was for many of them not a vision of the good life but an incident of industrial warfare. "The coöperative movement among the Finns," S. Nuorteva told the Coöperative League of America in 1917, "is but a side issue. All the societies have been established by socialist locals, and have been used as schools in which the workers might become more efficient, and might be more capable of working industrially and politically in the class struggle."

The same might be said of all the immigrant coöperatives. The religion of their members was not the life more abundant here and now. They either reduced consumers' coöperation to a sort of commissary department of the proletarian producer in his struggle with the capitalist, or they denounced and fought it savagely as inimical to the socialist ideal and method. These, significantly enough, were political rather than economic, and the aspiration to create some sort of socialist political party and to compete in elections for political office was more dynamic and more effective than the dull meticulous routine of conducting coöperative enterprise. The professions were socialist and the practices capitalist, and they remain so, everywhere, including Russia.

§ 9. COÖPERATION IN THE GHETTO: ALBERT SONNICHSEN AND HYMAN COHN

THE APTEST ILLUSTRATION of this situation occurred among the Jews in the metropolitan area of New York City. The Jewish settlement there was a consequence of a series of pogroms which began in imperial Russia about 1882, and were renewed with increasing frequency until the Great War. The articulate minority of this settlement were wage-earners, largely garment-workers, who had been students and intellectuals on the other side, and like all the students and intellectuals of Russia during the period, revolutionists laboring at the risk of their lives and liberties to educate and arouse the masses of their people. Socialism was to them an orthodoxy, more passionately held than Judaism; it repeated the Messianic promises of the older religion with a different vocabulary; it provided a naturalistic explanation of the oppression and injustice which they saw everywhere around them, and of which they themselves were especial victims; it gave them a basis for combating the Jewish inheritance which was the condition of their sufferings and it united them to the rest of mankind from which they had been traditionally cut off; and it provided them with a method and a plan for expressing the righteous anger which filled them. They established a socialist ghetto where they told each other in Yiddish that the workers of the world were members of one another, with one interest and one destiny.

In these things they were not different from other enclaves of liberty-seeking immigrants, establishing a new life in the sweet land of liberty! Nor was their intelligence different. All classes of immigrants met the problem presented them by the American scene with about the same readiness and skill of adjustment. But the Jews of that generation had in addition the skill of dialectic. They were intellectuals. Indeed they were intellectuals first and men of intelligence afterward. They would rather divide principle from practice than modify principle by the test of practice. The teachings of the church were to be kept pure, regardless of the behavior of the churchmen.

This industrially sweated, intellectually febrile and strange community caught and held the fascinated attention of the new generation of native reformers. The Spanish War had been fought and won. Theodore Roosevelt had begun to moralize about trusts in public and to compromise his integrity with their makers in private. A new unrest was developing in the agrarian Middle West, and in the cities good citizens were much exercised over slum conditions and political corruption. Social settlements which had begun as religious missions to the deserving poor, were changing into foci of advanced thought for the missioner-settlers as well as the natives. Churchmen were beginning to translate their own gospel of salvation into the more secular languages of other sects: many felt that religion should be brought down to life, and men like George Herron and organizations like the Interdenominational Christian Socialist Fellowship were forerunners of the present social-worldly trend of the churches. The generous impulse, which later came to its term in the abortive Bull Moose movement, with the slogan "human rights *vs.* property rights," expressed itself among the educated minority in the colleges by the profession of Socialism. "Parlor socialists" became a stick to beat a dog with, and much of the "parlor Socialism" went down to the social settlements of the East Side and took fire from the slum Socialism of that area.

A maverick among those regulars was Albert Sonnichsen, later a secretary of the Coöperative League of the United States of America. California-born son of the Danish consul to San Francisco, he ran away to sea at the age of fifteen, and joined a knowledge of the laborious life to a memory of the cultured one. Somewhere on that early way he learned Marx and Socialism. He had served in the navy during the Spanish-American War, had been captured by the Filipinos and for ten months had been held as prisoner of war. While in the Filipino jail he had started to write and found enough satisfaction in the exercise to try, on his release, to make it a profession. Naturally he drifted east; in New York he secured a post on the New York *Tribune*. From that he quickly passed to a job with McClure Phillips and Company and from that to the position of foreign correspondent for the New York *Evening Post*. He spent two years in the Balkans, the latter part of them in the field with Macedonian revolutionists. When he returned to the United States, something had happened to Sonnichsen. On his way home he had sojourned in England and become awake to Consumers' Coöperation, learned all he could of it, and brought it as a gospel to New York.

With a dozen others, mostly young fellows, recently out of college, he had organized a "Coöperative League of America," scraped together $100, and opened a grocery store somewhere in the Bronx. Among the members were a letter carrier, a policeman, a real estate dealer, a mulatto and a Catholic. They met regularly on Saturday nights to discuss principles and improve practice, but neither discussion nor improvement developed sufficient strength to resist the panic of 1907, and the shop and the League went the ancestral way of so many predecessors. The society disbanded. Sonnichsen, on the strength of his sojourn in the Balkans, got a job with the United States Immigration Commission, investigating Slavic immigrants in the Middle West, and remained there for two years.

Among the members of his League of individuals was one Hyman Cohn. A very Jewish-looking Jew of Russian birth and Talmudical education, Cohn was destined for the rabbinate but chose shoemaking in the belief that the latter offered prospects for a better and a more honest living—reading Maimonides' *Guide for the Perplexed* had aroused doubts. He found, however, that though he would not be a poor rabbi he did not become a good shoemaker. When Cohn reached the United States, in 1895, he was twenty-five years old, educated in the Judaistic way and self-taught in other ways. His efforts to earn a living in America were typical of his time. First he peddled. He peddled potatoes; he peddled vegetables; he peddled fruit; he peddled notions and dry-goods. In Boston he spent fifteen days in jail for peddling without a license. Then he tried buttonhole-making in New York, then peddling old clothes. Some one of his contacts brought him among the Davidsonians. The Davidsonians were a group of Jewish young men who gathered around Professor Thomas Davidson, a learned and eloquent Scotch philosopher with a flair for Plato and a humanistic passion, who took delight in feeding the intellectual eagerness of his young Jews with what he regarded as correct doctrine. For a time he conducted a sort of one-man settlement on the East Side, and has left his mark on many a distinguished American thinker and man-of-letters. Among the Davidsonians Cohn found friends who taught him

English and lent him books and gave him new ideas. He turned from peddling to storekeeping, from storekeeping to teaching Hebrew, and from teaching Hebrew to drumming dry-goods. The same year he joined Sonnichsen's Coöperative League, becoming the forty-eighth member. The year was 1907. Cohn had been a member of the Socialist Party since 1902, and as such had been buying from one or another of the stores of the socialist New York Industrial Coöperative Society. But that coöperation possesses an ideology and technique of its own he had no inkling. These he learned from Sonnichsen and other members of the Society. But it was the reading of Mrs. Webb's *Coöperative Movement in Great Britain* which provided him with a definite doctrine and made him a complete convert.

He could not endure that the Coöperative League should die. He agitated for consumers' coöperation in the socialist ghetto. He preached it in and out of seasons. He called meetings—the University Settlement on Eldridge Street could always provide a room free of charge—at which he was often the only attendant.

It was at one such League meeting that Sonnichsen found him when in 1910, he returned to New York, and had the secretaryship of the League forced on him. The League membership in fact counted more than one hundred persons and it had already been confronted with a split and a new society. Among the members had been Piet Vlag, caterer to the Rand School. He and several others broke away. They started a coöperative wholesale with the idea that it should organize the local societies it was to serve. The initial funds were supplied by a wealthy friend, but the scheme collapsed. What survived of it was Vlag's journal, which he called *The Masses* and published monthly. This organ survived because its voluntary contributors took possession and transformed it into a lively and amusing literary periodical with a "revolutionary" point of view.

But the Coöperative League, with Cohn for its prophet, carried on undisturbed. Cohn's eagerness had earned him the nickname of "Coöperative Cohn." He preached coöperation impartially to comrades and "boorjooi," to his customers for his dress goods and his bosses. It was the boorjooi contact that led to the typical adventure of the coöperative hat store. Persuaded by a hat manufacturer who held a fifth interest in a small factory on the East Side, the League opened a hat store on Delancey Street, with the good-will and blessings of all the comrades and their organs, including the *facile princeps* among them, the *Jewish Daily Forward*. The store was an instant success, so much so that the League decided to take over the factory, and to open two more stores. But the factory could be maintained only if the stores were able to sell all the hats it produced, and they were not. The League then reached out for more coöperative customers. Sonnichsen wrote to groups in New England and the Middle West, without results. The League found itself being ruined by its own overproduction; its factory had to make more hats than its members could use. At the same time, competitors in private business threatened to withdraw their advertising from the socialist press if it continued to advance the League's cause, and a group of rascals attempted to capitalize the good-will developed by the League by soliciting membership in a nationwide coöperative society—"the Rochdale movement adapted to American conditions"—at the price of two dollars per head.

To organize the racket, a prominent labor leader was put in charge of an army of canvassers. Retailers were induced to part with money as earnest for the trade the newly organized consumer groups were to bring them. And the whole scheme was loudly advertised in the socialist press. The advertisers won on both fronts. The *Jewish Daily Forward* denounced the League and its works as a diversion of the socialist movement from its proper objectives, and even told inquirers that neither the organization nor its stores existed. The *Call* continued to publish the profitable advertising of the racketeers. By the time Cohn had secured the endorsement of consumers' coöperation first by the state socialist convention and then by the national convention, it was too late. . . .

The League spread itself on propaganda. It won the attention of the metropolitan press. It aroused the fears of editors of trade journals. But still it struggled to pay its overhead charges. The coming visit to the country of William Maxwell, of the Scottish Wholesale, seemed an occasion that might be employed to advantage. Sonnichsen communicated with him in Glasgow, and a dinner was arranged at Greenwich House under the joint auspices of the Coöperative League and the Settlement. The party was a cross-section of social and intellectual leadership of the Metropolitan area. The English and Scottish story and the personality of the man who told it could not fail to make a profound impression. Dr. James P. Warbasse, upon whose self-devotion the subsequent history of consumers' coöperation as a national movement in the United States so largely turned, was present and according to Sonnichsen a few days later joined the League, but not apparently as an active member. But the menace of bankruptcy through the overproduction of hats was not offset. Debts mounted and fears grew. Cohn and Sonnichsen, together with the generous creditors who cared about the coöperative idea, staved off disaster. The factory and the branch stores were disposed of, and the League dissipated. Sonnichsen withdrew from the movement for the time being. The remnants of the League were salvaged and the remaining members staked the fortunes of their movement on a coöperative restaurant.

§ 10. EVOLUTION OF THE COÖPERATIVE LEAGUE OF THE U.S.A.: JAMES PETER WARBASSE

BUT THE SEED had been sown, consumer coöperation was a known ideal, and with all the uncertainties of social wind and weather, was yielding harvest. There was hardly a section in the metropolitan area which at one time or another did not have a society. In the course of time, a Federation of Jewish Coöperative Societies was set up: mostly restaurants, bakeries, butcher shops, agricultural societies, a grocery or two, a school. Some of the societies were affiliates of the Coöperative League.

For the idea of the League stayed alive; only its organizational form perished. Its first form had been voluntary and unincorporated: its body was the grocery that Sonnichsen tended and its soul the Saturday night meetings of the active members. The second form was based on the remnant that

Hyman Cohn had saved and led into the hat venture. It was incorporated under the laws of the State of New York, and it was suffused with the socialist attitude and point of view. "The Coöperative League has been organized," declared the prospectus, "(1) in the hope of establishing successfully in New York a coöperative society of consumers similar to those societies which have succeeded so well in various European countries; (2) with the ultimate aim of assisting in the development of coöperative production and exchange, by joining or helping other coöperative attempts, so as to build up in the midst of present society the foundation of a new industrial system which will in the end take the place of wage slavery, when the workers in one way or another bring about the abolition of capitalism.

"The League seeks its members among those who are already convinced of the necessity of abolishing capitalism; and its constitution provides that a portion of the benefits shall go not to the individual member but to the cause he is supposed to have at heart."

The first step was to be a coöperative bakery. This, if patronized by the members of certain Jewish organizations, was to save them annually $450,000 on bread and leave another $150,000 "toward the spread of their ideas." All the European methods had been surveyed and canvassed, and the method proposed by the League, its organizers believed, "is better adapted to the conditions of this country and of New York in particular than any which has yet been tried." Share capital was to be five dollars and not interest bearing. One dollar of this payable on admission, could be divided into four weekly instalments. The balance had to be paid up within the year, and out of purchase dividends if the member so desired. The amount paid in was to be returnable on call. In addition there were monthly dues of five cents. The bread was to be sold in the general market, at the market price. The "surplus"—the word profit does not occur—was to be divided annually as follows: 75 per cent for distribution among the consumers as purchase dividends; 5 per cent for an educational fund; 20 per cent to public causes consistent with the purposes of the League, designated by the consumers: in addition each member was to be bound to the League with "sickness and accident benefit" which would insure him, when sick or disabled, a three-months' supply of bread without cost, in the same amounts as he had been buying.

We have already seen what happened to this form of the League. It could not survive its leaders' enthusiasm and logic. Over-extended, in hats, it died during a period of general prosperity, to come alive in a new form during the depression of 1914–15. This depression was the first effect of the World War on the national economy. The upshot of Theodore Roosevelt's bull-moosing about human rights as against property rights had been victory for the "new freedom" and the election of Woodrow Wilson to the presidency. The "new freedom" was with difficulty getting itself enacted in fiscal and corporation law when the murder of Sarajevo broke up the socio-economic equilibrium of Europe and divided her peoples into two embattled camps. The United States entered the doldrums of strict neutrality. "War babies" begotten of European need were still *in ovo*, war-prosperity was still to come; but the economic activity of peace times had already gone. The transition from the prosperity of peace to the prosperity of war took about eighteen months and these eighteen months were a time of depression. It was in this period that the present Coöperative League of the United States was organized.

The moving spirit this time was James Peter Warbasse, president of this third League since its inception. An American of pre-Revolutionary stock, with an independent fortune, by profession a surgeon who had won distinction both as a technician and a writer, Dr. Warbasse's first known contact with the coöperative movement occurred in his student days in Germany and was renewed at a Greenwich House dinner to William Maxwell. He was then forty-six years old. The practice of his profession had not failed to point out for him the misery which is the lot of the average person in our modern economy, and he had concerned himself with the movements of philanthropy and reform which came and went among the comfortable but sensitive and humanitarian intellectuals of the metropolitan area. Socialism and other radical cults had intrigued him, but he found no meat in them. Temperamentally, as well as by professional training and experience, he was disposed to require for the correction of social evil a method more immediate and direct than those of Socialism and the other cults looking toward a millennium too long postponed, and one more continuous and fundamental than the makeshifts and stratagems of philanthropy and social reform.

In consumers' coöperation he recognized what he had been seeking. He came to see it as a method of human association by which men could satisfy every need, procure every good and every service more quickly, more cheaply, more excellently and more harmoniously, than by any other method. Warbasse believes that the coöperative technique can replace that of the profit corporation, and the state itself. His contacts with the movement in New York, its confused socialist-coöperative mentality, its tendency toward rigid dialectic and loose management, its disposition to seek variations and shortcuts instead of hewing straight to the Rochdale line, convinced him of the need of a central clearing-house for the movement whose function should be educational and advisory and whose field should be nothing less than the whole nation. Meeting after meeting was held at his home in Brooklyn and the form and function of a national organization thoroughly discussed. Finally, in 1916, the Coöperative League of the United States was launched, with Warbasse as its first and only president, Scott Perky its first secretary and Peter Hamilton its first treasurer. The *Coöperative Consumer,* founded in 1914 by Albert Sonnichsen, was taken over and he continued to edit it. Membership in the League was open to individuals and societies. A dozen societies, including some from New England and Pennsylvania, were represented. There were many individual enthusiasts. It was agreed that the membership fee should be no more than one dollar. Space for an office and library was taken at 70 Fifth Avenue, and the League set to work to federate and unify and serve the hundreds of coöperative organizations scattered throughout the country. The official organ was circulated; pamphlets, model by-laws, audit systems and the like, were printed in thousands, news releases were prepared, inquiries answered, advice given, and all the innumerable demands met that come to an educational and propaganda organization.

From the first, the income from membership, pitiably inadequate to meet the small wage bill and the cost of printing, was supplemented by contributions from Dr. Warbasse. In effect, he financed the work of the League. He gave himself without stint to the propagation of the coöperative idea, travelling, lecturing, writing, corresponding, expounding always the orthodox Rochdale method, and developing its implications. He familiarized himself with the status and character of the coöperative movement in every state in the Union, and eventually in every country in Europe. In 1919, he gave up his practice, to devote himself entirely to the movement, and has remained its head and front since. Through the League which he headed, local societies and regional federations began to make contacts with one another; the Rochdale method began to stand out clear from foreign entanglements; a unification of the coöperative organizational consciousness began. Shortly before the end of the World War, when the League held its first convention in Springfield, Illinois, it had listed and classified upward of three thousand coöperative societies scattered over the continent.

§ 11. THE COÖPERATIVE MOVEMENT DURING THE WORLD WAR: TAIL TO THE TRADES-UNION KITE

WAR CONDITIONS favored the movement. "War babies" were being littered all over the country. The cost of living began to mount; the diversion of production to military ends caused shortages in all consumer commodities from food and clothing to housing.[6] Wages followed slowly, and not without many

[6] About this time Hyman Cohn, active, voluble and eloquent as ever, developed his concept of the coöperation of the City Block. Some years earlier he had organized a Tenants' League—"a mutual benefit association of the people who have to pay rent." The annual dues were one dollar, payable in monthly instalments of ten cents. The League undertook volunteer sanitary inspection and control, a better housing agitation, legal and financial aid to members in danger of being dispossessed and planned to go into coöperative housing. The League got action from city departments where other means had failed and secured a considerable

often bitter strikes and threats of strikes, and at first far behind prices. The office of the League was flooded with inquiries from all sections of the population—government employees, trade-unionists, college professors, farmers, even politicians.

Among certain sections of the trades-union movement—conspicuously among miners with a Welsh and English tradition and leadership—a vestigial idea of coöperation had endured from the beginning. The mining industry in the United States was in a condition of competitive disorganization and inhumanity not unlike that of England. Intellectually and emotionally the miners were in a state of unrest, and the leadership, drawn largely from English stock, was inclined to define the trades-union program in terms more comprehensive and thorough than "a fair day's pay for a fair day's work." John H. Walker, at one time or another president of a district of the

following. Its success led to a plan of the coöperative reorganization of the whole municipal economy in block units. With Sonnichsen's aid, he wrote the plan out and it duly appeared, under the title of *Coöperation in the City Block,* as a publication of the Coöperative League, price two cents. The plan was to organize for coöperation as Tammany organized for politics. Each block was to form a society, the members of which were to pay dues of a dollar a year. The society was to elect a captain, who was to be made a special officer of the Board of Health and the tenement house department. The captain was to appoint two assistants. Their immediate task would be to enforce sanitary and housing laws. The block societies would combine into a Home League which charged itself with housing of its members, who would receive a "purchase-dividend" in proportion to the rentals they paid. The League would raise capital in the form of shares taken in a minimum amount of three hundred dollars by each member, paid for by an initial cash investment of fifty dollars and the balance by purchase dividends. The League would establish a Credit Union for each block to serve as the fiscal agent of its enterprises. After the shares capital had been paid in, rent-dividends were to be held to pay for repairs, meet arrears, build roof-gardens and sun-parlors, establish block stores and restaurants, hire nurses and teachers for the children, etc., etc. Cohn, as usual, got a following for this plan and struggled passionately to see it through, and as usual, failed. He added the words "consumerize" and "consumerization" to English as she is spoke in the United States. He invented a slogan: "Consumerization converts rent payers into home owners." His idea of the Block Unit was taken up by others in other places in connection with family welfare work and certain promotional activities. It is the most promising idea for urban coöperative organization thus far advanced, and sooner or later some organizing soul who is hard-boiled and knows the ropes will put it successfully to work.

United Mine Workers of America, and president of the Illinois State Federation of Labor, had been in and out of the Socialist Party from before 1900. To him and his rival and collaborator, Duncan McDonald, consumers' coöperation meant a worker-commissary in industrial conflict as well as a defense against high prices.

In the spring of 1915, they called a convention in Springfield, Illinois, and formed the Coöperative Society of Illinois. The following year, the name was changed to the Central States Coöperative Association. Walker was president from the first, and from 1917, Duncan McDonald was secretary-treasurer. The association was treated by its leaders as an instrument of the trades-union movement and the American Federation of Labor was induced to endorse it in 1917 on this ground. With money supplied by labor unions two wholesale societies and a chain of seventy groceries were opened. It was Walker's idea, like N. O. Nelson's, that in the United States the coöperative movement would grow better from a center outward. He wanted a single unified national wholesale system which should proceed to organize locals as a national trades-union organizes locals. He called this notion "the American plan" and in spite of the strongest protest from the League, persisted in developing it. The Rochdale plan was conspicuous by its absence. The Central States Coöperative Wholesale Society was organized to serve the Central States Coöperative Association which hoped to make it the nucleus of a national wholesale.

For a time, the enterprise prospered, in spite of the bitter quarrels at the yearly coöperative conventions caused by the rivalry between McDonald and Walker. War prosperity had begun to seep down to the rank and file of Americans, and if war millionaires multiplied *in excelsis* the standard of living of the whole nation also rose not inconspicuously. Employers were heard to complain that employees were spending their high wages on silk shirts instead of materials proper to their station in life. As the War came to its close and Hun hysteria gave way to the Bolshevist phobia liberals and radicals turned with one mind to the problem of making effective the Wilsonian ideals by which "the war to end all wars" and to "make the world safe for democracy" was rationalized and justified. "Reconstruction" flowed in every variety from every variety of tongue and pen.

And one variety of reconstruction was consumers' coöperation. The mentality of the time favored Walker's "American Plan." Under the leadership of Dalton T. Clarke, a Pittsburgh lawyer who became convinced of coöperation and gave up his law practice to advance its cause, the miner societies in that area had been confederated into another association, as the Tri-State Coöperative Society. This also set up chain stores in communities where no coöperative existed and sent missionaries and organizers into unorganized communities. Soon an attempt was made to bring the two groups, the Central States Association and the Tri-State Society, together in line with Walker's "American Plan." In 1919, the Illinois State Federation of Labor invited all coöperative societies to a convention which brought together Dalton Clarke, Duncan McDonald and John H. Walker. The convention created the National Consumers' Coöperative Association, with Dalton Clarke as president and Duncan McDonald as secretary. The Association was to undertake the creation of a nation-wide system of stores on the Rochdale plan. Although the antagonism between Walker and McDonald broke up the meeting in a row, and the hoped-for consolidation was not effected, wholesales and stores were established and a membership drive was undertaken which drew in large numbers of trades-union members. The organization was financed by the trades-unions—mostly miners—from their reserve funds. The National Association operated for a year or two. Its overhead, however, absorbed its share capital; fire in the wholesale house destroyed a large proportion of the stock; the post-war depression caused a slump in prices which forced sales below cost, and the endeavor to save the remnant by altering the management was not successful. The association declined. So likewise did that of its bitter enemy, John Walker, and for the same reasons.

So the contemporary trades-union phase of coöperative interest ran its course. The officers and staff of the Coöperative League of the United States stood by, helping as they could with information and advice written and personal, pointing to the record elsewhere, stressing the time-tested, fundamental character of the Rochdale method, but to no avail. Among the trades-union coöperators what was primary was not the consumer, but the organized rank-and-file producer. The lower prices of the coöperative store were to be merely accessory to the higher wages of the competitive trades-unionists. Their mentality was still as pecuniary and capitalist as that of their employers. They were still wage-minded, not life-minded.

CHAPTER X

THE CONSUMER IN AMERICA: III, COÖPERATION IN THE DEPRESSION

§ 1. "NORMALCY" OR FAREWELL THRIFT, WELCOME DEBT!

MEANWHILE, the War to end all wars and to make the world safe for democracy had been won and the peace to end all peace and to endanger democracy throughout the world had been dictated. Woodrow Wilson had, like Matthew Arnold's Shelley, intoned his long soliloquy, flashed his luminous wings in the void, and was to go down before the votes of his countrymen, to the defeat of all his purposes. All the war-time regulations were to be repealed save the Espionage Act. The moguls of the Republican Party, considering programs and slogans, and observing the interest of the powerful trades-unionists in consumer coöperation, meditated on making it a plank in the party platform. They decided, however, that "normalcy" was a safer election slogan. Harding was elected. The Ohio gang was chosen to administer the affairs of the nation. The new freedom and the new safety were bartered for "normalcy." Everything was to be as it had been in the balmy days of big business before Wilson and before the War. The planned economy such as it was, of war time, was abandoned. Wilson himself held that it should be let go, without taking thought or considering consequences.

But the structures and methods which the war economy had built up were not so easily to be torn down. The new economic relationships of the United States to the world could not be altered. The world's old debtor had become the world's new creditor, and this could not fail to govern foreign policy, with or without isolation. "Normalcy" did not mean the actual abandonment of the essential war-time economic structures; it meant only the abandonment of government regulation, government supervision and government control. It meant that the organized employer would have a free hand in a ruthless and bloody warfare against the organization of the employee. It meant that agreements would be made and prices fixed without fear of interference or punishment from government. It meant that the nation's resources—like its oil reserves—would, with the paid help of faithless cabinet officers, be quietly pirated by predatory business; while, for a smoke-screen, the alien was officially denounced and attacked, and the agents of government, sworn to defend it, violated the Bill the Rights in every practicable and impracticable way.

The contraction, the disorganization, the industrial warfare and the intolerance which constituted "normalcy" became the inevitable post-war depression. Especially was this a farmer's depression, for "normalcy" in the agriculture of the nation could mean nothing else than a fall in farm values, a reduction of acreage, a diminution in the number of farmers. The industrialization of agriculture had been doing these things before the war; war needs arrested the process and gave to farmers a passing and factitious prosperity which collapsed with peace. Businessmen formed "open price associations" which fixed prices on consumer goods while wages were thrust down. The farmers turned to government with their traditional demands; again there was talk of third parties and attempts to organize them. The Harding administration passed the problem on to the Federal Trade Commission and in short order the Federal Trade Commission returned with findings recommending among other things trust-busting and fostering coöperatives. Harding threw a sop to farmers and laborers with pronouncements in favor of coöperatives. . . .

It was a short depression. Even while it lasted, the national standard of living remained considerably above a pre-war level. Harding died and Coolidge succeeded him in a *laissez-faire* administration which observed the amenities but otherwise deferred reverently to the bankers and industrialists. There was an upswing in the automotive industry which lifted the whole confused network of the nation's business. Real wages continued to rise. "The requirements of existence," Coolidge told Congress in his report on the state of the country, in December, 1928, "have passed beyond the standard of necessity into the region of luxury. Enlarging production is consumed by an increasing demand at home and an expanding commerce abroad. The country can regard the present with satisfaction and anticipate the future with optimism." The country, but not the farmer. By comparison the farmers did not prosper. Their burden of debt grew greater, not less. Invention, industry, special boards to serve farmers financially, morally and socially, brought amenities to country life but no independence to the ordinary farmer. Chiefly, the rich owners of the great industrialized farms benefited.

Nor was this Coolidge prosperity a healthy thing in the cities. The "enlarging production" was not consumed by an "increasing demand" which it naturally found, but by an pseudo-increasing demand which it artificially made. Foreign trade consisted in lending Europeans American money so that they could import and pay for American goods while higher and higher tariffs shut out foreign goods. The home market was developed similarly, as a debtor's market. Farmers had to go on borrowing as the prices of farm products fell. Thrift, which masters had always held up to servants as the great virtue, fell into contempt. Spending was now the great virtue. Wage-earners were urged to house, clothe, feed, educate and transport themselves on credit. Every necessity and even more, every luxury, was offered on instalments—real estate, cars, pianos, sewing machines, phonographs, radios, washing-machines, mechanical ice-boxes, garages, houses. Americans were urged to acquire, to use, houses and instruments, automobiles and books, stocks and bonds. Legal ownership of the goods remained in the seller until the last payment was made; the seller had the right to take possession of them at the first failure to pay.

Instalment buying raised the American standard of living upon a foundation of quicksand. If it expanded the American's field of consummative enjoyment, it made this enjoyment conditional upon a peonage of debt. It caused the debtor to be more anxious than ever regarding his economic security, the safety of his job, the stability of his status in his community—a status defined by the number and variety of his consummatory possessions. To mitigate, to repress this feeling of insecurity, he became orgiastically reckless. Since any day might be the last of his enjoyment of his unowned possessions, why not enjoy as many as possible so long as possible? Today we live, tomorrow we die! So to hell with everything. To this mood the riches and delights of prohibition drinking brought their own strengthening. . . .

§ 2. AFTERMATH I: THE DEPENDENT FARMER TAKES TO COÖPERATION

INSTALMENT SELLING is necessarily speculative. It increases the usual price to the market as a sum the seller can exact for his additional risk. As it was worked, it was self-defeating, for the high-pressure salesmanship undermined the buyer's basic feeling of security regarding the future on which its returns depended. It meant pyramiding indebtedness without proportional increase of income. This pyramiding was to some degree forced on the producer by his own indebtedness. The debt charges were so many and so varied, that only by working at top speed and producing the utmost and selling it at the highest price could such components of the industrial economy as, for example, General Motors, carry on. So the producers were forced to create their markets among already saturated customers. The dealer organizations became still more important and larger than the productive establishments. Publicity men and advertising agents became to them prophets and wizards who would save them from falling into the abyss on whose verge they actually felt themselves to be. The publicity men also enriched American English with a new word. The word is "consumptionism." Consumptionism is the name for all the ways which producers employ to get consumers to take their surplus product off their hands. Hyman Cohn's "consumerization" is its exact opposite.

Herbert Hoover was elected to the presidency when the wave of consumptionism was near its apex. At the beginning of his administration, the United States was the most richly endowed and prosperous country in the world. It had half the world's iron and steel, two-fifths of its coal, seven-tenths of its mineral oil, one-third of its water-power, endless fertile lands with surpluses of corn and wheat and cotton and lumber, a great, free public school system and a busy and happy population all in debt. By the end of 1929, the country's total interest-bearing debt was more than 154 billions of dollars and the interest-charges were nine billions. From 1927 on, canny economists were predicting collapse, and canny captains of finance who had become the actual masters of the nation's economic establishment found themselves forced into the bull-market boom of 1929 with which Coolidge prosperity crashed to its climacteric.

A point came when credit could be neither had nor taken. At that point the whole precarious structure caved in. The permanent victory over poverty fell down and went boom! People couldn't believe it. Instead of writing off losses, they attempted to borrow; instead of trimming overhead and wages to the rising gale of depression, they labored desperately at face-saving. The Hoover administration's Farm Board tried to peg farm prices above the world market by buying up 500 millions in cotton and wheat; its Reconstruction Finance Corporation pumped 2¼ billions into banks instead of businesses, farmers and wage-earners and so made sure that the banking crisis which followed would follow. Prices fell; rents fell; but wages fell faster. Municipalities, railroads, other corporations found themselves unable to meet their obligations. More and more workers went from the shops upon the streets or wandered country roads, unemployed. It cost the farmers more to produce their stuffs than they could receive for it. It became cheaper to burn corn for fuel than to sell it for food, no matter how many millions might be starving for lack of it.

Sharp clashes occurred, from New Jersey to California, between industrialized farmers and the agricultural laborers they seasonally employed. The degradation of the "hired man" into the agricultural proletarian had come with the chemical and mechanical transformation of agriculture and the corresponding development of agricultural capitalism. Like the degradation of hired labor in industry it was concurrent with the rise of the general standard of living and the economic stress on consumption throughout the nation and the formation of agricultural marketing associations and the like. The agricultural laborer is a recent and new vocational category in the national economy. There are today upward of three millions of him, and they work under the worst conditions and at the lowest wages of any vocational group in the country. They work beet fields, or the citrus plantations, the cotton and tobacco fields, they work in canneries and fruit packing houses. The occupation is seasonal and intermittent, extremely hard, and altogether joyless. Their employers are the harshest and least moralized of all American employers, and the law provides the employees less protection than any other craft. They are the constant victims of vigilantes and hired gangsters. Although more than two hundred organizations are open to them, which through collective action might improve their lot, few are affiliated, and much of the vigilante terrorism of 1934–35 had for its motive to inhibit organization. The civil war between the employing farmer and the rural worker was and remains a projection of the farmers' general situation. The employer's violence is here an index of his insecurity.

At best able to meet their debts with difficulty, the farmers now failed to meet them at all, and one country bank after another had to shut down, more than five thousand between 1930 and 1932 alone. Then came the Farmers' Holiday and similar movements. And there came an intensification of the movement toward coöperative organization.

Coöperation had had the blessing and endorsement of government departments since the end of the War. It had figured more and more largely in the minds of the farmers as the irresistible pressure of industrialization and finance grew stronger and spread over more territory. As we have seen already, marketing and the purchase of producer goods had become an established associative practice, but purchase tended to extend from producers' raw materials to consumer-goods in spite of unhappy experience with coöperative stores during the post-war depression. So far as farmers were concerned, the depression had not stopped. As the agricultural arts kept improving, the production of cotton and wheat and tobacco and pigs and cattle kept increasing, and the farmers' market kept shrinking. It shrank, for one thing, because his foreign market was largely cut off when the United States became the world's creditor; a creditor country is compelled to import; a creditor country requires free trade, as the English learned early in the nineteenth century. It shrank, for another, because of the resumed production among his former customers.

At the same time the farmers' home market was saturated. In spite of apple weeks and orange weeks and milk weeks and what weeks, in spite of fancy packaging and the most fanciful advertising, very little of the industrial worker's increase in wages went for foodstuffs. At the turn of the century the average wage-worker was paying half his wages for food—the Chinese peasant is still paying four-fifths—but in 1930, food cost the wage-earner only one-third of his wages, housing cost him about one-seventh and clothes one-tenth. The balance was presumably available for health, education, travel, entertainment and the amenities. This, however, refers only to the *average* wage-earner who does not exist.

With the actual wage-earner the case was different. As a matter of fact, he could very well have used up the entire amount of the farmer's surplus, and like Oliver Twist asked for more. In 1929, at the very height of prosperity, twelve million American families were living on a subsistence diet, eight million had only the essentials, five millions more had only a little leeway, and only two million were really well-fed. Of the houses they lived in nearly half were slums, and a large proportion of them without running water, plumbing or central heat. At that, they were housed better than the farmer—for of ten farm houses only one had a bath, one and a half had running water or electric light, three and a quarter had telephones. As for medical and dental care—only 10 per cent of the population ever had a physical examination, 20 per cent ever could see a dentist and 40 per cent could ever afford a doctor. At the very least two million were unemployed. Obviously, even in prosperity the average American's margin for health, education, travel, entertainment and the amenities was negligible. He needed in 1929, and needs even more now, much of the farmer's so-called surplus or overproduction.

But between him and the farmer there stand some two hundred thousand corporations—processors who take control of the milk, the meat, the grain, the cotton, the wool, the silk, the lumber which the farmer produces, and the metals and coal which the miner digs. They process, that is, they prepare for sale and perhaps consumption not as much as the people need and can use, but only so much as they can sell for a price, and they it is who fix the price they pay to the farmer and the price they take from the worker. As the annual income of twenty million American families was then under $2,500, it is clear why so many Americans lived only at subsistence.

The farmers' destruction of crops, uprooting of fruit trees—600,000 peach trees were uprooted in California in 1931—was a natural if not an intelligent reaction to this situation. The creation of the farmers' marketing coöperatives was a more intelligent consequence, and the step from marketing to purchasing was logically next.

Already buying fruit seed, feed, fertilizer coöperatively, the displacement of horses by motor vehicles compelled within the decade the organization of coöperatives specializing in the purchase of petroleum products and motor accessories for farm use. There are now upward of six hundred such coöperatives, federated into ten or a dozen wholesales, and they are multiplying. They are organized on Rochdale principles, and associated into a number of wholesales, such as the Midland Oil Company, and the Consumer Coöperative Association, formerly the Union Oil Company, Coöperative. These societies have passed automatically from purchase to manufacture, from manufacture to general distribution through coöperative filling stations; the Consumer Coöperative Association has recently voted to establish a grocery department. Their average saving to the members on petroleum products has been during the past five years fifteen cents on every dollar.

Through these specialized coöperatives, particularly, coöperative purchasing has justified itself to the American farmer. At the least, he has found in it a mode of defensive association and procedure, such as the trades-union is to the wage-earner, and on the whole, a more successful one. In the market, it brings him the advantages of collective bargaining over his produce, as the trades-union brings it to the wage-earner over his labor. In field and orchard, in hen yard and cow shed and barn, it means better quality of fertilizer and seed and feed, of fuel and oil and sprays, of paints and twine, at a lower cost in money, in time, and in sheer human effort. These profits, these savings, come to him as the direct result of working together in such a way that the labor of all is to the gain of each. It is still only this gain that the average farmer sees in coöperation. To his mind, during the decade preceding the great depression, the coöperative process did not look toward an economy of plenty so much as a counter-manipulation of scarcity in a competitive world, and all his education by government agencies and agricultural economists have confirmed this frame of mind. As seller he coöperated to get higher prices; as buyer to get lower costs. Through coöperation he succeeded. But his relative position in the national economy did not improve.

§ 3. AFTERMATH II: NEW FORMS, NEW IDEAS, NEW GROUPINGS

IN HIS LONG SLIDE down the incline of depression, the farmer developed a number of variants from the standard consumer form. One of the more interesting of these—especially from the point of view of the farmer or worker without money—is the Eastern States Farmers' Exchange. The members of the

Exchange are not societies but individual farmers. They invest no capital and they pay no dues. A farmer becomes a member by securing something he needs through the Exchange. He continues to be counted as such through two calendar years dating from his latest purchase. All purchases are for cash, and delivery is made direct to the purchaser. There are now some 50,000 members who were spending, in 1935, upward of $12,000,000 through the Exchange. The goods are all producers' goods—feed, seed, fertilizer. The Exchange is governed by a Board of Directors of whom one-third are elected at each annual meeting, in a ratio commensurable with the distribution of the members through the Eastern States. The Board designates an Executive Committee from among its members, to manage the business of the Exchange. The paid staff is in the position of a civil service: none is elected to the directorate or may have any interest in the concerns with which the Exchange deals.

The organization was founded in 1918, in Springfield, Massachusetts, where coöperation has been a hardy perennial from the first, by a body of public-spirited citizens from all walks of life. The initial capital was borrowed on a note endorsed by three businessmen, and has been paid off. In its seventeen years' operation under Rochdale rules, it has not only paid large purchase dividends, but accumulated a capital reserve of more than $1,500,000, in accord with a provision in the constitution that one-third of the savings must be retained as reserve for future growth. In Minneapolis, Minnesota, the Midland Coöperative Wholesale has been similarly financed by purchase savings: but this society issues share capital to the members of the retail societies composing it.

With the farmer's slide down the incline of depression came not only new coöperative forms, but the realization of the primacy of the consumer. As against the "strictly business" point of view of so many farmers' marketing and purchasing coöperatives, there appeared here and there, particularly in the Middle West, a recognition of the continuity of the consumer economy with the democratic aspiration of American life. By 1930, this recognition came to be explicitly expressed as a program. Thus the Consumer Coöperative Association, one of the most successful and prosperous of the Oil Coöperatives among whose customers are now European coöperatives, printed at the masthead of its monthly journal, *Coöperative Consumer,* the following:

Our Program

We seek a better life for the common people, of farm and city, through Coöperation. We stand for:

1. The organizing of all consumers into local Rochdale Coöperatives for joint purchasing of their needs and supplies; and the organizing of all farm producers into Producers' Coöperatives with the aim of eventual direct marketing through Consumers' Coöperatives, eliminating all profit-seeking and speculation.

2. The organizing of all local Consumers' Coöperatives into regional Wholesale Coöperatives for wholesale purchasing and manufacture.

3. The organizing of all regional Wholesale Coöperatives into National Coöperatives, Incorporated, for production, distribution and international coöperative trade.

4. The union of all consumers *against* exploitation, ignorance, political oppression and enforced poverty; *for* universal plenty, freedom, democracy and education.

The appearance of associative variants and the growth of the consumer consciousness were accented by the formation of regional federations—not so much wholesales, which are perennials, as regional leagues, affiliated with the Coöperative League of the United States. There are today four such leagues, representing the Central, Eastern, Northern States, and California. The great majority of their membership are farmers. Among the organized wage-earners, miners, railroad men, and until recently, textile operatives, have prevailed—that is, employees of nationally depressed industries. Local nuclei of garment workers—associated mostly with the Amalgamated Clothing Workers of America—and national-cultural enclaves such as the Finns and the Jews, present the next order of strength. The consumers' coöperative movement of the United States made its way from the World War into the world depression with a surer step, a higher morale and a clearer realization of its own meaning and method than ever in its history before, though this is not saying a great deal.

But it was trying the coöperative method on every kind of consumer interest, from edibles to education, from rents to recreation—and on the whole successfully at last.

With the advance of the depression, moreover, came the usual crop of new organizations, and a great upswing of interest and discussion. Organization was more noticeable among the white-collar salaried vocational groups than among organized working-men; the philosophy of this organization was the trades-union philosophy brought to its logical conclusion. New societies were formed in many regions, and in New York the new philosophy of organization is now favored among teachers, clergymen, engineers and college students. This philosophy, as we have seen, accepts the principles of capitalist-socialist economics. It regards competition as the rule of trade, and combination as a purely competitive instrument. The trades-union is simply a pressure group organized for "control at the point of production." But its members confront not only employers who pay wages. They also confront producers and middlemen who exact prices. As they combine to maintain wages, so according to the new philosophy they should combine to lower prices. Organization on traditional coöperative lines, the argument continues, has proved unsuccessful in the United States. Indeed, it is both undesirable and dangerous, for it involves setting up a store, accumulating and managing property, and thus falling victim to all the fears and timidities which go with ownership. Where it does succeed, it becomes a visionless penny-pinching. All that the worker needs to do to defend himself as consumer, is to organize on the same principles and use the same methods he does as producer.[1] He should aim at collective bargaining for goods and services, he should be ready to call consumer strikes, to picket, to boycott, in order to enforce fair prices, good quality, and union wages and conditions of labor among the merchants and manufacturers with whom he deals. In short, he should

[1] "Consumers cannot take over the business of the country. And why should they? Let the owners bear the onus of running the business, but let the consumers organize and squeeze them from one side and labor from the other. Then labor and the consumers do not bear the responsibility for the defects in the business system, but neither are they exploited." —E. J. Lever.

be ready, through organization as consumer, to wage the same industrial warfare he wages as trades-unionist. If the labor movement has been backward in the United States, if it has lost more strikes than it has won, it is because it has neglected to build up its commissary department simultaneously with its combative organization. It has been deluded by the idea that coöperative purchasing must be a matter of stores, when it need be nothing more than purchasing organized on trades-union principles. The Rochdale rules work as readily in purchasing so directed as in stores.

In this gospel extremes meet to contrary ends. Mr. Tugwell calls for the organization of consumers as a pressure group in order to establish a balance between wage-earners, employers and the general public. The gospel here summarized is especially concerned that organized labor shall organize its consumer interest—first, to protect its flank; second, to become habituated in the arts of purchase according to standard specifications checked by laboratory tests, so that it may, without the limitations and burdens of ownership, educate itself in the principles and methods of consumer coöperation, thus making itself ready for ownership. At present the consumer interest is not ready; and so, while a permanent coöperative structure finally involves ownership, ownership now is only a handicap.

The propounder of this philosophy of consumer organization also undertook to implement it. His name is Edward J. Lever. A gaunt, restless, eloquent, thin man in the early forties, Lever is of the older American stock. He grew up on a farm in Pennsylvania, developed a taste for machinery and became a machinist, and thence a trades-unionist with a vision of the industrial scene and the working-man's problem rare indeed in the present generation of native leaders of organized labor. A member, and for a period an organizer of the International Association of Machinists—a constituent of the American Federation of Labor—his experience there convinced him of the necessity of a specially directed professional and cultural education for workers planning a career in the trades-union movement. He founded and for a time directed, the Philadelphia Labor College, and passed from that to the faculty of Brookwood Labor College. He participated in the organization of the Brotherhood of Utility Workers, and for some time served Consumers' Research as vice-president. There he found that giving consumers advice without making sure that it will be followed couldn't do much for consumers. But he could not persuade his colleagues to this view. Accordingly, he called together a group of friends and acquaintances, among them a lawyer, a public accountant, an engineer, a labor leader, a professional economist, and proposed the formation of a consumer society which should combine the trades-union pattern with the technics of a research institution. During a year, frequent meetings were held, and the proposal discussed pro and con.

Finally, in November, 1932, the association was organized under the coöperative law of the State of New York as Coöperative Distributors, Incorporated, and on January 25, 1933, the organization was publicly launched. The capital was to be $20,000. The organizing costs were contributed mostly by Lever, and the labor similarly given without return by the founders and their friends. Shares were set at five dollars. Membership was both individual and group—any existing non-profit organization is eligible; while the central body organizes consumers' clubs *ad hoc*. "Bankers, business proprietors, distributors and their executive officers whose products and services are sold to the ultimate consumer, persons holding elective political office . . . or professional politicians" are ruled out from membership. The members are recruited mostly among the white-collar and professional groups; working-men are not numerous. Individuals must take at least one share, groups, two. They receive a fixed dividend according to law. Members of local consumers' clubs pay yearly dues of two dollars. Of this one dollar goes to the central body and is credited to share capital for the club. The board of directors reported to the third annual meeting a membership of thirty-two coöperative and other non-profit organizations and forty-five clubs with a local membership of over 1,200 and 1,024 individual members belonging directly to the parent organization. The annual meetings elect six of a board of directors of nine members, three for two years and three for one. This board chooses from its own body a president, a vice-president, a secretary-treasurer and a manager. The organization acts as its members' middleman for goods and services of every sort. It purports to work entirely according to Rochdale rules, but its price-policy is varied according to the bargaining situation, and for many commodities it has been able to set a price considerably below the market. It maintains a laboratory which makes tests on request for both the organization and the members; it manufactures certain commodities, mostly cosmetics, it publishes a monthly—*The Consumer Defender,* with a "technical" section listing goods and prices; it concentrates on organization and education, and maintains a labor committee which is supposed to make sure that concerns selling to Coöperative Distributors maintain union standards and conditions. For the Consumer Clubs it undertakes to make collective bargaining arrangements for coal, gas, oil, milk, laundry, and the like. It provides them with a "model Collective Bargaining Agreement." Coöperative Distributors, Incorporated, is a member of the Coöperative League of the United States. To date its practice is still far from its theory; and the likelihood that the two may coincide is remote. . .

A similar pressure group, but without the militancy or the prepossessions in favor of the producer-as-such, is the National Coöperative Association of Washington, D. C. Its six thousand members are government clerks and former members of the military service, for whom it secures better service and lower rates for milk, gas, laundry work, and insurance. It maintains a store and a medical clinic.

§ 4. AFTERMATH III: THE NEW DEAL AND THE EXPLOITATION OF THE CONSUMER

MEANWHILE, the national economy had crashed. Early in 1929, the American spirit rode high with its stocks and bonds. Although the unemployed numbered more than 2,000,000, the confidence was greater than ever in the "job for every man" and the final triumph over poverty as Mr. Hoover had promised when he accepted the nomination to succeed Calvin Coolidge. The policy later to be described as "rugged individualism" seemed to vindicate itself by better than good works. Late in 1929, collapse, with the swift transformation of rugged individualism into ragged individualism, and the consequent electoral exchange of this individualism for "the new deal" on behalf of the "forgotten man"! Launched when the country was in a state of jitters, with thirteen to seventeen million disemployed, the still-employed sweated, the banks failing one after another, the shops idle, the factories shutting down, the "new deal" created more than a score of financial, industrial, agricultural and relief agencies, employing about 150,000 people, in the attempt, in its turn to provide "a job for every man" and bring that "final triumph over poverty." It devalued and reflated the dollar. It entered into a "new partnership" with business; it organized all the nation's industries under some six hundred "codes of fair competition," as in 1921 some had organized themselves in "open price associations," but imposing publicity and governmental control. It provided "a new charter" for labor by requiring, first under Section 7A of the late N.R.A., that employees must be organized as they choose if at all, that they shall receive not less than a certain minimum wage and work no more than certain maximum hours, and by setting up a machinery for the handling of labor disputes. It promoted laws to regulate and supervise banks, stock-exchanges and other financial enterprises. It advanced the government regulation of railroads and public-utilities; it undertook to ease the burden of debt on the farmer and subsidized him to reduce crops of all sorts. It appropriated billions of borrowed dollars for public works, relief, the protection of youth and old age; it slightly raised the tax-rate in the higher income brackets; it enacted an unemployment and old-age insurance measure. Willy-nilly, between the spring of 1933 and the summer of 1935, the national economy came back to life and the new life is reflected most conspicuously in profits. Senator Wagner told the Senate:

The profits of all manufacturing and trading corporations, which were $640,000,000 in 1933, rose to $1,051,000,000 in 1934, a gain of 64 per cent. During the same period the earnings of banks and other trust and investment institutions rose from $210,000,000 to $240,000,000, an increase of 14 per cent. . . . If we contrast the first half of 1935 with the first half of 1934 we find that the profits of the General Motors Corporation have increased 20 per cent; the profits of the auto accessory industry have gone forward 49 per cent; the profits in building materials have risen 98 per cent; the profits in electrical equipment have increased 112 per cent; the profits in machinery are up 65 per cent; the profits in textiles are 19 per cent higher; the profits in merchandising have mounted 10 per cent. Nowhere in the record of business cycles do we find a parallel improvement.

Indeed, if the stably prosperous year 1926 be taken as 100, then the New Deal lifted dividends and interest to 150 or 175; while wages crashed at 60. They regained only one-tenth of their value in 1929. Reëmployment has borne no proportion to disemployment, and more is being produced by fewer workers. Americans without jobs number 11,000,000; of whom nearly half are either on relief or holding pseudo-jobs, on work relief, or are enrolled in the Civilian Conservation Corps, or employed by the Public Works Administration. Wages have been forced up, but lag far behind prices, and the average American with a job is little better off than the average American on relief. The cost of living is lifted without effect on wages; to win wage-increases has called for legislation, innumerable strikes, some long and bloody. Although the Supreme Court invalidated the Codes, the decision came too late to save the small business, which was first used as the measure of price and profit, and then squeezed out by the great corporation. "Fair competition" was made an expression for no competition and price-fixing. The codes were so framed that they definitely put the consumer at the mercy of the producer.

The same thing held, and held even more conspicuously in agriculture. The policy of the Agricultural Adjustment Administration was to replace competitive plenty with collusive scarcity. Assuming that there are too many farmers, who produce too much cotton, too much grain, too much pork and beef and mutton for the market; the Administration undertook to reduce this supposititious superfluity by ploughing under or removing from production ten million acres of growing cotton, forty million of wheat; by killing millions of pigs, by imposing processing taxes and otherwise establishing artificial scarcity. This it did in face of the fact that millions of American families exist at or below the level of subsistence and lack enough food and clothing and housing decently to live and to grow. Its purpose was to raise prices to consumers of these necessities in order that their producers might secure their needed relief; but few or none of the benefits accrued to the multitude of the producers—the tenants, the share-croppers, the agricultural laborers—who really needed them. In effect, the consumers, outnumbering these producers by millions, were levied upon for the benefit of the American *kulak*.

In a word, the New Deal, knowingly or unknowingly, sacrificed the consumer to the producer at every point in the national economy. As even the Durable Goods Industries Committee, formed at the request of General Johnson, reported with unconscious irony at the end of May, 1934, there is "an insufficiency of consumer purchasing power largely caused by unemployment resulting from the low activity of the durable or capital goods industry."

By basic principle, the New Deal gives priority to production over consumption. Its sponsors hoped, through stimulating production, to restore prosperity. But they accomplish, mostly, the sacrifice of the consumer to the producer. The New Deal's economy of planned scarcity in agriculture and its trend toward collusive controls in industry leave the consumer holding the bag. As we have seen,[2] its efforts to protect the consumer were, when honest, perfunctory and ineffectual; and there is grave doubt whether the structure of the Consumers' Advisory Board and the powers given it were meant to serve as more than a sop to the public.

§ 5. CONSUMERS' AND PRODUCERS' COÖPERATIVES UNDER THE NEW DEAL

ONLY WHERE CONSUMERS were effectively organized on their own account, in coöperatives, did the New Deal give "the consumer interest" sufficient support to enable the consumer to make a real fight for his rights.

[2] Chapter V, § 3.

The record in the petroleum industry is representative. Invited by the President to prepare a code of fair competition, the masters of this industry met to that end in Chicago in June, 1933. The coöperatives were not invited to this meeting, which agreed upon a code and on July 25th submitted it to the Recovery Administrator in a public hearing. The oil coöperatives and the important farm organizations, aware of what was happening, sent to this hearing, Howard A. Cowden, the president of the then Union Oil Company, Coöperative, to represent them all. His argument was reënforced by a statement from the Farm Credit Administration. Nevertheless, in the committee of eight which General Johnson appointed to reconcile conflicting views in a new Code to be drawn and submitted to him within two days, the coöperatives were not represented, and had to ask permission to meet with the Committee. A whole evening was given to discussing the coöperative position. The code as framed, prohibited purchase dividends and contained other rules which, if put in force would have destroyed consumers' coöperation in petroleum products. The rules protecting the coöperative technique and structure were written into the code only in consequence of the intervention of Dr. Warbasse, the late Mrs. Rumsey, Donald Richberg, General Johnson, and finally the President.

This was bitterly resented by the leaders of the profit-seeking corporations. The President and the Administrator were publicly denounced, and a threat was made so to interpret the petroleum code that new societies could not be organized, or new members admitted to existing societies, or petroleum departments set up by coöperative societies not yet dealing in petroleum products. The reply of the coöperatives' representative was, to secure an executive order redefining the rights and powers of coöperative organization. But a campaign of malicious whispering made necessary a second order to clarify the first, and it looked at last as if the dispute were settled. It was not, however. Balked in one direction, the enemies of coöperation turned to another. They now attacked the classical coöperative practice which credits dividends to non-members toward the purchase of a share of stock. Harold Ickes affirmed that it could be done and various State Code Committees passed resolutions that it couldn't. The coöperatives asked for a public hearing, and when their representatives arrived in Washington for it, found themselves confronted with written rules signed and ready to mail. One rule would have put upon them the burden of making a metaphysical distinction between oil products which the farmer consumed in production and those he consumed otherwise; purchase dividends were to be paid only on the former. Another rule gave the committee power to decide when a coöperative could establish a branch and when not—i. e., to control of the growth of coöperatives. In addition, the enemies of coöperation had made their own definition of coöperative organization. The hearing nullified the rules. And as against their definition of coöperative organization, an official one was secured from the Administrator, which safeguarded the essentials of the coöperative structure and method.

But until the Supreme Court decision which invalidated the whole N.R.A. enterprise, and abolished all codes, the coöperatives found themselves called upon to exercise the utmost vigilance and to mobilize all resources, personal and political, to safeguard the coöperative principle. Throughout the period, codes were being continually rewritten in the hope of catching them off guard; they were subject to misrepresentation and vilification at meetings, in trade papers, among the rank and file of their own membership. Methods of unfair competition were devised within the framework of the codes. Refiners proposed not to sell to coöperative wholesales; they planned a price war in coöperative territory; and finally, if they didn't have their way, to withdraw from the petroleum committee. That the coöperatives were able to hold their own is due partly to the advantageous position of the farm coöperatives under the law, and the power of the farm movements. The heart of the assault was laid bare when a representative of Standard Oil interest said to the representative of the coöperatives at a meeting of the Petroleum Code Committee: "You represent the consumer while we represent the stockholders and our interests are therefore different."

As with petroleum producers, so with the producers of fertilizer, iron and steel, and coal. They wrote codes with the intent of hurting if not destroying the coöperatives. Nor did the housing and restaurant codes as first written lack regulations nullifying one or another coöperative technique. When such regulations failed to carry such nullifying intention, the tendency was general, to threaten reprisals by boycott or price war. Not only were there attacks on the coöperatives and on the administrative authorities vindicating their practice, but the old custom of the Bureau of Statistics of the United States Department of Labor of publishing bulletins reviewing the coöperative record and analyzing coöperative principles was denounced, by a department store executive, as a fostering of consumers' coöperation to the disadvantage of private retailers.[3]

Per contra, E. A. Filene, one of the great figures in retail merchandising, announced the project of organizing a nationwide chain of coöperative department stores along lines suggestive of N. O. Nelson's adventure a generation earlier. The projected enterprise is to be built from the center outward, for two reasons—first, because, as the English Wholesale has learned, it is no longer possible for a small local store to compete single-handed against the modern chain structure, and second, because distribution now involves the same qualities of scientific management as production.

Today, the projector argues, a coöperative chain will need to unite the strongest features of a department store privately-owned, with an organization combining the strong points both of chains and mail-order houses. The Rochdale principles would govern the society, except that the financing, the determination of the associative form, the policies and the administration of the coöperative chain should be vested in a central organization. At the end of ten years, this control should pass

[3] "There is reason to believe, however, that consumer coöperatives, if fostered by government agencies, may sustain an unwarranted growth. In that event, the damage to privately owned distribution agencies would be irreparable." From a letter written by J. H. Namm, president of a New York department store, to the Business Section of the New York *Times,* to complain of the contents of Bulletin No. 598, entitled *Organization and Management of Consumers' Coöperative Associations and Clubs* (with Model By-Laws).

to the members, or if it appears to their advantage, at the end of five.

Significantly, if complaints of consumer coöperatives were numerous, there were no complaints of the self-help or producers' service-exchanging coöperatives organized mostly in the West with the aid of relief funds provided under the Federal Emergency Relief Acts. At one time as many as 500,000 Americans figured, in one way or another, as members of these self-help groups. Business opposition to actual producers' coöperatives forced their closing. The others are essentially evanescent, and prosperity is likely to dissipate them entirely. . . .

The endeavor toward coöperative production was most highly organized and articulate under the Tennessee Valley Authority. There a company was incorporated, the Tennessee Valley Associated Coöperatives, Incorporated, and a variety of self-help coöperatives were organized and put under the direction of officials of the Authority who were to serve as managers and guides, and to educate the coöperators in coöperation until they should be able to coöperate by themselves. With the usual consequences.

No capitalist complaint against producer-coöperation under the New Deal need be anticipated. The case is different with consumers' coöperation: that grows by what it feeds on.

§ 6. ENGINEERS, POLITICIANS AND COÖPERATIVE ORGANIZATION

As WE HAVE SEEN, the foremost advantages of the New Deal have gone to the stockholder rather than to the consumer or wage-earner. The disturbances which gave rise to it, and those which it gave rise to naturally brought to birth the usual flight of schemes and stratagems to enable Americans to live happily ever after. Endeavors to save the nation from the capitalist predicament ranged from analyses of the national economy to prove or to disprove that abundance was inevitable, to the organization of new political parties and the ordination of new cults. Technocrats hurried to demonstrate that America's power to produce was monstrously beyond its actual production; [4] more or less orthodox economists hurried

[4] Harold Loeb and Associates, *The Chart of Plenty*.

to demonstrate that it was only within 80 per cent of its maximum.[5] Both may have had some comfort from the publication of the findings of a seven-year study of production in the United States. This study had been initiated by the American Society of Industrial Engineers in 1926, and had been directed by Messrs. L. P. Alford and Joshua E. Hannum. It was purely technological, unrelated either to business cycles or economic gospels. It analyzed the major industries in terms not of money but of man-hours. It charted productivity, wages and salaries, working hours, plant and organization capacities, and the relation between industrial and agricultural prices. Although the findings are predestined to be ignored by both our political and business leaders, they are indispensable to any realistic definition of fundamental policy for the national economy.

They show that productivity is independent of the business cycle and increases as the skill and dexterity of workers and management increase, the ratio being 6 per cent to 8 per cent yearly. They show that low wages go with low productivity and vice versa; that short week periods are better than long ones; that small plants have more operative effectiveness than large ones; and that the disadvantage of the farmer in relation to the industrial worker is due to the fact that the unit of farming is proportionally too small. Messrs. Alford and Hannum declare that the productivity both of agriculture and of industry is indefinitely extensible; but only as the standard of living is raised can this productivity be absorbed. There is hence no need to stabilize production of any kind at a low standard of living. The need is continuously to raise the standard of living.[6]

That is, the findings of the engineers is an affirmation of the primacy of the consumer. The organizational implications of this primacy were, of course, not discussed, not being a theme of the research. On the other hand, political parties

[5] Harold Moulton and associates, *America's Power to Produce,* (Brookings Institute).

[6] Thus engineers, in whom Veblen placed the hope of the future, vindicated his distinction between industrial and pecuniary employments, and his judgment that the latter are irrelevant to the former, and confirmed the teachings of Ira Steward that the habits and desires of the multitude are more important in the upkeep and growth of an industrial economy than the profits of entrepreneurs.

are concerned first and last with organizational patterns. To the Republicans, Democrats, socialists, communists and Farmer-Laborites of pre-depression days, were added the Continental Committee, Father Coughlin, Farmer Labor Political Federation, Huey Long, the Progressive Party of Wisconsin, the Utopian Society and the Workers' Party. Of these, the Farmer-Labor Party, the Farmer Labor Political Federation and the Progressive Party of Wisconsin definitely favored coöperative organization—for farmers. They appear to have done so, not because they have realized the primacy of the consumer, but because their constituencies are prevailingly agricultural, and because the farmers are one vocational group in the United States who are definitively coöperators. The American farmer still approaches coöperation as a producer, but, as we have seen, the shift to the consumer point of view is under way.

§ 7. AFTERMATH IV: THE CHURCHES TAKE TO CONSUMER COÖPERATION

IT IS the Protestant churches that have turned to consumer coöperation with the greatest ardor and the clearest understanding. The conversion was natural enough. From the Renaissance on, the institutions of religion had begun to undergo dislocations, first because of the pressure of commerce, then of humanism, then of science, and finally of industry. The effects of these pressures were cumulative. The first two eventuated in the Protestant Reformation which shifted the seat of religious authority from the ecclesiastical establishment to the personal conscience, and gave on earth that importance to the individual soul which the church universal claimed for it in the hereafter. It transformed the church as an institution from a divinely-ordained supernatural organism into a personally-determined earthly organization, into a congregation gathered upon the vision and sanction of the individual conscience, with an authority following from its consent. The one church became thus diversified into many chapels each with an equal claim to be divinely inspired and sanctioned.

During many generations the religious life of the Christian

world was a warfare of each of these rival claims against the others, and a struggle of all to resist and overthrow the truth of the sciences. Political and social circumstance led to a stalemate among the rivals, bringing about first a condition of armed neutrality which was the initial phase of religious tolerance, and later a genuine tolerance in which each, living for its own vision, suffered the others to live for theirs. As science entered more and more deeply into the daily life, transforming its commonsense, altering its immemorial ideas about nature and human nature, transforming its notions of God and fate, and compelling the churches to accommodate themselves to its discoveries and implications, it not only altered religious doctrine, it modified associational pattern; it brought former rivals together in a concerted endeavor to save themselves from destruction by the forces of the new world.

The industrial revolution changed this world still further. Its tendency was to force religion from the center to the far circumference of the world's attention. Science and industry are inexorable secularizers and the frame of mind induced by the operation of machines and their laws leaves little room for the frame of mind needful to the upkeep of religious establishments, especially such as are based on consent. Even the intolerable hardships coincident with the industrialization of society, to which the Wesleys applied Methodism as earthly consolation and otherworldly remedy, are insufficient to support remedies of this order. Socialism and Marxism—the type of consolation and remedy these hardships could support—they generated autogeneously; and Marxism, being a religion itself true to the religious type, declared eternal enmity to all traditional religion because it regarded all traditional religion as the enemy of the suffering multitudes of religionists.

The total result among these multitudes was not so much antagonism to established religion as indifference, and while antagonism often vitalizes, indifference kills. Even where a church is, as in England, "established" and state-supported, death by indifference is intolerable. Owen's attacks on Christianity, which brought his movement the enmity of the clergy of all denominations, were life-giving to the denominations. Their characteristic treatment of Dr. King hurt them more than if they had let him be, since it turned the sympathies of their members away from them to him. Hence, to priests truly convinced of their vocation, the misery of the multitudes which the prosperous and their priests attributed to their irreligion, becomes a witness of the betrayal of their religion by the priesthood. They feel the burden laid upon them to invest the old teachings with the new doctrines, and to give new life to the old gospel with the new practices. This was the burden which made Christian Socialists of characters so unlike as the saintly Maurice and the robustious and tory Charles Kingsley. This is what made the faith and work of Christian Socialism. In the United States this is what led to the formation of the futile Christian Labor Union in 1872, the Church Association for the Advancement of the Interests of Labor in 1887, the formation of the Society of Christian Socialists in 1889, and finally to the osmosis of ideas and attitudes from secular Socialism to churchmen and church groups which resulted in the formation first of the interdenominational Christian Social Fellowship and then the Church Socialist League.

In many ways, this assimilation of Christianism to Socialism was a more risky and heroic adventure in the United States than in England. Although "the Churches of Christ" in America were by first intention protestant and revolutionary, by ideal democratic, personalist and consummatory, their congregational government and its voluntary ground put them under a double hazard. Not only did the swiftly growing secularization of the land but the progressive impoverishment of the multitudes, especially on the country-side, threaten the very physical survival of churches and sects; it tended to put the clergy among the lowest paid and least esteemed of the professional classes, and left the upkeep of the church economy dependent on the good-will offerings of the rich and powerful. These required in return divine sanction for their works and ways, the sanctification of things-as-they-are as fulfilments of God's will. And this, like the rich and powerful everywhere, they received. Conventionally American churchmen have approved and defended slavery, for whites as well as blacks; attacked manhood suffrage, labor unions, free public education, equal rights for women; defended financial oppression, industrial exploitation and war.

If the total effect was to keep pulpits on a certain income level full and to empty more and more pews on the countryside, it must be remembered that even ministers of God cannot live by his spirit alone, however all-powerful they might deem it. The ministerial incumbents who sanctified the established order by that fact cut themselves off from any genuine fellowship with those who in Christ's name denounced it. Employing diversified modern symbols, they continued to preach sin and salvation from sin; submission to scarcity on earth for the sake of an eternal consumption of treasure laid up in heaven; while the others more and more reaffirmed the beatitudes of Jesus in the arguments of Marx, and preached the justice and righteousness of the equal enjoyment of wealth produced on earth. Once more within the church itself the City of God stood away from the City of the World.

Meanwhile, the national passage from an agricultural to an industrial economy, with its scientific and secularizing culture, its great swift mechanical consolidations of the mental and material equipage of the American spirit, forced the hitherto diverse and mutually antagonistic churches into an analogous association. The Protestant sects combined into the Federal Council of the Churches of Christ in America and under a forthright and unflinching leadership, not easily, not all at once, but definitely, projected the church interest into the enduring struggle which is the heart of American history—the struggle to transform the preamble of the Declaration of Independence from a confession of faith into a way of life. All that the ministerial sanctifiers of the *status quo* had condemned, the Council in the course of time approved: all they had defended, the Council finally denied and denounced. They made surveys, published reports, adopted resolutions; ministers preached and wrote and labored, led strikes, did sentry-go on picket-lines with the *quondam* followers of John Wesley in the van.

But for more than a generation, their Kingdom of Heaven to be ordained on earth was to be a kingdom of producers.

They, no more than the Christian Socialists, could escape the contagion of opinion from the producer-dominated world. Almost from the beginning of their redemption of the Christian churches, they were aware of consumers' coöperation. W. D. Bliss, who had been a member of the Knights of Labor and knew of their stores, drew the articles of his faith almost entirely from the English Christian Socialists. Walter Rauschenbusch interpreted the consumers' movement as "the beginnings of a higher business morality," and understood them as devices of management rather than as ideals of life.[7] The representative of the Federal Council who served on the American Commission for the Study of Coöperation in Europe, came closer to envisaging the consumer economy of life potential in the movement. His report, printed in the annual report of the Federal Council for 1914, summed up:

> The sympathetic participation in and promotion of the coöperative movement on the part of the church is a logical and almost necessary result of the existence of a movement of such a character, since many of the ends for which the church is striving are effectually accomplished by these institutions, while these institutions in their purpose and endeavors, necessarily command the sympathy and allegiance of every sincere and disinterested churchman.

But the issue was not momentous enough to lead to any action. The World War first obscured and then perverted all the issues of right and justice with which the churches had been concerning themselves. But during the disturbed period of reverting from a war to a peace economy, when men's minds were taking flight in dreams of "reconstruction," "a new car" and "a new world order," the Council undertook as one of seventeen items in the program adopted on October 2, 1919, "to study the coöperative movement as developed in Europe and America and standardize the best methods and practices for the conduct of coöperative societies." The bishops of the Catholic Church had already that same year included coöperation in their "program of social reconstruction" as a device to reduce the cost of living and to "train our working people and consumers generally in habits of saving, in careful ex-

[7] *Cf. Christianizing the Social Order* (1912), Chapter VII.

penditure, in business methods and in the capacity for coöperation." Little seems to have come of either of these characteristic recommendations, save inquiries at the office of the Coöperative League; and occasional resolutions by this church conference or that to the effect that consumers' coöperatives should be encouraged. Church action was focalized rather on the issues of labor against capital, modernism against fundamentalism, peace against war. Church thinking was socialist, church language was Christian.

When, in consequence of the march of events in Russia, Communism became not only a thing to curse with among the nation's hearsters and demagogues, but a subject of disturbed discussion among spiritually-minded Americans, many came to feel between Christianity and Communism a certain incompatibility never-to-be-overcome, and an itching doubt about the happiness of this amazing marriage. Yet, among all the schemes and stratagems of the times, they could see no fitter mates. The nation's swift descent into depression accented the dilemma. The country churches were confronted with an insoluble crisis of men and means. The city ministers found themselves called upon to make good their claims for the superior saving power of the church in the face of a misery mounting to despair. They had to overcome the rival claims of depression-spawned panaceas, and especially, the matter-of-factness and logic of the Marxist faith, to all appearances fully vindicated by events.

These needs brought American churchmen to consumers' coöperation, again. And this time realistically and, it is to be hoped, lastingly. Religious journals, church conferences, committees, assemblies, brotherhoods, journals, took up the serious discussion of coöperative principles and practice; classes and study circles are being arranged, texts and syllabuses printed and distributed; churches either organize coöperative societies, join them or become them. The views and works of Kagawa, the Christianized Japanese busying himself about the formation of coöperatives among his fellow-countrymen, became a theme of somewhat hysterical and emulative rediscussion. Many found in consumer coöperation the escape from the logic of Communism. One made the title of his book about it *Christ's Alternative to Communism* and characterized the Kingdom of God as "a coöperative society" "with individual freedom at its heart." [8] In a word, the beatitudes of Jesus were now found, not in the arguments of Marx, but the practice and principles of the coöperatives.

Whether, with the upswing of the business cycle this exaltation will pass and these energies die down, it is too soon to say. In the modern world the condition of the churches is such that they must perforce attach themselves to another vision or perish. In their present crisis they have come to a realization of the primacy of the consumer, and of the significance for spiritual values of the consumer economy. They are better aware than they were of the continuity between this economy and the religious conceptions of their inheritance. But as for building it into the infinite details which make a way of life—before such tasks their history shows churches and churchmen more successful at profession than at practice. To the churches the coöperative movement is the ultimate challenge and test. . . .

[8] E. Stanley Jones, *Christ's Alternative to Communism* (Abingdon Press, 1935).

BOOK III

THE CONSUMER'S FUTURE

CHAPTER XI

MONEY, CREDIT, AND THE CONSUMER

§ 1. IS FINANCE ORIGINAL SIN IN POLITICAL ECONOMY?

TO STRESS the fact that the nerve center of our modern economy is its financial system is to stress a truism. But there is little in human relations that needs so much stressing as their truisms, for it is by the neglect of the truisms that most human disasters come. The obvious, usually the ignored because it is obvious, is obvious through being like the air we breathe, pervasive and essential. The very attributes that lead to its neglect and forgetting harshly penalize the neglect and the forgetting. The eternal vigilance which liberty exacts is vigilance regarding the obvious. And nothing in the works and ways of contemporary credit-enterprise calls for so much vigilance as the fact that its corporate structure, whatever form be given it, is a function of the traffic in money and credit as these are manipulated by bankers and brokers. The art of these traders in faith appears so autonomous, so independent of the material and technological realities for which money and "paper" are ostensibly but signs and symbols, that social philosophers like Veblen and his school find an irreconcilable antagonism between the realities and the symbols. They attribute all the evils of the modern economy to the perversion of industrial processes by pecuniary interests. More orthodox economists recognize the evils but deny their pecuniary causation; the conventional ones are inclined to minimize, even to deny the evils.

Within the walls of Academe academic curriculi accord to finance the high place it holds beyond them. "Money and banking" and "corporation finance" figure mightily among courses in economics, and their treatment implies that money is the measure of all things: of things that are, that they are: of things that are not, that they are not. Intermittently condemned by philosophers, accursed by farmers and workers, reformed and regulated by legislators, "viewed with alarm" and "pointed to with pride" by political parties, the traffic in cash and credit is generally respected and taken for granted. Its rôle as the leading instrument of financial oppression and industrial exploitation, as the surest and safest of all the channels through which force and fraud make themselves effective in the government of the business world is only periodically and never effectively a matter of public concern. Testimony to the record is coeval with banking and broking. You read it in the proverbs current all over the globe, which warn the borrower against the lender; in the Hebraic prohibition of usury for the defense of the poor producer; in the Hellenic condemnation of it for the protection of the rich consumer; in the anathema upon trade and usury by the mediæval Church; in the legion of secular statutes enacted since the ecclesiastical bans were ignored or denied and their authority was reinterpreted. So self-repeating are the condemnation and restriction, that the record is sometimes construed as evincing some inherent original sin, some inborn total depravity, in finance as such. No other economic domain more infallibly or ruthlessly demonstrates the rule of *caveat emptor*. To some every relation between bankers and brokers and their customers is an evil nascent and bound to come to birth unless unflinchingly checked; not a few reformers or Utopia-makers endeavor to devise politics which shall do without either money or credit.

Yet no associative form has yet been imagined and no economy conceived which did more than vindicate the functions of money and credit and condemn their names, while several—like Proudhon's Exchange Bank—simply elaborate or extend one or another of their activities. How, indeed, can any economy that in any significant degree divides labor, extends trade in space and prolongs it in time, operate without money and credit? Or, if without them, without the same things by other names? Civilization is as dependent on the functions they designate as it is on language. Their acutest critics—the Veblenites for example—have been able only to demonstrate their attendant iniquities, not to show how to do without their services. Services and iniquities appear in fact to hold relations to the financial function such as marriage and prostitution hold to sex. Finance appears to be indispensable to any advanced, and certainly to every advancing, economy. Like all other patterns and events which occur in history or in nature, its values are consequences not of its character but of its uses. Good and evil are not qualities inhering but relations taken on and left off; ethical meaning follows from employment, not birth; it is a consequence of a frame of reference which changes with each and every item of the frame.

§ 2. ORIGIN AND CHARACTER OF COÖPERATIVE FINANCE

THE CONTRAST between corporation finance and coöperative finance points this moral and adorns this tale. Both come, wherever they operate, under the law of the land. As a rule, however, the statutes directed to the control of corporations were enacted after the corporations had worked their iniquities upon the peoples: the statutes progressively restrict, control, forbid: they make the range of the corporation narrower. On the other hand, the laws governing the organization and management of coöperatives were enacted after coöperatives had demonstrated their benefactions to the people. On the whole and in the long run, each new statute extends their scope and power, defends their name from abuse and their principle from prostitution.

The sources of this difference is one of the richer jokes of a social history which is mainly jokes. The earliest coöperatives had no standing in the law. Voluntary associations of the poorest of the poor, they could not become legal entities, corporations or joint-stock companies. So far as the law was concerned, they were non-existent. Hence they could not hire land to work or build on or houses to meet in; they could not own capital or any other property; contracts made with them were not binding; pledges violated were not punishable. Having no legal existence, they could neither sue nor be sued. Every legal step they took had to be taken through others, usually their own members or officers, who as individual subjects of His Britannic Majesty, did come under His Majesty's law. But if a secretary was dishonest, a treasurer corrupt, a manager a swindler or a thief, the society was at their mercy: it had no remedy against them beyond taking the law into its own hands. Men who associated with one another under these conditions needed to have intimate knowledge of each other's character and faith in each other's integrity; they could coöperate only on a basis of complete mutual trust, or not at all.

Nevertheless, life was too hard and temptation was too great. Theft and fraud did occur; and even if rarely, often enough to keep coöperators remembering that they were possible, and constantly in search of means to make them impossible. The first such legal means was the stratagem of organizing under the Friendly Society Acts. The Rochdale Pioneers organized under the Act of 1836. This, without rendering their society a joint-stock company, endowed it with a legal existence. It gave the society standing before the law; the members could turn to the courts for protection—not much, but better than nothing—from chicanery at the hands of officers or trustees or creditors; they could sue and be sued as a body. It relieved them from paying stamp duties and it in some degree regulated and supervised the investment of their funds, giving them a chance at government securities. On the other hand, the Act forbade business with any other than their own members, and this had the salutary effect of keeping membership on an open basis and making increase in membership a necessity.

The legal identification of consumer coöperative societies with the principles and purposes of "friendly societies" was the second factor which distinguished the coöperative from the usual business corporation. Already Adam Smith had pointed out that such companies as the British East India Company—or any other corporation—deprived the individual stockholder of the responsibility for the uses of the money which his stock represented; it made of him an absentee owner with only vicarious control over his property; it made of its actual managers, negligent, inefficient bureaucrats associating together with an unfriendly intent toward the public. "People of the same trade seldom meet together, even for merriment and diversion, but the conversation ends in a conspiracy against the public, or in some contrivance to raise prices." Friendly societies of necessity had an opposite intent. They were non-competitive. They were organized, not for profit but for mutual aid: whether with sickness and death benefits, loans of money, or purchase of goods.[1] The rich and powerful did not need friendly societies and did not organize them; each and every one of them was able, presumably, to take care of himself. It was different with the poor and powerless who did need them and did organize them. Their friendly societies were regarded by the holders of political power as they themselves were regarded by the lady of the manor and the curate dispensing her charities: predestined to eternal damnation through drink, thriftlessness and ignorance, and to be supervised, guided and admonished so far as these generous occupations didn't interfere with comfort and convenience. The fact

[1] The "friendly society," in the form of the fraternal order, figures among the major associative patterns in the United States. While never, or hardly ever, coöperative in the Rochdale sense of the term, neither is it a corporation. In structure, purpose and function, the average fraternal order is a hybrid between a religious cult and a mutual insurance company. Most fraternal orders maintain secrecy and employ an elaborate and highfalutin' ritual with many degrees of initiation, grandiose and extravagant titles and the like, as spiritual parachutes to keep their dues and payments on a safe financial level. There are scores of such orders in the United States, with ten million members, more or less, and a decreasing business, which they are endeavoring to offset by moving, not very consistently, toward the methods and actuarial basis of commercial insurance companies.

that the first consumer coöperatives could secure a modicum of legal protection only by organizing as friendly societies, though they needed it perhaps less than the joint-stock company, protected them against themselves and their members. It reënforced the tendency toward one set of business habits as against others, and these habits have become the characteristic of *bona fide* coöperative enterprise. Especially important was the frugal investment clause.

On the other hand, the mothering intent of the Friendly Societies Act limited the scope and functions of organization, restricted growth and tended to keep societies in a state of prolonged infancy. The wave of producers' association which Christian Socialist effort set in motion led to the drafting, and adoption in 1852, of the first Industrial and Provident Societies Act by which coöperatives as such were established as legal entities, the restrictions of the frugal investments clause were withdrawn, and societies were permitted to enter upon undertakings that had hitherto been open only to joint-stock companies. Later legislation still further extended the scope and power of the coöperatives. Since the sponsors of all the enabling acts were Christian Socialists or authorities like John Stuart Mill, Bellenden Kerr, or Lord Shaftesbury, the original moral outlook and providential attitude of the law was altered in tone but conserved. The total effect was to make of coöperatives a business enterprise somehow without a business meaning.

As the coöperative movement spread to countries other than England these traits of the English law were stressed and elaborated. Certain of the rules laid down by the Pioneers became universally parts of coöperative law: that, for example, membership must be open; that control must be democratic; that shares can receive only a fixed interest and must be non-transferable; in many cases that transactions must be for cash; that a purchase-dividend must be paid. If some laws, like those of Switzerland and Belgium, for example, handicapped the coöperative by making each member liable for his society's obligations with all he possessed, others limited his liability to the extent of his investment, and still others made the liability not individual but collective. Often, especially in the case of credit coöperatives, governments made themselves partners in the enterprises, and inspected, audited, supervised and imposed penalties for deficiency, as well as lent money or arranged credit.

§ 3. CORPORATION AND COÖPERATIVE FINANCE UNDER AMERICAN LAW

COÖPERATIVE LAW in the United States is defined by a similar frame of reference. Where there is no coöperative law, coöperative societies must either remain unincorporated or must incorporate under the general corporation law. If they remain unincorporated, the members are jointly and severally liable for all their societies' obligations. If they incorporate under the law of corporations they almost inevitably cease to be coöperatives, as coöperative principles are often in direct opposition to corporation rules. Coöperative law, by specifying the power and form of coöperative organization, by limiting the liability of the members and defining coöperative standards, protects the integrity of the coöperative principle. Although there is no national legislation in America dealing with consumer organization as such, what legislation does exist is indefinite and ambivalent enough to apply when need arises, not only to consumers' but to producers' societies. This is the Capper-Volstead Act, which was designed to do for farmer organizations what the Clayton Act ostensibly was to do for trades-unions—relieve them of the onus of the Sherman Anti-Trust Act; put them beyond classification as "conspiracies in restraint of trade," especially with regard to price-fixing. As a good many farmer organizations, largely marketing organizations, sometimes function far less as coöperatives than as trusts, the law makes the Department of Agriculture the judge as to whether a price is or is not contrary to the public interest, and gives it power to order reductions of price or to dissolve a society practising price-fixing.

The attitude of certain executive branches of the American government—the presidency, the department of labor, the federal trade commission—has already been noted: coöperative organization is defined, studied, protected and recommended as a defense against financial oppression and commercial exploitation, although nothing very consistent and practical is done to advance coöperative organization. Substantially, coöperation in the United States is a local issue and its legal status is defined by the laws of the states, not of the nation. To date coöperative laws of some sort have been enacted by thirty-two states and the territory of Alaska. In many instances they began as laws for the benefit of farmers and were later generalized to apply to all forms of coöperative association. As far back as 1830, New York State used to charter mutual insurance companies by special acts, and in 1857, passed a coöperative fire insurance law. But the first state to authorize consumers' coöperative societies as such was Michigan. A bill, enacted in 1865, provided for the organization of coöperatives of mechanics and laboring men. Massachusetts adopted a more general bill the following year, and other states came along as opinion and circumstance permitted or required. Sometimes the laws were put on the books without any clear recognition of their import. At others, especially in those states whose citizens had a tradition of coöperative practice from Europe—for example, Wisconsin and Minnesota—not only was there a clear understanding of the implication of coöperative law among its enemies, but every effort was made to obstruct its passage and to defeat it; or failing that, to nullify it by amendment and otherwise. The defeat in the Minnesota legislature of the coöperative banking bill of 1934 was due to such causes.

In general, coöperative laws require that a society organized under them shall embody the associative pattern by which it is distinguished from a corporation. Where corporation stock is regarded as personal property which may be freely bought and sold upon the open market, coöperative stock can as a rule be sold back only to the coöperative society, and must be bought direct from the society. Coöperative stock is set at a fixed price and is paid a fixed rate of interest; like labor, it receives "a wage." The price of corporation stock fluctuates and its "earnings" vary; and these fluctuations and variations need not, and as a rule do not, indicate corresponding changes in the material establishment and technological activities which the stock represents. Often, indeed, one is made the opposite of the other. . . . Coöperative stock signalizes membership in a coöperative society; corporation stock signalizes ownership of a marketable "security." Not infrequently a limit is set upon the number of shares of stock a member of a society may own, but whether he owns one share or one thousand, he has one vote and one only, in the affairs of his society, and its government is therefore democratic; its decisions are a consensus of the majority of its members. In corporations, shares vote, not the owner: a man with one share has one vote, a man with a thousand shares has a thousand votes; one majority stockholder can impose his will upon a hundred thousand minority-holders. The government of corporations is oligarchic. Decisions are the coercive power of the majority of dollars. . . .

Coöperatives tend as a rule to maintain a strictly cash business; corporations prefer to use credit—"other people's money." Corporations pay "dividends" on stock, and seek these dividends at the expense of all the other components of an enterprise. Coöperatives pay "dividends" on business done by each member, and such business depends on the other components of the enterprise. Corporation dividends are largely unearned increments—the excess of income over cost and this cost itself contains unearned increments; coöperative dividends are savings—the reduction of income to costs and the reduction of costs. Both are called profits: but corporation profit is what Veblen calls "a legitimate right to something for nothing," while coöperative profit is a fruit of labor and the return to the owner of his own.

The rules of coöperative financing, government and procedure, when compared with those obtaining for corporations, are distinctly limiting. They compel the valuations of coöperative enterprise to stay as close to their physical foundation as is morally possible in a political economy whose spiritual climate tends to vaporize all real structures and functions into the forms of money values. A share of coöperative stock represents exactly what it purports to represent, no more and no less. It cannot be watered. It cannot represent "promoter's costs," banker's commissions, brokerage charges, "future earnings," market-rigging, and the other items by which the enduring actuality of an enterprise is stretched like the skin of a balloon, so thin that to touch it is to break it. It cannot be juggled, as investment bankers have juggled merely commercial stocks, shuffling old values into a sleight-of-hand creation of make-believe new assets. It cannot be employed by a minority of the members to control and not uncommonly expropriate the majority; or to deprive any member of his rights, or to entrench enemies of the enterprise in power over it, as happens with corporation stock. Money and credit in the coöperative enterprise function in their legitimate rôles of facilitating and smoothing the making and exchange of goods and services, instead of frustrating or aborting these functions.

§ 4. FAKE COÖPERATIVES

IN SPITE of its limitations under the law, coöperative economy has, as we have seen, consistently grown and prospered. It has come through war and inflation and depression with a soundness and vitality which more conventionally financed enterprises have been far from able to match. The word "coöperative," hence, has a value of eulogy which the word "corporation" lacks, and its employment by rascals as bait to catch innocents with has created in America a tendency to put statutory limitations on the use of "coöperative." When, during the Great War, coöperation became a matter of widespread interest both in certain sections of the organized labor movement and among intellectuals, a number of "wild-cat" corporations were organized with "coöperative" in their titles and prospectuses although they had all the features of a get-rich-quick scheme and none of the true coöperative structure. Their prospectuses duped hundreds of thousands of Americans whom they fleeced of a sum estimated at about sixty million dollars. They operated under such all-embracing corporate titles as "The Coöperative League of America," "The Coöperative Association of America," "The Consumers' Association of America," and so on. Essentially stock-selling schemes, promoting chains of groceries, restaurants and cafeterias and banks, they all sooner or later came into the courts. The most notorious was the Coöperative Society of America, organized and sponsored by a captain of industry who had been among other things business manager of Chicago's "most pretentious newspaper" and president of a Hearst property in the same city. Between 1917 and 1921, this hearster and his mates cost 81,000 Americans something like $15,000,000. The Coöperative League of America was a Pittsburgh corporation. Its name, apparently chosen *ad hoc,* was often confused with the national federation of coöperative societies, the Coöperative League of the United States. Ostensibly it was to engage in coöperative banking. Its organizer had been a figure in the Coöperative Society of America of Chicago. In the course of three or four years he cost American citizens several millions of dollars. Another spawn of this fertile fraud, the Coöperative League of America, was the Wisconsin American Rochdale Company organized in 1925 with headquarters at Milwaukee. . . .

§ 5. CLASSICS OF CORPORATION FINANCING

ONE OF THE PRIME TASKS of the Coöperative League of the United States has been to keep friends of the coöperative movement informed of the existence and menace of these fake coöperatives. They are a peculiarly American phenomenon and seem to be an autogenous toxin of the American economic structure. A cynic might say that the chief difference between them and other creations of corporation-finance is that they got caught, exposed, and that their promoters were, in one or two instances, punished. Some corporations escape altogether, others are only exposed. The great exposure occurred in 1911 when a committee of Congress investigated the United States Steel Corporation and brought the classic pattern of corporation financing to general public knowledge. This corporation, one of the two or three great industrial concerns in the world and the greatest in the United States, has the form of a holding company. According to the reports of the United States Bureau of Corporations, it is a combination of formerly actual and potential competitors, brought together to coerce the consumer instead of fighting each other and to take gargantuan profits from the sale of the trust's "securities" to the public. Capitalized at $1,400,000,000, more than one-half of this capitalization was wind and water; $150,000,000 represented salesmen's tips and commissions, direct or indirect promotion costs and underwriting; $700,000,000 represented "reserves" of iron ores valued by the Bureau at only $100,000,000. While common bondholders were handed a fixed dividend of 5 per cent on the money they actually paid over to the corporation, millionaire owners of ore lands leased by the trust to make its monopoly safe received extortionate royalties on those lands. During the decade 1901–1910, the average rate of profits on the trust's tangible assets was 12 per cent. The congressional investigation brought out that the directing powers, bankers and brokers and their lawyers, had used the steel industry as merely a springboard for bond issues; that they had inflated and shuffled "securities" which they had issued regardless of the rights of the stockholders or the welfare of the industry; that they bought from each other properties for the trust at excessive prices and sold trust property to each other at prices too low; that, themselves makers and masters of a gargantuan combination of employers and managements, they would viciously prevent the combination of their employees in trades-unions, compelling them to labor under cruel and killing conditions at a bare subsistence wage; that they impartially bribed and debauched the major political parties; that they limited output, fixed prices, arranged agreements in restraint of trade, and made more money out of stock-operations than from the manufacture of steel; that, finally, the earnings of the trust were not due to the efficiency of its management, their ability to make the best steel at the least cost, but to the trust's control of ore and transportation; to rebates, and other discriminatory advantages, economic, financial and political, obtained by methods even more questionable.

The record of the Steel Trust during the quarter of a century since these findings were reported reveals little or nothing in mitigation. The lapse of time may perhaps have refined methods of corporation finance, but it has not reformed them. Although the nation passed during the period from steel and steam to electric power, the financing and manipulation of power-companies has followed the classic lines. A recent investigation by a committee of the United States Senate of the methods of the Associated Gas and Electric Systems, brought into the field of public attention the place of finance in this industry. A holding company capitalized at $900,000,000, controlled by a "voting trust," which invested no money but drew all the profits, the Associated Gas and Electric System sold shares in the open market at $50 and $75 which later did not bring half a dollar. Its promoters developed it by floating securities to pay for operating companies, on which they based a new capitalization to float more securities to buy more companies. Even during a great depression they paid themselves large salaries. By the traditional tricks of stock transfer they took at one time paper profits amounting to $17,000,000; and actual cash of $3,000,000 between 1929 and 1934, this at the depth of a depression, when the stockholders were receiving no dividends and the stocks were practically worthless. They spent fabulous sums on political lawyers, on lobbyists exerting pressure on members of Congress, and on publicity. For the large amounts of the stockholders' money, for the high prices exacted by the service companies of the system from the consumers, no tangible return by the holding company is recorded. The Federal Trade Commission unqualifiedly condemned it.

Theoretically, a holding company, like a coöperative wholesale, is supposed to reduce the cost of materials and equipment; through the pooling of resources to provide its component corporations with better goods and services at lower prices; to provide superior engineering skill, better accountancy, better legal advice, safer financing. Actually, holding companies appropriate, for little or no service rendered, profits and surpluses that should go to stockholders as dividends and to consumers as improvements of services and reduction of costs. Even when honest, holding companies uniformly lay an unnecessary additional burden on the consumer; and when financed as they often are financed, by a pyramiding of watered stocks and fictitious assets, they defraud the stockholder as well as gouge the consumer. The offspring of one law—the Sherman Anti-Trust Act—which they were invented to evade, the holding companies have called out a host of other laws, whose head and front is that creating the Securities Exchange Commission to control and police the nation's financial establishment.

§ 6. CLASSICS OF COÖPERATIVE FINANCING

CONTRAST such structures and their financing with the great consumers' coöperative combinations—the wholesale societies of Great Britain, the Scandinavian or other countries. These societies are the direct antitheses of holding-companies. They do not hold, they are held. They are the creatures and servants of their member-societies. The flotation of securities, the watering of stock, the creation of "voting-trusts" are impossible; the stockholder cannot be defrauded; the consumer, who is the ultimate owner, can only be benefited. The societies have their problems and difficulties and run their dangers; but those of financial fraud and manipulation are not among them. They survive and grow because of their superior competency, because they can do the same job better than their rivals, because they can make and sell better goods in greater quantity at lesser costs. The English Coöperative Wholesale Society was created by retail coöperatives in 1863. In 1864, it paid a fixed interest on 2,455 shares of capital stock and purchase dividends of one and one half pence in the pound to societies whose members numbered 18,337. In 1890, the number of members was 679,336; the interest-earning shares numbered 342,218, and the purchase dividend three and one eighth pence in the pound. In 1912, the number of members had risen to 2,160,191; the number of shares to 1,916,151 and the purchase dividends to four pence. The growth, in the frame of reference set by the general economy of Great Britain, is steady, sure, consistent. By the end of 1933—a low point in the great post-war depression—the wholesale society had a total capital of about $420,000,000, and was paying a purchase dividend of four pence in the pound. The membership had risen to very nearly 7,000,000, associated together in 1,150 societies, whose own share capital amounted to nearly $650,000,000 receiving about twenty-five millions in interest, and the dividends on purchases came to nearly ninety-five millions. Add to this that you have a business of nearly one and one-half billion dollars with not one cent of water or wind; which in its nearly seventy-five years of struggle and growth has never failed to pay each and every one of its members interest on share capital or dividends on purchases.

Or turn from Europe to the United States. Take such a coöperative as the Eastern States Farmers' Exchange. This society, as we know, had its start in the concern of a number of wise public-spirited New Englanders over the position of the American farmer. They organized it to help him to help himself. They wanted to finance it as coöperatives are usually financed, but the farmers were too poor or too suspicious, or both, to invest in shares. The initial capital available to the Exchange was a credit in a bank, backed by notes for $42,500 signed by Horace A. Moses, and twenty-nine of his friends. These notes were made payable to the Eastern States Agricultural Trust, which was organized for the purpose; the Trust was later increased to $103,000. With this credit, the Exchange began to serve its constituencies. Its first intention was to deal only with local societies, but as many of these disintegrated in the panic of 1921 it began to serve the individual farmer directly as a broker for feed and other farm necessities. In a short time it was able to work on its own credit and borrow capital, when it needed to, from commercial banks. Before this state was reached, manipulators had organized a feed pool, and in order to secure feed at a reasonable price, the Exchange was compelled to make contracts a year in advance. The price for such a contract was a guarantee-deposit of nearly half a million dollars. To provide this guarantee the Exchange organized the Eastern States Agricultural Credit Corporation. Through this corporation the promissory notes which the farmers deposited with their agreements to purchase from the Exchange were rediscounted with the Federal Intermediate Credit Bank at fifty cents per dollar of collateral, and the amount called for by the guarantee obtained. But the exactions of the feed speculators and dealers made it clear that the Exchange must itself undertake manufacturing. A mill was available in Buffalo at $300,000, but no cash to buy it with. Again Horace Moses and his friends met the difficulty. The Eastern States Coöperative Milling Corporation was organized, and stock bearing interest at 6 per cent was issued. Moses and another each took $100,000 of this stock; the remaining $100,000 Moses lent the Corporation on a demand-mortgage for the amount, also at 6 per cent. It was arranged that the stock should be retired in ten years through equal half-yearly payments. It was retired in seven; the mortgage was transferred to a Buffalo bank, and the Exchange was in full possession of the milling corporation. So a working plant was developed without share-capital and freed of indebtedness through the application of the purchase dividends of the members. These numbered in 1934, 56,000; and their transactions with the Exchange amounted to $12,300,000. Besides clearing off, during its seventeen years of activity, its indebtedness, the Exchange has invested another $300,000 in doubling the capacity of its mill and has paid more than $2,000,000 in purchase dividends.

§ 7. WHY THE COÖPERATIVE WHOLESALE SOCIETY WENT INTO BANKING

THE FINANCING of the Eastern States Farmers' Exchange depended on the good-will of interested individuals, the availability of credit in commercial banks and the mobilization of the credit resources of the farmers whom the Exchange served in the ordinary way of business. It is, however, open to the Exchange, as its enterprises progress, to make itself independent of external aid by employing a portion of its own gains to create its own implements of finance. This is what the English consumer societies did. They were early in their history confronted with a problem of cash surplus. Many members, instead of withdrawing all their surplus dividends, whether in goods or cash, left a portion in the keeping of their stores as a savings deposit; still others deposited cash savings from their wages with their stores. The stores employed these deposits in the conduct of the coöperative business and paid interest on them, at first at somewhat less than the market —then at the market. Nevertheless, they accumulated at some points more rapidly than they could be used, while at others there was a lack of necessary capital.

As the scale of enterprise grew larger, the principle of cash transactions tended to break down. The direct exchange of money for goods was workable, even if sometimes inconvenient, between a member and his store. But as between the store and Wholesale Society, the store and the general market, it could not be consistently adhered to. Efficient buying, intelligent expansion of activity, inert capital and other business contingencies sooner or later necessitated borrowing or lending, for which "investment" is but another name. It called for commerce in money and credit, that is, commerce in promises to pay, in acknowledgements of indebtedness, in expectations to be paid, and in pledges. These pledges were sometimes given in the form of actual goods but mostly in the form of other acknowledgements, promises and expectations written down on papers called negotiable instruments; bank notes, promissory notes, bills of exchange, stocks, bonds and checks are such negotiable instruments. All this required treating promises as if they were things; it required acting on the faith that a promise would be replaced by a performance, a debt by a payment, credit by cash, and cash by a consumable commodity; ultimately it required acting on faith in the character and integrity of some individual or association of individuals, very few of whom ever knew one another. At one point or another, the coöperative movement had to make itself a place in the credit structure of the national economy.

The credit-system or debt-structure of the business world is an impersonal system of belief whose sustaining force is the personal faith of each individual believer. A break in the faith of any one man can bring about the collapse of the whole system. The faith starts at the bank. At first men left their treasure with merchants or goldsmiths for safe-keeping in their strong boxes. They expected to receive back exactly the same objects they had put in; and they paid the banker a fee for keeping it safe. This practice is continued in the form of letting safe-deposit boxes. But it is not banking. Money or "securities" kept out of circulation are deprived of their function by whose virtue they are money or "securities." Circulation is their life. Banking is an activity dependent on this life. The men with the strong-boxes got permission to circulate the treasure entrusted them, and undertook to return to the owner, not the identical objects, but their equivalent in money or bills, either all at once or in instalments on demand, or after a certain time. In effect, those trusts became, and they remain, loans, which the borrower banker is free to use as he chooses. And they are loans made absolutely on faith. The banker gives no security and the depositor asks for none. That consequences have often been disastrous to depositors, and that movements for the guaranty of bank-deposits and the like arise perennially, is not surprising. What is surprising is that the degree of betrayal of depositors is so comparatively small.

Banking, as a positive instrument of the modern economy, serving a vital function in the making and moving of the goods of life, is postulated on that act of faith. As a vocation, it is the practice of the exchange of debts at a profit, within whose domain a considerable division of labor has developed, and special functions such as bill-broking, discounting, stock-broking, foreign exchange, have tended to autonomous establishment. Technically, banking consists almost entirely of bookkeeping and accountancy, and as such is subject far more than other businesses to tricks, falsifications and frauds. This is recognized alike by the law and banking practice. Both have been fertile in ordinances to protect creditors from the frauds of debtors and debtors from the oppression of creditors. As banking got its start in a world where borrowers were mainly princes of the church and the state able to exact involuntary loans and bound only by their own whims to repay, law and custom have perhaps favored the creditor, and when commerce and industry brought him to power, have provided new rationalizations for the age-old oppression of the debtor which the Bible forbids. To the average wage-earner or professional worker, credit, which is as often a necessity to him as to the "businessman," is normally available only at usurious rates, even from establishments proclaiming themselves friends of the working-man organized to protect him from the usurer. This was among the causes of the Rochdale rule of requiring cash transactions.

That the Wholesale would need sooner or later to engage in banking, simply for the welfare of the great consumer enterprise, was early recognized. The attention of the British coöperators had been called at the Congress of the Coöperative Union in 1869, to the benefits which the members of Schulze-Delitzsch and Raiffeisen banks enjoyed in Germany. But at the time the leaders were concerned how to find profitable employment for the accumulating capital of the Wholesale and of the retail societies, not how to serve the credit needs of their members. Nor do these needs ever seem to have been so urgent among members of British consumer societies as elsewhere. To some of the leaders, like Ludlow, the creation of a central coöperative bank, separate from the Wholesale and autonomus, was desirable besides, in order to give greater unity to the movement; and at first it was such a bank that was contemplated. But J. T. W. Mitchell argued that to create a separate and distinct establishment apart from the Wholesale, was to create two executives for the control of one capital, and in the end his view prevailed.

The C.W.S. set up a banking department, not without misgivings. The law, which because of its assumption that working-men need more policing and discipline than other classes, enfranchized coöperative enterprise but grudgingly, had to be amended; and the needed changes did not come till 1876. The Wholesale began its traffic in money and credit under the old law, serving simply as an institution of "deposit and loan," not a bank, and making call loans at interest 1 per cent less than the Bank of England rate. Meanwhile, the great wave of "union shops" owned and conducted by unions and their members, had begun to rise. The coöperative Ousebourne Engine Works was meeting with discrimination from commercial banks, and for its sake, and in satisfaction of a widespread feeling in certain sections of the coöperative movement, a bank was organized in Newcastle. This, named the Industrial Bank, was, as it had to be, a joint-stock company; its organizers promised that all profits in excess of 10 per cent would be "equally divided between capital and custom." Its creation focalized the issue and concentrated the controversy at a point of practice. The surplus of the coöperatives cried for fruitful investment, and the bank, the engine works, and a whole host of producers' "coöperatives" affirmed a prior claim on consumer resources. Coöperative sentiment favored such a claim. The Wholesale lent, and lost, thousands of pounds. The Industrial Bank and the Engine Works both failed, and the union shops kept falling by the wayside. The situation of the Wholesale itself became very precarious: "The Wholesale Society," Mitchell told much later, "was in very great straits" and, unable to secure help from the commercial banks it had done business with, did secure it from the Rochdale Pioneers and the Heckmondwike Society. By 1876, parliamentary action enabled the Wholesale to engage openly and fully in banking; votes of the membership confined the banking operation to true coöperative enterprise.

§ 8. THE STRUCTURE, DEVICES AND CONTROL OF THE WHOLESALE'S "BANKING DEPARTMENT"

WITHIN THE LIMITS set by the capitalist-industrial frame of reference which environs the coöperative movement, the banking department deals in credit as the groceries department deals in cocoa. The wealthiest and most powerful coöperative financial institution, the C.W.S. Bank, is distinguished from private banks of the same order in that it is a tool of the consumer movement and an agency of the consumer enterprise. The movement and the enterprise are the masters of the bank; the bank is not and never can become the master of the movement and its enterprises; it can never exceed or transform the legitimate and proper functions which banking properly serves in the modern credit-enterprise economy. The situation is the exact opposite in the non-coöperative world. There the bankers, lending other people's money, have made themselves dictators of the borrowers' business, displacing technological by pecuniary standards, and reënforcing the domination of the producer in the national economy.

The C.W.S. Bank, which is typical of coöperative banking enterprise, is owned directly by the coöperative societies which own the Wholesale, and through the societies by their individual members. This ownership develops automatically from the act of joining a coöperative society. The bank's services are available not only to member organizations, but to any association of men, a trades-union for example, which is not competing with or controverting coöperative practice and principle. Its function is to provide fruitful employment for coöperative capital within the field of the coöperative movement and in such a way as to help it grow in strength and quality. It provides credit for member societies, "accommodation for the various departments of the Wholesale"; its interest charges tend to be lower than those of the Bank of England, and its interest payments at the market-rate. In July, 1934, it had some 70,000 separate accounts; and the society-members, through their savings facilities, millions such; its assets were over $400,000,000, of which some 340 millions were in medium or long term investments such as government bonds; fifty millions in short term investments; twenty millions in overdrafts or loans to customers and twenty-five millions in cash on call. The "profits" on the financial transactions of the bank return ultimately to the consumer member as a component of his purchase-dividend: That is, he gets his banking service at cost.

§ 9. WHY CREDIT HAD TO BE SOUGHT COÖPERATIVELY

ALTHOUGH, historically, certain aspects of banking are functions of the needs of great gentlemen of leisure engaged in vindicating their freedom and worth through conspicuous consumption, banking as we know it today developed as an accessory to production and is largely now the producers' master. The needs of the ultimate consumer for credit hardly come into its purviews. The average man makes small loans whose handling may cost as much as the interest that may be collected from him amounts to, and in the main he is left to the usurer, the money-changer, and the modern "private banker" and joint-stock companies and loan sharks who specialize in lending money to simple citizens at rates which in one way or another remain usurious, either because the average man is so easy a victim or so great a risk. "How is it," asked Abbe de Lammenais, four years after the Rochdale Pioneers established their consumers' coöperative, "how is it the worker cannot borrow? Simply because he has no security to offer except just his work in the future. That future guarantee can only become real and certain by means of combination. Union eliminated the uncertainty which hitherto made the security worthless and the loan impossible."[2] Risky as they are held to be, even without union the total volume of these small, consumer loans easily holds its own with the volume of greater producer transactions: In the industrially undeveloped areas like China, India, and the near East, there are hardly any others whether for consumption or production. Nor are the numbers, the business and the profits of the usurers and their mutants by any means to be sneered at in industrially-developed countries like England or the United States or Germany. Always, the consumer's need for credit has been as imperative as his need for goods and clothing; more often than not he could not secure the second without the first: always, consequently, he has been at the mercy of the usurer, whether this usury was exacted in the form of excessive prices for goods or exorbitant interest for money.

In England, freedom from this bondage was sought among industrial workers through the creation of the consumers' coöperative society and the endeavor to keep all transactions cash transactions. For agricultural workers cash transactions were out of the question. Farmers had no wages, coming in regularly, to depend on; their need of credit for production was even more urgent than their need of credit for consumption. Thus, in the coöperative organization of the agricultural workers of Great Britain and Ireland, under the leadership of Sir Horace Plunkett and George Russell, credit societies were of first importance. At the same time, it turned out that the endeavor to do without credit in the consumer coöperatives grew more and more doubtful, as the coöperative enterprises grew larger and more varied.

§ 10. CREDIT UNIONS: BÜRING, SCHULZE-DELITSCH, RAIFFEISEN

THE CHARACTERISTIC modern forms of credit coöperatives were developed in Germany, where freedom from the bondage of

[2] *La Question du Travail* (1848).

the usurer was sought through the creation of coöperative loan banks. The forms there developed have proved even tougher and more adaptable than the consumers' stores. They have been diffused throughout the world, and employed with the same success in Europe, in Asia and in the Americas, in countries with populations all peasants and in countries with populations mostly wage-workers.

The earliest form of credit coöperative was devised by Büring in the eighteenth century. A land-mortgage credit organization, it was intended to serve the credit needs of German landowners and independent farmers and was postulated on the collaboration of the government. Under Büring's scheme, landowners of a certain locality formed a society whose members assumed joint responsibility for the debts of the society. Each pledged his property as security. The society thereupon issued bonds in an amount equivalent to the value of the total properties pledged. It lent any member a sum, in the form of these bonds, not to exceed two-thirds of the value of his property-pledge. He then sold the bonds in the market for what they would bring, and he had twenty-five years in which to repay all charges—interest, costs and principal—and the corresponding value in bonds was redeemed when he completed his payments. The method was sanctioned and implemented by Frederick the Great. The Federal Credit Administration of Mr. Roosevelt's New Deal has adapted this technique to American uses.

The true credit coöperative was not devised, however, until almost a century later. Its inventor was the Prussian lawyer, Herrmann Schulze-Delitzsch, born in 1808. A judge's son, he grew up in the turmoil of revolutionary romanticism and democratic struggle which marked the history of the younger generation of post-Napoleonic Europe, without coming to that new philosophy of revolution whose classical utterance was the *Communist Manifesto*. His outlook was political, his spirit humanitarian, his method that of the modern social worker. His experiences as a liberal member of the Prussian National Assembly of 1848, and his treatment by the government thereafter disillusioned him regarding political effort as a means of salvation. They rendered him wary of the state. Industry was just beginning to make its way in Prussia, and the hardship that came with it to the townsmen of the lower middle class, was even more conspicuous than that coming to the peasant who was still too much a serf. Schulze-Delitzsch, working in philanthropic loan and provident societies, conceived the idea of an extensive coöperative enterprise that might develop into a total economy. But nothing came of this idea. The urgent need seemed to be for credit, and it is the coöperative organization of credit among urban workers that Schulze-Delitzsch devised. From 1850, when he established his first loan bank, to the day he died, he was the director and philosopher of the loan bank movement. Under his plan, state aid was rigidly excluded. Members joined voluntarily, each buying one share and not more than one share. The shares came high. The liability of the society, as the law went then, had to be unlimited; the range of its banking activities limited: it was able to accept savings and deposits from non-members and to discount bills of exchange. Its government was not altogether democratic. Management was delegated to paid officials responsible to a committee which usually did not function, and the control by the members was limited. Interest was paid at the market rate and the profits were divided—one-fifth as reserve and the rest as dividends to members.

The need which the Schulze-Delitzsch societies served was so urgent and their service so obvious that they multiplied rapidly. In 1859, they formed a central organization with Schulze-Delitzsch to head it. But they did not create a central financial instrument: for this they used the Bank of Dresden which set up a Coöperative Department *ad hoc.* The central organization labored, like its English analogue, to overcome the limitations and invidious distinctions due to the law of the land. Schulze-Delitzsch secured the promulgation of the first Prussian coöperative law in 1867. An imperial statute changing and limiting liability was procured in 1889, and other liberties have since been gained. But essentially, the structure created by Schulze-Delitzsch remains.

What Herrmann Schulze-Delitzsch was to the dislocated urban craftsman, his junior of ten years, Friedrich Raiffeisen, was to the agricultural worker. Deeply responsive to the authority of the church and further regimented by army service, this son of a village burgomaster became himself a burgomaster in his twenty-seventh year and worked at this profession for twenty years, passing by invitation from the service of little German town to little German town. In 1865, failing health caused his retirement from this form of public service, and with the income from a small business to support him, he devoted himself to the promulgation of his plan for agricultural credit coöperatives. He had had, as burgomaster, a diversified experience of coöperative organization. In 1846, he started the *Konsumsverein* at Weyerbusch which operated a mill and a bakery—not of course on Rochdale principles; it was long before the Germans learned of the English movement or the English of the Germans—and throughout his professional career he initiated numerous *Hilfsvereine* and loan-banks. It was through his occupation as mayor that he came to realize the importance of credit for the multitudes, and when he retired he wrote down his views in a book: *Die Darlehnskassen-Vereine als Mittel zur Abhilfe der Not in des Landischen Bevölkerungs* (Lending-fund Society as an Agency of the Relief of the Agricultural Population). The book had an immediate influence. It passed through five editions during his lifetime.

The Raiffeisen system of coöperative banking was designed for his country's poorest, the uneducated peasants, socially still close to serfdom. It was based, like the first consumer-coöperatives in England, on personal character, mutual trust and knowledge. Unless the law required it, an individual joining a Raiffeisen society was not obliged to buy a share of stock. Shares were set at ten marks payable in small instalments, to make membership easy where the law made shareholding a condition of borrowing. The society's liability was unlimited. It received deposits and savings, and it made loans. The decision as to loans was as a rule made by a board of directors elected by the members and serving without fees. A borrower gave his note which had to be endorsed by two neighbors. Being an implementation of mutual trust for the service of individual needs, the society, both by intent and by method of operation, needed to be small, local, and rather intimate. It charged and paid a lower rate of interest than that which prevailed in the city, and in the course of time added to its first job of supplying credits to its members, marketing, purchasing and processing services. The profits were not paid out but held in a common fund which was employed to make improvements and to finance the other forms of coöperative endeavor.

The record of the Raiffeisen societies sufficiently testifies to their success. By 1872, there were enough of them to federate and establish the first regional coöperative bank; and in 1876, the National Central Agricultural Bank was organized. Through the Central Bank a surplus accumulated by any local society could be transferred, in the form of a loan, to some other society whose cash was insufficient. The Central Bank also lent money to the trading coöperatives, or engaged in trade itself, slightly in the manner of a Consumers' Wholesale. The Raifleisen enterprises won the approval and support of the Prussian government. It set up a state bank for the purpose of lending the Raiffeisen societies money at low rates of interest and on the ground of the government's actual and possible investments, it organized government supervision and auditing of the societies' work and accounts.

§ 11. DIFFUSION

THE WHOLE DEVELOPMENT provided an example which other governments did not fail to imitate and endeavor to improve upon. Italy, France, Belgium, Austria-Hungary, the Balkan countries, Ireland, India, Japan, all encouraged agricultural credit societies on the Raiffeisen pattern. Most followed the Prussian example of lending to the societies at low interest rates and requiring state supervision and audit. In the more democratic countries—Italy and Ireland, for example—the initiative was taken by liberal humanitarians like Luzzatti, Wollemborg, Horace Plunkett, George Russell; it was Henry Wolff, a president of the International Coöperative Alliance, who introduced the plan to India. Lately it was extended in China.[3] In some countries the governments gave no aid. But by the beginning of the present century the value of the credit union for the agricultural population was recognized throughout the world. It flourished in places and among peoples where no other form of coöperative organization seemed able to take root.

§ 12. CREDIT UNIONS IN THE UNITED STATES

AMONG THOSE is the United States. Here also it owes its development, under the name Credit Union, to the labors of a humanitarian and liberal who, having accumulated a fortune in commerce, withdrew from business to work, as *Who's Who* declares, at the "promotion of the better organization of production and distribution in the United States and Europe, in order to lower cost, eliminate waste, increase wages and profits and raise the general standard of living." This man is Edward A. Filene. Born in Salem, Massachusetts, seventy years ago, the eldest son of a Jewish tradesman, he went from the public schools into his father's business in Boston, and with his brother led in the building of the prosperous department store under the firm name of Wm. Filene's Sons Company. In 1908, while on a visit in Germany, he learned of the Raiffeisen societies and their spread, and it seemed to him that they would be very valuable to the plain people of America. Canada had had such societies since 1900. In that year the French Canadian journalist Alphonse Desjardins, with the approval and coöperation of churchmen, got together a dozen odd inhabitants of the parish of Levis in the province of Quebec, and with a capital of twenty-six dollars started the *Caisse Populaire de Levis* as a near-Raiffeisen bank. Participants received the earnings back in the form of dividends on savings. By 1908, the capital of the Levis bank was closer to $100,000 than to twenty-six dollars; its loans to members were close to $400,000 and it had fellow societies in a number of

[3] During 1934–35, Max Brauer, a pre-Nazi leader in the German coöperative movement, organized credit and purchasing and sales coöperatives among the peasants of the Shansi Province in China. His work had to stop because the Nazis threatened to recognize Manchukuo if Brauer were not dismissed by Nanking.

other parishes of the Province. Desjardins set up a similar *Caisse* among French Canadians in New Hampshire with equal success. When Filene returned home, he made contact with Desjardins, and with Pierre Jay, then bank commissioner of Massachusetts. Jay, reacting to the depression of 1907, had come, in the course of searches for a way out, upon the record of the people's banks and was recommending them to Americans.

Between Filene, Desjardins and Jay, the terms of a bill were set down which should make the credit union, under the supervision of the Commissioner of Banks, a legal form of banking in Massachusetts. The bill was presented to the legislature and became a law in 1909. But no unions followed. Education and guidance as well as legal authorization were needed. Filene and a number of other Massachusetts citizens, among them Louis Brandeis, united to meet the expenses of a quiet educational campaign. Both the War and the peace were a distraction, but the effort was at no time abandoned. By 1921, it took the form of the Credit Union National Extension Bureau. The idea was that the Bureau should teach the nation as Massachusetts had been taught. The costs were underwritten by Filene. With headquarters in Boston and Roy F. Bergengren as executive secretary, the Bureau started on its several objectives of securing adequate legislation in the different states of the Union, educating the public in the theory and practice of coöperative banking, fostering and aiding the formation of credit unions, federating the local into state organizations and combining the state organizations into a national association.

These objectives were reached in little more than a dozen years. In August, 1934, the Credit Union National Association was formed and on March 1, 1935, it took over the assets and liabilities of the Extension Bureau and the Bureau was liquidated. In its twelve-odd years of labor the Bureau had placed coöperative banking laws on the statute books of thirty-three states and of the District of Columbia; it had secured the enactment of a federal law which enables and controls the formation of credit unions in states with no laws of their own, or in states with bad laws or with an administration inimical to the movement. It had established an *entente cordiale* between the movement and the Farm Credit Administration. It had brought the idea of the credit union to all manner and condition of men: Mr. Bergengren claims "sixty well-defined types of successful credit-unions." He probably means sixty different bases of association intimate enough for the mutual faith necessary to credit coöperation: occupational, geographical, religious, political, social and the like. These "sixty well-defined types" at present embrace more than 3,000 unions and 750,000 members. Their resources amount to upward of $60,000,000; their credit turnover goes toward the billions, and they are still growing. They have survived the depression—and the same holds for the European credit cooperatives—as brilliantly, or more so, as the consumers' cooperatives. With the replacement of the subsidized Extension Bureau by the self-supporting National Association, the national headquarters have been moved from Boston, Massachusetts, to Madison, Wisconsin. The organization's new home has been named Raiffeisen House.

§ 13. THE UNSOLVED PROBLEM IN CREDIT: SERVICE OR RULE OF THE CONSUMER INTEREST

OF THE VARIOUS TYPES of coöperatives which are associated together in the International Coöperative Alliance, the credit unions are, if we except the Russian societies, the most numerous and the most powerful. They are the most immediate and direct concern of governments, and receive the greatest degree of government backing and are subjected to the completest government supervision and control. The law, which protects the poor man's credit when he entrusts it to his fellow, and by comparison neglects it when he entrusts it to a commercial banker, hampers as much as it safeguards. Everywhere, it is in the same need of reform as were the laws of England governing the organization and management of cooperatives. There is no intrinsic reason why the credit union, especially when organized on a national scale, with the character and resources of the multitudes of citizens guaranteeing each and all, should not exercise, within the coöperative movement, all the legitimate functions of commercial banks, and enjoy the same privileges. No uninvidious argument has yet been advanced why the loans made by credit unions should be limited to their available cash, while the business of commercial banks is conducted on a cash reserve averaging about 10 per cent of its total. No legitimate reason has been given for the handicap allowed to commercial banks over credit unions through the checking privilege. All the reasons reduce themselves to the presumption that the people who organize coöperative societies—whether for purposes of consumption or production or credit—are somehow less competent, less provident, more shiftless, than those who organize commercial or manufacturing, or financial joint-stock companies.

But the record shows how false all that is. "Private" business in all fields has blown up while coöperative enterprise has stood firm. Everywhere legislation is directed to regulating and controlling private business in its exploitation of other people's money. This has been one of the major objectives of the American New Deal. This is why the nation's palladia, such as Liberty and the Constitution, are being conscripted for the benefit of the sacred cows of the competitive credit-enterprise economy, and invoked to sanctify an attack by Big Business against New Deal measures which are terrifying innovations in the United States and time-worn commonplaces in England and the other industrial countries of Europe.

That these measures are destined to the same rôle and fate in the national economy as their ancestors, the anti-trust laws, is hardly to be doubted. The remedy against the iniquities of our banker economy is to strengthen its democratic alternatives, to remove the restrictions upon coöperative banking without removing its safeguards. The credit union is not dealing with other people's money, it is dealing with its own. Its basic purpose is not pecuniary profit but the life more abundant for its members. Automatically it tends, as did the Raiffeisen Banks in Germany, toward the investment of its surpluses in other forms of coöperative enterprise. Thus, as the consumer society found itself moving from the handling of goods to the handling of credit, so the credit societies move from the handling of credit to the handling of goods. But credit and finance are imponderables, highly abstract and symbolic, the power of faith in an ultimate consumer-value which may never be realized. Where they pay the piper and call the tune there is always a danger that the fullness of life may be made secondary to a balance of debits and credits. In an adequate consumer economy, this may not be. Its banking structure and credit system must be the servants of consumption, and only that. In the fact that the autonomous and independent credit union is far more than the consumer organizations compatible with the economic *status quo;* in the fact that the credit union is the most prevailing form of coöperative society, in the fact that it gets the full moral and financial support of the most anti-democratic and reactionary type of government, such as that of Japan, there resides a neglected problem of coöperative theory and practice: It is the problem of shaping the development of the existent coöperative banking structure so that, like the Banking Department of the English Coöperative Wholesale, it may ever serve and never rule the consumer interest.

CHAPTER XII

THE ORGANIZED CONSUMER AS EMPLOYER

§ 1. THE MASTER-SERVANT RELATION IN THE INDUSTRIAL ECONOMY

WE USUALLY think of employers as persons who hire and fire employees. We hardly ever remember that this is a secondary and derivative activity, that they can do it only after an enterprise has been planned, capital invested, a plant constructed and implemented, material to work on provided, and arrangements have been made for the disposition of the finished product. Giving employment, in a word, is an intermediate step in a long series composing an "industry" and depends for its continuance on both what goes before and what follows after. In the expression, "capital and labor," "capital" is used as the synonym for employer, but means far more than this employing function. Like "labor" it is an abstraction; "Labour," in the words of Stanley Jevons, "is any painful exertion of mind or body undergone partly or wholly with a view to future good." But to the mind of the modern world "capital" and "labor" mean "employer" and "employee." They mean the master-servant relation, and they mean it for a state of the social mind whose conscience is much disturbed regarding the morality of this relation. The meaning is comparatively recent. It is a creation of the financial-industrial economy. With it go certain corrective conceptions regarding the ethics of unemployment, the "right to work" and "social security."

These conceptions did not exist either when "labor" was a household of slaves or a village of serfs. Whether as living chattels among other men's personal possessions or as immovable growths of other men's soil, the multitude of producers presented no problem of security or unemployment; they claimed no "right to work." For themselves, the problem was liberty, and the right they claimed was the right *not* to work—the right of free contract, choice of occupation, and the other "liberties" designated by the French Bill of Rights, and fought for, over the continent of Europe, a hundred years after. The nineteenth century was more than half over before the last German ceased to be a serf; it was 1861 before the Russian Czar issued his liberating decree, and many decades more before any of the Russian multitudes could take practicable advantage of it.

Everywhere, from Newcastle to Nijni-Novgorod, the development followed a relatively self-repeating pattern. Freedom and mobility brought "insecurity" and unemployment in their wake. As causes of unemployment they are prior to the *crise pléthorique* and perhaps underlie it. For they made the way of industrialization easier. The serf, detached from his lord, as a prisoner in jail is detached from his warden when his time is up, became in the same manner a man "unemployed." His unemployment was an aspect of his freedom. That not only changed his status, but made available his hitherto harnessed energies for the vindication of this freedom, in which resided all the equality with his masters that he knew. Liberty empowered him to pass from the level of the mere producer who works without living, to the level of the consumer who, if he works, also lives.

Unfortunately, the liberty had come to him defined and implemented for an agricultural economy. The new economy of finance and industry permeated it, distorted it, and limited its fulfilment. It shackled the western spirit more firmly than ever to the delusion that production takes precedence over consumption and that the consumer exists for the sake of the producer. It elaborated and sanctified the prevailing employer-employee relation. It made of the employee a wage-earner. As a wage-earner, however, his struggle for his living and his life ceased more than ever to be a struggle with nature. It became entirely a struggle with human nature, and with human nature more than ever impatterned by property and driven by its passions. The employer was the man of property entering into free contracts with men of no property. The one-sided use of property in such contracts nullified the freedom which made them possible. For much property in the hands of one man confronting many with little or none gives him the same advantage over them as arms over the unarmed. If I hold what you require merely in order to keep life in your body, I can compel you to do what I require in exactly the same way as a bandit with a gun in his hand can compel you. And this, in the industrial-financial world, is what the employer did to the employee, capital to labor.

We have already discussed the characteristic efforts to break down this compulsion: the philanthropic Owenite movements, the struggles for political enfranchisement, the nationalisms, the new religious evangels, the socialist movements, and the trades-unions. Of these efforts the socialist movements and the trades-unions have survived in the form of enduring separate institutions with a developed doctrine and discipline. Even the consumers' coöperative societies, it must not be forgotten, began in England as producers' effort toward self-liberation and producer autonomy. They had been going and growing nearly half a century before they discovered for themselves something of the full meaning of being a consumer, and that entire interval had been punctuated by endeavors to subordinate the coöperative movement to "self-governing workshops"; failing that, to give these workshops a privileged place in the movement, or at least to give its employees a considerable share in its direction and its "profits." By the time these endeavors lapsed and the paramountcy of the consumer was taken for granted, the trades-unions had established themselves in the economy of England in their present form. The motives and methods drawing from Owen, from the Christian

Socialists, from the example of the French, fell into desuetude. Where trades-union organization had been employed as an instrument to obtain other than trades-union ends, such as the political franchise or the furtherance of Socialism, these ends were now treated as means toward characteristic trades-union purposes: the progressive extension of union standards of wages, hours, and conditions of labor.

In practice, this meant that union members had ceased to regard themselves as producers endeavoring to vindicate their rights and liberties as citizens of industry, or their trades-unions as implements of their struggle toward industrial self-government. In practice this meant that producers accepted and acquiesced in the conception of themselves as employees working for employers, and used their trades-unions as means to establish and enforce a competitive advantage in the employee-employer relation. In practice this meant that the organized producer acquiesced in the different functional relations of employer and employee to the enterprise which provided the employee's employment,[1] and limited the employee's stake therein to the competitive value of his job. Thus trades-union principle and practice confirmed the separation of labor from life, of occupation from personality, of production from consumption. Labor, occupation, production, were dispositions of one's energy for a money-wage; life, personality, consumption, were the expenditure of that wage in self-renewal and delight, to be realized elsewhere than on the job, and in other forms than work.

Whatever may be said of the psychology or the moral outlook underlying the separation, its practical consequences cannot be described as entirely unfortunate. The organization of producers as employees only, on the whole and in the long run, prospered. The trades-unions became permanent powers to which aspirants with wider aims attached themselves. From the early 1870's, when a parliamentary act recognized the unions and their endeavors as a lawful part of the social structure of Great Britain, they have grown in numbers, wealth and strength. Business cycle has followed business cycle, and the trades-unions have suffered all the changes and chances of

[1] *Cf.*, above, the remarks of E. J. Lever, p. 276 n.

that succession; they have weathered winds of doctrine from syndicalists, socialists, communists and tories; they have expanded a labor lobby into a labor party; once, their leaders even became ministers of a labor government: they have also called and lost a general strike.

Nevertheless, the drama of this story is surface-change, remote from the growth and work of trades-unions as employee-organizations. Consisting in the main of associations of skilled laborers, confederated in a Trades-Union Congress which has less jurisdiction over its members than the A. F. of L., they evidence no uniform organizational pattern. Industrial, craft and general unions come together and do the best they can. A large percentage of British labor is still unorganized; in 1932, trades-union members counted only five millions out of the total number of British citizens gainfully employed. But they have a status from which American labor organizations are still remote: a yellow dog contract cannot be drawn; collective bargaining is universal; trade agreements—national, regional, local—such as the New Deal sought to make part of its "codes of fair competition," are an old story; machinery of conciliation and arbitration of disputes is maintained by the government, and its use is required by law, without denial of the right to strike.

§ 2. EMPLOYER-EMPLOYEE RELATIONS IN THE BRITISH COÖPERATIVE MOVEMENT

AMONG the 1,060 unions represented in the Trades-Union Congress is the National Union of Distributive and Allied Workers. In this union are enrolled, as a *sine qua non* of their employment, all the employees of the consumers' coöperative movement in Great Britain. In fact, they are more than a preponderant majority of the Union. They work under a general agreement between the Union and the stores affiliated with the Coöperative Union, and under another arrangement with the Coöperative Wholesale Society adapted to its diversified labor-structure. The agreement is the usual type prevailing in England. Its first concern is wages, hours, conditions of labor, and definition of the handling of disputes. These, if they cannot be settled by direct negotiation, are referred within seven days to the National Conciliation Board, which was set up by the union and the coöperative in 1926. The Board, consisting of twelve members and a chairman, is chosen in equal proportion by each party from panels. At least two members on each side must be from societies and unions which are not parties to the dispute. The Board must deal with the dispute within fourteen days, and while it is being decided strikes and lockouts are prohibited.

The Board's decisions may be unanimous; they may represent a majority of representatives of both sides, or be handed down by the chairman alone. A unanimous decision is automatically binding, but the other two are binding only by prior agreement between the disputants. Neither the right to strike nor to lockout is surrendered. Both have occurred; but very rarely. As a rule, if the Board fails to come to an acceptable decision, direct negotiations are resumed and in the course of time a consensus does develop. In the negotiations the side of the coöperatives is defended by an official labor adviser and all the problems of union relationships are handled by a labor department of which the adviser is the chief officer. The unions are represented by the appropriate trades-union official, usually the general secretary.

The Wholesale, with its diversified occupations and its necessity for drawing a good many different agreements, has another sort of machinery. A special sub-committee of the board of directors is designated to deal with trades-union relations. Directly responsible to this committee is the labor and personnel department, whose duty it is to deal directly with the employees and their representatives. The desirability of simplifying the situation is recognized by both sides and they are together studying the possibility of a single comprehensive instrument defining the relations between the Wholesale and its employees. It is the testimony both of the coöperatives and the unions alike that employer-employee relations obtaining within the coöperative movement are better far than those outside. Wages tend to be above the average; hours follow the custom of the country and are, if anything, a little shorter; and working conditions are far better. Many of the stores contribute to pension schemes, sickness and death benefits, old-age insurance, over and above the contributions required by the law of the land. They carry on what American business calls "welfare work"; they maintain schools; they provide training courses for employees, and give scholarship grants to encourage them to study. Similarly, the Wholesale offers to pay tuition fees of employees attending evening classes, pays wages above the established rate in fifteen industries and at the market in the rest, and provides universally better conditions of employment.

In some of the societies employees who are members are eligible to election to the board of directors; others provide for employee-representation in the management, so that the interests of employees may be properly protected; still others, like the Royal Arsenal Society, continue to maintain joint advisory councils for the mutual good and welfare of employers and employees. According to the general secretary of the National Union of Distributive and Allied Workers, the employer-employee relationships within the coöperative structure are themselves coöperative. "The operations of the National Conciliation Board for the coöperative service," he declares, "have been attended with considerable success. . . . Apart from this result in promoting and maintaining amicable relationships, the Conciliation Board has been the means of facilitating lengthy discussions on a variety of matters concerning the development of coöperative trade. Very useful means of joint effort by the managerial and operative sides have been found in many instances out of Conciliation Board proceedings or out of negotiations connected therewith." And a high official of the Wholesale declares: "The extension of coöperative production and distribution extends the value of employment of wage-earners under guaranteed trade-union conditions, and coöperative employment means greater facilities for organization and more regular employment. . . . The C.W.S. and the retail societies can justly claim that as a corporate body the movement is an enlightened and progressive employer and as the cardinal coöperative principle is the production of goods and the provision of service for use and not for profit . . . it is the movement's desire to see that its goods are produced under as nearly ideal conditions as its existence in a competitive world will permit."

§ 3. EVOLUTION OF THESE RELATIONS

THIS COMMENDABLE STATE of things is a development of little more than ten years. The events which led up to it involved the transition within the coöperative philosophy from the principle of the primacy of the producer to that of the primacy of the consumer. They covered an interval during which the consumer ideal was itself dominated and beclouded by the necessary entrepreneur activities of the consumer organization: The consumer, as employer in a competitive world of employers, fell into its characteristic competitive attitude and behaved like a producer producing for "profit." This period arrived in England about the time British trades-unions had consolidated their gains and their power had begun to expand in the British heavy industries. Concurrently, the principle of the paramountcy of the consumer was becoming definite in the consciousness of the leaders and the rank and file of the consumer movement, but had little effect on the widespread practice of sharing profits and of paying a bonus to labor over and above wages. The practice was challenged in 1893, and was abandoned by stages between 1914 and 1922. Bonuses were demanded by the employees, and held to be a moral debt of the coöperatives. It was argued that the net gain of the cooperatives was of the same nature as the profit of a profit-seeking concern.

But as J. T. W. Mitchell had made clear, all the difference between cost and price which remains in the treasury of a consumers' society after its books are balanced and before the dividend is distributed, has been put there by the consumer in the first place. It isn't something added from outside; it is something redistributed from within. Its relation to wages is altogether different from that of profit to wages. Although it is called profit or dividend, it is neither: it is a saving measured by spending. Even if it be true that the employee has a moral title to a share of the profits of private business, he has no kind of claim whatsoever to any of the savings of coöperative business. Those he may share only as a fellow consumer, and if he is not one, it is the simplest thing in the world for him to make himself one by joining the society which employs him, and thus becoming also his own employee.

Not that the bonus made a great deal of difference in the actual standard of living of the coöperative employee. He belonged to one of the most depressed and least organized of the occupational groups in the United Kingdom. Hours were everywhere long and wages low, conditions of labor often vicious. The worker as grocery clerk or bookkeeper or counter boy, employed by persons who in another relation are coal miners, engineers, locomotive drivers, textile workers, etc., found himself in a tangle of conflicts and coercions no different from those he encountered in private employment; the worker as employer found himself confronted by heedlessness, evasion, soldiering and sabotage of the same sort that profit-takers complained of. This is in the nature of things. The relation between employer and employee is intrinsically such that it cannot always be harmonious and pacific. As even in the happiest marriage there are bound to be quarrels and disagreements between husband and wife, so between employer and employee. These are part and parcel of the intrinsic weather of life, and the problem is always how best to minimize and offset their undesirable consequences.

During a considerable period undesirable consequences tended to develop, and to develop abnormally. Competitive pressure led committees and store managers to emulate their competitors in exploitation. Although the hours of labor in the coöperatives were slightly fewer than the sixty or seventy hours that prevailed in the same competitive field, and the wages were slightly higher than the prevailing pound per week or less, conditions were not any better and the chief advantage of the coöperative employee over the non-coöperative was that his job was steady.

The decade, from 1890 to 1900, was a penny-pinching one and many complained that the consumers' coöperative movement was setting dividends above decency. In 1893, William Maxwell, leader of the Scottish society, called indignant attention to conditions of employment in the coöperative movement. At the Congress of the Coöperative Union of that year he gave ample reason for the employee organization which had begun to form a year or two earlier. The women in the movement took up the issue. In the course of time the Women's Guild joined with the Amalgamated Union of Co-operative Employees—which had been expanded, in 1895, from the Manchester and District Coöperative Employees' Association, organized by J. H. Hallsworth in 1891—to campaign for a minimum wage for adults and a general improvement in standards and conditions of coöperative employment. Such a minimum was voted by the Coöperative Congress in 1908, and a united board created to prepare and propose a scale. The societies, however, disregarded the suggestions of the Congress and behaved as if a joint commission of trades-unionists and co-operators which had been created in 1881 to serve as arbitrators in disputes did not exist.

And so far as its authority went, it didn't. The employees concluded that the organized consumer as employer was no better than the private producer. They accumulated a strike fund and started an aggressive campaign. The philosophy of this campaign involved a restatement under the new conditions of the older Christian Socialist notions concerning the primacy of the producer. They invoked against the consumer organization its own principles. They based their demands on an abstract logic regarding wages and conditions rather than a realistic regard for the state of the industry in a competitive market. They demanded participation in management in terms of a philosophy of control which later, at the hands of intellectuals, developed into guild Socialism. Whatever differential advantage they received from the coöperatives they accepted as their due, and they pressed demands which it never occurred to them to make of private employers. During more than a decade their pressure on the coöperatives was so successful that they ceased to heed the import of the very agreements they themselves made and their tactics took on something of the character of a racket. Often they imposed terms which forced this or that store to operate at a loss.

So notable were the achievements of the Amalgamated Union of Coöperative Employees that a great many members of other unions sought to transfer their membership to it. Thereupon followed jurisdictional disputes, dissensions which terminated in 1916, with the resignation of the Amalgamated Union of Coöperative Employees from the Trades-Union Congress. To this the Congress replied by outlawing the Amalgamated and calling upon the coöperatives to boycott all affiliated with it and to employ only workers who were members of affiliates of the Trades-Union Congress. The tasks and duties brought by the conditions of the World War seem to have done little to mollify the general exacerbation. But by the time the war came to an end the coöperative employees' union amalgamated with the National Union of Warehouse and General Workers, and this finished the jurisdictional dispute. The conjoint formation called itself the National Union of Distributive and Allied Workers and in 1919 rejoined the Trades-Union Congress. Employers of the members of this union are now not exclusively coöperatives. This fact influenced the character of the general agreement to be drawn. It relaxed the pressure on the coöperatives. In the strikes which the Union called the same year it is significant that the deciding multitude of the coöperative membership sided with their employees against their managements and from these strikes there grew the present pattern of relationships between employers and employees.

These employees are mainly manual laborers, clerks, transport workers—the rank and file of the operatives in the consumer structure. The "brainworkers"—the secretaries and managers—have their own organization, with its own history of transformations and readjustments. This organization is less like a trades-union than a professional association. Compared with the pay of men of similar executive rank in corporations in other private business, the salaries its members receive are low, and they are little concerned to make them higher. The great gulf between the wages of management and the wages of the operative staff which characterizes non-coöperative business does not exist. The executives feel themselves the leaders of a movement, not the pursuers of a fortune, and their organizations are the vehicles of this feeling. The secretaries had formed an association in 1908; the managers in 1912. In 1914, the Union of Coöperative Employees attempted to absorb them and hold them in its ranks, on a theory, not consciously worked out but applied, which could be called syndicalist.

Of course the attempt could not long succeed. Although the managerial and the operational functions are supplementary and interdependent, and are means to an industrial end, they approach this end from opposed starting-points. To management, labor is necessarily an agent in the execution of a plan of enterprise; to labor, management, be it the most freely chosen leadership, is necessarily magisterial and coercive. No amount of "self-government in industry" can change this functional relationship. It obtains wherever many men work together for a common end. In science, in sports, in play, in religion, as well as in war and in industry, some must command and others must obey. The Soviets learned this from defeats of their efforts to secure production by a technique of factory control which, ignoring this condition, paralyzed soviet industry; and they are today operating on the opposite principle; employing all the dehumanizing devices of "scientific management," in the organization and direction of their plants emulating the methods of the Ford Motor Company and the United States Steel Trust, and reconciling the contradiction with their communist orthodoxy by calling the tyranny "socialist competition." Elsewhere, social agencies, voluntary scientific or research organizations, trades-unions themselves, have learned the same lesson. No employer, with the best will in the world, can avoid falling at one time or another into exploitation or injustice; no employee, working with the most devoted concentration and loyalty, can avoid falling into slackness and sabotage. For these reasons an eleemosynary organization like a federation of charities and a semi-public research organization like Consumers' Research, have found themselves confronted with strikes. For these reasons a trades-union in one occupation, in its rôle as employer of workers in another occupation, may find its offices picketed by its striking employees.[2]

As the record of the "self-governing workshops" shows,

[2] Local 1,733 of the Silk and Rayon Workers' Union was in 1935 fighting a strike of the Office Workers' Union.

these divisions of labor, the differences of function between management and operation, are not abolished by identifying the two, and except where an individual works alone, and for himself, the identification serves only to arrest production. This is one of the reasons why economic democracy is unattainable in exclusively producer terms.

Whether or not these observations were in the minds of the managements of the British societies, their action was naturally determined by them. In 1917, general managers, heads of departments, cashiers, accountants, buyers, propagandists, organizers, teachers, secretaries, organized the National Union of Coöperative Officials. This association of officials is a trades-union in the same sense as the association of men is a trades-union, but from the first its collective attention was directed to the problems of their profession, and continues to focus there. Themselves employee producers, they are answerable to the great body of consumers who employ them for the adequate conduct of their employers' business: abundantly to provide them, as ultimate consumers, with the necessities and comforts of life in an ever better quality at an ever lower cost.

To the successful attainment of this end, the liberty, the well-being, and the participative interest of the employees, from the highest to the lowest, is a means indispensable; and the organization of this means through the autonomous association of employees for the purpose of suggestion, criticism, consultation and safeguarding themselves from exploitation and oppression is a necessity. But in the very nature of things it is only and always a means, not an end; it must remain forever secondary, subordinate to the end, as production remains secondary and subordinate to consumption. The right and power of possession and control, hence the responsibilities of management, must remain in the hands of the consumers.

It took the consumers' coöperative movement of Great Britain some fifty years to arrive at this view of the employer-employee relation. No less than the trades-unions an employees' movement par excellence, it began with the doctrine of the primacy of the producer. It operated on the assumption that the doctrine was workable, and discarded it reluctantly, and with many a backward glance, after fifty years of expensive experimentation and testing. It took another twenty-five years to come to the present machinery both for dealing with employer-employee conflicts, and for facilitating employer-employee coöperation for the common end.

This machinery embodies the freest, the most efficient and the most hopeful organization of the employer-employee relationships devised to date. Its logic leads to a nation-wide confederation of employees. All the workers of each small, local industrial or agricultural establishment would associate themselves into a corresponding guild or union; these would come together in their national confederations of shoe workers, automotive workers, building-trades workers, physicians, teachers, etc.; and these national associations would compose the nation-wide confederation of producers, which would correspond to the Consumers' Coöperative Wholesale or the Coöperative Congress or both. Its task would be the production-engineering of the national economy and the safeguarding of the producer from exploitation in the process. It would discharge all the functions which the trades-unions are ideally supposed to discharge. But its attitude toward the coöperative as employer would not be primarily combative, but primarily collaborative. Its government would be as democratic as that of the national consumers' organization and its relations to the member-organizations similar. It would, of course, not be quite sovereign. It would be answerable to the consumer-organization for the quality, quantity and variety of the goods and services produced, even as the consumer-organization would be answerable to it for the standards and conditions of work.

§ 4. EMPLOYER-EMPLOYEE RELATIONS IN THE COÖPERATIVES OF BELGIUM, CZECHOSLOVAKIA, DENMARK, FINLAND, FRANCE, NORWAY, PALESTINE, RUSSIA, SWEDEN, SWITZERLAND

As England, so the other countries in which the consumers' coöperative movement has grown to wealth and power. Most of them are prevailingly agricultural, not industrial. All are confronted with the problems and prospects of industrialization, at least of agriculture. Most, even the completely agrarian and individualistic, operate in a social and political order which had, before England, followed the Bismarckian precedent of establishing certain types of social insurance—such as insurance against unemployment, sickness, old age, and the like—as a part of the law of the land. And employer-employee relations are conditioned, of course, by this context.

In Belgium, all employees of coöperatives are members at once of the consumer organization and of their appropriate trades-unions. When disputes arise in large societies, they are referred under a national agreement to mixed committees representing both parties; in smaller societies to mixed committees representing the management and the personnel; some societies provide for employee representation in the directorate.

In Czechoslovakia, the employees of the coöperative movement are associated together as a separate section of the national organization of trades-unions. Relations between employer and employee are governed by a general agreement which provides for a mixed conciliation board, with the president of the National Trades-Union as chairman, to deal with disputes. Under the agreement the decision of the board is final, and strikes are ruled out. As in Belgium, the state is a partner to an unemployment insurance scheme, but the coöperatives maintain additional funds, allocated from their surplus, for superannuation, sickness, disablement, funeral expenses. They allow longer vacations than the required legal minimum, provide for the continued training of their employees, and often pay the employees' income tax out of the surplus. As consumer members, employees are eligible for election to the directorate.

Denmark, far more agricultural than Belgium or Czechoslovakia, presents a somewhat different picture. Conciliation is obligatory under the law of the land. Disputes are not infrequent; strikes occur. An agreement obtains between the Danish Wholesale and the federated trades-unions. In the bacon factories it does not formally include the white-collar workers, but they usually get the benefit of its terms. The agreement between the dairies and the union is obligatory only when it is unanimously accepted. Distributive stores situated in towns have agreements with their workers; those in the country do not. Nevertheless, the relations between employers and employees in the coöperative community of Denmark have been signally amicable: only two strikes and lockouts are recorded in twenty years.

Finland is also an agricultural country, and a poor country, poorer than Denmark, with a later start in the coöperative movement, and a division along social and religious lines into two consumer organizations, one of which may be described as conservative, the other as progressive. The employees of both are organized in two trades-unions, one consisting of the office, shop, depot and transport workers; the other of operatives in the provision and produce branches of the coöperative enterprise. Both unions are members of the Central Union of Finnish Trades-Unions. Between them and the coöperatives there is a general agreement which determines hours, wages and conditions of labor. Minima are established by law; but generally speaking, coöperative practice is, within the limitations of the competitive field, to do rather better than the law requires. The coöperative societies do not participate in the unemployment funds which the unions maintain, but they help in accident and life insurance; provide a sickness allowance of one to four weeks on full pay and sometimes participate in an employee sick fund. They provide professional instruction and make separate grants for school attendance. Since 1932, disputes are referred to a permanent board of conciliation consisting of three representatives from each party, with the chairman drawn alternately now from one party, now the other. Unanimous decisions are binding; majority decisions may be rejected in favor of the minority view; a tie is referred back to the respective organizations; failure to reach a decision leaves the complainant free to seek such remedies as he thinks wise. Strikes and lockouts occur, but very rarely. Employees are not eligible to election as directors.

In France, as in England, there has survived a small association of producers' coöperatives, or self-governing workshops, which have an older tradition than the consumer societies and in their own view at least, stand coördinate with them in value and superior in principles. The members of these workshops are called masters; their employees, helpers. The helpers are members of their respective trades-unions. Disputes are dealt with under standard agreement with the *Confédération General du Travail.* All the workshops practise profit-sharing and employment in them is comparatively stable. The several other advantages so characteristic of the consumer organization are rare; some workshops allow vacations on salary; some make contribution to sick benefits; some maintain apprentice schools or arrange for continuation studies. Work is done both on an hourly and on a piece basis. Strikes are infrequent.

The relation between the French self-governing workshops and the general trades-union movement is not very different from that obtaining between any other profit-sharing employer and organized labor. The relation between the C.G.T. and the consumers' coöperative movement postulates a basic difference. Organized labor in set terms gives the consumer movement a preferential position. The fifteen-year-old general agreement declares:

> Consumers' coöperative societies are institutions which, in their nature, seek no profit whatsoever, and through their objectives, constitute elements of a new society. Trades-unions, hence, are under obligation to bear this fact in mind in all relations they are called upon to enter into with the coöperatives. Conversely, it is the duty of the latter to find ways and means of organizing their labor force according to union requirements. At the same time, the consumer coöperative societies are never to be placed at a disadvantage (*en état d'infériorité*) before their private competitors, lest they disappear or no longer perform their full service for the consumer, especially for the working people who are the greater part of their membership.

Following this preamble it is generally agreed that the coöperatives will employ only trades-union members, through the offices of the unions. Wages, hours and conditions are to be those prevailing in the market, but as is usual, the coöperatives do better than that. Since social insurance is an undertaking of the government's it does not figure in the agreement, but the coöperatives add a voluntary subvention to the state tax for *apprentissage* or technical education. Disputes are referred to arbitration. There are no strikes, and the C.G.T. binds itself not to call out the employees of the coöperatives even during a general strike. A permanent national mixed commission is maintained to serve as guide and adviser and to render other *bons offices* regarding all matters that the parties to the contract submit to it jointly. Employees are rarely elected to the board of directors of a French coöperative.

In Norway coöperation between the coöperative movement, at least between its Wholesale organization, and the trades-unions is even closer. All employees of the Wholesale are required to be members of the Office and Shop Workers' Union, the Transport Workers' Union, or the Food Workers' Union. In the retail societies, union membership is not required, although the larger the number of employees, the more likely is enrollment in the union. Only from 20 to 25 per cent of the employees of the retail societies are organized. At the same time, the standards and conditions that obtain in the Wholesale tend to define the level of retail employment. Under an agreement, made in 1915, between the coöperatives and the National Federation of Trades-Unions, the coöperatives undertake to boycott non-coöperative concerns against which strikes are declared and the union pledges reciprocity. Disputes are referred to a joint committee and are considered without any interruption of work. The right to strike is not abrogated, but there have been only two strikes in the Wholesale since 1906. Employees have the right to elect one representative to the board of directors and one to what would correspond to the general council of the coöperative movement. Among the retail societies, conditions are more variable, but the tendency is general on the part of the union to demand, and on the part of the coöperatives to establish, even without demand, an employer-employee relationship on a level higher than that prevailing in the country.

Palestine presents a unique but paradoxical and confusing picture. For in Jewish Palestine consumers' coöperation has developed since the War and almost exclusively as an instrument of the producers' organization. Mostly an agricultural economy with an organization whose ideals and methods have been defined by and adapted from principles of industrial organization of the continental type, the Jewish labor movement in Palestine is associated into a sort of one big union which includes teachers and physicians as well as unskilled workers, and brings together samples of every mode of agricultural coöperative ever attempted elsewhere, besides a number brought out by the Jewish experiment. The consumers' aspect of the experiment does not appear to be very important. The Rochdale principles, it is said because of the peculiarities of the Palestinean problem, are not observed, and the technique of production and distribution, the allocation of surplus, the methods of management and control, are highly centralized. Practically speaking, however, so far as there are advantages in Palestine, they are all on the side of the employee.

The same cannot be said of Russia; and it cannot be said because in Russia the employer is the state and the state is a dictatorship of the proletariat, but not by the proletariat, and ambiguously for the proletariat. The same rules that govern the control of employment in the non-coöperative enterprises of the U.S.S.R. govern the employment of workers in Centrosoyus. The coöperatives, however, are charged with maintaining special training schools for the staff. Some ten million roubles are said to have been appropriated for training restaurant workers only. The organization maintains fifteen universities in various districts, but it is the government which guarantees insurance and "cultural services for the toilers." As the dominant point of view in Russia is a producer's point of view, much in this respect is left to the trades-unions who exact membership dues of 2 to 1 per cent of the wages of each worker and expend close to three-fourths of this income on "culture," maintaining workers' houses, "palaces of culture," trades-union clubs, and similar establishments, whose organization and membership are said to be voluntary and elective. The national income is divided by the central government into four parts, of which the bulk goes for reserve toward industrialization and toward armament. A modicum goes for social insurance, public health education, "public feeding," etc. The residue is allocated to individual consumption, distributed, in accordance with the quantity and quality of labor rendered by every toiler, in the form of individual wages. Concerning the adequacy of the service in Russian coöperatives, then the world's largest, W. H. Chamberlain said in 1929, "The element of corruption cannot be overlooked in reviewing the difficulties of the new system of economic administration. . . . The consumers' coöperatives, for instance, lose ten million rubles a year in embezzlements, which are especially common among the rural societies. . . . The ill-managed, bureaucratic trust, which puts out defective goods at high prices, and the negligent coöperative which allows its cashier to run off with the funds and stores its potatoes next to leaking kerosene tins, can be just as much of a plague to the consumer as the grasping monopoly or profiteering middleman under capitalism." [3]

This sort of thing is not to be found in the freer coöperative organizations, and is being driven out in Russia.

One of the freest of these organizations is that of Sweden. All the employees of the coöperative movement are required, as in England, to be members of their appropriate trades-unions. Employer-employee relations are based on a general agreement which is applied with specific variations according to the character of the case in dispute. The agreement provides for a committee on conciliation which arbitrates disputes. As usual, conditions of employment, wages and hours are better than those which prevail in the country in non-coöperative industry. There is no unemployment insurance, but the organization contributes 2 to 3 per cent of its wage-bill toward old-age pensions. It maintains a special school for employees, but like most of the coöperatives, it does not allow the election of employees to the directorate.

Essentially the same principle, but somewhat more middle-class, is the arrangement in Switzerland where a joint agreement providing for collective bargaining on tenure, vacations, wages, etc., governs the relations between employers and employees.

Of course the history of the employer-employee relation in each country varies according to the local situation, the prevailing tradition, and the other differentiating factors. The English record, English experience and practice provide the base as usual. The total picture is the picture of a movement starting at a great many different points and progressing concentrically and convergently toward a common standard pat-

[3] *Soviet Russia* (Little, Brown, 1929).

tern. The record shows a development in which accidents neutralize each other and the steady force flowing from the primacy of the consumer lays a general ground plan for the determination of employer-employee relations.

§ 5. THE RELATIONS IN THE UNITED STATES: THE STATUS OF THE AMERICAN TRADES-UNION

We turn now to the United States. Here the relation between the coöperative movement and organized labor reflects very precisely the conflicts and ambiguities which characterize both the coöperative and the labor movements in America. Although the United States is one of the most highly industrialized countries of the world, coöperation had had its most lasting development among American farmers, and in the form of marketing and purchasing societies. The latter buy mostly producer goods, not consumer goods. That is, in the American movement consumption is still secondary to production, and consumer organization is an instrument to a producer end. The most widespread and most powerful form of urban and wage-earner coöperative organization is the credit union. This fits more readily and smoothly into the trades-union context than other forms of coöperation. Not that consumer coöperation has not had its day among wage-earners, organized and unorganized. But at present it stands simply as a survival here and there, expressing a purely local or personal interest. However persuasive the pincers argument of Coöperative Distributors may be and however cogent its philosophy of consumer-trades-union relations, the fact still remains that those relations were much more prevalent in the past than they are today; and that this philosophy appeals more readily to unorganized intellectuals than to organized wage-workers.

In addition to the prevailing producer mentality, there are many reasons for the indifference of American organized labor to consumer-organization. The "American Dream" embodied in the availability of free land, the push upward which successive waves of immigrants gave the earlier comers, the powerful democratic idea and its political implements have had the effect of keeping labor organization in the United States backward in plan and undeveloped in structure.

The action of these positive influences has been reënforced by the inhibitions of legislative enactment and judicial decision postulated on an early capitalist notion of employer-employee relation which began to be modified only with the adoption of the Clayton Act. Trades-unions of the type that have become standard in England did not begin to grow and gather power till well after the turn of the century. Organizational gains have largely waited upon social and political crises, like wars and depressions. Thus, in 1920, at its height because of the World War, the American Federation of Labor had enrolled only five million members. Twelve years later this number had fallen, only partly because of the depression, to less than two and one-half million. There are internal causes which prevent it from holding the gains it does make and making the gains it can and should. Among these are the race[4] and sex prejudice which lead it to neglect Negro and women workers; the invidious caste and religious distinctions which lead it to ignore unskilled and immigrant labor and to prefer the comparative security of craft unionism, with its monopolistic aims and scarcity techniques, to the open industrial unionism which would enroll every employee in an industry, and establish a united front of collective bargaining vis-à-vis the employer. This is one of the reasons why, in spite of much protestation, nearly thirty million wage-earners in the United States remain shut out from the unions, and a permanent threat hence to union strength and effectiveness. From them are drawn the two and one-half million employees enrolled by their employers in company unions.

Under Article 7A of the National Industrial Recovery Act, which President Roosevelt called the charter of labor, some of the more militant unions in the American Federation of Labor put on an effective organizing campaign and Federation mem-

[4] Analogous factors may be observed in the organization of Polish trades-unions: of South African and Australian. The clothing workers and one or two other American unions are doing what they can to overcome the racial prejudices.

bership has come to about 80 per cent of its 1920 strength. There are now some four million workers in its 102 member unions. Of these unions twenty-five are exclusively craft unions; fifty-one are amalgamated craft unions, certain of the needle trades, the textile workers, the miners and the brewers are industrial unions; most of them are "international"; they have jurisdiction in Canada and sometimes Cuba. What would have happened without this "charter," if the unions had been left entirely to their own resources, may be gathered from the consequences of the depression of 1921.

Although the "charter," together with the rest of the National Recovery Act has been nullified by the Supreme Court of the United States of America, as contrary to the Constitution, governmental approval of collective bargaining is provided by the Wagner Bill. Assuming that the Supreme Court permits this bill to operate, it does little more than to permit trades-unions to organize. It does not endow them with the legal status they enjoy under the laws of England or the other democratic European countries. American trades-unionism, far more than labor in Europe, must depend on its own strength and power of organization, and this is not very considerable.

The "open-shop" anti-union employers' associations which exist mainly to prevent employee organization are "class-conscious" as their employees are not. They hate trades-unionism and all it implies, and fight it with every available weapon, calling their purpose and activities "the American plan." They are the chief supporters of strike-breaking organizations and the powers that construct and maintain company unions. Although they denounce class-distinctions and class-struggle as economic doctrines, their program and methods generate and maintain them as economic facts. Ironically enough, they vindicate Marxism by wilfully creating the very situation they condemn.

It is far otherwise with the average American employee. Not many regard themselves as permanently a member of the employee class. Each knows that in the voting booth, where he exercises his prerogative as a citizen, he is the equal of his employer. He believes that he can be, and aspires to make himself, the equal of his employer in the industrial field. Since he encounters his boss at the theater, the baseball park, the motion picture house, at the prize fight, on the same level as at the voting booth, he feels that he has the right, and therefore the power, to meet him in the same way on the economic field. The result is that his trades-union does not stand to the American working-man for the associative pattern of a way of life. He regards it as a business similar in kind and purpose to the business of the employer. This attitude has made it possible for American trades-unionism to develop business and even racketeering features of a sort that Europe does not know. It is moved neither by social vision nor by class interest. Its vision is the same as that of the employer. Its interest is, with some exceptions, to get its leaders if not its members into the class of the employer. With a vision and interest of this sort for drive, it can do little more than make haste slowly, even though it may, incidentally, improve the working conditions of its members.

After the depression of 1929 arrived, after it was slowly recognized that unemployment is likely to be a permanent and growing aspect of the present form of the American economic establishment, American trades-unionism found itself compelled to pay attention to the realities of its place in the national economy. It was forced unwillingly and not altogether honestly to consider the foundations of its internal structure and external functions and to review the import respectively of craft unionism and industrial unionism for its survival and growth. It was forced to recognize the company union for the growing menace it is.

For the company union is a menace not only as the employers' evasion of trades-unionism, but as the center for an autonomous and separate union movement analogous to that which grew in the men's clothing industry in 1914. When, under Article 7A of the National Industrial Recovery Act, the unions affiliated with the American Federation of Labor began to organize employees in their respective industries, the employers endeavored to circumvent them by swiftly organizing company unions. Sixty per cent of those counted in the fall of 1935 had been organized within the two preceding years, and many of them in establishments like the steel industry which the American Federation of Labor had consistently failed to organize. As was bound to happen, these unions are beginning to defy and to challenge the authority of the employer. They are beginning to associate together for purposes of collective bargaining on wages, hours and conditions of labor. Their association is taking an industrial and not a craft form. They count most numerously in the steel, rubber and automotive industries, and they have a point of view which has analogies in harmony with the older vision of the Knights of Labor and might come into the present attitude of the British unions. The leaders are a more intellectual type. They may become pace-makers and standard-bearers for the older trades-union movement in the United States. They will certainly intensify the bitter warfare of employer against employee throughout American industry. Should their rise fail to bring forth a new type of leader and to generate a reorganization of American trades-unions which will make them more effective servants of their members than they have heretofore been, even a constitutional Wagner Bill and every other form of support which the government may bring, will serve only to confirm the *status quo* and its evils.

§ 6. AMERICAN TRADES-UNIONS AND CONSUMER ORGANIZATIONS

Now, however much they improve upon the *status quo* they are not likely to gain so much from it as from a parallel and coördinate organization of consumers. But it must be organization as consumers through and through; it must be founded and implemented upon the primacy of consumption. The philosophy of consumer coöperation which sees it as merely an employee weapon in his struggle with the employer for the industrial surplus, is plausible but unwarranted by the record. So long as trades-unions organized consumers' coöperative societies as the commissary branch of their struggle with employers, their attention was divided and both organizations suffered. Little survives of the establishment set up by the Knights of Labor, the Sovereigns of Industry, and the Illinois miners, but the autonomous consumer organizations have been more durable even in the United States.

Unfortunately, consumer coöperative societies in America have thus far given as little evidence of power and unity as the American trades-unions. They have not been especially conceived to win trades-union interest, participation and coördination. The agricultural marketing and purchasing societies carry over into organizational policy the personal attitudes of their members toward employees; and many of the vigilante groups, whose behavior toward agricultural workers has earned the reprobation of the enlightened public opinion of the United States, are recruited from members of coöperative marketing and purchasing associations of fruit growers and the like. On the other hand, societies with a genuine coöperative tradition, like the Finnish ones, urge their employees to unionize. Many coöperative dairies, insurance companies and similar organizations require their employees to be members of appropriate unions. Some consumer societies, often with the most enlightened coöperative memberships, find that differences of color, nationality, sex, religion, make employee organization too difficult to undertake and too unsafe to encourage. On the other hand, the Coöperative Workers' Union, in which are enrolled practically all the employees in coöperative stores of Upper Michigan, Northern Wisconsin and Northern Minnesota, provides in its constitution that "no working-man or woman shall be excluded from membership in the union because of creed or color." This union was organized, indeed, to make place in the labor union structure for those who because of one thing or another are shut out of the usual A.F.L. unions.

On the whole and in the long run American coöperative societies have not reached a consensus of theory or practice and have developed no corpus of custom or statute rule regarding employer-employee relations. The state of the labor market, the judgment of the directors, the custom of the industry or the region determine wages and conditions. Employees as such are rarely represented on the Boards. No effective internal checks on managerial exploitation have yet established themselves. As in England before the formation of the Amalgamated Union of Coöperative Employees, American coöperative employees have the same standing as employees of private industries of similar character; and, as in England, the standards and conditions of employment in coöperatives are, nevertheless, better than those prevailing in non-coöperative services. Wages tend to be higher than the market, hours rather shorter and working conditions much more sanitary and pleasanter. The gradient of development is not well defined, but the facts suggest a form of employer-employee relationship similar to that prevailing elsewhere in the consumer coöperative movement.

§ 7. EMPLOYER-EMPLOYEE RELATIONS IN COÖPERATIVES: RETROSPECT AND PROSPECT

To SUM UP. As a matter of ordinary psychology, conflicts between people who have a common background, common aims, and common enemies are easiest to settle. This is why, on the record, the consumers' coöperative has been the best employer of labor. The needs which led working-men to form trades-unions also led them to set up consumers' coöperatives. The trades-union was the older formation. Embodying the first associative endeavor of industrial workers to overcome the hardships of their condition, it was not by itself successful, and it was first supplemented by consumers' coöperation and later on by Marxist Socialism and its doctrine and program of class struggle. In a certain sense trades-unions have been the field-force of this struggle, so far as it in fact exists. Their activities have consisted in setting up through combination, wherever possible, a monopoly in the "labor market" (called usually the "closed shop"), and of winning from the employer higher wages, shorter hours and better working conditions for his employees.

But what they win for their own members, they win at the expense of wage-earners in other industries organized in other unions. The higher wages they secure for a few are paid for by higher prices exacted from multitudes. Thus, the trades-union tends to seek the monopoly of employment in each industry, and the special high wages it is able to exact in this way is made the basis of general high prices. Whether the money wage be high as in the United States, or low as in England, wages lag persistently behind prices, and real wages—that which money brings in food, clothing, shelter, medicine, insurance, recreation, and other necessities and comforts of life—are thus kept at the lowest possible level instead of being lifted to the highest.

Nor, as the record shows so clearly, can the lift of real wages be accomplished through the program and methods of trades-unionism alone. It can be accomplished only as workers realize themselves as consumers, and as consumers organize. In England, producer trades-unionism gained strength from consumers' coöperation. The Rochdale Pioneers went from defeat as trades-unionists to victory as coöperators, from the status of employees as producers to the status of employers as consumers. And so with all consumers' coöperatives. When they become employers, they are employers whose members are at the same time the employees of others. Thus they are in conflict with the business world on two fronts. First, as workers, more and more members of trades-unions confronting employers; second, as coöperators competing with profit enterprises. It is natural, hence, that in their rôle as employers, their sympathies and interests shall be with the trades-unions rather than with the employer. Although different countries show considerable variations of practice, the coöperative movement as a whole does take collective bargaining for granted. There have been no disputes over the recognition of union; disputes over the closed shop have been rare, disputes about wages not very frequent, and about conditions of work, practically nil. Most of the disputes that do arise turn on questions of jurisdiction and on the preciser definition of trades-union standards. On all counts they are far fewer in number and far less serious than when the employer is merely a capitalist producer, seeking profits in a competitive market.

The wage bill of the coöperatives tends always to be higher than that of private enterprise, and this fact, together with the general attitude of the coöperatives, constitutes a disadvantage in the warfare carried on by private enterprise against coöperatives.

Nevertheless, the tendency of the unions has been to accept the labor policy of the coöperatives as their rightful due and to demand from them all sorts of things which, when coming from the private employer, they regard as great concessions and privileges. Often, they unduly handicap the coöperatives. Indeed, it has been so easy to get results from the coöperatives that the unions have tended to cling to this easiest way. The record shows that they neglect the still unorganized employees in non-coöperative enterprises, although those immensely outnumber the coöperative employees and although their wages are so low and conditions so inferior as considerably to increase the competitive burden of the coöperative as against non-coöperative business. Private entrepreneurs, when they make agreements with trades-unions, often demand that the unions shall organize the non-union market, and thus overcome the latter's differential advantage. They demand it as a measure of protection for themselves and urge it as a measure of defense for the union, since wages, like water, will move toward the lowest level unless prevented.

But this cannot be prevented unless the breach between labor and life, production and consumption, is healed. The recognition, in Sidney Hillman's phrase, that "the workers are the industry," [5] is a step on the way, but is not sufficient.

> There are [declared Hillman], hundreds of manufacturers in the clothing industry who are unfit to manage a peanut stand. Some of them honestly cannot pay decent wages for the sufficient reason that they do not know how to run their business profitably without exploiting labor. Time and again, in literally numberless cases, we have had to lend them our experts to fix up their payrolls, to straighten out incredible tangles, to introduce the most elementary efficiency methods. We help them for one excellent reason: The clothing workers must make their living out of the clothing industry—just as their employers. Until now labor has fought mainly from a sense of outrage against exploitation. Henceforth it will fight more and more from a sense of industrial and social responsibility.

It will, in a word, guard its industry—but at the expense of other industries and other workers. This is the life principle of a producer-dominated economy. It cannot be abolished so long as men are organized as producers only. Let the economic base be shifted to the consumer and production be reduced to

[5] *Cf.* H. M. Kallen, *Education, the Machine and the Worker,* Sec. 17.

an activity of consumer-organization, and the workers will no longer have to identify themselves with the industry. They will be free to subordinate the industry to themselves, their labor to their lives, and to organize accordingly.

In view, hence, of the realities of any working-man's life and any working-man organization, the coöperative movement could become one of the most potent aids of the trades-union in its struggles, and the trades-union a powerful reënforcement of coöperative growth. Trades-unions and the coöperatives might even establish permanent joint advisory councils to consult on the problems of "industrial and social responsibility" the two share in common; and to deal with the differences which in the nature of things, must arise.

Such councils could, in the course of time, grow into a nation-wide structure in which each worker, blue shirt and white collar alike, enters twice into association with his fellows: First as a consumer, with all his fellows; then as a worker, with the members of his trade or profession.[6] This growth would benefit by certain changes in the structure of the trades-union to make it correspond to the expanding structure of the coöperative Wholesales. As consumer coöperation grows and tends to enter more and more into production of what is consumed, it reaches out to fields, factories and transport, and ultimately to the basic raw materials of the national economy. A great coöperative wholesale, deprived of the characteristic coöperative organization and control, would be a vertical trust. The trades-union movement, however, has until recently maintained its organization on the horizontal level, and tends to stick to the associational pattern of the craft unions rather than to seek confederation into industrial unions. Only by changing from craft to industry can working-man organization catch up with employer organization. For the craft union neither expresses nor gets any use from the functional interdependence of workers with one another in the performance of their work. The industrial union does.

As usual, employer-organization has far outdistanced employee-organization with respect to this aspect of associa-

[6] For the argument on this point see H. M. Kallen, *A Free Society*, Chapter VI.

tion. The cartel and the vertical trust have been with us for several generations, and while these were taking shape, labor leaders were denouncing industrial unionism as Bolshevism or anarchy, and workers' organization was unnecessarily handicapped because of the antiquated and mistaken principle on which the labor union was constructed. But there cannot fail to be an end to all that.

From the standpoint of the consumer, the organic interdependence of different crafts in the production of an identical commodity is far more important than the external similarities of the same craft in the production of different commodities. In terms of the pair of shoes on the wearer's feet, all the operatives in the factory who participate in making shoes constitute one shoemaker. And technologically, each operative depends on the others in the same way that their ultimate joint product depends on them all. Herein lies the rationale of industrial unionism. And herein is another reason why, in a complete consumers' economy, the most desirable organization of producers would be the vertical or industrial.

The consummation of this coöperative order is still remote. But the successful beginnings are at hand. The essential identity of purpose and friendliness of attitude are there. And sooner or later their implications will be realized in joint action of the coöperatives and trades-unions looking to the final achievement of a consumers' economy.

The details of such an action are, of course, countless. They will vary with the geography, the state of the industrial arts, the prevailing political atmosphere and the other items of the social context of each country. They will be of one type in England, another in Finland, another in the United States, another in Italy, another in Russia. But nevertheless, the employer-employee relation in a consumers' economy is simpler to work out, with all of its varying details, and its promise of freedom and appropriate equality, and a good life for each member of it is more likely of realization than in any other type.

CHAPTER XIII

EDUCATION IN THE COÖPERATIVE MOVEMENT

§ 1. *Early Victorian Education and the Rochdale Pioneers*
§ 2. *Competition beween Autonomous Coöperative and Workers' Classes and Public Schools*
§ 3. *Competition into Coöperation: The Rôle of the Women's Guild*
§ 4. *Autonomous Education of Producers*
§ 5. *Vocational Trend of the Coöperative Educational Establishment in Britain*
§ 6. *Education in Denmark*
§ 7. *Coöperative Schooling in Finland*
§ 8. *And in the Soviet Union and Spain*
§ 9. *The Educational Enterprise in Nova Scotia*
§ 10. *Education and Democracy in the United States*
§ 11. *Consequences to Special "Workers' Education"*
§ 12. *Consequences to Coöperative Education in the United States*
§ 13. *The Basic Problem in Coöperative Education*
§ 14. *Vocation or Culture: the False Dilemma, unless Prevented!*
§ 15. *The Permanent Task of Coöperative Education*

§ 1. EARLY VICTORIAN EDUCATION AND THE ROCHDALE PIONEERS

FROM ITS BEGINNING the consumers' coöperative movement has been concerned about education. But neither the nature nor the content of education has had the same meaning all the time. In its first phase the coöperator's idea of education was something antecedent even to the organization of the coöperative technique and the specific economic functions of the movement. In a sense coöperation could have been regarded as an instrument of education rather than education an instrument of coöperation. This was in no small degree Robert Owen's view, and in so far as the Rochdale Pioneers held any philosophy of education at all, they followed Owen. To Owen, it will be recalled, education was the foremost agency in the liberation and elevation of men. It would place "the lowest in the scale many degrees above the best of any class which has yet been formed by the circumstances of present or past society."

Owen's hopes for education spread to all his followers. They were revolutionary hopes projected in a world in which education was the unappreciated privilege of the privileged classes and regarded as beyond the capacities of the multitudes. Their instruction was left to the churches. The Church of England especially charged itself with the duty of indoctrinating them concerning the high place of the rich and well-born and disciplining them in submission and obedience to those high ones. The dissenting sects were less tied to the *status quo* in the national life; their Sunday schools taught something a little better than submission, but they too were concerned with subservience rather than liberty. The ideal of education which had been a commonplace in democratic thinking from the time of the American Revolution—a free, non-sectarian, tax-supported, publicly controlled system, open to young and old from kindergarten to university—had not even entered the dreams of officialdom. Working-men aspiring to education had to educate themselves and the autonomous undertaking by working-men's associations to organize classes and lectures and other means of learning developed into a component of the institution of education in England.

The conflicts and concerts of industrial England's educational history drew approving rationalizations from John Stuart Mill and Herbert Spencer. These great champions of liberty were justly opposed to the regimentation of the mind; they saw public education as a new device to subject thought and knowledge to the control of exclusive authority. Such authority, they felt, must, as always, crush spontaneity, banish or destroy alternatives, perpetuate error and defeat truth. Therefore, although they favored universal education, they wanted it to be a voluntary achievement, not a governmental undertaking; they remembered what the church had done to the human mind, and they were afraid that government would only emulate the sacred precedent. Owing to these not unjustifiable fears, the champions of liberty—as Huxley later had occasion to point out—played directly into the hands of the powers of reaction. The endeavors of the multitudes of England at self-education were launched in part as an expression of this *laissez-faire* rule, in part as a defiance against the reaction. Its forms range from the creation of classes in the three *r's* to the publication of millions of penny pamphlets on various subjects in the arts and sciences.

During more than half a century these pamphlets had an enormous circulation. They helped, with the classes, in some degree to supplement and more completely to overcome the deficiencies and handicaps of the fifteen thousand church schools charitably open to the very young. After the adoption of the Reform Bill of 1832, the private education of the middle class was carried a step forward through the increase of secondary schools aspiring to be like Rugby and Harrow, but parvenu in structure and spirit, aping only the worst features of the aristocratic public schools. Concerning their work Matthew Arnold wrote, by implication: "Our middle classes are the worst educated in the world. The education of the middle class is vulgar and unsound, our body of secondary schools is the most imperfect and unserviceable in Europe." Since the education of the middle classes was modelled on the education of the aristocracy, whom Arnold later described as barbarians lording it over the lower castes of Philistines and populace, the character of the schools of Victorian England is not difficult to infer.

It is within this setting that the educational enterprises of the British coöperative movement took form. Set down by the Rochdale Pioneers as one objective of their society, they integrated education so little with the society's work during its early years that they failed to make provision either for supporting it out of the society's funds or for organizing it as a coördinated society activity. Inasmuch as their passion for and faith in education was as strong as their passion for social justice, their failure to provide for it would suggest that they regarded education as a separate and equal function, calling for independent institution and financing; and that its absorption into the sphere of organizational influence was a consequence of circumstance and experience rather than purpose.

At first the members of the society used to meet once a week in the room behind the store to discuss various subjects, not all connected with the business of the society. The news room and library which eventually followed this was supported primarily by voluntary contributions of tuppence a week, the society adding a subvention of about twenty pounds a year. This was in 1849. The rule making it obligatory for the society to contribute a certain proportion of its "profits" for educational purposes was not adopted till three years later, the amount designated being 2½ per cent. Other societies followed the precedent of the Pioneers. The result was that a coöperative educational activity, in no sense to be regarded as a system, grew up. It answered in the coöperative movement the same sort of needs as the working-men's educational enterprises served in other movements.

§ 2. COMPETITION BETWEEN AUTONOMOUS COÖPERATIVE AND WORKERS' CLASSES AND PUBLIC SCHOOLS

MEANTIME tax-supported, universal compulsory schooling had become a public issue. The adoption of the Reform Bill of 1867 had doubled the number of voters in British elections. The obligations of suffrage, it was universally felt, called for an equipment of literacy and knowledge not yet attained by the British multitudes. "We must," said one champion of educational reform, "educate our masters." To accomplish this purpose the best and the most devoted minds of England associated together as the National Education League and challenged the monopoly of learning by the well-to-do and of teaching by the church. In response to this challenge the churches and their patrons organized the National Education Union, mobilized the schoolmasters, most of them servants in their employ, and put the old Earl of Shaftesbury, who had championed the factory laws and helped to pass the Workmen's Provident Act, at its head. The Union battled the League with every weapon at its disposal. Its defeat was signalized in the adoption of the Education Act of 1870.

The resistance of ecclesiastical and feudal reaction prevented the Act from being much. It merely permitted localities to establish free schools for needy children between the ages of five and thirteen, if they wanted to; whether or not attendance should be compulsory was also left to local option. It was a bill whose effect the taxpayer would hardly notice. The Bill of 1876 made school attendance compulsory until the age of ten. Secondary education remained unprovided for and the youth of England were left to their own resources if they desired more than the mere ability to read and write and cipher. Perforce working-men's organizations had to supply to poor Englishmen engaged in gainful occupations whatever advanced education they could secure for themselves. The great liberals of the times, especially the leaders in science and art like Thomas Huxley, Foster, Tyndall, Ruskin, Morris, and others, coöperated with the workers' clubs to this end. Some of the classics of the period—essays from the pens of Ruskin and of Huxley—came to birth as lectures to working-men.

About the same time that Parliament made its first doubtful step against British illiteracy, old England's coöperators undertook to make education an established general feature of the English coöperative movement. Pursuant to a resolution of the Congress of 1870, lecturers were secured, classes were established. In 1873, an affiliation was effected with the science and art department of the South Kensington Museum. According to G. J. Holyoake, between 1883 and 1886, four to five hundred students were enrolled each year in classes in science, art and technology.

Meanwhile, free public education spread as rapidly as the law and the resistance of the clergy and the squirearchy permitted. The tendency to make use of the public schools was pervasive; they drew away large numbers of pupils from the autonomous workers' classes. Before long local coöperative societies found themselves appropriating money for education without pupils on whom to spend it. In such coöperative schools as continued to carry on, interest shifted from the general and humane to the vocational and technical. At the same time, intellectuals who had entered the movement either though their Christian Socialist affiliation or directly from the universities, reaffirmed in another language and with reference to the narrower specific problems of the time, the doctrine of Owen regarding education. Thus, Arnold Toynbee and Professor Stewart repeatedly insisted that the function of cooperative education is to train the members for citizenship in a coöperative democracy and urged a curriculum which should equip students to meet the problems, moral and technical, of democracy and coöperation.

With the help of these and other academicians such as Ackland and Sedgwick, the Central Board added education to its administrative responsibilities and in the first years of the eighties, coöperation became as such the theme of study. Its ideals, of course, but especially its techniques and its methods received progressively greater attention. The first technical pamphlets were produced at this time: a manual of coöperation and a work on auditing. A syllabus followed. Prizes were offered for papers on education. The Congresses kept stressing the movement's educational duties; but interest moved more and more from the field of general subjects to the field of vocational training. By the nineties, systematic classes in coöperation made their appearance. Syllabuses on bookkeeping, on management, on elementary and advanced coöperation, and the like, had to be provided to meet their needs. There were not enough teachers, either, and the problem of training such had to be met. The depression of 1892, by its effect on the societies and the Wholesale, threw the question of general economic theory into the foreground: and pointed the need of a study dealing with general problems in terms of their bearing on the coöperative movement.

§ 3. COMPETITION INTO COÖPERATION: THE RÔLE OF THE WOMEN'S GUILD

IN 1891, the local government boards had opened up opportunities for secondary education to the children of the poor. A new education bill had provided for evening and continuation schools; and in many areas the discussion of the coöperative movement had been made a unit in the syllabus of those schools. By 1896, the Coöperative Union was offering certificates to those passing examinations in coöperative courses.

None of this work would have developed with such speed and effectiveness as it did, had it not been for the Women's Guild. Organized in 1883, on the initiative of Mrs. A. H. Acland, it was the foremost instrument in implementing the original Rochdale premise that the coöperative society must be an open society which all human beings are free to join and to participate in, regardless of faith, race or sex. The Guild, without wanting to, found itself under the duress of conducting a constant fight against the traditional conservatism of the male even in such a movement as the coöperative movement. It enabled the daughters and wives of working-men to deal with public issues on their own terms. It mobilized their power and influence to bring women into public administrative offices not only in the coöperative movement but in local government boards. It was a power in the developing struggle for equal suffrage. In the coöperative movement itself it was in many ways closer to the democratic realities of the consumers' interest than were the organizations controlled by the men or by the men's committees. The Women's Guild it is, that pushed the extension of the coöperative technique among the very poor; and in the educational activities of the movement its rôle has been the most persistent, unrelaxing and intelligent.

§ 4. AUTONOMOUS EDUCATION OF PRODUCERS

AT THE TURN of the century the general conditions of education within the nation had considerably changed, and with this change had had to go coördinate alterations of the educational program of the coöperatives. One of the alterations turned on the improvement of general public education in England; another turned on the consolidation of a specialized working class education in terms of the interest of the producer rather than the interest of the consumer. Nineteen hundred saw the establishment of Ruskin College; 1903, the organization of the Workers' Educational Association; 1909, the creation of the Central Labor College by a group of seceders from Ruskin.

These three institutions represent three ostensibly different trends of the education of producers tending toward a common objective in spite of the competition between them. Ruskin College was organized to provide higher education for trades-unionists and to train trades-union leaders. The Central Labor

College is the penetration of the Ruskin objective with radical Marxist ends; it was associated with the radical Plebs League as its highest educational instrument. The Workers' Educational Association described itself as non-sectarian, non-political and democratic. It sought and still seeks to bring, to those members of the laborious multitudes who desire it, the opportunity of a non-vocational higher education which would enable them to participate in the life and culture of their masters. It not only creates classes to be taught by men of university rank, it seeks to coördinate all existing agencies, to work on local authorities, and to bring to the worker, without any alteration of his economic relationships, the fulness of vision and life that any employer may attain through the established channels of education for the privileged.

In spite of the remarkable success of the Workers' Educational Association, English labor is tending toward a specific "working class education," an education of and for the workers. Starting with the efforts and methods of the Central Labor College, the tendency developed by contaminating the professionals from the universities with the point of view and the ethical attitudes of the self-conscious working class. It conceives its goal as "the cultural autonomy of the labor movement" and it presumes that this movement, of necessity and automatically, must develop a separate and distinct culture which has sometimes been called "proletcult."

Upon this ground of educational change and standardization outside of the coöperative movement come the last thirty years' developments within the movement. They are significant in that they reveal a trend toward a more and more completely vocational educational activity. The plan for this activity is partly response to a changing situation, partly the outcome of analysis and study. A special committee of inquiry on education appointed in 1897, had reported that the work of coöperative education is not to duplicate but to supplement the work of the municipalities and the rest of the system. It suggested focusing "on industrial economics and the duties of citizens," and it recommended the creation of a specially selected educational committee of seven. It defined the aims and tasks of the committee.

§ 5. VOCATIONAL TREND OF THE COÖPERATIVE EDUCATIONAL ESTABLISHMENT IN BRITAIN

The recommendations were considered but not all adopted. The educational work merely grew. Nineteen hundred and nine saw the organization of the first coöperative tours to visit coöperatives in other countries. The same year a sort of convention of all of the educational groups and agencies of the movement was held during Easter, and there has been an annual Easter meeting ever since. In 1911, a Men's Guild was organized, analogous to the Women's Guild. In 1912, the first proposals for a coöperative college were laid before the Coöperative Union. These proposals were not approved until 1914, and because of the World War could not be implemented until 1919. The success of the first summer school held in 1913, had meantime led to greater and greater elaboration of the summer school activity everywhere in the movement.

By 1915, its educational activities had become so diversified that a paid professional was added to the officers of the Education Department with the title "Adviser of Studies." He is now reinforced by a staff of thirteen teachers and functions as the principal of the Coöperative College at Holyoake House. In 1919, an attempt was made to raise some fifty thousand pounds to finance the college but the depression of 1920 limited the amount contributed to less than ten thousand pounds, partly on the ground that the other working-class colleges, the colleges for producers, were sufficient. Nevertheless, the Coöperative College was opened with the available money, and by 1923, housing was provided for students and classes and lecture rooms were organized in Holyoake House which had been allocated to this purpose. Both wholesale and retail societies subscribed scholarships, and arrangements were made to exchange students with Denmark, Japan, India and Australia. The curriculum of the College is essentially vocational and economic; the problems handled are those which persist in the administration of the movement and those due to the contingencies of the environing economy. Thus, war problems, such as the coöperative control of raw materials and prices—which became a matter of life and death in 1915, when private monopolies almost strangled the coöperatives—provide a point of departure for certain more general considerations. The rise of the chain stores provides another, and so on. The College tops the coöperative educational system.

This system does not stand alone. It functions in more or less coördination with the general school system of the nation and delegates much of the instruction in technical matters, like bookkeeping, etc., to the public schools and the continuation classes. Its relation to the producers' schools and the W.E.A. is not quite so integrative, but not unfriendly. Within its own field it has prepared and must continue to prepare new text-books and syllabuses, conduct institutes, summer schools, classes, correspondence courses, tours, and other activities of adult education, besides the regular schools and classes. During 1934, there were enrolled in the coöperative schools some 54,000 students, of whom 34,000 were either in the elementary or advanced schools, some 4,000 were adults taking courses in social sciences, and the remaining 16,000 were either taking courses in bookkeeping or other vocational subjects. The courses are classified into professional or vocational; social sciences; coöperative honors. They lead to degrees. Taking examinations is a voluntary matter and in recent years about 14,000 students have taken them annually. Those who pass receive certificates and are rewarded with summer school scholarships. The cost of this education to the movement is about $1,000,000 a year, exclusive of what is expended by the National Coöperative Publication Society which prints and publishes the textbooks, the literature and the propaganda of the movement.

§ 6. EDUCATION IN DENMARK

TURNING from England to other countries, we find that the story of education is different but analogous.

In Denmark, whose educational system has received, no doubt deservedly, the greatest amount of study and praise, co-operative education is almost exclusively professional. That is because education of the multitudes is an autonomous enter-prise having a nationalistic origin, intent and method. It is identified largely with the *Folkehojskoler,* or People's High Schools. They are the creation of a Lutheran priest, Frederik Grundtvig, a rebel in theology and in moral and social vision a nationalist with the outlook and temper of Fichte and Mazzini. The Denmark in which Grundtvig grew up was a feudal agricultural state demoralized by military defeat and driven to a reconsideration of the values of the national life by the necessity of recovering national self-respect and national honor without resorting to the military effort which would be foredoomed to defeat. It is this necessity which impelled Grundtvig, the rebel minister, romantic and mystically-nationalist poet, into political activities for which he had no talent but which developed into the enterprise of coöperative education of which he is the founder.

Curiously enough, one practical factor in this enterprise was a series of visits to England between 1829 and 1843. As compared with Danish, English life seemed to Grundtvig free and happy, and it is this English liberty and happiness, idealized, that he endeavored to transplant to his native country. He saw each congregation as an autonomous community whose members are directly in contact with the "living word" of God and are so instructed in the poetry and history of the nation that all three fuse in a single, unified, endowment of each and every Danish soul.

Education was to be not only a preparation for life but an expression of it and in continuous touch with it. The schools, hence, were to be set up and maintained by associations of parents, helped by the state but independent of it. They were to choose their own teachers and make their own curricula. The lower schools, in the course of time, came entirely upon state support, but the folk high schools, which were organized concurrently, have remained a charge upon those who use them; they only receive a certain help from the state. Their curriculum is indefinitely wide in range and their method is that of free election of subjects. But subjects not historical or religious are chosen against the background of history and religion formulated in the spirit of Frederik Grundtvig.

None of the impedimenta of the school organization or the academic structure is to be found. There are no degrees, no recitations, no assigned lessons, no examinations, no credits, no grades and no diplomas. Lectures suggest reading and are made the basis of discussion. Schools are organized as small communities of four or five teachers with their families and about one hundred students between eighteen and thirty years old. Teachers and students live together. The schools distinguish themselves from one another by the subjects they stress, and by the method of instruction. They run during a five-months' winter term for men and a three-months' summer term for women. Some of the schools are owned and managed by the teachers, some by religious organizations. State-aid takes the form of supplementation of teachers' salaries and subventions for needy students.

About 30 per cent of the adult population is regularly enrolled in these schools. The enrollment is a consequence of the development of the Danish coöperative movement, itself also inspired by British practice. But the educational work of this movement, which is both agricultural and urban, is not contrasted with the educational movement of the trades-unions and the socialists. The agricultural political party, the Social Democratic Party, the trades-unions, and the coöperatives all contribute to the upkeep of these folk schools. There are also other coöperative schools maintained more especially by the trades-unions and the Social Democrats. These schools too receive subventions from the local and national government. As a consequence, labor history, coöperation, economics, labor law and literature, figure largely in the curriculum and in the courses selected. The result is that the people of Denmark, a country primarily of peasants, has been described as the most literate, the most highly cultured, and the freest of Europe.

§ 7. COÖPERATIVE SCHOOLING IN FINLAND

THE PRECEDENT set by Denmark spread to Finland, Norway and Sweden. In the two latter countries however, coöperative education has developed along technical and professional lines. The picture is not unlike that of England.

In Finland, a distinction must be made between developments during Russian suzerainty and developments since the achievement of Finnish independence. A public system of a sort, requiring the attendance of urban children between the ages of eight and fourteen was set up under an ordinance passed in 1866. This public school system supplements, and has been treated as a competitor to, the religious school system. Under that system every parish is divided into school districts with a teacher for each district. The teacher spends the school year touring his district; he remains in each village from four to eight weeks. Toward the close of the last century rural communities were ordered to establish secular schools. Since the World War secondary or intermediate schools have been set up. These draw more than two-thirds of the youth of the land; they prepare for the university or for the Polytechnic Institute. Instruction in both is free.

In the setting of this more general political development, there is to be found, first, the special coöperative business college at Helsingfors, and second, the Workers' Schools topped by the Workers' Academy. The business college has a Finnish-speaking section and a Swedish-speaking section. It offers a two-years' course looking to preparation for managerships and offers special courses for branch managers, bookkeepers, and other vocations. This technical work is supplemented with lectures on coöperation as such, and on general economics. Tours are arranged, correspondence schools, summer schools and itinerant lecturers are provided.

The arrangements suggest England, and in point of fact, the English precedent may be said to be followed naturally and easily throughout the coöperative world, with the exception of Denmark. As in Denmark, the Finnish coöperative educational movement had a strong nationalist trend; it affirmed the cultural and spiritual life of the Finns against the efforts of Czardom to Russify; it gave this affirmation practical force through the organization of the agricultural coöperatives. The very name of the initiating society tells the tale: it is *Pellervo*. *Pellervo* figures in Finland's national epic, *Kalevala,* as the god of fertility and good harvest. The *Pellervo* Society was formed in 1899, by Hans Gebhard, an agriculturist at Helsingfors University. A straight consumers' coöperative society had been attempted by another professional as far back as

1866, but was barren of results. But Gebhard was endeavoring to solve the problem of the farmer and together with Mikael Soininen, later the head of the State Education Department, he studied how to promote "the economic improvement of the people by means of coöperation, and to establish a bond between the various different coöperative societies in the country." They concluded that only education could accomplish this end, and so developed *Pellervo* as the educational highway to coöperation in Finland. After a careful survey of the record of other countries, Gebhard and his assistants prepared textbooks, syllabuses, rules, contracts, rules of adjustments between employers and employees, trained students, and finally distributed them and his educational material among the villages and farms of his country. The current phase of coöperative education in Finland is the consummation of the activities and program of *Pellervo*.

§ 8. AND IN THE SOVIET UNION AND SPAIN

But the most interesting development of coöperative education, whether it survive or not, is to be found in Russia. The revolutionary enthusiasm which aimed within five years to transform a nation of individualistic peasants into industrial and agricultural producers' collectives, regardless of their wishes and desires, and a nation of illiterates into an educated people, turned its energies to education with greater enthusiasm and more significant effectiveness than perhaps in any other field of Soviet enterprise. As the return to traditional methods and practices of schooling ordered by the communist executive shows, expectation far exceeded accomplishment; nevertheless, the gains have been greater than in other fields. Bolshevik Russia, counting among its citizens more members of consumers' coöperative societies than were to be found in the rest of the world, started its coöperative enterprise in the primary schools. The children are organized into consumers' cooperatives which procure the commodities satisfying their own wants,[1] and learn coöperative habit from childhood.

[1] There is one such school, quite the reverse of communistic, in Palestine. This is the school of the Parents' Education Association of Jerusalem.

This learning takes place, however, in a context of social ideals and economic technique postulated on the primacy of the producer. In many respects the ideal of education as a liberating process contradicts this postulate; for education when it is liberal and liberating, is itself unconsciously premised on the primacy of the consumer. Nevertheless, the social atmosphere, the press of the productive enterprises, the five-year plans and the like, function in such a way as to abort and distort the liberating effect of the new education. They make and keep consumption secondary. They emphasize vocation, technique, skill and industrial and financial specialization and tend to generate the servility of spirit which goes with this sort of training. The arts and the sciences are compensatory to them. Being, moreover, governed by the Marxist premise and conception, they function in relation to the realities of life and work as the religion of Czardom functioned before the revolution.

Thus the coöperative movement proper is deprived of the range and scope which the coöperatives have educationally in other countries. It now provides the usual technical training which it carries through to universities—one in Moscow, established in 1918, another in Leningrad, opened by Centrosoyus in 1922. The function of both is to train officials and operatives for the coöperative service within the limits and the framework of the Marxist preconceptions.

That a contradiction is involved must be obvious. The consequences of this contradiction it is still too early to prophesy. Everything depends upon the degree in which the coöperative habit of life, organization and thought can become constitutional to the folk-ways of the new Russia; and this, in view of the record, is a problematical matter.

Another country in which instruction in the coöperative theory and practice has been ordained by law is republican Spain. The republic recognized the coöperative movement as a constituent element of the national being and the decree giving coöperative societies a legal status represents a consensus among the leadership of the coöperative movement in Spain and the best minds in the government. The educationally significant part of the decree is the fact that coöperation is made a required subject of instruction in the elementary schools. The ordinance requires not only verbal teaching but the organization of children's coöperative societies. The aim assigned to these societies is the development of the discipline and doctrine of coöperative organization as a habit of life among the children. The societies are required to be exclusively children's societies, although adults naturally will have the right to advise and guide them. The societies trade in school materials and items of personal use and are permitted to trade in any other relevant thing.

The elementary training is to be followed by a progressively more advanced education in coöperative discipline and doctrine in all the schools of higher learning.

The enterprise is still in process and both budgets and staffs are not what it had been hoped they would become. Education in coöperation, with all other aspects of the movement, is to be under the supervision of a special department of coöperation under the Ministry of Labor.

§ 9. THE EDUCATIONAL ENTERPRISE IN NOVA SCOTIA

ON THE AMERICAN continent coöperative education has developed in a unique and significant way in the Province of Nova Scotia. In that primitive and rather arduous land of farmers, fishermen and miners, the problem of holding the population had become a critical one for all institutions with a vested interest in continuity. Emigration was steady and consistent and even the development of the coal fields at Cape Breton and the steel industry at Sydney did not check the decrease of population. Toward the turn of the century a number of the faculty of St. Francis Xavier University, led by Dr. Hugh MacPherson, gave their attention to the realities of the situation. They came to the conclusion that it could be met through the development of a coöperative habit of life, through the cooperation both of producers and of consumers.

The creation of such a habit, they felt, would depend not only on setting up appropriate coöperative organizations, creameries, wool-growers' associations, stores and the like, but especially, on education. The coöperative societies were first reinforced with a People's School along Danish lines. To this adult men came for six weeks, and until 1928, such forums where priests and lay leaders could meet for discussion and analysis were conducted everywhere. In 1928, the University set up an extension department and headed it with Professors M. M. Coady and A. B. MacDonald. Under the leadership of these men community industries such as lobster factories, saw-mills, timber societies were organized, to produce for the open market or for the needs of the community, as well as credit unions, marketing societies, and stores. These enterprises are distributed mostly in the seven eastern counties of Nova Scotia. With them go study clubs that undertake "study which leads directly to action with measurable results." In 1934, there were 952 such clubs with an enrollment of close to 8,000 members. Clubs are organized at a meeting called under the auspices of the Department; they choose their own leaders and their own subject; the Department supplies, without cost, the material of study in the form of books, pamphlets, travelling libraries, and publishes an Extension Bulletin. The University caps these activities with a short course for coöperative leaders every winter. Since 1933, some 129 students have come to Antigonish for a term of six weeks to get training in business arithmetic, business English, bookkeeping, citizenship, economics, coöperative business practices, the history and principles of coöperation, community programs, debates and public speaking.

On the record this is one of the most successful educational enterprises in the coöperative movement. It is significant that in it principles and practice, theory and action are kept interdependent. Although the curriculum has a wide range, its focus is coöperative business and its margin may be literature, public speaking, social, economic and political problems. That is, its subject matter is not the dead past but the living present, and the past is significant only in so far as it can be employed to illuminate and improve the present. The consequence has been a raising of the standard of living, the creation of many more opportunities for the young of the country than there had been heretofore, and the elevation of the level of culture.

§ 10. EDUCATION AND DEMOCRACY IN THE UNITED STATES

WE TURN NOW to the United States. Here the educational problem of the coöperatives is very different from that which they faced in other countries. The difference follows from the different national attitude toward education and the different educational tradition of the land. The first English education act was not adopted till 1870. Almost a decade earlier, Henry Ward Beecher was in England defending the embattled Americanism of the North against the effects of the sympathy of British aristocracy with the slaveholding rebels of the South in our Civil War. He addressed himself mostly to the workingmen of England. One of his addresses concerned "the Success of American Democracy." The ideal of the equality of men, he argued, implied their liberty. The powers of government came from men and were for men. Governments and institutions were not masters but servants; the people themselves were the masters; and therefore each had the right and the need to be enlarged and developed as fully as possible. This right and need implied education.

The education of the common people follows, then, as a necessity. They are to be fitted to govern. Since all things are from them and for them they must be educated to their function, their destiny. No pains are spared, we know, in Europe, to educate princes and nobles who are to govern, no expense is counted too great to prepare the governing classes for their function. America has her governing class too and that governing class is the whole people. It is slower work because it is much larger. It is never carried so high because there is so much more of it. It is easy to lift up a crowned class. It is not so easy to lift up society from the very foundation. That is the work of centuries. And, therefore, although we have not an education so deep nor so high as in some other places, we have it broader than it is anywhere in the world; and we have learnt that for ordinary affairs intelligence among the common people is better than treasuries of knowledge among particular classes of the people. . . .

And so there comes up the American conception of a common people as an order of nobility, or as standing in the same place to us that orders of nobility stand to other peoples. Not that, after our educated men and women of genius are counted out, we call

all that remain the common people. The whole community, top and bottom and intermediate, the strong and the weak, the rich and the poor, the leaders and the followers, constitute with us the commonwealth. . . .

In America there is not one single element of civilization that is not made to depend in the end upon public opinion. Art, law, administration, policy, reformation of morals, religious teachings, all derive, in our form of society, the most potent influence from the common people. . . .

Although these remarks were an *ex parte* statement in the development of a special plea, they sufficiently approximate the facts. The American approach to general education differed from the European from the roots up; and the difference was so signalized by official and unofficial foreign observers. Essentially, it followed from the democratic idea. Its starting-point, if not its way and its stopping place, was man as consumer. Education was to be the prime tool to equality, liberty, fraternity, the paramount assurance of democracy.

This philosophy of education was embodied in resolutions of the Continental Congress to the effect that "schools and the means of education shall be forever encouraged." The practically contemporaneous grants of 640 acres of land for every township northwest of Ohio, upon which our state university system is based,[2] were endeavors to implement it. George Washington's admonition in his Farewell Address:—"Promote then as an object of primary importance, institutions for the general diffusion of knowledge. In proportion as the structure of government gives force to public opinion, it is essential that public opinion should be enlightened"—followed from it. But most of all, it was intrinsic to the principle and practice of political equality, the parity of men as citizens given effect through the institution of manhood suffrage.

This is why the working-men's party of the late 1820's and early 1830's agitated for a system of tax-supported public schools "equally open to all"; why they fought against the in-

[2] Today close to 120,000,000 acres of the public domain pay part of the bill of free public education, especially of the state universities. The land grants led to the interesting paradox of a free state university organized before a free tax-supported elementary school.

vidious distinction between the schooling of the rich and that of the poor, a fight in which the more prosperous, public-spirited citizens joined so that the Free School Society changed its name to the Public School Society.

Throughout the country, and especially on the frontier, the faith in education was a function of the faith in democracy. Free public education was advocated as the chief power "to check aristocracy" and the advocacy was followed by efforts "to make the common school the best school" and thus to overcome the invidious advantage of the private schools and academies. As Horace Mann, who did as much as any one to turn that aspiration into achievement, wrote in one of his reports as secretary of education to the Governor of Massachusetts, "God places the right of every child that is born into the world to such a degree of education as will enable him and so far as possible will predispose him to perform all domestic, social, civil, and moral duties. . . . We can cite no attribute or property of the divine nature for giving birth to any human being and then inflicting upon that being the curse of ignorance, of poverty, and of vice, with all their attendant calamities." [3]

In sum, if democracy was the method by which men safeguarded their equal rights to life, liberty and happiness, education was the instrument through which democracy was enabled to perform its task. It implied the special training of teachers and to some degree even the selection of women for this training, women being chosen because of the superior tact and moral power natural to female character. Of course the tendency of men to enter other more profitable vocations might have had something to do with the feminization of teaching: however that may be, the development of teacher training schools as an integral part of the movement toward free, tax-supported, public education, from the elementary school through the university, derives from this democratic passion. Even the English, who rather despised American ideas and American ways, looked upon the early development of American education as something to praise and emulate; Macaulay, arguing during the early 1850's for a slight improvement in the education of the English multitudes, cited the United States as a model.

[3] *Report to Governor Briggs,* November 29, 1849.

§ 11. CONSEQUENCES TO SPECIAL "WORKERS' EDUCATION"

IN A COUNTRY where tax-supported, non-sectarian, publicly controlled, free, compulsory schooling to high school grade is the rule, the interest of working-men as such in specialized educational establishments is naturally limited. Workers' education has consequently had a much more sporadic and tendentious character in the United States than in educationally more under-developed countries. It has been determined much more by the contagion of example from abroad than by the actual needs at home. Where it developed it concerned itself either with the promulgation and spread of the teachings of a special cult like Socialism, or with the improvement of such vocational training as that of "walking delegates," "business agents" and so on in labor unions. Thus, the Rand School of Social Science, which was organized in 1905, is a sectarian institution, analogous to church schools and concerned, perhaps too much after the manner of the Y.M.C.A.'s, to advance the special sectarian interests of the Socialist Party; and a more recent Workers' School educates for the revolution, whatever that may mean. The wave of trades-union colleges and the organization of the Workers' Educational Bureau (reorganized in 1933), which came during the reconstruction excitement in the period immediately following the Great War, has been dissipated. One or two labor colleges, endeavoring to train trades-union leaders and officials, survive, not too prosperously. And recently the Affiliated Schools for Workers have taken up the tasks of the lapsed trades-union schools and colleges. The activities of general education which are carried on by the W.E.A. in England have in the United States been taken over by the adult education movement whose central body is an adult education council largely financed by grants from the Carnegie Foundation. The general school system tends to absorb these activities as a part of its regular task and the depression has called out new efforts in new directions which may still further extend the rôle of government in the upkeep of education in the United States.

§ 12. CONSEQUENCES TO COÖPERATIVE EDUCATION IN THE UNITED STATES

UNDER THESE CONDITIONS, the direction of events in American coöperative education can be forecast readily enough. The record already indicates it. A generalized structure of the kind that obtains in some of the countries of Europe is not to be found. There is much activity, but no order; much enthusiasm, but no framework of principle to give direction and steadiness to the educational enterprise. Different coöperative groups have their local institutes, publications, summer courses, and the like. In variety and quantity, if not in quality, they compare favorably enough with the similar materials and activities elsewhere. As in Europe, the tendency is for these to be primarily technological and to concern themselves first and last with vocational and technological problems. After the depression of 1929 imparted an unprecedented momentum to coöperative growth, especially in the agricultural sections of the nation, one or two states, where the coöperative movement is strong, found coöperation important enough to include in the school curriculum, either by law, or by administrative order. Thus, the Department of Education of the state of Minnesota attempted to produce a syllabus and textbook on social subjects which was to include a unit on coöperation. The state of Wisconsin has put a statute on its books requiring the whole school system of the state, from common school to university, to prescribe "adequate and essential instruction in coöperative marketing and consumers' coöperation, and making knowledge of coöperation one of the conditions for a certificate to teach economics, social studies or agriculture." The officers of instruction in the state are directed to prepare the necessary syllabuses and other materials to be used in this instruction.

The lack of straight American material is not limited to Wisconsin, and the wealth of it existing abroad, especially in England, has not yet been surveyed and reshaped to serve American needs. The need for such material is nation-wide, and its preparation must necessarily depend on more than assembling the record and rearranging it for classroom use, whether in a public school or a coöperative institute.

§ 13. THE BASIC PROBLEM IN COÖPERATIVE EDUCATION

FOR, apart from expense, the organization of coöperative education must depend upon the philosophy which guides it, and the habits of life which are to fulfil it. That it is confronted by the barriers of the prevailing educational atmosphere and of the ruling passions of the masters of school policy goes without saying.

Assume that coöperation, its philosophy, its history, its methods, its achievements, have become as they should and will, a permanent part of the curriculum of the American school system, from primary school to college. Assume that every child who graduates from a grammar school knows much more about coöperation than he knows about the American Revolution, the Declaration of Independence and the Bill of Rights. Why or how should this information make any difference in his life and labor? Why should it signify more than the information that the moon has another side which is never seen from the earth or that the sun is 93,000,000 miles away? Why or how should it make any more difference than the teachings of the Christian churches or embody, any less than those, an organization of desires without attainment, a system of hopes denied by events, of beliefs falsified by experience, of professions belied by practices?

Coöperative education, as practiced in most places, does not yield a hopeful answer. Far more than the coöperative establishments it is devised to serve and to sustain, the coöperative school is exposed to the prevailing weather of opinion, it is directed, without knowing it, toward accepting the prevailing ideal of human personality as the coöperative goal, and toward acquiescing in the current doctrines of conformity or of rebellion as the coöperative doctrines. The education of the consumer coöperatives comes to nothing that can be called characteristically and uniquely coöperative. Coöperative schools, consequently, tend everywhere to develop as trade-schools merely, similar in principle and purpose to the schools maintained by the Ford Company and other gargantuan producer organizations. Largely as coöperative doctrine may figure in the course of study, its bearing on the technological part is like that of a Sunday school lesson on the daily life. For in a producer-dominated world, whose schools and colleges draw their ideals, their emotions and their techniques from the ways and works of its overlords, standards and methods of the majority perforce contaminate and distort all the minorities, whatever their discipline and doctrine. In countries where there is no democracy, such as Italy, Germany, and Russia, the state orthodoxy is imposed by superior power; coöperative education is reduced either to a technological discipline subordinated to anti-coöperative doctrine, or to a discipline unillumined by any doctrine whatsoever, a body of blind skills directed nowhere.

Now, since scientifically, the techniques of production and distribution are the same everywhere, the skills required by cooperative business are not any different from the skills required by capitalist or Fascist or communist business. The practice of the arts of agriculture, of dairying, of manufacture, and of distribution, does not depend upon a social philosophy any more than skill in making or shooting firearms depends upon a social philosophy. Capitalist American and Nazi German munitions are bought by communist Russia and there made communist by being put to communist uses. Russia's communist cereals and coal are bought by Fascist Italy; and there made Fascist by being put to Fascist uses. American systems of accountancy employed by Russian state trusts are by the mere fact of this employment transformed into communist methods. Capitalist French financial techniques applied by Russians to Soviet ends in Soviet banks become in virtue of this application Russian and communist. The Rochdale pioneers were Englishmen but their method is the free inheritance of all the races of mankind. Not nature but affiliation determines the political or social category of any industrial process or financial device, and affiliations are external and ever changing. Trade and industry would be impossible if they were not.

What is true of the industrial arts is even truer of culture, of the fine arts and the sciences. The cultural equipment of mankind is neutral to every special interest and available to all. Its life and growth anywhere depend upon its freedom everywhere. Without the absolute free exchange of thoughts, discoveries, inventions, mental starvation sets in and civilization lapses. Although Newton was a deist the Newtonian mechanics is none the less equally employed by Nazi pagans, communist atheists, Catholic Fascists and capitalist Protestants. The self-proclaimed German "Aryans" find that they cannot without condemning themselves to sickness and suffering, discard the principles and methods of modern medical science, although Jews have so largely shared in discovering and perfecting them. Shakespeare was a very Elizabethan English Englishman, but the works of Shakespeare play a major rôle in the literary tradition of all the peoples of the world, including the German. Although Marx was the founder of a new religious system, his work has been employed by all other peoples as well as the Germans among whom he was born and his beloved "masses" to whom he addressed himself. Jesus was a Palestinean peasant and his doctrine was addressed to the lower classes of his kind, but he and it have been used over and over again by different peoples in different connections for different purposes, peoples and purposes at war with each other more frequently than at peace; and the life and sayings of Jesus which they employed in these wars have survived them to enter again into still other contexts and to develop consequences in still other directions. Every achievement is a growth of a particular soil and the work of an individual person struggling to live and to fulfil himself among his fellows upon this soil. Once, however, it has come to birth, it becomes capable, without any diminution of its local geography and personal origin, of a world-wide reference and implication. Like the air and the sun, it enters the common heritage of all men, available, unless prevented, for the uses and enjoyment of all.

§ 14. VOCATION OR CULTURE: THE FALSE DILEMMA, UNLESS PREVENTED!

HISTORICALLY, the multitudes of men have been, and throughout much of the world still are, kept from the enjoyment of this inheritance by deficient education, and kept deficiently educated because too poor to go to school. Education has been the monopoly of the rich, and through education, culture.

Throughout history, education has been conditioned on scarcity rather than abundance, kept a special privilege of the consuming classes; denied to the producing multitudes so that the subservience of the producer who produced without consuming toward the consumer who consumed without producing might be perpetuated. In democratic terms, education is the means by which this common fund of skill and culture is made available to each and every human being, regardless of race, faith or sex. The democratic idea of education implies the primacy of the consumer.

Yet the practice of education in democracies has tended to maintain the invidious distinction between consumer and producer and to keep the liberal education and the vocational sharply apart. Liberal education is the education of the "gentleman"; vocational education is the education of the commoner and since the industrial revolution, never the twain shall meet!

The traditional opposition between the two has been perpetuated in new ways under the new discriminations produced by producer dominance. What is known as culture, which is the name for the accomplishments and equipment of a gentleman, has been recessive before the rise and multiplication of technological and professional schools, with the social and financial pretensions of the more ancient universities and colleges, aiming to train the producer as capitalist-master. These schools are designed to impart the knowledge which is power, power over things. They belittle and cut themselves off from wisdom, from the knowledge which is freedom, freedom through that insight into the relationships of things which is a philosophy of life whose material is knowledge and whose method is self-expression. In the light of what we know concerning the mind and heart of man, concerning the dynamics of character and formation of personality, this division is diseased. For to living men of flesh and blood power has meaning only as it leads to freedom, only as it is freedom, and freedom is freedom only as it is a living of the life more abundant.

Unfortunately, the division of labor, on which the achievements of power depend, has not so far permitted the complete fusion of power with freedom. Whatever it be applied to, the labor of laboring millions remains servile. Labor is labor because it is servile, servile in employer as fully as in employee. In the essential nature of human life, the producer and his production must remain subordinate to the consumer and his consumption. But although production must be subordinate, it is not to be separated from consumption. Indeed to separate them is to tear apart the life which they together enchannel. Yet the older educational activities of the laborious sects and the current practice of the free public schools and universities push this separation to ever greater extremes, extending to its logical limit the idea of an absolute vocationalism which expresses the actual dominance of the producer.

§ 15. THE PERMANENT TASK OF COÖPERATIVE EDUCATION

In view of this situation what else must be the permanent task of coöperative education if not to restore the natural relationship of producer to consumer, and without weakening energies or skills of production, to frame them properly within the aspirations and activities of consumption? Coöperative education must stress first, last and always the primacy of the consumer. It must provide a vivid and dramatic ideal of human personality in a consumer economy. It must define this personality in terms of a habit and vision of life, extending the democratic idea of education from its political to its economic base. It will seek to make culture available in that abundance which it seeks for food, clothing, shelter, and other traditional "necessities" of life. It will show how these "necessities" themselves depend upon culture, upon the common heritage of the arts and the sciences, and are the produce of this heritage; how it follows hence that the separation of vocation from culture is as false as it is invidious, and that the activities of a grocery clerk, a tailor, a coal-miner, a household servant, can exist in the conscious minds of the persons practising these arts amid the living context of all the arts and sciences upon which they in fact depend. The task of coöperative education is to enable the coöperator to become deeply aware of this context as it really is, and aware through the patterns and perspectives, the principles and aspirations, the hopes and habits of the coöperative way of life.

What this way of life implies we have already seen. It implies a philosophy which takes for its starting-point the multiplicity and variety of human beings, each unique, each different from the others. It affirms the equal right of each personality to live, to grow, and to fulfil itself according to its nature. It appreciates human association, whether in the form of a church, a state, an industry, an art, a science, a sport, a game, or any other institution, as a device the better to accomplish this end. It sees association as basically free and voluntary; as coming to rest on consent, from whatever it may have begun in. It sees the method as always that of a team whose members work and play together on the rule of *live and let live,* and so far as possible, on the rule of *live and help live.* It sets their unity and cohesion in their aim: To enlarge and perfect the personality of each through the creation for all of an abundance of the positive goods of civilization. It draws its methods from the precedents set by the coöperative competition and competitive coöperation of the scientists, the inventors and the artists; it declares that what keeps industry going and trade alive has the same technological character; that it is the method of working engineers and honorable merchants. And finally it affirms that the coöperative method devised by the Rochdale pioneers liberates the economy of civilization from its burdens of financial oppression and industrial exploitation, enabling it to develop into the consumer economy of a free society.

To give point to this teaching and incarnate this philosophy, coöperative education will have to depict and bring to life an identifiable coöperative personality-image which should be able to hold its own in a producer's world. This it cannot do either by courses in public schools or by the sort of instruction now to be had in the coöperative schools. These generate the educational climate of opinion in which coöperation must live and grow; and properly, the coöperative movement must suffuse them with attitudes and programs favorable to it. But they can never of themselves turn the trick. The movement requires in addition an autonomous coöperative system which will take a child from kindergarten through college, teaching him everything that he needs or desires in the perspectives of the philosophy of the consumer. His instruction would need to be continuously "practical." It would start with his joining the other members of his class in a consumers' coöperative of their own, and through it serving their individual needs according to their capacity. It would continue thus, from class to class, with ever-expanding activities of organization, management, administration, control, carried on in the context of a curriculum of reading and study to illuminate the activities, to aid in analyzing them, reflecting upon them, judging them and their relations to rivals and competitors. This it would reënforce with the arts and play, all moving from the core of coöperative association out to the frontiers of culture and beyond, and back again.

Such a school would provide a yardstick by which the effectiveness of education in and for a coöperative way of life could be measured outside the coöperative system. It would indicate what educationally hurts and what helps. It would have the same bearing on the future of coöperation as the schools of the Christians had on the future of Christianity. Whether it could prevent the intellectual and spiritual debacle that finally came to established Christianity is on the lap of the gods. By nature and habit, education is a follower, not a leader. It looks backward rather than forward; it transmits the past far more than it plans the future. Education for a consumers' world would need to subordinate the transmission of the past to its reorganization for a different future, and to date the schools of the world have not shown themselves able to do this. Nevertheless, the attempt must be made. For world-wide consumer coöperation is an adventure into the unknown. It involves taking the risks of self-stultification and self-defeat, as well as all the other risks that free action, innovation, and discovery require. That the adventure will succeed is not a foregone conclusion; but that mankind will lose more by failing to undertake than by undertaking it, *is* a foregone conclusion.

CHAPTER XIV

THE CONSUMER ECONOMY AND ITS RIVALS

§ 1. REPRISE: THE TWO LEISURE CLASSES

LET US RECALL once more the pattern of the time between 1914 and 1936.

From 1914 to 1919, the whole world was busy as never in the history of civilization before. Everywhere people were passionate, eager, and religiously absorbed. Everywhere production developed at an unprecedented tempo. Concurrently, as we have seen, sheer consumption reached a scale unheard of in history. For it was the time of the World War, and as consumer, war is the aristocrat of aristocrats. Its consumption consumes utterly. It is capital consumption, producing nothing. It not only uses men and goods; it uses them up. It not only makes no return whatsoever on the investment, it causes further losses. Thus, by 1919, a world-wide political economy had been broken down; a third of France had been devastated, much of Poland and the Baltic countries had been reduced to wildernesses; even the primitive economy of the Russian Empire had been dissipated and the remnants were being morcellated by revolution and civil war.

So many millions of lives and billions in capital had been consumed without leaving a wrack behind, that it looked as if it would take at least a generation to restore and rehabilitate the devastated areas. The surviving soldiery returned home full of hope and eager to be taken up again in the economy of peace.

But nothing of the sort happened. There were not jobs enough to go round. The devastated areas of France were restored within a decade, and to a latter end which was better than their beginning. Outside Russia, the Slavic peasant soon found himself lacking a living and lacking land. In Russia, civil war gave place in the course of time to what those opposed to the new faith recognized as the old social pattern of mastery and subjection, but rationalized with new dogmas, new slogans, by new rulers with new names. And all over the western world, in Italy, in Austria, in Germany, in England, and in the United States, men went about unemployed.

Veterans demanded and received bonuses. A factitious business developed, and the countries of Europe passed through cycles of inflation and deflation; governments tried this and attempted that; economists analyzed and prophesied, but the number of men without employment increased regardless. To the already unemployed were added brothers and sisters who had grown up only to find there were no jobs. In 1929, at the height of "prosperity" in the United States, there were millions of people so forced into the leisure class. In spite of briefer work days, 100 men were producing in 1929, what approximately 140 men had been producing in 1919. In 1933, at the nadir of the depression, men were producing in 38 hours what it had taken them 50 hours to produce in 1929.

Why? Because of that displacement of men by machines which is called "technological unemployment"; and because of that intensification of "efficiency" systems by managements dispensing with men, which is called "rationalization" of shops and factories.

Need it be repeated that this displacement of men by machines was no mere post-war phenomenon? That it goes on as a constant function of industrial expansion? That, since the middle of the last century, it has been forcing upon unwilling poor men what they seek willingly through riches—membership in the leisure class? And that this leisure is an imposed leisure, not a chosen one? Recall how it occurs simultaneously with an increase of goods, both durable and perishable, more than enough to sustain them all and to meet all capitalist requirements for expansion of business and profits, but not so employed: how often, indeed, they are destroyed to prevent their being so employed. England, let it be remembered, paid, throughout this period, a "dole." The Germanic countries also paid various types of unemployment insurance. Still "surpluses" accumulated with no market to sell them in, so that they therefore ate up profits, and were attributed to "overproduction."

We know that this process is cyclical and cumulative. In our industrial economy, "surpluses" of goods and men increase; they do not diminish. Even the artificial scarcities imposed by monopolies and governments do not diminish them. Only war can genuinely diminish them, and that is why they are a threat of war. Alone a country like Russia, rich in natural resources but undeveloped, where basic scarcity is genuine, is a sincerely pacific country, when permitted by its neighbors.

Consider the record since 1919. It is the record of a series of struggles over markets, dumping, tariffs, rationing, planning, and other issues, occasioned by "surplus goods." These struggles have exacerbated nationalisms, and provoked autarchic fantasies. Their high place is the military psychoses of Italy, Japan, and Germany.

"Surplus" men have made possible the formation of private armies. These armies in the past have gone by the euphemisms of "political parties"—the Fascist Party, the National Socialist or Nazi Party. But the record shows that these parties were first groups of idle young men seeking freedom in fantasies of association. Then they became armed bands subsidized by bankers and industrialists anxious about their profits and prestige. Now, having developed into armies, the "parties" are the pretorian guards or janissaries of the rulers of those countries. As parties they are sheer consumers. From the point of view of the economy of either nation supporting them, they have no productive function. They serve only to consume, without producing, national wealth. They consume, indeed, far more than their members would receive through unemployment insurance or other methods of social welfare.

An analogous situation obtained in the United States prior to the repeal of the Eighteenth Amendment. Whereas in Italy, a considerable proportion of the unemployed population was absorbed by the Fascists, and in Germany by the Nasties or Nazis, in the United States they were absorbed by the liquor traffic, with its *duce* or *Führer*-like Capones and their private armies, here called "gangs." Since the repeal of the Eighteenth Amendment, a proportion of the American unemployed section has been absorbed by the Civilian Conservation Corps, and similar New Deal enterprises; but there remain still some ten million without work. . . . It is clear that the forms through which the idle seek their salvational occupations vary with the country and its circumstance; the basic economic relationships express the same principles.

In Russia the situation differs in certain fundamental respects. During the Soviet Socialist Republic's most insecure and dogmatic period peasants died by the millions of famine. Even now with the first "Five Year Plan" of industrialization accomplished; and the second "Five Year Plan" making headway so that food, shoes, clothing, and other necessaries are no longer so scarce in Russia, a state of abundance cannot be reached for many years. Even at any pre-Revolutionary best, these things were insufficient in Russia; and as for the comforts of more complex western polities—they were then not even thought of. Russia is a revolutionary country under an implacable dictatorship of, if not by, the proletariat, and her basic power-economy has been obscured by many other factors as well.

Of these the most important is her revolutionary religion, Communism. Italy opposes it by another religion, Fascism, and Germany by a third, Nazism. Each has its echoes and partizans in the United States . . . Each offers itself as a revelation of the Kingdom of Heaven on earth and as the sum of salvation from the insecurities and dangers, from the fears of imminent disaster which beset the men of the machine age since 1929. None of the three, moreover, presents itself as merely revelation. Each is incarnate in a national economy, each is a fact as well as a faith, a practice as well as a principle, a march of social events as well as an ideal and a program. Like any other religion—Christianity, for example—each operates in two dimensions, profession and practice, whose contradictions and contrasts must always be kept in mind. In each country consumers' coöperation had the stature and status of a national institution, and could have been expanded into a national economy. Nowhere was it done. Salvation was defined, imposed and to some degree accepted in terms directly contradictory.

§ 2. SALVATION ACCORDING TO DICTATORSHIP

As conceptions of the nature and destiny of man and of the relation of the individual to society, Communism, Fascism, and Nazism are historically and logically interdependent. Their relationships are organic. Philosophically, Nazism and Fascism are meaningless without Communism. They presuppose Communism and derive a great deal of their significance from the fact that while they purport to be negations of Communism in certain respects, they are repetitions of Communism in other respects.

Thus, all three are *totalitarian* systems. They hold that society or the state is a whole, separate and distinct from the individuals which compose it. They assume that the individual is merely an organ or tool of this whole and that, except in relation to this whole, he is nothing. They impose on him submission and obedience. If he lives, it is for its sake; if he dies, it is for its good. He owes it all he is or can be, and his life must be a continuous repayment of this debt. As Dante once said of God, they say of the state: "In its will is all our peace."

For all three the essence of the state is embodied in a dictatorship, incarnated in a single individual, whom the Fascists call *duce* and the Nazis, *Führer*. According to some observers, a certain contamination from this practice has reached the communists in Russia; "the word *vazht* is now used in the Soviet Union with solemnity and without qualification, exactly as *Der Führer* is in Germany or *Il Duce* in Italy." These *duces* or *Führers,* or *vazhts,* these heavenly states become man and walking on earth, theoretically hold the decision of life and death for their subjects.

Finally, all three postulate a Devil or Adversary, whatever it be, and hold the belief that their schemes of salvation are predestined by the nature of things to victory over it. Here again, the communist view is the key to the others.

§ 3. THE MARXIST FAITH

THE MARXIST FAITH calls itself "dialectical materialism." By "dialectic" it means what Hegel meant. But where Hegel called the stuff of the world "idea," Marxism calls the stuff of the world "matter." It describes this matter as characterized by an inward conflict or polarity, so that whatever exists implies at the same time the existence of its opposite. Everything actual is a tension between a positive and a negative pole, a process of antagonism and conflict. Everything is inwardly at contradiction with itself. It consists of opposites which cannot live without each other but can live with each other only in a state of war. In human history, this polarity and conflict at the heart of all being expresses itself as "the class struggle." It is a dialectical activity, and is manifested by events endowed with an inevitable direction. The activity is such that the rich grow ever richer and the poor grow ever poorer. The wealth which the labor of many men produces aggregates and compounds itself in the hands of a few, and the many are left with nothing but misery. The misery and the wealth are poles of one another reciprocally dependent and reciprocally at war. In the fullness of time, the struggle will culminate in a tremendous collapse, which is known as "the revolution." The revolution will be followed by "the dictatorship of the proletariat" and the dictatorship of the proletariat will, in some way not revealed in the Marxist scriptures, flower into a classless society "where the free development of each is the condition of the free development of all."

Presumably, for Marx and his followers, as for Hegel and his, the inherent dialectic of nature comes to its end with the attainment of the condition that they regard as desirable and satisfactory. For Hegel, the Prussian monarchy of his day was apparently the *terminus ad quem* of the universal dialectic process. For Marx, the desired classless society was the *terminus ad quem*. Marx was as absorbed in his dream as Hegel in his privileges. Hence, indignant critic of Hegel though Marx was in other respects, he accepted without examination the curious paradox that the *eternal* dialectic action which both ascribed to the nature of things must run out and come to a standstill when the heart's desire is attained; Marx's "classless society" has no beyond; with it attained, eternal polarity has collapsed into eternal identity; eternal struggle into eternal peace; mankind has reached its heaven and is at home.

This heaven is only rationalized by what is peculiarly Marxist, not characterized. Its characteristics are those which all lovers of equality and freedom for all men assign to heaven, regardless of sect or party—the *free* development of *each* is the condition of the *free* development of *all*. The same humanitarian passion, the same moral indignation, which moved the makers of the French and American Revolutions, also moved Marx and his comrades. Alike they labored to overcome the parasitical tyranny which the privileged classes who lived without working practised upon the exploited classes who worked without living. Like Rousseau, Marx reasoned away the inequalities among men. Like Jefferson, he affirmed that all men were created equal. The sympathies of the men who made the eighteenth century enlightenment were so fixed upon the essentially human that a royalist Samuel Johnson could in his *Dictionary* describe patriotism as the last resort of a traitor. Similarly, Marx, like Bentham, the Mills, Owen, Cobden, Mazzini and other liberals of his generation, affirmed the essential international ground of nationality, stressing the economic as well as social and political interdependence of peoples. Marx, in doing so, gave greater weight than his contemporaries to one among the diverse conflicts which provide historians with their most exciting material. For the Marxian imagination envisioned men as primarily members of warring economic classes rather than as subjects of divinely elected kings or citizens of sovereign political commonwealths. And hence he rebelled against classes as the revolutionaries of a generation before had rebelled against kings; he brought to the working multitudes his gospel of class-consciousness and class-war in order that they might the more quickly attain to the classless society which was his dream.[1] Communism, or its less militant form, Socialism,

[1] The brilliant Sidney Hook, by disregarding the Marxian metaphysic and stressing this phase of Marx's work and thought, has been able to reconcile it with the pragmatic liberalism of John Dewey. The reconciliation witnesses the unconscious pragmatism which is natural to all men; it does not identify Marx's consciously held faith.

has for this reason gripped the imagination of countless high-minded and kind-hearted people.

Intrinsically not a scientific hypothesis, but a religious faith, Communism employs the logic of Hegel in the language of economics to preach a crusade against the inequities of the "existing social order."

It exalts the working-man; it makes work the foundation of all values; it rewrites history as a war between the working-man who creates the values and the capitalist who only exploits them; and it infallibly demonstrates the victory of the working-man-creator over the capitalist-exploiter as the predestined, inevitable conclusion of the eternal war. It frames every worker in a gratifying cosmic setting. It mobilizes his many personal hatreds and discomforts upon a generalized enemy it is his very life to fight. It leads him to feel that he has a heroic place and rôle in the fulfilment of a universal destiny. It gives him, as the political philosophy of freedom cannot, a sense of personal dignity.

Correspondingly, the first plans and enterprises of Marxism were also cosmic and wide-ranging. It ignored all the day-to-day items of individual difference, local color, and associative perspective. Its organization was to be international, its revolution world-wide, and all of its achievements as totalitarian as the autocracy which it rejected. The march of events being the outward aspect of nature's inward dialectic, enterprise that was merely individual, piecemeal, and self-contained could not possibly succeed. Its principle was "All, or nothing."

But events gave the principle the lie. Until the Russian Revolution, the Bolshevik philosophy was the philosophy of an impotent but caustic minority. The Socialism that prevailed in continental Europe as the doctrine of a political party in opposition, or even of a party with power, was reformist; a program to be carried out piecemeal, step by step, in terms of the common life of the common world. It is this same thing in Russia today, and Trotsky, prophet of Bolshevism militant and universal, is in exile from the socialist state he helped establish, still conspiring for a totalitarian revolution. The battle for freedom goes on much as it had gone on before Marx, except that its techniques have been altered by the new conditions of technology and organization due to the spread and change of industry. Even in Russia, attempts, outside of agriculture, to establish and maintain producers' coöperatives have been replaced by a regimentation of producers not unworthy of the early days of British or American industry, and the idea of the worker as consumer is still tangent to the prevailing modes of economic thinking and planning.

For in Russia the Marxian scheme of salvation has been established as the national orthodoxy, and the Communist Party has set up as the true church, entrusted with the Marxian deposit of faith, and the fulfilment of its gospel in the works and ways of men. Thus the rebellious and hopeful of other countries look upon Russia as a century ago Europeans had looked upon the United States. They see it through the rose glass of the Marxist prophecy, which translumines dull things at home into glorious things there, and wicked ways in America or England to revolutionary grace and true salvation in the Soviets.

§ 4. FASCISM, NAZISM, COMMUNISM AND THE SERVILE STATE

It is to these aspects of Communism that Fascism and Nazism oppose their contradiction. Fascism is a gospel of salvation to those who fear to lose what they possess more than they hope to find what they need. In Nazism need presses more fiercely. But both are gospels of the *status quo* made secure, rationalized, and held firm by a rigorous discipline of "law and order." Their most characteristic clergy are industrialists, financiers, armament manufacturers, trades-people threatened by chain stores and the like, scared intellectuals dependent on patronage, and white trash. The symbol of Fascism is the band of sticks and the headsman's ax to beat men with. The symbol of Nazism is the swastika or double-cross which the German sadistocrats oppose to the Cross.

Where Communism affirms the substantial equality and interchangeability of men as workers, Fascism and Nazism affirm their utter inequality. The Nazis declare that all the values of civilization are concentrated in an invention which they call "the Aryan race," and they decide as suits their convenience who shall be acknowledged members of this race and who not, even Jews not excepted, although they have elected Jews, who are unarmed and helpless and without a defender, to the rôle of adversary in their myth of Nazi salvation. According to this myth mankind is divided into the Aryan and the human races. It is the manifest destiny of "the Aryan race," concentrated in the fortunate sovereign state of which Hitler and his company are the leaders and masters, to save the human race by ruling it. The Nazis look forward to a cultural and political empire, won by arms, and maintained by fraud and force, which shall be the great pedestal of Wotan's chosen people. . . . The Fascists recall the splendor which was Rome and insist that history must repeat itself under Mussolini, moving Italy to an imperial destiny outshining that under the Cæsars.

Where the communists preach the class war, and international coöperation, Fascists and Nazis preach class coöperation and international wars. Where the communists describe the Kingdom of Heaven as a classless society, Fascists and Nazis describe it as an autarchic hierarchy of castes composing the national body and national soul. Where the communists hate capitalism and predict its inevitable overthrow, Fascists hate Communism and affirm wherever they find themselves that it is their mission to defend the world against the communist adversary.

So much for the gospels, their resemblances and differences. When one turns from profession to practice, from idea to event, in certain obvious respects the differences dissolve and in these respects there is little to choose in fact between the existing communist rule and the existing Fascist rule. So far as the policy of dictatorship goes, Stalin in Mussolini's place or Mussolini in Stalin's would not need to change a single act in order to conform to their different gospels. The conflict of theory seems to present no obstacle to a similarity, almost an identity of practice.

If there be a consequential difference, it is in favor of the Russian practice. Since the Russian Revolution was a repudiation of certain mediæval evils of exploitation, it has brought corresponding freedoms to the subjects of the Russian dictatorship. Thus, it affirms and maintains, not altogether platonically, the principles of nationality and cultural pluralism within its borders. It designates race prejudice as counter-revolutionary. It has enfranchised women, protecting them where on biological grounds protection is required; otherwise treating them on an ostensible parity with men. It is establishing a nation-wide system of schools, which of course must indoctrinate in the Marxist orthodoxy, but which tangently serve to advance education. It has redirected law, medicine, penology, into channels of social welfare. It has given the physical sciences unreserved support. But all these benevolences, which are *vieux jeu* in democracies like England or the United States, and are there the fruits of free effort and individual initiative, are imposed by command from above, not achieved by consent from beneath. At its present best, the socialist Soviet Republic is a paternalistic tyranny with democratic aspirations, operating on the analogy of a model dairy farm or a well-kept hospital. The individual must do as he is bid, ostensibly for his own good, but he is free neither to discover for himself nor to choose what his good is nor what way to attain it.

Italy and Germany repeat the tyranny, but not the benevolence. Germany reverts to the mediævalism from which Russia emerges. Russia, moreover, makes at least a promise of democracy which Italy and Germany scorn and repudiate. At the present writing, in all three countries the state as an actual fact consists of the members of the civil and military bureaucracy, with their spy systems, their secret police, their armed partizans. They are the state because they are in actual possession of the agencies and armaments of government. Those constitute the power which minorities seize and must hold in order to maintain themselves as the *de facto* masters of the multitudes of the people and their possessions. Holding the coërcive arms of government, minorities are able to practise a constant terror against the great residual majority, and to suppress those civil liberties of conscience, of speech, of press, of assembly, and the like without which the opposition so essential to good government of any kind cannot exist. So the government of Russia has been able to put away thousands of the intellectuals who dared to differ from it, to deport other thousands, besides tens of thousands of peasants, and with the spirit and sincerity worthy of a

Torquemada, to permit, even to force, millions of peasants to die of famine for the greater glory of "collectivization" or a "Five-Year Plan." In these respects there is little to choose between what Stalin's bureaucracy has done to peasants in Russia, and what Hitler's and Mussolini's have done to dissidents and workers in Germany and Italy.

The economic structures which actually obtain in the three countries go by different names, but have the same essential form. In anatomy and in function, the Russian Soviet is not distinguishable from the German cell, or the Italian corporation or guild. Nor are the state trusts distinguishable from the cartels, and such, of the Fascist polities in authoritarianism, though they may be in composition and ideal. All three alike forbid strikes and lock-outs, determine wages and conditions of labor by ukase from above, and impose by statute regimentation under an industrial hierarchy. All three alike require the arts, the sciences, and religion to conform to their several prescriptive orthodoxies. And all three alike practise an inquisition, which out-Christians the classic Christian one, against their heretics and heresies.

Although their theories of property are different, they reduce in practice to the same essential technique of control. Ostensibly in Russia the means of production, the land, the natural resources, are collectively owned and the ownership is vested in the state. In Italy and in Germany they are privately owned and the state exercises an unlimited taxing and controlling power. But on the record, collective ownership in Russia presents no technological advantage over the private ownership in the other countries, for such collective ownership cannot help being even more absentee than the ownership of capitalist and Fascist countries. The employment of field and factory, of money and transport, must necessarily be delegated to employees. It has been subject to the same form of graft, exploitation, sabotage, waste, and invidious handling as among capitalists, Nazis, and Fascists. Although Russian law prescribes procedures, rules, wages, hours, working conditions that compare favorably with the best that can be found in the rest of the world, the Russian government, nevertheless, maintains an industrial police and spy system and administers draconian punishments in order to control managements and men. The contradiction is revealing.

Thus, from the point of view of the average Russian peasant or worker, as from the point of view of the average consumer anywhere, the socialist administration of state-owned properties constitutes, no more than the Fascist coercions of private ownership, any improvement upon the prevailing European and American systems. On the contrary, under them the consumer's standard of living has fallen, not risen; his food, his clothing, his shelter—not, however, his ideas, as in Italy and Germany—have been reduced in quantity, quality, and variety. He has been compelled to accept what was offered, without alternative, where he should be choosing what he desired. The communists deplore this for Russia. They point to the announced increase in consumer goods during 1935. They declare the existing state of things to be transitional. Socialism, they say, is not yet here. It is being "built," and the end justifies the means.[2] Their view, with its contradictions between professions and practices, its doctrinal compensation for present existing evil by future non-existent good, is duplicated by the views of the Nazis and the Fascists. It is no news in history. Neither is the paradox of claiming to make a man free by enslaving him or full by starving him. Wheat from tares and figs from thistles are easier miracles. Soviet Russia's Communism has been and must remain for the most part a dream and prophecy of freedom, not a working way to freedom. But the Fascism of Italy and the Nazism of Germany have been and must remain entirely dreams and false prophecies of security, but not working ways to security.

To date, none of the three is a free society or a safe one. They are equally servile states. A servile state is one in which a minority imposes its rule on the majority and subordinates the well-being of all the people to its own fortunes. The form of the government does not need to be that of a dictatorship. Any form of government is susceptible to the servile perversion. A

2 For a full analysis of the fallacy of this notion see my *Individualism—An American Way of Life.*

church undergoes it when the priesthood or its hierarchy is exalted over the congregation. It occurs in a nation whenever the minority holding the implements of public control—especially the police and the military—tend to make loyalty to the government the same as loyalty to country and people. It works by extirpating liberty from the idea of the welfare of the nation, and by reducing the people to subjection. Lenin belittled liberty as a "bourgeois conception"; Mussolini and Hitler ridicule democracy as falsifying the meaning of history and the conditions of the well-being of nations. In the United States the same sort of thing can be noted as Constitution-worship. The worshippers are anxious to maintain the social, economic and political *status quo* regarding collective bargaining, the position of the Negro, the rights of women, the labor of children, the license of bankers and industrialists to continue and repeat the malpractices which precipitated the depression of 1929–1935. They demand a reverent assent to this condition under the name of "loyalty to the American form of government."

Against the background of political folk-ways from which this view emerges, it is but a rehearsal, in a different language, of the older self-idolization of hereditary monarchs governing on the principle *"l'état, c'est moi."* Today, instead of kings we have dictators. Instead of aristocracies we have communist, Fascist, Nazi or other types of minority political parties who by force and fraud have appropriated to themselves the agencies of social control and who are thus able to impose loyalty and conformity on the great residue of the people. Announcing, *"le pays, c'est moi,"* they force the multitudes into subjection and peonage and call it liberty. They set up servile states where they did not exist before and seek to maintain them where they did.

Now in a free society not only the government but the form of government is changing and changeable. Political democracies are such because they are organized for the purpose of changing governments. Their means is the competition of at least two, and sometimes many, political parties, for the privilege of controlling during a set time the instruments of government, especially the police and the military power. The essence of the democratic form of government is the right and the power of the people continually to choose between political personages and political forms. In the Constitution of the United States this is established and guaranteed by the article providing for the amendment of the Constitution. That alone, so long as the United States remains a democracy, cannot be abrogated, amended or altered in any way.

What is really American in the American form of government is the liberty of amendment by the people, from below. Servile states fix the forms of government. They abolish this liberty. Wherever it is restricted the people are in danger of subjection. Subjection of the people is a fact in Russia, tempered, perhaps, by benevolence. In Italy it is naked and cruel fact. In Germany it is a horrid and murderous fact. Even the subsidizers and supporters of Nazidom now recognize that Germany is a servile state under a *soi-disant* inalterable rule; her masters have been at no pains to hide it, Thyssen is in personal flight and impersonal capital, not excluding perhaps Hitler's and Goebbels' and Goering's own, has been in flight ever since Hitler traitorously seized power and began the economic and cultural starvation of the German people. The actual Italian record—the mounting national debt, the falling standard of living, the loss of hope and the passive resistance among the masses, with their depressing effect on heart and mind—have been decently obscured by the masters of Italy driving the nation on to war. Like the masters of Russia, they are suave in the ways of publicity and understand better than the Germans the arts of suppressing the true and exploiting the false. But if the Russian dictatorship has taken something from the men of Russia, what it has added is not all illusion. Nazism and Fascism have added only illusion. So far as Italy and Germany have carried on, it is despite their new cults, in whose signs these lands have been conquered, not because of the new cults. In both, the leisure classes are more than ever two and not one. Fascism and Nazism have been simply added burdens laid upon their respective national economies; still deeper impoverishments, not enrichments, of the Consumer, who is Everyman. They have not solved, they have only aggravated, the problem of Adam Smith.

§ 5. THE PROBLEM OF ADAM SMITH IN MODERN DRESS

Adam Smith was led to analyze economic behavior because he saw a possible abundance kept from becoming an actual one by a corpus of common law and of administrative practice which choked off the freedom of men to work and to invest their capital in trade and manufacture. His endorsement of the rule of *laissez-faire* was a consequence of his concern for abundance, which grew, he believed, only as each man freely labored to satisfy his own wants. The man so laboring tended more and more to concentrate and specialize and thus to make himself ever more dependent for things he needed, but did not make, upon exchanges with other men who were making things they did not need. This dependence enabled him to consume more and better goods of all kinds than he could if he had attempted to serve all his needs by himself. The free individual activities of each automatically merged with all. Their clash as well as their concord went to the making of spontaneous and automatic coöperation, which transformed scarcity into abundance. We know that, so far as Adam Smith's idea of coöperation through freedom has actually obtained in the business of the world, this abundance has come. Scientific and technological advances, quantity production, improvement of quality, increase in variety, are all traceable to this coöperative competition or competitive coöperation which is the logical conclusion of *laissez-faire.*

As already observed, during the century and a half since the publication of Adam Smith's *Wealth of Nations,* the principle of *laissez-faire* has been continually worked, but even more continually obstructed. Although the wealth of nations *has* increased beyond Smith's most generous dreams, the problem which his work analyzed and his program purported to solve is, if anything, more acute and vexatious than ever. Invention and ingenuity have transformed natural scarcity into civilized plenty and ancient waste into present-day wealth. Men are largely accessories to machines, and that displacement of human labor by mechanical appliances known as "technological unemployment" progressively decreases the proportion of jobs at which is produced all of the wealth and more, necessary to maintain the progressively increasing number of the men without jobs.

This has led to a variety of ironical consequences. In 1935, machines working at capacity can produce at least three times what they had been producing at the height of prosperity in 1929. But unless what is produced is not consumed but sold, production stops. Now what, and how much, is sold depends on the purchasing power of the average consumer. The purchasing power of the average consumer comes to him as wages. But as the automatic production of goods to buy increased, wages finally decreased; that is, purchasing power was decreased; goods could not be bought and remained in the stores; though the supply was available, and though people needed the things, they could not buy. Their insufficient purchasing power was called "low demand." But it wasn't "low demand." Indeed, at no time in the history of industrial society has the production of the necessities of life been sufficient to meet all needs. It was not need which limited demand. It was price. Prices had so outdistanced wages that wages could not catch up with them. Thereupon employers, being unable to sell what they produced, discharged their employees, and added to the technological causes of unemployment the more familiar ones. Since it was no longer possible for wages to follow prices upward, prices began to follow wages downward, to the point where buying and thence producing might resume. But at no time did prices reach that point. For low prices are a consequence of "low demand"; "low demand" obviously cannot be a consequence of "low prices."

Consider prices in *Russia,* in *Germany,* or in *Italy* and compare them with the *de facto* standard of living in those countries. The comparison lays bare the causal connection between high prices and low standard of living. It shows that the notion that some inner bond exists between high prices and prosperity is a persistent delusion of politicians, businessmen, and their academic apologists and interpreters. We find the denizens of a world whose productions are always exceeding consumption manifesting a feeling of economic insecurity their ancestors of Adam Smith's day would not understand. For the multitudes, freedom to work has become the permanent threat of unemployment; freedom to invest the permanent threat of financial misappropriation and the use of one's investment for exploitation; collective abundance has become personal poverty; unplanned plenty, planned scarcity.

We already know the reason why. In actual economies, *laissez-faire* remained only a logic; *equal* liberty never became a fact. In the greater financial-industrial fields monopoly overtook free competition before it ever got started and is master of both the economic and political scene. It sunk the man in the worker, life in labor. It made consumption a body-servant of production; it attached men to machines and contaminated them with the destiny of machines—to live to work until scrapped. Because men are many and jobs not so many, it was able, without lifting the biblical curse from labor, to elevate work into a right. In its train of consequences come the business cycle, the constant drive toward international monopoly in certain industries; toward national autarchy in certain states; the continuous warfare by the methods of protective tariffs, commercial subsidies, dumping, colonization, manipulations of money and credit, and competitive armament culminating in actual military collision.

The excuse usually given for these developments is "national necessity" created by economic scarcity. Rulers of countries like Italy, Germany, Japan, assert that their populations are greater than their lands can support and that they must have lands and markets to feed their populations. But to get lands and markets they make war. Hence they demand of their already too numerous people to increase and multiply so that they may produce armies to take forceful possession of the room their alleged numerical excess requires. They demand still greater overpopulation to overcome the evils of overpopulation; and they glorify the military spirit, national armament, industrial peonage, and political tyranny on the same grounds. Their totalitarianism and aggression contaminate the mind of the world. And even in countries with free institutions like France, England, the Scandinavian lands, and the United States, they spawn sects and parties that demand, sometimes in the name of liberty, a similar regimenting of the bodies and souls of free citizens.

But as a rule the methods of the countries with free institutions are of another sort. To them also prosperity means the maintenance of scarcity under conditions that, left to themselves, would create abundance. They wage a war against plenty. This was the fundamental principle underlying the New Deal and determining the technique of its Industrial Recovery program. The Agricultural Adjustment Administration, the National Industrial Recovery Administration, and other agencies of "recovery" have sought to fix prices, to reduce the number of hours of work, to raise wages, but especially, in agriculture to limit production. In December, 1933, the former administrator of the NRA, General Johnson, declared that public policy should be looking toward a six-hour day and a thirty-hour week, and implicitly acknowledged how futile the policy was in solving the basic problem of unemployment. "If we return," he said, "to the 1928–1929 standard of prosperity, there would still be four million unemployed."

Obviously, the devices of the New Deal at their very best could be only palliative, and were. They did not touch the fundamental cause of unemployment. And as administered, they had to fall far below hopes, promises, and possibilities; they had to become components of widespread industrial warfare, of conflicts involving the animosities which arise when old ways are challenged and when fear of loss—whether of property, prestige or profit—becomes stronger than any hope of gain.

Practices and programs of the type just discussed have another than an objective ground. In the light of the present state of the sciences and arts of agriculture and of industry, it is not true that any country is so overpopulated that it need rob any other country of land or goods. Material and spiritual abundance can be brought forth everywhere; even deserts have been made to, and do, bloom again more readily than ever. Over-population is not a sign of the poverty of a land; it is in the first instance a sign of a land's growing fertility, and in the second instance a sign of political incompetence and technological backwardness, a sign of cultural lag. Over-population means that a state's political and economic masters are thinking in terms of envy and of institutional survivals, not in terms of the actual conditions of human life and how to alter them. They are more concerned to conserve and extend ancient "rights" for privileged classes—rights of property, rights of prestige, rights of status—by means of economic and military aggression, than to bring a greater abundance to their peoples by setting up democratic parity of such rights by the obvious means. To accomplish the latter would require altering the distribution and use of lands and factories, democratizing their control, and reorganizing education so as to put at the disposal of the multitudes the entire social heritage of skills and knowledges.

Predatory adventure abroad appears more natural, because more primitive and more customary, than administrative and technological reconstruction at home. It is closer to the animal passions of the human heart; it more readily enchannels greed, purges fear, and exalts vainglory. It is self-interest, but not the self-interest which Adam Smith had in mind. It is not guided by an insight into the causes and conditions of human well-being, nor is it a method of controlling and directing those causes on behalf of "the national interest." It is simply a gargantuan extension of the sort of animal behavior that leaps and writhes and roars and bites at its own wound instead of seeking with quiet intelligence the scientifically ascertainable medication. Types like Hitler and Mussolini—and militarists anywhere—are, together with the programs and doctrines of their cults, testimonies how deep-rooted and wide-ranging this animal reaction is. They are but rushes and clawings and roars which give voice to a sickness of society they do not envisage and cannot cure, and which only aggravate the disease. They are the most conspicuous garbage of the problem of plenty in modern dress. Repudiating *laissez-faire,* they embody as the state that which trusts, cartels, banks, incarnate as finance and industry in the name of *laissez-faire*. Together, they are why the problem of Adam Smith lives and grows more aggravated to this day.

§ 6. THE PRESENT STATE OF THE COÖPERATIVE MOVEMENT

TOGETHER, by and large, they produce the economic climate in which the coöperative movement must live, move, have its being, and bring to completion its trend to an economy of freedom and abundance working with the methods of freedom. In this air and temperature the free society of a consumer economy does not stand clear. To the general mind the very perspectives of the movement toward it becloud it. The vision has not yet been elicited with the necessary sharpness from its implications in the structure and activities of the world's coöperative establishments. Of the one hundred-odd millions of coöperators and more on the globe, almost two-thirds were counted in the Soviet Union. About two-thirds of the remainder—some forty millions—are found in other European countries, and the rest are scattered in the Americas, Asia, Africa, and Australia. Only about 100,000,000 were counted in the International Coöperative Alliance. Of all these millions, about one-third are organized consumers first and foremost. The members of consumer organizations as such number perhaps twenty millions outside of the Soviet Union and were once seventy-five millions inside. The farmer marketing and purchasing coöperatives, which show themselves thus far as dominated by a producer interest, count about twenty-three million members, of whom some fifteen million are in the Soviets. Other producers' coöperatives count some three million, five hundred thousand members of whom about three million live in the Soviet Union. The credit unions count some twelve million farmers and two and one-half million urban industrial and white-collar workers. There are none in Soviet Russia. The building and loan associations count some fifteen million members, and the coöperative housing societies, perhaps a million outside of the Soviet and two million in the Soviet Union. All these organizations count as coöperatives because the relations of their members are governed by the Rochdale principles of association, especially the principles of one-man, one vote, dividend on purchase, and fixed interest on share-capital.

The field of the coöperative endeavors extends, of course, far more widely than the major divisions indicate. Insurance is naturally one of the important coöperative activities, but the coöperative method is applied to the protection of health, to hospitalization, to recreation, travel, transportation, education, to the building of roads, the supply of water, gas and power, and the organization of traction and telephone.[3] In one place or another a society will be found engaged in satisfying coöperatively every conceivable need of its members. Most of such societies are classified, not incorrectly, as consumer societies: And they are contrasted with the self-governing workshops of producers' coöperatives, the agricultural or farmers' coöperatives, and the credit unions. So far as numbers, financial strength and psychological type define the coöperator, the credit union and agricultural organizations weigh more heavily than the straight consumer societies in all countries except Sweden and England. But if basic ideology is a criterion, coöperation is a growth of the industrial soil and its fruit and goal is consumer organization. Moreover, unless the application of science to farming is arrested, and the use of machinery forbidden, agriculture is sure to be industrialized within a generation or two, and this makes the general displacement of the producer by a consumer organization with its characteristic psychology almost a foregone conclusion.

It is to be expected that the consensus which embodies the principles and policies of the movement should reflect the diversities of character, interest and action that enter into it. Certain conflicts are perennial; they arise wherever different human beings try to work together; the most military or ecclesiastical regimentation is as unable to repress them as the freest coöperation. Among them are the spontaneous emulations of men and groups, which develop often into vested interests of place and power, with their consequent machine politics.[4] The one antidote against them is the continuous active participation of all members of a movement in its labors and deliberations. Against this, however, inertia and indifference constantly work. No way has yet been found to keep an issue permanently momentous, or a mind alert without a lapse. Habit dulls the edge of the sharpest danger; everything is born an adventure and dies a bore. The overwhelm-

[3] *Cf.* J. P. Warbasse, *Coöperative Democracy.*

[4] *Cf.* The competition between societies, managers, and wholesale that keeps recurring.

ing desire for security which moves the present generation is itself a child of this basic inertia. It leads to timidity and slowness of action; it is the sustaining emotion of the illusion, not by a long shot confined to coöperators, that economy consists in saving rather than in spending wisely. It underlies the provincialism and stodginess which mark large areas of the coöperative population. It animates the persistent tendency to "penny-pinching" as against the expansion of the personality. Because of it, coöperators have often shown an undue caution, a certain smug content with the *status quo*. Fearing to lose what they own more than they desire to become what they can, they fall into a state of arrested development; they tend to straddle or evade basic issues instead of forthrightly gripping and settling them in the light of the fundamental philosophy of consumer coöperation.

Indeed, a study of the debates at the Congresses of the International Coöperative Alliance suggests some ambiguity of mind as to this fundamental philosophy. In view of the record, the activities, and the program of the Alliance, the coöperative movement is the residuary legatee of the internationalism, the free trade philosophy and practice, and the hopeful democratic idealism of the humanist libertarians of the early Victorian age. Economic nationalism is its contradiction. The current policy of governments aims to cripple the coöperative movement and to prevent, or at least to hold back so long as possible the organization of international exchange of goods and services between the coöperatives of different countries. But the Alliance carries on its positive coöperative work regardless, and its affiliated members show themselves at home to have a resiliency and an adaptability which make them in a crisis, natural trustees for the upkeep and expansion of the national economy. These qualities appear to be accompaniments of the Rochdale economic principles and program: democratism; political and religious toleration. Only on these does there appear to be a complete consensus; in the face of the nationalist and autarchic contagions, the members of the International Coöperative Alliance are working out devices to exchange credit, goods and services on the same terms and under the same principles as individuals do with their societies and societies with their wholesales.

Yet on the issues between social and political militancy and neutrality, between racial and religious partizanship and coöperative tolerance, the consensus is not so stable nor its pattern so clear. As their countries, so the coöperators are disturbed, and some of the leaders feel that it is the better part of valor to conform. Others insist on the need of militant action against the forces of reaction wherever they appear; still others on the necessity of a clear and forthright effort to secure acceptance on any issue of coöperative policy as it would follow from coöperative principles; but to acquiesce in whatever decision has finally been reached.[5]

§ 7. COÖPERATION, POLITICAL ANTAGONISM AND THE CULTURAL LAG

IN VIEW of the record, the last policy is the wisest and most fruitful one for the coöperative movement as a movement. Its one sole task is to live and to grow into the fulness of a consumer economy. In the accomplishment of this task coöperators are opposed, not only by an inward lag which leads such usually careful observers as H. G. Wells *ex cathedra* to declare them incapable; [6] but by the whole institutional and cultural

[5] *Cf.* Albin Johansson, Director, Swedish Coöperative Union, *The Rôle of International Coöperation in Present Day Economic Development.* Paper read and report submitted to the Fourteenth International Coöperative Congress of the International Coöperative Alliance, held at London, September, 1934.

[6] "One may doubt whether this movement, as it exists at present, will ever crystallize out into that promised new world. That new world, it would seem, needs something more, much more, than is to be found in this sane and discreet extension of membership and activities. It may be overtaken by other forces, more powerfully and rapidly constructive. It is significant that the coöperative movement has failed to take root in America. . . . The modernization of economic life has reached such a point in America that the possibility of small progressive crystallization has passed. . . . The coöperative movement is seen to grow, but without animation. Members are primarily interested in the dividend. How many would attend a public demonstration in favor of the coöperative commonwealth? No one boasts that he is a member of this great movement; no one's eyes brighten at the mention of it. It causes neither pride nor exaltation. A Glasgow housewife would not 'go past the co-op,' but no Glasgow man would be proud to be told that he looked as if he had been rigged out at the co-op.

complex which constitutes their environment. This environment was not made for them and is not primarily favorable to them. They happened in it, as more or less spontaneous variations. The configuration of their growth is due, of course, to their inward drive and outer struggle. If state, church, labor union and school have now and again favored them, they have perhaps not less frequently fought them. The credit-enterprise economy from which the coöperative system is a mutation has been and will remain their natural competitor. The coöperatives live most immediately within this economy. They are subject most of all to the pushes and pulls, the strains and distortions of its business cycles, its invidious competition, its monopolies and coercions. One of its effects has been the establishment, in the ordinary wage-worker, of a producer mentality which permeates the trades-unions and is among the most powerful forces that hold back the integration of the trades-union interest with consumer organization. The power of the state is a permanent menace: it can cripple overnight or kill in a day what has taken generations to grow. The varieties of state Socialism or capitalism—communist, democratic and Fascist alike—organize men as producers only. In all of them the organized producer holds the unorganized consumer at his mercy, and the employer holds the employee. The state, ostensibly purposing to enforce justice between the opposed parties and to render unto each his right, actually tends to side with the producer and employer. When, as is the case with Russia, Italy and Germany, the state is either the producer itself or a partner of the capitalistic producer, it develops a consistent unfairness to the consumer and the employee. Let the record of Code Administration under the American NRA testify. The state's organic relation to Big Business is notorious, and the threat of taxation of the purchase dividend in England and the Scandi-

The co-ops supply good, honest goods, but without distinction or novelty. "Which is not to say that the coöperative movement will be so much defeated and disappear as to be overtaken—as it has already been overtaken in Russia and Italy—and incorporated in bolder and wider enterprises with a more explicit plan and a deeper emotional drive." (H. G. Wells, *Work, Wealth and Happiness of Mankind,* p. 290.)

navian countries, the actual employment of brute force in Italy and Germany are but recent examples of the menace to coöperatives through the state.

In a word, the institutional environment exerts more than enough external pressure upon the coöperatives to cause them to compensate for any deficiency of inward drive they may be suffering from. At the moment, the defense of its own survival, and its own growth in its own domain, are as much as the coöperative movement can well manage.

But more, there is no urgency which calls it to go beyond this self-defense. Indeed its self-defense is its best attack. Unlike business-enterprise, consumers' coöperation does not need to assault competitors in order to live and grow. It works by a different method and grows by a different principle. Its method is the teamwork of individuals, who pool their resources and by joint effort satisfy their individual needs as they occur here and now. The method of its rivals is cataclysmic and revolutionary in its beginnings and oppressive and tyrannical in its end. "You are nothing: the state is all," the rivals tell the men and women whom they offer their salvation. Consumers' coöperation abhors and excommunicates this nullification of human individuality. To the principle of "all at once or nothing," it opposes the principle of evolutionary growth and progressive learning. To totalitarianism it opposes federal democracy. To the technique of irresponsible leadership and paternalism, it opposes the technique of responsible free election. It holds the task of any national economy to be, setting free, encouraging, and helping to perfect the diversities of human nature: through economic organization to enhance the equal liberties of different men. Hence it needs only as fully and completely as possible to be itself, to fill out its form and perfect its functions. It is not at war with the existing economic system or mores. It calls for no revolutionary break with the past, and is not battling the present. It is doing to capitalism what capitalism did to the pre-capitalistic economy—displaced it by performing the same task better, by bringing, item by item, step by step, a freer and more abundant life to more human beings. It is displacing capitalism as the automobile displaced the horse, the electric light, the lamp; scientific medicine, old wives' remedies; not by attacking and harming the competitor, but by doing his work in a better way, a shorter time, at a smaller cost, in greater freedom, and thus superseding him as one species of the same genus of plant or animal supersedes another.

Hence the more the coöperative movement minds its own business the surer it is to become the business of everybody. The more strictly it adheres to the principle of social and political neutrality today, the surer it is to absorb into itself the loyalties of all sects and parties tomorrow. Only where a government, an industry or some other institution threatens to attack the coöperative integrity is the movement or any member of it called upon to seek alliances, to develop organs of defense, or to wage war. Thus, the kidnapping and perversion of the Italian coöperatives by the Fascists, the rape of the German coöperatives by the Nazis, led to the exclusion of the coöperatives of those countries from the International Coöperative Alliance; the assault of Big Business upon the British coöperatives by means of a tax on the purchase dividend led to the formation of the political British Coöperative Party. The assimilation of the Russian coöperatives by the Soviet government, on the other hand, led to nothing at all: it seemed not to have had any serious effect upon the integrity of coöperative organization and methods but had led instead to an increase in the rate of growth—until the producer-minded, all-powerful government decided to abolish the coöperative in favor of the state trust. However, within the limits of forceful destruction, it is the movement's best service to the progressive and humanitarian forces of the world to extend its organization and its methods. To strengthen them is to keep itself growing ever larger and stronger and more self-sufficient; to stay wide open; to cross all boundaries, alike geographical and political; to bring together every shade and variety of character, faith and opinion, and to familiarize them in the community of the diverse which the consumer economy institutes, and to habituate them in the organization of liberty which coöperative method presents as the way of life.

CHAPTER XV

TOWARD A CONSUMER ECONOMY: HELPS AND HINDRANCES

§ 1. RANGE AND DRIVE OF THE CONSUMER INTEREST

CAN THE CONSUMERS' coöperative movement incarnate its vision without doing in its own way the same violence to human nature as its rivals and competitors, without getting involved in the cruelties, the oppressions, the exploitations and injustices which characterize Communism and Fascism as fully, if not more so, as they characterize capitalism?

On the record, if the consumers' coöperative movement cannot, none has yet been born that can. The most serious disability attributed to it has been attributed by its staunchest friends and wisest interpreters.[1] However open in principle the coöperative associations were, and however eager organized coöperators were to draw all sorts and conditions of men into coöperative society, certain sorts and conditions were automatically unable to reach to the advantages of this free association. To obtain at all, coöperative society presupposes, Mrs. Webb reasoned, a certain geographical proximity, a certain standard of living, relatively steady employment, and more or less "regular" habits. The casual laborer, moving in short irregular intervals from job to job and home to home, living at or below the level of subsistence, is too destitute to have even the poor pennies with which the weavers of Roch-

[1] *Cf.* Mrs. Sidney Webb, *The Coöperative Movement in Great Britain,* Chapter VIII.

dale began, too mobile to keep loyal to any organization; and there are millions upon millions of him, whose life problem has thus far not been met by the method of coöperation, whether as producer or consumer. Not only are the multitude of the industrial poor not coöperators; they are not trades-unionists. Equally irregular, but for opposite reasons, are the fashionable rich, with their hunt for variety and change. They also stay beyond the reach of voluntary coöperation. Together with the multitudes of the poor, Mrs. Webb thinks, they must be compelled to coöperate, though by different methods. Like children, they must be indoctrinated and disciplined until they have grown into the social maturity needful to voluntary coöperation.

But this judgment, like the judgment of the Webbs' regarding the susceptibility of transport, gas and water works and other public utilities to coöperative ownership and control, is too hasty. To date the issue has been abstract and somewhat platonic. In England, neither the coöperative organization of the submerged nor the coöperative ownership and control of public utilities has become a momentous option, requiring a choice. There are still too many people *above* the subsistence level to win to the consumer movement and still too much to do in other directions to bother about deviating from the past on how to own and manage public utilities. And both are even remoter from urgency in other countries. Nowhere have they been faced and studied as practical programs requiring to be implemented and justified against alternatives. Even without a dynamic wisely-directed educational establishment, coöperative membership can be at least as voluntary as citizenship is today in free countries; share-owning can be as universal as taxes and the purchase-dividend or usage-profit perhaps even more widespread than share-holding.

For though a few more than one hundred millions of the world's billion of men and women are associated together in one form or another of coöperation, the principle and method of the movement renders it in the nature of things indefinitely expansible. The more it has grown, the more it is able to grow.

Its ways and rules need to be reconciled, not so much with

the casualness and destitution of the laboring multitudes as with their mobility. This reconciliation is a problem in the techniques of accountancy; a bookkeeper's problem, and the ingenuity which has solved the perplexities of the credit-enterprise structure can be relied upon to do at least as well for the expansion of coöperation. Public utilities, mines and railroads can be owned and managed on Rochdale principles no less than fields and factories.

But more than that, the great depression of 1929–1935 has repeated the demonstration of 1844 in Rochdale that even in this new and very different age destitution is no insuperable obstacle. Thus, in 1934, twenty-five or thirty of the unemployed citizens of Grand Island, Nebraska, formed the Grand Island Self-Help Society. They assembled a capital of $24.99, and with this undertook the coöperative serving of their individual needs. A year later their capital had increased by 300 per cent, they had goods on their shelves inventoricd at five times the original capital, and had sold a second little group of unemployed a "washtub full of groceries" to begin their own coöperative adventure with.

Again, the most depressed section of the population of the United States is the Negro. No workers anywhere in our industrial or agricultural society could be more destitute, marginal and mobile. In Gary, Indiana, there were 20,000 Negroes, lowest of the low, poorest of the poor. In 1932, half of them were on relief and most of them somehow not in receipt of the relief that was their due. A number fell in the way of discussing the situation, trying to figure out what they could do about it. It was a present situation—present hunger, present thirst, present need for shelter and warmth and medicine. It had to be met now, on the spot. Meeting it couldn't be postponed until after a proletarian revolution or a socialist election or a Ku Klux Klan raid (so that Mother Red Cross could practise her well-known benevolence); hunger and cold and sickness and death wouldn't wait. The one way to deal with them here and now, the discussion revealed, was the coöperative way. Some twenty families scraped together about $24 and formed a buying club, and in less than a year the buying club grew into a store. It wasn't much of a store. Its directors were millhands and unskilled laborers, out of work; its manager and one clerk were without any experience; it was dark and poorly located and not too clean. The merchants around made fun of it. They predicted it would "go bust" before it started. But it hasn't gone bust. The membership of the, now, Consumers' Coöperative Trading Company of Gary, Indiana, has increased from 20 to 400. Its turnover for 1935 was more than $35,000; this is greater by one-third than the maximum sales of the greatest long-established Negro-owned grocery store. It is today the largest Negro-owned grocery store in the United States.[2]

Does it not seem, that if either the physical or the psychic urgency is sufficient no level of human life in the modern world is too low to be reached and lifted by the coöperative movement? But time and place must adhere. A great material urgency or a great spiritual urgency may be required to set the salvational activity in motion. Once started, however, it appears, at least as surely as any other, able to go on its own momentum. The material urgency happens: natural catastrophes, strikes, depressions, may be enough to direct self-preserving action into coöperative channels. The spiritual urgency can be induced; there must be the desire to coöperate. The desire to coöperate can be animated only through an ideal and vision of self-improvement; that is, of a consumer economy. The vision can be brought into action by education on any level of development, that of the child or that of the adult. The feel and form of coöperation may be taught, as we have seen, by any kind of organization—state, church, patriotic society, no less than the movement itself. Any may undertake to awaken men and women and children to the meaning of liberty for themselves and its attainment through the organization of liberty in the form of consumers' coöperatives.

The basic point of departure is the fact that the business of a consumer society is able, from the very moment it starts, to furnish from within itself the materials and conditions of its own success. It is one institutional structure which grows by what it feeds on and feeds on itself. For its intent can never be anything but democratic abundance. Founded on the wants

[2] *Cf.* J. L. Reddix, *Consumers' Coöperation* (October, 1935).

of the consumer, it mounts and spreads as they multiply and diversify. This means that "the store" can grow without limit. It is not bound like the producers' organizations of the producer economy by inner and outer competition. Producer societies, no matter how democratically conceived and organized, are always restricted to their own exclusive development: They tend automatically toward monopoly; their prosperity rests on scarcity. Such a scarcity maintains itself not by endeavoring to do better than the competitor but by destroying the competitor. It lessens jobs for workers as well as goods and quality for consumers. This is another reason why—apart from those which have become evident in the survey of the function of the organized consumers as employer—a consumer economy is a more desirable thing for the multitude of producers purely as producers. For the multiplication and diversification of wants generates a corresponding multiplication and diversification of occupations. It means, not the shutting out of careers but the opening up of careers; an enlarged opportunity to choose occupations; and, under coöperative rule the completest possible transformation, within the limits of effectiveness, of the servilities inherent in the employer-employee relation into industrial citizenship.

§ 2. TOUGHNESS, FLEXIBILITY AND INTELLIGENCE OF THE COÖPERATIVE MOVEMENT

COMPARED with the capitalism from which it is a variant, and the Socialism, the Fascism, Communism, Nazism, and other forms of state mastery which are its competitors, coöperation has grown more rapidly, more surely, more stably, in any measured period, than each and all of them. In a hundred years, capitalism had hardly begun to effect the modification of feudal society which the coöperative movement is obviously accomplishing in capitalist society. In fifteen or twenty years, Communism, Fascism and Nazism have simply depressed and impoverished the populations whose economies they rule.

Furthermore, the coöperative structure and method reveals itself to be possessed of a flexibility, a toughness which enables it to survive and to grow, without losing its integrity, in every variety of social context. It is not merely that the movement prospers alike in England and in India, in Japan and in Russia, in Ireland and in Denmark, among every variety of race, color, sect and political affiliation. It is that, short of destruction, it is able to survive, even increase, in the noxious atmosphere of Fascist Italy and amid the material and spiritual poisons of Nazi Germany. To some degree this may be ascribed to the political "neutrality" of the movement, to its policy of avoiding "entangling alliances," to its nonpartizanship. But this "neutrality" itself, it must not be forgotten, is an expression of the very essence of democracy: It follows from the recognition of the parity of opinions, faiths, races, cultures, and other differences which call people to separate and exclusive allegiances. In effect, coöperative neutrality acknowledges the right of each of these to be. It rests upon accepting the individuality of individuals and the inviolability of the individual conscience, and presents itself to individuals and to groups as the method of combining their diversities without sacrificing them; of combining them in such a way that the prosperity of each becomes an enrichment of all and the strengthening of all becomes a reënforcement of each.

In this acknowledgement of the individuality of individuals as the prime dynamic in action resides coöperation's claim to be closer than any other movement to the passions of the human heart. By its technique of reconciling them with one another, of developing action upon a consensus born of free deliberation it allies itself with the scientific social intelligence and establishes itself as the paramount method of economic association which this intelligence has thus far been able to devise.

But the consumer movement may be called intelligent for still other reasons.

One is the immediacy of its action, the fact that the benefits it brings do not need to wait upon a change of heart in individuals or a revolution in society.

Another is that being immediate, this action does not break from the institutional course of events: it merely alters directions and changes forms. The record shows much talk of "production for use," but the prevalence in practice of the idea and feel of private property, profits, and the price system. Resting on the democratic insight of the parity of the different, requiring their equal liberty, the movement cannot wish to replace private property with state ownership. It is aware of the difficulties and dangers that come with the absentee-ism intrinsic to public ownership, and its democracy rejects absentee-ism. Therefore it combines the principle of individual ownership with associative use. It grows by extending the principle of private property, so that ultimately there shall be no human being so mean as not to feel that he owns, as part and parcel of his proper personal property, enough to meet well the needs of his body and to satisfy the requirements of his soul. Such an extension may bring about a change—undoubtedly it will bring about a change—in the legal form of ownership; but it will intensify and spread, rather than break with, the working psychology of possession.

Consumer coöperation also confronts "the profit motive" intelligently. If profit be the increase which is the more that comes out of the less that has been put in, if profit be the difference between the less possessed and invested and the more desired, whether as material or as psychic income, the profit motive cannot be expunged from the human heart; it can only be redirected. This the coöperative movement does. Its attitude toward profits is its attitude toward property: It may employ another word for the satisfaction of this desire for increase; it may speak of "plenty" or "abundance." But what else are these than the excess of value over investment in labor or goods, the increase which the Bible blesses and all men desire? Without profit in this sense of the word, there cannot be a consumers' economy, a life more abundant. And the general measure of the difference between cost and gain, its bookkeeping and accountancy, so to speak, gets defined in the well-known price system. This too, the consumers' economy preserves, employs, and employing, transforms.

Thus the special technique and ideology of consumers' coöperation tend little by little to effect a profound alteration of capitalist society at its roots in the habits and character of the individual. Conditioned to the attitudes and ways of consumer coöperation, a man will regard property, for example, as personal and private as ever, but its meaning will have changed. As a coöperator, he cannot be a mere absentee owner, receiving rents or dividends; he must be a functional owner, participating in direction and control. He continues to use price as his yardstick, but under coöperative conditions it is a price with consumers' gains, not pecuniary profit. The speculative production of things to sell becomes to him an activity imaginable but not experienced; he knows but the sure production of things not merely to be used, but to be used up, to be consumed. Price figures in his mind alone as the money-sign of the cost of producing, handling and distributing the goods of life under consumer control.

Moreover, because of the primacy of consumption in his psychology, the coöperator becomes more than ever aware of and sensitive to personal differences, the uncontrollable liberty of taste and sensibility, the uniqueness of the personal equation, as well as the mutual contagion and consensus of these equations. Such awareness brings new strength to the democratic principle of voluntary association, the rule of one man, one vote, upon which are based the associative form and government of consumers' coöperatives. Hence, classes, sects, castes and the like, become recessive; they cease to function in his mind as instruments for identifying individuals. He comes more and more to acknowledge individuals in their individuality, and his associative rule changes from "Live and let live" to "Live and help live."

§ 3. COÖPERATION VERSUS OVER-POPULATION AND WAR

THE EFFECT of such changes on the peace of the world are easy to infer. Other things being equal, the competitive-producer economy organized in corporations can be displaced with increasing speed and effectiveness by a coöperative-consumer economy organized in coöperative societies.

As this happens the essential causes of unemployment are bound to diminish and ultimately to disappear. Unemployment itself being a consequence of over-population and over-population nothing more at bottom than a deficiency of institutional resources to maintain the population, it must follow that where resources are adequate population cannot be excessive. Thus the concepts of an economy of abundance and of over-population are mutually repugnant. Abundance is the excess of the goods of life over effective demand. It exists where a population enjoys all that it desires and possesses more. That the sciences imply such an abundance we know, but it is clear that this implication has little chance of being made explicit in contemporary policies. To date coöperation presents itself as the sole existing economic techique which can, without revolution, abolish both unemployment and over-population and thus, the external causes of war.

That it can abolish war cannot perhaps be claimed. There are inner conditions which are usually unacknowledged and always rationalized and disguised. Certainly the claims of a national necessity imposed by scarcity of land or resources are often of the flimsiest, and sometimes not even flimsy. In the modern world very few wars have been due to a genuine scarcity. It rarely happens that peoples truly suffering from scarcity become organized military aggressors. The millions of China, of Ireland, of Italy before Mussolini, of Japan before the World War, never thought of using their need as a justification of military aggression. Indeed, they never thought of aggression. On the record, wars have been waged only by powers that felt themselves able to do so, that is, sufficiently prosperous, well-armed and sure of victory to risk the event. Their motives were as a rule not need but greed, "national honor" or simply the overflow of envy and malice. First they emulated, then they hated, then they endeavored to destroy. This is the story of the motives driving to the World War. That cost four million casualties and four hundred thousand million dollars in property. It brought social upheaval to many of the participating countries, depression and poverty to the others. According to an authoritative study by the Carnegie Endowment for International Peace, out of the cost of this War every family in the United States and Canada, in Great Britain and Ireland, in France, Belgium, Germany and Russia could have been provided with five acres of land at $100 per acre and a $2,500 house with $1,000 worth of furniture; every city of more than 20,000 inhabitants could have been endowed with a five-million-dollar library and a ten-million-dollar university. From the remainder a fund could have been dedicated which at 5 per cent interest would yield a salary of $1,000 a year each to 125,000 teachers and 125,000 nurses, and still enough be left to buy and pay for every single item of value that composed the total wealth of France and Belgium in 1914.

These facts are sufficient to falsify all notions that war is an advantage to anybody who wages it. Norman Angell proved that long ago. That it is waged, therefore, is due to quite other motives than economic necessity or national advantage. War springs from the spontaneous passions of the human heart, its appetite for combat, and for the sort of expansion and release of life which the gratification of these emotions brings. These springs cannot be dried up. If not war, they call for William James' famous moral equivalent. Now there is widespread agreement regarding what such an equivalent can be. It is war against nature instead of other men. It is labor, and what Marx called "the administration of things." To the modern mentality labor is mostly servile and holds only a servant's place in its war-like philosophy of life. The labor corps of the Nazis, the work battalions of the Fascists are compulsory and are suffused with the Fascist and Nazi creed that life is glorious only as it is murderous. Russia has come closer to redefining the moral equivalent as a sublimation of the war-like disposition, but also the prevailing ideology of the Soviets is war-like and life is a class war looking to "the peace that passeth understanding" of the classless society.

Many observers have seen in the Civilian Conservation Corps organized under the American New Deal a similar moral equivalent. This, more nearly pacific than its analogues elsewhere, is however only a remedial and transitional depression-phenomenon. Nevertheless, it is closer to the moral equivalent than any of its rivals and competitors. A consumer economy could easily adapt it to its own institutional organization and integrate it with the total structure of its educational system.

§ 4. HOW COÖPERATIVES, LABOR ORGANIZATIONS AND CREDIT UNIONS CAN CONVERGE INTO A CONSUMER ECONOMY

THE GENERAL FEATURES of such an economy are not difficult to designate. Its basic difference from its rivals would lie in the fact that it defines its structure and its function in terms of consumption and not in terms of production. In a producers' economy consumption is supposed to exist for the sake of production and as a consequence the multitudes work without living and the privileged live without working. The system separates the activities of the personality as producer from the character of the personality as consumer, labor from leisure. This separation establishes itself in the form of industrial castes and classes and develops the conflicts of interest which vex industrial society and which are the preoccupation of revolutionists and reformers. In effect it creates the population problem, remembering that it is an ancient difficulty and modern superstition. It starts in the fact that in order to live, men must eat; in order to eat, they must work; in order to work, they must have land and implements to work with. If they cannot get them for themselves and their children freely or by fair exchange, they will take them from other people by force or fraud. The conduct pattern is immemorial; it has lived on as an unconscious component in the commonsense of the ages, regardless of relevancy or reality. It is the premise on which Plato postulated his Utopian Republic, and it has coerced political idealists after Plato as certainly as political realists. The generations since Malthus have been more aware than those before of the unconscious premise concerning group relationships which the hypothetical race between population and sustenance sets up. "Neo-Malthusianism," "the population problem," are expressions which signalize this awareness. The variously-conditioned developing modern interest in sexuality, the spreading endorsement among all groups and classes of contraceptive knowledge, are reënforcing indications. But the paramount ones are the politics of autarchic nationalist states like Italy or Germany or Japan.

Although science and industry have established a mastery

of the earth and the creatures thereof which, rightly employed, could solve the population problem, the advantages they have created are being applied only to intensify the problem. The ancient "law of tooth and claw" enchanneled in the habits of pre-industrial man-to-man competition bars the way to the establishment of new habits of coöperation, which the modern state of the industrial arts evokes and tends to enforce. Those to whom leisure is a privilege of birth or wealth tend to oppose with every means in their power the extension of a like leisure to those upon whom it has been an imposition of their helpless poverty. The masters of industry and finance fight with all their resources against shorter work days and shorter work weeks for the servants of industry and finance. Wherever we turn, we see the progress of the industrial arts, by whose means we could so easily solve the population problem, adding, to the human surplus which nature breeds, the surplus which the labor-saving machine throws out of employment.

In every country, the generations which grow up without a living or a life-work to look forward to, join the generations of the disemployed who have only employment to look back upon, and live together with them in anxious idleness.

Yet why work?

Those who are privileged or adroit enough to live without working have no wish to work; and those who work, do so moved by the inveterate hope that their labor today may enable them to live in leisure tomorrow. How recent among us is the exaltation of work and how the glorification of the working-man still wears a revolutionary and heretical aura! How long is it since the Congress of the United States declared in the Clayton Bill that labor is not a commodity? And thereafter as before, have not men continued to treat labor as nothing else than a commodity? Nor has the seller of his labor been more reluctant than the buyer so to treat it. A sign of meanness to the pagan ancients, a degradation following a divine curse to the Christian mediævals, labor, regardless of its nineteenth-century assumption to aristocratic dignity and excellence, continues to be esteemed as something to escape from, not something to seek. A richly endowed leisure is still the sign of social election. "The right to work," that paradoxical and ironic right, sets up a claim on something in itself undesirable and undesired because it is the approved way to the securing of something desired. The goal of desire is for each man such a fulness of his proper life as always has been the privilege of the men of the leisure class alone. The leisure class *is* the leisure class because it consumes without producing. The fulness of life is attained in the consumption which not only uses the goods of life but uses them up.

Now a consumers' economy distinguishes itself from a producers' in that it does not regard work either as a right or a duty; it regards work as a means. The one right paramount upon which it seeks to rebuild the world's economy is the right to the good life. Consumers' coöperation treats production purely as an occasion or a condition or an instrument of consumption. Hence within the framework of consumers' coöperation there cannot occur between organized consumers and organized producers that exacerbated conflict about hours, wages and conditions of labor which keeps breaking into non-coöperative economies. Employers and employees being simply the same people in different rôles, a consumers' economy would have neither place nor reason for the separation of labor from leisure. True, we are consumers by nature and producers by necessity; perhaps production is but a necessary evil that we would not suffer in a world which was made for us; but it does not follow that the natural conflict between our disposition and our necessities need extend beyond our individual hearts. The interval stretching from desire, through labor, to the satisfaction of desire need not be so long and so difficult as the prevailing producers' economy has made and keeps it, even in so-called communist societies.

That leisure which gives managements and stockholders access at will to the sports, the arts, the sciences, can without conflict be extended to all employees. In a consumers' economy employing the implements and resources of modern technology, no member of the consumers' society need be under the divine curse to earn his bread by the sweat of his face for more than ten or twenty years of his life. All may enjoy the blessings of leisure from birth to their twentieth year, and from their fortieth year till they die.

Inasmuch as every one would be a personal owner of the tools and materials of collective production, he would, as owner, exercise the rights of property as they are currently understood but without the disposition toward the creation of artificial scarcity which poisons this exercise at the source. He would be an employer, but at the same time, he would be a worker, working, however, not for another first but for himself first. In feeling as well as in fact, he would be his own employer and his own employee. The invidious distinctions between those who live without working and those who work without living would disappear. They would be replaced by emulative distinctions of skilled effort toward the enhancement of life. The daily duration of this effort, moreover, and the number of years would, if the theoretical and technological control of nature continues to advance as it has, become automatically smaller. The dream of a four-hour day would realize itself at least as certainly as Ira Steward's dream of the eight-hour day.

The steps by which this condition might be reached can be sketched broadly, even if the details can be determined only after some of the steps have been taken.

They would start at three points, and converge into the consumer economy. The first is the existing coöperative organization as a going concern. The inner subordination of all other interests—farmer, producer, credit—to the consumer interest, and the rapid and planned multiplication and confederation of consumer societies can develop with increasing precision and security.

The second is organized labor. Although the use of consumer-organization as the "commissary department" of the trades-union struggle with the employer must necessarily be transitional, it can add significant speed to the transition from the producer to the consumer economy. Trades-unionists are in a position greatly to strengthen their bargaining power, to bring the immediate trades-union objectives more readily within their reach, to increase real wages and considerably to enlarge the lives of their members by devoting themselves seriously to consumer organization. Lever's campaign of collective bargaining pressed simultaneously at the two poles of the national economy—production and consumption—would, if consistently and wisely conducted, bring about an enormous expansion of the lives and liberties of the working multitudes. For the good life is at once a function of its material conditions, its comforts, easements and luxuries; and of the leisure they make possible, the energies they set free to pursue other ends than a mere livelihood. Such dual collective bargaining would on the one hand rapidly raise the standards and conditions of employment which concern the consumer as worker; improving wages and hours and greatly widening the area of trades-union organization; on the other hand it would invincibly enrich the standards of living, which concerns the worker as consumer.

The third point is the financial surplus of the multitudes. The unexpended pennies of farmers, wage-earners, white-collar workers, like the little drops of water and the little grains of sand which make the mighty ocean and the continental land, are the substantial pecuniary wealth of the nation. They constitute, as has been already noted, an accumulating surplus, pressing for investment; held by private savings banks and insurance companies and used primarily for the pecuniary advantage of the bankers, insurance men and their ilk. These pennies are a surplus of unspent wages, not unspent profits or interest or rent; their spending by the professional financier is done at the depositor's risk, not the financier's. Nor does it bring the depositor any return in the enrichment and expansion of life. If the spending were coöperative, such a return would be automatic. The application of the consumer principle and the coöperative method to the employment of this financial surplus by extending coöperative distribution and production would be a powerful engine in the modification of the competitive-producer into a coöperative-consumer economy.

Through the multiplication of coöperative banks and credit unions, and the widening of their range and powers under legal safeguards, the savings of the working multitudes could be employed to dissipate the invidious distinctions, the dependence and servility which these savings now serve to maintain. More and more employees would become their own bankers and their own employers. More and more members of the younger generation would from childhood on be enabled to grow up in purely coöperative setting and acquire the habits and outlook of the coöperative way of life.

§ 5. THE NEW CONSUMER CONSCIOUSNESS: SOME TOOLS AND TRAITS

ONE IMPORTANT consequence of this would be a certain identification of the now invidiously different fields of experience for the nation's young. The present artificial diversity lays down the psychological basis of that misunderstanding, that deficient sympathy, that certain blindness in human beings which, far more than conflict of interest, underlie class wars. For in a specifically negative sense it is true that all men are born equal. It is true that babies, regardless of race or faith or sex or the wealth and station of their parents, would all die unless tended. Rich and poor, black and white, Aryan and human, are equally helpless, equally dependent. The quality, the skill and the intent of the tendance they receive, its materials and implements, have much to do with setting their characters, enchanneling their sensibilities, directing their lines of growth. All that is said to be fixed by the end of the second year of life. An infant which has for two years been reacting to the conditions of a Negro share-cropper's hovel in the South or an unskilled laborer's cold-water tenement in the North will have been started with a very different basic mentality from one that has been reacting to the luxurious equipment and expert handling of a Vanderbilt or Morgan household. Between the two there will be qualitative differences which follow from the qualitative differences of the stimuli that their childhood experience has absorbed and built into their mentalities; and the farther they grow from the starting-point the wider apart they are likely to grow, until they become the psychologically different species on which Aristotle bases his notion that slaves are a biological variety of the human race—tools with life in them.

Now the establishment and maintenance of a common, "standard," infant environment would have the effect of liberating and guaranteeing in later life the expression of natural as contrasted with nurtural differences. In a free society this single level would be continuous. Those who believe that freedom can be attained only by means of revolutionary violence want to establish the unity and continuity of the common environment, by leveling downward. They want to impoverish the rich, lower the mighty from their seats, degrade the noble and enslave the free. This is precisely what is ruled out by the program and method of consumer coöperation, seeking an economy of abundance. The coöperative movement grows from strength to strength, not by making the rich poorer, but by making the poor richer; not by lowering the mighty but by exalting the low; not by enslaving the free, but by freeing the enslaved. It levels up. It embodies a plan and a method by which everybody may fulfil as completely as possible his spontaneous desire to be as good as his betters without becoming the same as his betters.

Consider the implications of this attitude with regard to social judgment upon labor. It is clear that the producer prejudice provides the psychological underpinning for the caste structure of producer-dominated society. The general consensus of the academic economists defines work as painful effort. And it is the ineluctable fact that the basic labors of man are the disagreeable and unpleasant ones. The tasks of the hewers of wood and drawers of water, of the miners, the farmers, the fishermen, the sewer diggers, the cleaners and sweepers, engage the largest numbers of people and receive the smallest returns. At the same time they call for the most allegedly painful and unpleasant labors; the most slavish, the most unworthy; they go with practically an animal standard of living and culturally a sub-human mentality. The tasks of the bankers and brokers, the actors and singers, the managers, and lawyers, the priests and poets, the engineers and teachers, are regarded as the most pleasant, the most "liberal," the most worthy; they employ the smallest number of workers and receive the greatest returns.

Now, as a rule there is a line of continuous progression from the conditions of infantile nurture to the field of adult occupation. It is rare that a boy born with a silver spoon in his mouth becomes a street-cleaner or a miner, and it is rare that a boy born in a cold-water tenement becomes a professor or a banker. Coöperative economy would break up this continuum in so far as it can be broken up. It would try to expose all the children of the coöperative community to a similar range of experience. It would study anew the distinction between pleasant and unpleasant labor, and were this found to be an inevitable and valid one, coöperation would make sure that every growing child should have full opportunity to experience both.

Not improbably, the conclusion would come early that the distinctions between pleasant and unpleasant labor, between servile and liberal activities, are invidious; that they are due to convention or habit far more than to the material and conditions of the labor or its nature as an activity of the personality. We must not forget how war glorifies the most disgusting conditions and materials, how it ennobles the most servile activity, so that enterprises hateful and rejected of the leisure class in peace-times become prizes they fight for in war-times. Nor must we fail to recall how hardship makes the glorious vacation of the rich man, how he then goes for days unshaved and unbathed, sleeps on the hard ground, amid vermin, and performs the most servile and arduous labor; and how sedulously he refrains from all of these things if they are the servile acts performed for a wage.

Vacation exalts and beautifies what *vocation* besmirches and casts down. The difference is not in the act, nor its materials nor its conditions; the difference is in its institutional relationships: these establish it as labor or art, pain or delight, servile or liberal. Fundamentally no action a human being can perform is intrinsically unpleasant; even the most delightful call for a certain component of pain and hardship and insecurity, and this component looms large in all holiday effort, all sports, all the arts and sciences to which the terms *free* or *liberal* conventionally apply. Our nature craves it no less than it craves ease and pleasure. But in the work of the world, our dominant culture has measured it through invidious perspectives of the producer-dominated economy.

In the equal liberty of the consumer economy these perspectives would be dissolved, leaving only the uninvidious differences of quality. The beginning would come with the beginning of supervised growth, that is, of education. Painful and unpleasant tasks would be part of the curriculum of the coöperative nursery and continue in the living experience of childhood and youth at school, set in the ennobling perspectives of the consumer philosophy of life and directed to the enrichment and strengthening of the growing personality. The discipline and doctrine of coöperative freedom could be enchanneled, transmitted and advanced through adapting the now only remedial Civilian Conservation Corp to the more generous coöperative purposes and extending their labors to mining, to farming, to sanitary engineering and the other key industries of the community life. No child need grow up without participating in these activities as education. No adult need remain in them unless he wants to as vocation. All can perform them with the same feeling and vision that accrue to vacation adventures and war tasks. Each can be treated as a focus of culture and personal growth, and given the importance in the current of life that now comes to it only when it is a special aspect of warfare, exploration or vacation.

The total consequence would be that the hard work of the world would be washed clean of the meanness and servility which now attaches to it. It would be done by the young during the school years as a part of their education. It would be done by those living at the age that craves and seeks hardships, those most able to assume them and to enjoy enduring them. This would necessitate an extension of the required school period for all young people until the twentieth, perhaps the twenty-fifth, year. If, on the one hand, it would generalize the social prolongation of infancy, it would, on the other, reduce the gap which now obtains in the schools and colleges between true physiological maturity and social responsibility. Infancy is prolonged wherever adulthood is artificially postponed by enabling persons not infants to live in the state of dependence, security and irresponsibility of infants. This is the case especially with the children of the rich in the colleges.[3] It is the condition that used to be expressed by the word "collegiate," and is a consequence of the irrelevancy of academic curricula to the living urges and passional drives of youth. It is because of this irrelevancy that the "extra-curricular activities" loom so large and that sports such as football acquire and retain all the momentousness of an adult occupation. Football saves those who participate in it from the rôle of adults required to conduct themselves like children. It gives them the chance they spontaneously crave for self-support and self-management, intellectual effectiveness and moral responsibility.

A system of society wherein education puts all the basic arduous occupations of life on the level of football at the football age, enables the young to acquire the configuration of habits which is social adulthood at the age it is most desired and most readily learned. By the time the young have "graduated," they will all have had the sort of experience that today only war gives, and their personal diversities will be at once more inward and significant and more on a par. The prolongation of schooling has been steady if not consistent during industrial times. Partly it is a known consequence of the drive to democracy; partly it is an unconscious result of the same dislocation of men by machines which, during a hundred years, has each year raised the norm of the permanently disemployed. Schooling for a time withdraws men and women from competition in the labor market; and it lengthens and spreads as the number of competitors multiplies. In America alone each year this number is increased by nearly a million although accident, death and age decrease the multitude of competitors by a much smaller number. The competitive-producer economy is of itself pushing them more and more into its educational system, and prolonging the school-years, but without making education relevant.

Here again the coöperative consumer economy would only

[3] *Cf.* H. M. Kallen, *College Prolongs Infancy* (John Day Company).

redirect and rationalize what is already going on. As a result, the coöperative enchannelment of the energies and ambitions of the young in the years of learning would release them for whatever life-work they desired in the years of maturity. None would need to be gainfully employed beyond the age of forty and none would need to be condemned to infantile futility after the age of fourteen. We should come at last into the abundance which today science and machinery can provide us with. The combination of institutional survivals and producer-dominance which holds it back would have been dissolved and washed away. In their place would work a consumer-governed economy where abundance would be as conventional, as automatic, as scarcity is now. Like the capitalist organization it displaces, it would be the dominant pattern in a context of survivals and anticipations. Being an organization of liberty, it would serve as the economic ground-plan in all societies and cultures. But like the common anatomy of the human frame, it would in each come to a different specific embodiment according to locale, region, climate, and cultural tradition and all the other items that are assimilated into the constitution of a personal or group individuality. It would vary as people vary from one another. Its pattern would be such as to harmonize the differences without coercion, to impart order to liberty. Therein it would really embody the economics of freedom.

EPILOGUE

TWO THOUSAND AND FORTY-FOUR A.D.: PRESIDENT ROBERT ADAM OWEN SMITH LOOKS BACKWARD

FORECASTS should be left to weathermen, statisticians and fortune-tellers. They hardly belong in a philosophical analysis and interpretation of a great movement. But when this movement's structure is so clear, its functions so unmistakable and its direction so definite as those of the coöperative movement, its shape in the unknown is at least indicated, and the imagination can, without too great strain, design its future form upon the empty screen of time. Imaginative definition of the undefined future used to be an obligation of the philosophers, who ever since Plato have been tracing the trajectory of civilization upon the void. So then. . . .

The year is 2044 of the Christian Era. The date is August 15th, the day of the foundation of the Rochdale Society of Equitable Pioneers. During half a century now this day has been a world-wide holiday, celebrated by all the races and faiths of mankind. But this year the day is momentous as never before. It is the two hundredth anniversary of the beginning of the Consumers' Coöperative Era. The official celebration of the festival takes place in Rochdale, and radio and television add it instantly to the local ceremonies of all the continents and islands of the earth. Over the International House at Rochdale flies the rainbow flag of the Coöperative Union of the World. The two houses of government, the House of the Consumers and the House of the Producers, are assembled in joint session. The President is in their presence to address the commemoration speech to the peoples of the world. Precisely at noon the carillon played at Rochdale resounds around the earth. President Robert Adam Owen Smith enters the great chamber with the International Executive Commission of forty comrades. The members of the two Houses rise as the President mounts the rostrum. The coöperative hymn is sung, the audience resume their places, and the President begins.

He is a young man, American born, less than fifty years old; his voice reveals the rhythm, the somewhat nasal timbre and precise articulation of American speech. He speaks slowly but with obvious feeling. The projecting machinery which makes him visible and audible to his fellow-coöperators everywhere in the world does not obscure him from his immediate audience. The machinery is now so compactly built and so cunningly devised that, like the lighting mechanism of the great hall, it is out of sight. The figure of their President, the form and color and movements of the living man of flesh and blood that stands and talks, is present to all the congregations of the earth. His voice is as clear in Australia and in Argentina as it is in Rochdale or New York.

"My fellow Coöperators," he says. "My fellow Coöperators, Two hundred years ago a tiny company of oppressed and hungry men came together in a new association, conceived in liberty and organized to the end that the concerted action of all might bring the life more abundant to each. Now, two hundred years after, we have come from the far places of the earth to the birthplace of this association to do homage to its founders and in its birth to commemorate the birth of abiding freedom and plenty for all humankind. The eyes and ears of the whole world are turned with joy and reverence upon this place today, not for what we say here, for our speech can enrich by no word the story which the place itself tells; nor for what ceremony we may here enact, for no solemn ceremony can make more momentous the import of what here came to pass without solemnity and without ceremony. Our world makes this day its holiday, not so much to do honor to those whose labors forever glorify it, as, by doing them honor, to relive in our own minds the ancient tale that no repetition can make too familiar; to avow the saving faith that no reaffirmation can make too firm. Knowing the bitterness and the horrors of our fathers' lives, we can the more resolutely determine that such things shall not mar the lives of our children; knowing the heroic wisdom with which our ancestors faced and overcame the dearths and dangers of their lot, we are enabled with ever firmer wills to labor in the preservation of the security and liberty and abundance of ours. We can the more highly resolve that what they established, we shall preserve; what they planted, we shall increase; that their bitter struggles and heavy labors shall be vindicated in our generous rivalries and happy leisure.

"On August 15th, one hundred years ago, nobody dreamed that this day would become the common holiday of all the peoples of the earth. Our fathers celebrated the hundredth anniversary of the founding of the Coöperative Movement piece-meal, without communion and without gaiety. The peoples of the earth were then embattled in the Second World War. In the spring of 1940, the ruthless cliques whose arms ruled the peoples of Germany and of Japan launched, from the east and the west a surprise attack upon the Russian Union of Soviet Socialist Republics. The attack had been preparing in the west from the days that the monstrous Nazi Party had raped and ruined the German Republic; in the east it was but the final step in a series of incidents manœuvered by the industrial-military oligarchy who were the masters of Japan.

"The entire world was at that time in the grip of a strange psychosis: Everywhere minorities were endeavoring to impose their special and limited interest, their special and limited doctrine and discipline as the sole rule of work and faith, overruling and excluding all alternatives. An intellectual and physical inquisition, with heresy-hunts, heresy trials and even *auto-da-fés,* spread like a slow poison also among the older democratic communities. The very sciences were driven under the yoke of conformity and almost stifled to death. About 1933, the race of armament had been renewed, at first secretly, then more and more openly, and the passion-blind nationalism which our own times find so difficult to understand moved into one imperialist military adventure after another—the Japanese in China, the Nazis in Austria, the Fascists in Ethiopia. The economic consequences of these piratical adventures threatened the security of the governments which entered upon them, and to save themselves they launched their concerted attack upon the Soviet Union. They endeavored to invest this sordid piracy with the glamour of a crusade. They claimed they were saving mankind from Communism, and called upon the world to join them. But by 1940 that cry of 'wolf' had been heard too often. Enlightened public opinion declared that if the social alternatives were only these two—Communism and Fascism—it was on the side of Communism. The choice which, in 1935 the people of England had made, in spite of the manipulation of their rulers, between Fascist aggression and Ethiopian primitivism, was repeated on a world-wide scale when the alternatives were piratical Fascist imperialism and Russian Communism. The former had the favor of only one section of the communities of the world. This was a parvenu demi-mondaine class who came to be known as 'hearsters' or 'hearstlings,' from whose activities the language has drawn the unsavory verb *to hearst,* which is now used with the same meaning in every language of the world.

"The hearsters served only to confirm the public opinion in its sympathy with Russia. Russia's place in the concert of nations had become firmer and more important as her inner economy improved. The tyranny of her dictatorship had relaxed, and the practice of democracy which was part of the way of life of her hundreds of millions of coöperators also under the height of the dictatorial tyranny, had been slowly, but perceptibly suffusing the ways of even government officials and communist fanatics. The world knew that the attack on Russia was not in reality an attack on Communism but an attack on freedom. The democratic powers knew that if Russia were conquered, they would be next to suffer assault. Even so, the Tories of England and financiers of France, preferring ruin to not ruling, were willing that Russia should be conquered; and in the United States they had their allies among the predacious journalists, financiers and industrialists while the demogogues shrieked about neutrality and keeping out of entangling alliances. In all three countries unlawful efforts were made to gag the free citizens and to silence their demand that the League of Nations should act promptly and aggressively. In the United States the leader of the hearsters instigated attacks by armed hooligan bands upon men and women doing their clear duty as citizens, and endeavored by force and fraud seditiously to suspend the American Bill of Rights.

"But the free peoples of the world were at last aroused. And not only the peoples but also the governments of Denmark and Norway and Sweden and Finland, of Switzerland and Czechoslovakia and Mexico and Spain, of Canada and South Africa and Australia as well as many of the South American countries, stood forthright for international action. Their insistence and the powerful American sympathy it aroused, forced the governments of Great Britain and France into line. During its session of 1941, the Council of the League of Nations devised a plan of continuous conciliation which came to nothing. This was followed by the notorious dawdling over sanctions which almost split the League, but late in 1942, all economic sanctions were applied at once and this was shortly followed by general war. Within six months, neutrality, entangling alliances, hearsters and all not withstanding, the United States was in. The *Führer* of the hearsters was arrested and tried for sedition; his property was confiscated and he was deported to Japan. To the Japanese, however, he was an undesirable alien, and they would have none of him. He finally found refuge among the lepers in one of the remoter islands of the Philippines and there died in the cleanness in which he had lived.

"The War, meanwhile, brought the usual economic consequences of war. The course which industry, transport and finance had run during the First World War was intensified a hundredfold. Attempts 'to take the profits out of war' failed miserably; but the war-like coercion of men and women into industrial and military peonage on the plea of patriotic duty and national necessity was more successful than ever. In all fields a gap yawned ever deeper and wider between wages and prices. Parliamentary investigations exposed extensive sabotage of the war organization for the sake of profits. Scandal befouled the governments of the great states and elections brought the liberal and labor elements to power.

"And what, now, of the coöperative organizations of England and France and the United States and the lesser countries? So long as it was believed that war could be averted, they brought the total weight of their influence to this purpose; they strengthened in every way that was open to them their neutrality of commerce and finance; they skipped the meeting of the International Coöperative Alliance which should have been held in 1942, and the celebration of the hundredth anniversary of the organization of the Rochdale Society of Equitable Pioneers they permitted to remain local and quiet. In all lands, they labored incessantly to offset rising prices by extending their consumer enterprises, and drawing as much as possible of the national commissary into consumer possession and control. They contributed to the exposure of the big-business speculation in the necessities of life, and actually kept down the cost of living. Managers and technicians, their sense of decency outraged and their honorable patriotism aroused, came in great numbers to take service with the coöperatives and do their part in protecting the multitudes from the rapacity of business in wartime. On general war issues the attitude of the coöperatives remained correct. By vote of special congresses of the memberships, the services of the coöperative organizations were put at the disposal of the war administration, and in England, the Scandinavian countries and Czechoslovakia the Wholesale Societies were formally entrusted with the task of feeding, clothing, housing and medicating the armed forces as well as the civil populations.

"The economic necessities of the democratic powers could be served only if there were an international agency continuously at work on a planned distribution of raw materials, transport and certain finished goods. The same condition had obtained during the First World War and had been met with only the greatest difficulty by bargaining and diplomacy. This time it was met by free and eager coöperation. Early in 1946, an international conference of the directorates of various national wholesale societies, banks and credit unions was called. This conference swiftly worked out and implemented as a war measure [1] a system of international exchange with a

[1] *Cf.* H. M. Kallen, *The League of Nations Today and Tomorrow.*

simple universal currency based on a standard gold coin with the same content everywhere. The International Coöperative Bank was assigned the task of serving as the International Clearing House; the International Wholesale Society was charged with the duty of serving as an international board of allocation and distribution. All barriers of monoply, all coercions made possible by the control of necessities were eliminated. In England, the directors of the Scottish and English Wholesales served as the Ministry of Economics, in a government of the Coöperative and Labor Parties. Soon after this government took power a new Defense of the Realm Act was voted which made it sedition to restrict in any way the rights of free speech, free press or free assemblage. It extended the techniques of collective bargaining and industrial self-government prevailing among coöperators to the private industries of the nation; so levied taxes as actually to take all the profits out of war and arranged for the conversion of every monopoly into a consumer-owned property. The Tories took advantage of the first clause of the act to resist the others with all their skill, but they failed miserably before the bar of public opinion, and the reorganization of the national economy took place with extraordinarily little friction. During the same session Parliament voted a measure directing the ministry to secure an agreement among the democratic allies that the liberation and rehabilitation of the coöperatives must precede any discussion of terms of peace.

"This was easy. In 1948, the International Coöperative Alliance called the historic Congress to which it especially invited the coöperators of the enemy countries. I need not rehearse to you the achievements of this Congress. Every child knows by heart its great *Coöperative Manifesto* which is the charter of our liberties and the ground-plan of their organization. Every child is taught at school the call to the peoples of Japan and Germany and Italy and their confederates to rise against their tyrants and to ally themselves with the free peoples of the world. What followed is a part of our glorious legend. The peoples rose. Even in India, the aged Gandhi and his followers abandoned their older plans of fighting the British rule for the program of coöperative organization. Very swiftly now, in the autocracies of the world, governments changed hands and form. A peace was negotiated, whose terms simply enacted the total program of the International Coöperative Alliance.

"My own country, as you know, had been, first and last, politically-minded. Our fathers felt and thought in terms of voting and legislation rather than of men and institutions, and as a result the oldest of the western democracies consisted of a visible government of elected officials who were no more than a servile front for an invisible government of bankers and industrialists. Those employed all the methods of force and fraud to impose 'loyalty to our form of government.'

"Now the great depression of 1929–1935 had awakened Americans to the import of the coöperative principle. They came to understand themselves as consumers, and to realize the coöperative union of the consumers as the next step toward the preservation of a living democracy in the United States. They recognized it as the sure way of embodying the ideals of Jefferson and Lincoln in the times of Edison and Einstein. The subsequent growth of coöperation in the United States became an amazing fact of American history. From the agricultural Middle West it spread in swift sure steps thoughout the land. Great merchants and manufacturers joined technicians and managers in putting their abilities at the movement's disposal. At some points it started as a wholesale which organized its local societies as its surpluses grew. At others it started in locals which confederated into wholesales. State legislatures vied with each other in enacting standard coöperative laws and prescribing coöperation as a subject of instruction in the public schools. Big Business, warned against the movement by its pundits and forecasters, used all its cunning and all its power to wreck it, resorting to arms as well as to financial oppression. Attempts were made to abort coöperative growth through politics. These were followed by efforts to buy the coöperatives out; these by attempts to cut them off from access to raw materials, to transportation, to tools. These endeavors having failed, armed gangs were employed to destroy coöperative establishments and murder coöperators. But the coöperators of America had been forewarned. They stood fast. They defended themselves. Their members grew in proportion to the assaults they suffered. In a short time they came into control of most of the nation's business, beginning with foodstuffs, clothing and fuel, and ending with power and minerals.

"Most ironical was the course of events among organized laborers. The federal union, then known as the American Federation of Labor, at first stood aside, insisting that consumer organization was not labor's business. As the coöperatives grew, however, they developed their own autonomous labor unions. These organized industrially, and made the typical coöperative agreements with their employers who were only their mates and themselves in another rôle. These agreements gave the coöperative employee so superior a status over the non-coöperative employee, that there were frequently premiums offered for coöperative jobs. The standards set by the coöperative movement forced up standards outside it. Independent unions detached themselves from the American Federation of Labor to ally themselves with the Amalgamated Society of Coöperative Workers. Company unions followed. It was not long before the Federation declined to a few leaders without a following. As everywhere in the coöperative world, a form of employee organization took shape which expressed, developed and perfected employee-functions in the coöperative structure. The Amalgamated Society of Coöperative Employees became a federal organization of industries and professions, whose societies of workers and managers elected the 'lower house' of the coöperative community, while the societies of consumers elected the 'upper house.' About the same time the nation's transportation systems were taken over by the government which acquired them with the funds from 'baby bonds' sold directly to the multitudes of the citizens, and plans were discussed which resulted in the present distributive ownership and collective management not only of railroads and shipping lines, but of all public utilities.

"By 1950, the consumer economy was under way in every region of the globe. England and Sweden provided the models and set the pace, and the rest of the world swiftly followed.

"My dear friends, six years hence we shall count one hundred years of unremitting labor first to establish and now to maintain the state of ever-growing freedom and plenty which it is our human nature to desire. One hundred years! Three, at most four, generations! Some among you were alive, infants in arms, children at the knee, when the great plan was implemented and the program launched. We have come to the pleasant place of this our age within the life-time of some single comrade. It is a miracle. But it is no greater miracle than the hundred years between 1810 and 1910! Upon the insights, the discoveries, the inventions of those great years our grandfathers and our fathers have built. They were not better than their ancestors, nor more richly-endowed; nor are we better men than they. But the bitterness of two great wars following each other swiftly had chastened our fathers' vision and guided their hopes. They were enabled at last to direct their ways as men toward harmony with the laws of things; and we can freely and happily follow in these new-old ways upon which the men of Rochdale daringly ventured in 1844, and all mankind now finds so safe and simple.

"And the ways are safe, they are simple. The animal passions in us have not been allayed nor has the evil of our natures been even mollified. We are as our fathers were, and their fathers before them, down to Adam and the primal ape. But we know a way now to gratify these passions without wrong, to work over this evil into good. We are freed from the needless and futile conflict between institutions and temperaments, between personal passions and institutional events. We know now how to judge the illusion which led the communists of Russia to endeavor to separate the administration of things from the government of men. Their prophet, Karl Marx, had mistaken the source of the ancestral tragedy. The tangency of church ways and state rule to scientific method and industrial organization made their tragedy. It caused conflict where there should have been peace and treacherous warfare where there should have been generous rivalry for excellence. We have abolished this tangency. We have rendered folk-ways confluent with machine-ways, and implanted the freedom of men upon the methods of science. We have organized liberty. With us, the government of men *is* the administration of things, the administration of things *is* the government of men. No more than our fathers' fathers do we deny the self its irreducible autonomy. No less than they do we affirm self-interest as the spring of action and the cause of progress.

"But with them, the idea that this self-interest must be enlightened was only a way of talking: They lived blindly, they labored blindly, they fought blindly. Driven by the dark passions in their hearts, they mistook greed for gratification, accumulation for wealth, cruelty for power and wish for wisdom. We know that men themselves are wealth and that gratification and power and wisdom are but the ways of the life more abundant whereof each man's biography must consist. We have made enlightened self-interest a way of living. We have illuminated passion with a knowledge of its nature and conditions and enchannelled it in the coöperative habits of the consumer-economy. In spirit our dark fathers were producers only, and as such servile in mind, competitive in habit, fearful, shutting each other out and being shut out. We who are consumers not in fact only, but in our very souls, live in a free society; our basic association is open and all the world's sorts and conditions of men live and move and have their being in it, comrades in their diverse individualities, peers in their inequalities.

"Such is our life. What was our grandparents'? One hundred years ago my own grandfather Robert Smith was ten years old. Born, the second of a family of three children, at the end of the Great Depression, in a city of the American Middle West, he grew up in a slum filled with tenements whose squalor the modern mind cannot even imagine. His father was a mechanic in a great tool factory; his wages were considered good for those days, but his employment was irregular, and we should regard his yearly earnings below any level of decency. There were hundreds of little boys in those tenements. They were educated together in a public school which carried them through a curriculum, grade to grade, as a carrier in a factory carries a car. Their education was assembled as a car is assembled, with the difference that the car held together. The teachers were dull and stodgy women whose sole equipment for their task to prepare the growing young for life was a prescribed ignorance of everything in life that mattered. They were a tragic company, sad and servile, with starved hearts and coerced minds, intimidated by male supervisors and the oaths exacted by the police state of those days. They were required to indoctrinate their charges in what was known as 100 per cent Americanism, or the heavenly and earthly superiority of things-as-they-were to all other actual and possible alternatives. Children were permitted to learn nothing for themselves according to their interests and needs; they were taught only what the masters of the system decided they ought to know. Nothing that they learned at school prepared them, either to earn their livings or to build their lives.

"My grandfather was only fifteen when he had to take a work certificate and find a job. From this he drifted to another, from that to still another, until his twentieth year. His whole existence was an aimless drift upon the tides of employment and unemployment, concentrated in securing a wage to keep the body alive, otherwise without direction and without goal. His physically most generous and adventuring years were socially his most futile and unhappy ones. Although the times possessed a correct knowledge and ripe wisdom concerning sex, the schools dealt with the young as if they were sexless intelligences. What my grandfather learned about women he learned casually and by accident, through obscene whispers and scrawls and lascivious communications of the older boys. Unequipped to see or care, he was condemned to move among the living arts and the sciences as if they did not exist. His knowledge was the misinformation and prejudice fabricated by the hearsters of the yellow press. His entertainment, when he could afford it, consisted in motion pictures, hearsted comic strips and athletic spectacles such as baseball games. In the course of time his father, my great-grandfather, succeeded in getting him a job in his own shop, and after much haggling, in securing his admission to his own union as apprentice junior. The union's officers and leaders as he describes them conform to the standard pictures of union officials of these times. They had the typical competitive producer mentality, given to petty jealousies, political manœuverings and small exploitations. They were harsh to Negroes and foreigners and fearful of enlarging memberships. They could not endure differences of opinion tolerantly. Their secret hope was to promote themselves from the employee to the employer status. They paid no attention to the relationship of the worker to the industry and of the industry to the national economy. They managed the business of the union by a sort of blind recollection and rule of thumb unilluminated by reflection and unclarified by analysis. Engaged on the task of collective bargaining, they yielded to their already far more powerful opponents all the advantage of knowledge of the industry, its competitive market and the other conditions that might affect the wages, hours and standards of the worker.

"But among the rank and file of the union there were many men of experience and wisdom, who had read widely and thought deeply. They were usually silent men, ironic when they did speak, who took little part in the affairs of the Union except in times of crisis, when wage cuts were threatened or discharges were in the air. One of these men was my maternal great-grandfather Adam Owen. He believed that he was somehow related to Robert Owen through his son, Robert Dale Owen and the life and writings of his magnificent ancestor were proud themes in his conversation. He took my grandfather into his house, introduced him to the literature and philosophy of coöperation, and to another conception of trades-unionism than prevailed among trades-union officials. From him my grandfather Robert Smith came to the faith that there was really a way by which men might save themselves from the spectre of insecurity which everlastingly beset them with fears of unemployment, disease, and hunger, and which made them the perennial victims of politicians with their flag-wavings, denunciations of agitators, foreigners and Bolsheviks to the greater glory of financial imperialism and industrial monopoly.

"My grandfather married my grandmother Roberta Owen when he was twenty-two and she twenty years old. She was employed behind a counter in one of the five-and-ten-cent chain stores that prevailed in the land in those days, and she did not resign her job when she married. They set up housekeeping in a three-room tenement on a mean street, furnishing it on the notorious 'instalment plan,' and having little left for food or other necessities after they had paid the exorbitant rent and the instalments. My grandmother wanted children but was afraid to have them. She had learned both from her father's ideas and her mother's burdens. She said she had no right to bring into the world children who would be born to misery, grow up in destitution, live in anxiety and die in poverty. But knowledge of effective contraception was in those days kept from the poor. My grandmother tells that she conceived five times and gave birth twice. Her first child, who was my father, was an unwanted child. But when it came she struggled to secure for it the advantages neither she nor her husband had enjoyed. It was she who moved my father to organize among his fellow-unionists that consumer society which became the parent of the beautiful and mighty cooperative institutions which are now Akron, Ohio. It was she who drew the other mothers of the neighborhood into a sewing circle which became a purchasing club and a study group and began the new era in the history of the woman's movement in America. You know that golden legend of our immediate past, and I need not rehearse it to you. But I ask you to rise in honor of the women of that age. To their courage, their perseverance, their unfailing hope and untiring labor, the new life of freedom and abundance which we enjoy owes its greatest debt.

"My father and my mother grew up when this life was in the making. They were children of the transition, when the forces of the Second World War were being liquidated, the consumer economy and the new education were being installed, and the conflicts and readjustments these brought with them tapped the energies of men to their depths and every soul lived and labored in heroic mood.

"Nor need we much look upon ourselves who are at maturity in these happy times. Who is there among us who does not feel in his own depths something of the spirit and posture of that transition? Who does not remember the gay and gallant argument which waged in all the tribunes and forums of those years, when the issue was joined between those who held that labor is the one and only source of value, and those who affirmed that the beginning of value is enjoyment, and its end delight, and that all things, labor included, are valuable only as they contribute to the conscious consummation of the personal life. The dispute finally found a consensus in this view, which is now a component of the commonsense of this our world.

"But it is fitting and proper that we should recall, on this happy commemoration day, what the roots were from which the argument sprang, and what the fruits which the disputants sought to grow.

"Throughout history, the many had sweated and slaved, with the labor of their hands and heads bringing to birth the shapes and services of life whose accumulation and remembrance compose civilization. They had sweated and slaved, but they had been prevented from consuming and enjoying. They had sowed but others had reaped; they had nurtured and tended, others had eaten. They had been the producers only, others had been the consumers. They had been the means, mere tools with life in them, others had been the ends, free lives with delight in them. And those who felt and understood the injustice of this division were filled with a righteous anger. Why, they demanded, should any one get who does not give? Why should any one eat who does not work? Without labor there can be no food; without work no human good whatsoever can come to be, no desire could be gratified, no wish attained, no life enriched.

"Those gratifications, this attainment, this enrichment is but labor expended and consumed. If they are value, labor is its energy and substance; its intensity and duration are their measure, its cost is their price. Let then the hire be worthy of the laborer. Let each give according to his capacities and get according to his needs. If there are any who will not work, neither shall they eat. The hunger- and poverty-stricken multitudes who are prevented from eating without working, have come to glorify work as a right and to mistake this bondage for freedom. But work is a duty, not a right. Those who would enjoy values must produce them; those who produce them have the first right to enjoy them. Down, then, with the exploiters! Down with the masters! Down with property! Down with all institutions which enable and justify the few to appropriate to themselves the goods made by the hands of the many. Let them work as the multitudes work, let them serve and sweat as the multitudes serve and sweat! Let the workers be the master! So alone can justice be done.

"Justice, in a word, must enfold a certain component of vengeance and punishment. Those who ascribed all value to labor and to labor alone, who proclaimed its dignity and glorified its future in their hearts could think of it only as painful, mean, intrinsically undesired and undesirable. Their plan of justice was but to extend the sentence of hard labor to all men; their proposals for a new order scarcely touched upon the extension of liberty and delight; they concerned mainly the redistribution of the painful and the disagreeable, of labor, as labor was looked upon by all classes of that bygone producer economy.

"The opponents of these warriors of righteousness were our intellectual ancestors. They established the tradition which we carry. Life comes first, they said, not labor; and the substance and form of life are taken up and defined by the processes of consumption. Every man can live without working, none can live without eating, nor can any work who do not eat. If men work, they do so not because they wish, but because they must. Labor is a necessary evil, not an indispensable good. It is ever a means, never an end in itself pursued for its own sake. In itself labor is without value; indeed, it is value's opposite, an activity disliked, diminished and avoided, not desired and enhanced and pursued. Far from being a right, labor is in itself an alienation of right, a burden upon life and an enslavement. Only when labor is joined to ends not itself does it attain value; but it is the value of a means and a method, not of an end and a result. It is not labor which creates value but value which generates labor. Labor signifies as a transition, not a dwelling place, and no man labors that he may continue to labor, but only in the hope that he may be freed from the serfdom of laboring. What, then, is the vaunted 'dignity of labor'? It is the compenetration of painful and servile effort with consummatory ends. By virtue of these it is set free and transformed into liberal art; it is suffused with diversified gratifications and enjoyment, so that delight reshapes pain, and life's work is made over into life's happiness. When this takes place and only then, can labor be described as value. But then it is value precisely because it has ceased to be labor and has become labor's fruit, the self-acquiescing and self-continuing substance of life itself, the means which is its own end, the way which is its own goal, the movement which is its own resting place. It has ceased to be production merely and has become consumption. Indeed, production as a separate and distinct activity has ceased to exist; working has been taken up into living, and living has become a free and creative consumption of its own energies in its own values. An individual biography is seen, from birth to death, like the Lord of the Hebrew Testament, as a consuming flame, not only using its own energies but using them up in its own aspiration and delight. By inborn nature and spontaneous disposition we are all consumers. By external compulsion and acquired habit we are made into producers. All our lives the consumer within us wars against the producer imposed upon us, the urge toward freedom and delight against the coercion into labor and pain. A free society must bring an end to this war. It must return the peace of childhood to our hearts. This is why a free society must be a consumer economy, dedicated to abundance, heightening each man's delight, enabling each to get according to his capacities so that according to them he might be able to give. For when value is so understood, the distinction between needs and capacities breaks down like the distinction between consumption and production. Now we know that capacities are needs, that needs are capacities, and that each individual's being is a unique and undefeasible configuration of them, to be sustained in its own way and developed toward its own perfection.

"Such was the issue; in these terms was it joined. It was not the argument which decided it, but the march of events toward a coöperative consumer economy. The philosophy of the primacy of the consumer and the consumer theory of value fell in naturally with the social action which brought all power to the consumers, and established it to endure in the commonsense of the world.

"To bring to its point our realization of the difference between our condition and that of our grandparents, let us look at our sons and daughters, who have grown up in this commonsense and know no other, and who enter into the full responsibility of citizenship in this year, the two hundredth year of our deliverance, 2044.

"The child born in 2023 has received during its infancy the best care knowledge and skill could provide. The nursery in which it grows into abilities to move about and to serve its own needs provides stimulation without fatigue, difficulty without oppression and danger without disaster. It is designed to be both an opportunity and a challenge. Its nurses serve it and teach it as little as possible; they know that their task is to guide it to serve itself, and free it to learn actively for itself rather than accept instruction passively from another. We endeavor from the nursery on to facilitate the satisfaction of our children's needs by their own efforts. In our schools we do not divide vocation from culture nor leisure from labor. Our schools are built like our homes, as places to live in, and our children learn by living. Teachers are not instructors but guides and friends, who know that all school activity must develop as personal growth and social use and that no activity may be without form and beauty. Our children learn what used to be called the formal subjects such as reading, writing, mathematics, history, the sciences and language as extensions of the practical arts of the daily life, such as cooking and serving, carpentering and plumbing, gardening and shop work, storekeeping and bookkeeping, drawing and painting and modeling. They practise these arts, not formally and abstractly, in order to acquire accomplishments, but functionally and concretely, in order to provide themselves with food and clothing and shelter and other necessities and comforts. But what they so do equips them with no mere vocational skill. It serves them also as a civilizing discipline which sets every practical task in the context of the scientific information and cultural embellishment which attaches to it. We apply the principles of the fine arts to all the physical activities from the swinging of a pickax to the shaping of a latrine, or the construction of a planetarium or the modeling of a planned city. No action passes by unillumined by its relevant scientific and cultural subject matters; no subject matter enters our curricula unembodied or unvitalized in some concrete project answering a living need and expressing a growing ability.

"The organization through which this work is arranged is, moreover, the children's own. Forming their consumer and producer societies in the primary school, they enter from their earliest years into responsibility for their grade and school economies, for the settlement of their own disputes and the expansion of their own activities. Since no theme and no project is forbidden them, the one requirement being that they shall complete the tasks they decide to assume duly and in good order, they divide into parties and argue out their theories and programs in their consumer assemblies. They deal with sex as freely as with cooking, for the implication of the insuperable fact that they are male and female is no longer kept from them, and they enter into puberty not ignorant, not afraid, and not ashamed, but splendidly.

"We recognize puberty for the critical transformation that it is, and we admit our youth at this time to a larger participation in the responsibilities of the common life. With us there is no sudden transition from school to world. The school imperceptibly opens up into the world, and the activities of the school boy and school girl become without a break the activities of the budding citizens. No people in our worldwide commonwealth of nations but initiates its youth at sixteen in the comradely sharing with their elders of both the responsibilities and the profits of the larger life of the community. With their teachers supervising, they organize into corps under their own leaders and assume the more elementary duties of the common life, analyzing, judging, discussing their tasks as they fulfil them, continuing, enriching and elaborating the disciplines and perspectives of the earlier years. Turn and turn about each corps performs the service which an earlier age had relegated to unskilled labor or a servant class. They clean and guard the highways and streets; they cook; they wait on table; they supervise their juniors. As they grow older and stronger they are promoted to the heavier, the more serious and disagreeable tasks: the sanitary labors, the road building, the mining, the fishing, the farming, the engineering, the policing and the like. There is not one among them, normally healthy, more than eighteen and less than twenty-two years old, who has not had his turn at each and every one of these arduous tasks. There is not one to whom it has not been a gay adventure, promising glory and fame. Formerly only prize-fighting, football, certain other exhausting and dangerous labors called sports were open to the young. And of course, occasionally there were wars. But now all these ways are open. What used to be called 'the dirty work of civilization' is their field of honor, whereon they attain their heroisms and win their glory and rewards. All the while they study deeply the tools and materials of their tasks, their theories and their methods. Led by a knowledgeable and experienced older citizen they meet in small groups and discourse upon the work in all its bearing upon the great adventure which is the history of mankind and upon the consumer civilization which is its present crown. Many work out new theories and insights; others invent improvements upon tools or methods or both. These are especially marked for honorable recognition, and their names are written upon the honor-rolls of their community.

"When their round of science and study has been completed, all take a general examination upon the content and interpretation of their experience. Those who pass it are then admitted to the ephebic oath and become full and free citizens of our Commonwealth of Consumers' Coöperatives. Unless they choose some other, they are automatically enrolled in the consumer society of their native place and invested with all its privileges and responsibilities: election to its offices, appointment to its committees, the exercise of any function a situation might require. This is the time, too, when the young man or woman with so rich and diversified an experience for guide, chooses his life-work. Again, unless the chooser wishes another, this choice automatically enrolls him in the appropriate producers' society of his native place: whether it be that of the miners or the farmers, the fishermen or the physicians, the teachers or the fiddlers, the prize-fighters or the bookkeepers, and so on. As a member of his professional or occupational group our citizen concerns himself not only with wages and the hours and conditions of labor, but with the improvement of its tools and techniques, the enrichment of its knowledge and the organization of its tasks. Here also he is eligible to election to local offices, or to the regional and national assemblies which legislate and manage the common interests of our national confederation of separate and distinct societies of producers. But if he serves in any assembly of producers, he may not serve in any assembly of consumers. And conversely. Although consumers and producers are but the same people in different functional relationships to each other, the difference of function sets up a difference of interest. Each must be embodied and served by a separate and distinct organization and the two organizations reconciled in a common action wherein the consumer interest automatically takes precedence. This is why locally, regionally, nationally, and internationally, we have two houses and not one. This also is why the Congresses of the unions of consumers have the decisive vote on the policies and programs which the directorate of both organizations jointly execute. That the method works as smoothly and happily as may be, I need not repeat to you, my friends. We have many disagreements—how, living men being what they are, can they be prevented?—but no strikes, no disorders, and especially no hatred. Our differences are settled as scientific differences are settled, through experimentation, and free discussion developing to a consensus.

"Should our young citizens wish to travel, they do so without passports and untroubled by problems of exchange. Their certificate of membership passes them wherever they wish to go and entitles them to the status of citizens wherever they wish to stay. The currency which was so diverse and confusing one hundred years ago is now of unified coinage and identical value all over the globe. Our international clearing-houses clear purchase-dividends from Australia to Labrador and from the Gold Coast of Africa to the Golden Gate of America. The old annoyances of customs duties, the old trade-barriers and other exclusions which kept our grandfathers unfriendly and apart are gone. Freer and more richly individual than ever our people are more than ever members of one another.

"Perhaps of all things that we take pride in, nothing more justifies it than this: That the world's national cultures, its local signs and colors have, since the establishment of our unified consumer economy, increased and multiplied astoundingly, and that, nevertheless, they interpenetrate and suffuse one another, so that all enrich and emphasize the identity of each in a great, free spiritual orchestration which is the common life of the nations. A member of any nationality or race or cult or sect finds himself a welcome and honored guest in the enclave of any other. Even anti-Semitism—that badge of the beast among our grandfathers—has faded away from our minds and the Jewish people, historic incarnation of group cohesion and group conscience, are as freely and happily as the rest of us a world-wide cultural confraternity in our world-wide brotherhood of peoples where Turks and Armenians, Negroes and Americans, Chinese and Japanese, are joined with Russians and Germans, Englishmen and Indians, Ethiopians and Italians, Scandinavians and Frenchmen, Portuguese and Spaniards, Icelanders and Filipinos.

"A young man of our time can find constant titivation of his intellectual curiosity and his emotions as he moves from the poetry and arts of one cultural group to another, from their scientific dispositions to their philosophic pronouncements, from their inner family organizations, their peculiarities of speech and opportunity to the common pattern of our basic consumer economy. At forty or, if he prefers, at forty-five, he retires from active participation in the processes of the community, and for ten years he remains a member of our reserve. He is free to pursue any and all avocations. He may make researches in the arts or sciences, develop sports or the practice of religion, or do nothing at all. If he is ill unto death and prefers to die no objection is made to his providing himself with the euthanasia of his choice. If he is well and lives on he finally comes to his death in serenity without illusion, mourned by those he leaves behind and unfearing of the end.

"For ours is a world of peace and understanding. We are not troubled by the problems of birth control and overpopulation which vexed our ancestors; we can produce enough to fill the wants of any population and cannot be overpopulated. In one hundred years our peoples have more than doubled in number but the arguments regarding the dangers and compulsions of overpopulation have been forgotten. We recognize that women are persons and that as persons it is their right, and only theirs, to choose how many children they shall bear and at what intervals. We have not found that this freedom has in any way diminished the number and the power of mankind. It is now three-quarters of a century since the last war. Yes, we have had our civil disorders, and we have settled them, sometimes with the police power. But we have not had wars. And perhaps we shall never again wage war. We have removed the most aggravating external causes of war and established the moral equivalent for its inward drive. Our war-like passions are being gratified by peaceful labors and our normal disputes are being settled by our national and international arbitral courts. When more than the courts' decision is needed to give them force, we have the means. But not once in three-quarters of a century have we needed to invoke these means. If there are collective law breakers among us, neither is there a lack of individuals so disposed. We, like our ancestors, have our criminals. Life being what it is, how could we not have them? But if we segregate them from the rest of us we do not do so to punish them but to protect their victims, and always we treat them as persons entitled to a life of their own so long as it does not interfere with the life of others. We help them to amend if they wish, and restore them to the larger community if they do, without loss of face or other penalty.

"Such is the life of man in our own times. I do not ignore its doubts and predicaments, its burdens and insecurities. But I may say without prejudice that it is a freer, a fuller, a braver and a more hopeful life than our grandparents knew, and let us pray that it is a lesser one than our grandchildren will attain.

"I have spoken. Now let the carillon sound again, and let us bow our heads in silence, remembering the twenty-eight weavers of Rochdale, their burden, their vision, their hopes and their labors. And when the carillon has sounded, let us depart to our appointed places to make a gay and gallant feast in their honor."

APPENDIX I

BIBLIOGRAPHY

The following books, periodicals, pamphlets, and reports have been consulted in the preparation of this work.

Books

ATKINSON, C. M., *Jeremy Bentham, His Life and Work* (London, 1905).

BARNES, Harry Elmer, and FLÜGEL, Felix, *Economic History of Europe* (New York, 1929).

BEARD, Charles A., *The Economic Basis of Politics* (New York, 1922).

— *The Rise of American Civilization* (New York, 1927).

BEGTRUP, Holger, *Folk High-School and Other Free Institutions for Adult Education in Connection with the Folk High-School.*

BLANC, Elsie Terry, *The Coöperative Movement in Russia* (New York, 1924).

BLOOMFIELD, Daniel (editor), *Trends in Retail Distribution* (New York, 1931).

BOJE, Andreas, BORUP, Ernst J., RÜTZEBECK, Holder (editors), *Education in Denmark* (Oxford, England, 1932).

BUCK, S. J., *The Granger Movement* (Cambridge, Massachusetts, 1913).

CALLENDER, G. S., *An Economic History of the United States* (New York, 1909).

CAMPBELL, Olive D., *The Danish Folk School* (New York, 1928).

CASSAU, Theodor, *The Coöperative Movement in Germany* (Manchester, England, 1925).

CHAMBERLIN, W. H., *Soviet Russia* (New York, 1929).

CHEN KUO-FU, *The Coöperative Movement in China* (Shanghai, 1933).

CLAPHAM, J. H., *Economic History of Modern Britain* (New York, 1927).

COMMONS, John R. (editor), *Documentary History of American Industrial Society* (Cleveland, 1910).

DIES, Edward J., *Solving the Farm Riddle* (New York, 1926).

DIGBY, Margaret, *Producers and Consumers* (London, 1928).

ENGELS, Frederich, *Socialism Utopian and Scientific* (London, 1892).

FABER, Harald, *Coöperation in Danish Agriculture* (London, 1918).
FIGGIS, John N., *Churches in the Modern State* (New York and London, 1914).
FILLEY, H. Clyde, *Coöperation in Agriculture* (New York, 1929).
FORD, James, *Coöperation in New England* (New York, 1913).
GEBHARD, Dr. Hannes, *Coöperation in Finland,* edited by C. Smith-Gordon (London, 1916).
GIDE, Charles, *La Coöperation* (Paris, 1910), translated as *Consumers' Coöperative Societies* (New York, 1922).
GJÖRES, Axel, *Coöperation in Sweden* (Manchester, England, 1927).
GOLDSMITH, Oliver, *The Vicar of Wakefield* (London, 1766).
HALE, W. J., *The Farm Chemiurgic* (Boston, 1934).
HALEVY, Elie, *The Philosophical Radicals* (New York, 1928).
HALL, F. and WATKINS, W. P., *Coöperation in Great Britain and Ireland* (Manchester, England, 1934).
HAMMOND, J. L. and Barbara, *The Town Labourer* (London and New York, 1917).
— *The Village Labourer* (London and New York, 1919).
— *The Skilled Labourer* (London and New York, 1919).
— *The Rise of Modern Industry* (London and New York, 1926).
HANNA, John, *The Law of Coöperative Marketing Associations* (New York, 1931).
HARRIS, Emerson P., *Coöperation, the Hope of the Consumer* (New York, 1920).
HOBSON, John A., *Evolution of Modern Capitalism* (London, 1910).
HOLYOAKE, George Jacob, *History of the Rochdale Pioneers* (London, 1892).
— *History of Cooperation* (London, 1908).
HOUGH, E. M., *Coöperation in India* (London, 1932).
HUME, David, *Essays, Literary, Moral and Political* (London, 1775).
JONES, E. Stanley, *Christ's Alternative to Communism* (New York, 1935).
JONES, Lloyd, *Life, Times and Labors of Robert Owen* (London, 1912).
JOHNS HOPKINS STUDIES IN HISTORY AND POLITICAL SCIENCE—*History of Coöperation in the United States,* Volume VI (Baltimore, 1888).
KROPOTKIN, Peter, *Mutual Aid* (London, 1902).
LECKY, Wm. E. H., *History of the Rise and Influence of Rationalism in Europe* (London, 1890).
LEVETT, Elizabeth A., *The Consumer in History* (New York, 1929).
LLEWELLYN, Karl, *The Law of Sales* (Chicago, 1930).
LOEB, Harold and Associates, *The Chart of Plenty* (New York, 1935).
LOWENTHAL, Esther, *The Ricardian Socialists* (New York, 1911).
MALLOCK, Wm. H., *Aristocracy and Evolution* (London, 1898).
MARX, Karl, *Capital, The Communist Manifesto and Other Writings,* edited by Max Eastman (New York, 1932).

—— *Das Kapital* (Hamburg, 1873); English translation by E. and C. Paul (London 1928).
MAXWELL, William, *The History of Coöperation in Scotland* (Glasgow, Scotland, 1910).
MERCER, T. W. (editor), *Dr. William King and the Coöperator, 1828–1830* (Manchester, 1922).
MERRIAM, Charles E., *American Political Ideas* (New York, 1920).
MERZ, John T., *History of European Thought in the Nineteenth Century* (Edinburgh, Scotland, 1896).
MILL, John Stuart, *Principles of Political Economy* (London, 1868).
MITCHELL, Wesley C., *Business Cycles* (Berkeley, California, 1913).
MORLEY, Henry, *Clement Marot* (London, 1871).
MYERS, Gustavus, *History of the Great American Fortunes* (Chicago, 1911–17).
NOURSE, Edwin G., *The Legal Status of Agricultural Coöperation* (New York, 1927).
ODHE, Thorsten, *Finland, A Nation of Coöperators* (London, 1931).
OGATA, Kiyoshi, *The Coöperative Movement in Japan* (London, 1923).
—— *Consumer Coöperative Movement in Japan* (Tokyo, 1929).
OPPENHEIMER, Franz, *The State* (Indianapolis, 1914).
OWEN, Robert, *A New View of Society and other writings*, Everyman's Library (London, 1927).
PAUL, Leslie A., *Coöperation in the U.S.S.R.* (London, 1934).
PERLMAN, Selig, *A History of Trade-Unionism in the United States* (New York, 1922).
PINKEVITCH, Albert P., *The New Education in the Soviet Republic*, edited by George S. Counts (New York, 1929).
PLUNKETT, Sir Horace, *The Rural Life Problem of the United States* (New York, 1912).
PODMORE, Frank, *Robert Owen, A Biography* (London, 1928).
POTTER, Beatrice, *The Coöperative Movement in Great Britain* (London, 1891).
RAUSCHENBUSCH, Walter, *Christianizing the Social Order* (New York, 1912).
REDFERN, Percy, *The Story of the C.W.S.* (Manchester, England, 1913).
—— *J. T. W. Mitchell* (Manchester, England, 1923).
Report of the Commission on Country Life (New York, 1911).
ROBERTSON, H. M., *Aspects of the Rise of Economic Individualism* (Cambridge, England, 1933).
RÜHLE, Otto, *Karl Marx: His Life and Work* (London, 1929).
RUSSELL, George W., *The National Being* (New York, 1930).
SCHLESINGER, Arthur M., *New Viewpoints in American History* (New York, 1922).
SMITH, Adam, *An Inquiry Into the Nature and Causes of the Wealth of Nations* (London, 1776).

SMITH-GORDON, C., *Coöperation For Farmers* (London, 1918).
—— (With C. O'Brien), *Coöperation in Denmark* (Manchester, England, 1919).
—— *Coöperation in Many Lands* (Manchester, England, 1919).
SOMBART, Werner, *The Quintessence of Capitalism* (New York, 1915).
SONNICHSEN, Albert, *Consumers' Coöperation* (New York, 1919).
SPENCER, Herbert, *Man Versus the State* (New York, 1884).
SUMNER, Wm. G., *The Forgotten Man and Other Essays* (New Haven, Connecticut, 1918).
TARDE, Gabriel De, *Social Laws* (New York, 1907).
TAWNEY, Richard H., *The Acquisitive Society* (New York, 1920).
TURNER, Frederick J., *The Frontier in American History* (New York, 1920).
VEBLEN, Thorstein, *Theory of the Leisure Class* (New York, 1899).
—— *The Engineers and the Price System* (New York, 1921).
WARBASSE, J. P., *Coöperative Democracy* (New York, 1927).
WARNE, Colston E., *The Consumers Coöperative Movement in Illinois* (Chicago, 1926).
WEBB, Sidney and Beatrice, *The Consumers' Coöperative Movement* (London, 1921).
—— *A Constitution for a Socialist Commonwealth of Great Britain* (London, 1925).
WILLCOX, O. M., *Reshaping Agriculture* (New York, 1934).

PAMPHLETS

COÖPERATIVE LEAGUE OF AMERICA,
COHN, Hyman I., *Coöperation in the City Block* (New York, 1917).
PERKY, Cheves West, *Coöperation in the United States* (New York, 1917).
WARBASSE, J. P., *The Coöperative Consumers' Movement in the United States* (New York, 1920).
COÖPERATIVE UNION, LIMITED,
AGNEW, P. J., *The Coöperative Movement and Trade-Unionism* (Manchester, England, 1926).
PALMER, R. A., *Employment in Coöperative Service*
—— *What Does Coöperative Employment Mean to You?* (Manchester, England, 1933).
FIPPIN, E. O., *First Principles of Coöperation in Buying and Selling in Agriculture* (Richmond, Virginia, 1934).
INSTITUTO NACIONAL DE PREVISION,
Asamblea de Mutualidades Escolares (Madrid, Spain, June, 1934).
La Comision de Mutualidades Escolares (Madrid, Spain, June, 1934).

INTERNATIONAL LABOR OFFICE,
The Coöperative Movement in Soviet Russia (Geneva, Switzerland, 1925).

WORLD PEACE FOUNDATION,
International Statistics of Coöperative Societies (Boston, Massachusetts, 1934).

ARTICLES

DOUGLAS, Dorothy, "Ira Steward on Consumption and Unemployment," *Journal of Political Economy*, Vol. XL, p. 532 (1932).

FEILER, Arthur, "The Consumer in Economic Policy," *Social Research*, Vol. I, No. 3 (New York, August, 1934).

HAMILTON, Walton H., "The Ancient Maxim *Caveat Emptor*," *Yale Law Journal*, Vol. XL (New Haven, Connecticut, June, 1931).

REDLICH, Fritz, "Wandlungen in der Absatzorganisation," *Jahrbücher für Nationalökonomie und Statstik* (Jena, 1932).

"The Ultimate Consumer," *Annals of the American Academy of Political and Social Science* (Philadelphia, Pennsylvania, May, 1934).

PERIODICALS

CONSUMER'S COÖPERATION (formerly *Coöperation*, 1924–35), Coöperative League of the United States of America (New York, 1935–date).

COÖPERATIVE REVIEW, Coöperative Union, Limited (Manchester, England, 1926–date).

MONTHLY LABOR REVIEW, United States Department of Labor, Bureau of Labor Statistics (Washington, D. C., 1926–date).

REVIEW OF INTERNATIONAL COÖPERATION, International Coöperative Alliance (London, 1920–date).

REPORTS

COÖPERATIVE LEAGUE OF THE UNITED STATES OF AMERICA, *Annual Congress Reports* (New York, 1930–date).

COÖPERATIVE UNION, LIMITED, *Annual Coöperative Congress Reports* (Manchester, England, 1885, 1892, 1900–date).

COÖPERATIVE WHOLESALE SOCIETY, LIMITED, *C.W.S. Annual* (Manchester, England, 1908–date).

FEDERAL FARM BOARD,
Bulletin No. 6, *Coöperation in Agriculture* (Washington, D. C., March, 1931).
— No. 9, *Statistics of Farmers' Selling and Buying Organizations* (Washington, D. C., June, 1932).
— No. 10, *Coöperative Marketing of Farm Products* (Washington, D. C., 1932).

GREAT BRITAIN, Parliamentary Papers, Royal Commission on Labour, *Sessional Reports, Précis of Evidence,* Vol. XXXIX (London, August, 1893).

INTERNATIONAL LABOUR OFFICE, *Results of Certain of the Enquiries for Instituting a Comparison Between the Retail Prices in Private Trade and Those of Distributive Coöperative Societies,* International Economics Conference (Geneva, Switzerland, May, 1927).

PALESTINE ECONOMIC CORPORATION, *Annual Reports* (New York).

UNITED STATES DEPARTMENT OF LABOR, Bureau of Labor Statistics, Bulletin No. 313, *Consumers' Coöperative Societies in the United States in 1920..*

— No. 314, *Coöperative Credit Societies (Credit Unions) in America and in Foreign Countries* (Washington, D. C., 1922).

— No. 437, *Coöperative Movement in the United States in 1925 (Other than Agricultural).*

— No. 531, *Consumers' Credit and Productive Societies* (Washington, D. C., 1929).

— No. 598, *Organization and Management of Consumers' Coöperative Associations and Clubs (With Model By-Laws)* (Washington, D. C., 1934).

— No. 612, *Consumers', Credit and Productive Coöperation in 1933* (Washington, D. C., 1935).

MIMEOGRAPHS

CENTROSOYUS (Central Coöperative Wholesale Society, Moscow, U.S.S.R.),

Work of the Coöperative Societies in the U.S.S.R.

Cultural Work of the Soviet Trade Unions (May, 1935).

Social Insurance in the U.S.S.R.

Wages.

GENERAL FEDERATION OF JEWISH LABOUR IN ERETZ-ISRAEL,

The Labour Coöperative Movement in Palestine (Tel-Aviv, Palestine, 1935).

APPENDIX II

DATA FOR THOSE INTERESTED IN ORGANIZING COÖPERATIVES

It is estimated that there are today some 3,000,000 Americans who are members of one sort of coöperative organization or another. The 3,000,000 are divided into 2,000 farmer supply associations, 2,500 societies for the distribution of petroleum products, 200 societies for the distribution of electricity, for medical care, for burial and so forth; 4,000 coöperative banks; 2,000 coöperative insurance companies, 750 urban distributive societies with stores, bakeries, restaurants, housing, and the like. These associations have an annual business turnover of about $400,000,000.

Most of the societies are members both of wholesale societies and of district leagues. The wholesale societies are buying, selling and manufacturing confederations; the leagues are unions of societies for purposes of education and propaganda. Practically all of them are affiliated with the Coöperative League of the United States of America, with headquarters at 167 West 12th Street, New York.

Subjoined is the official list of wholesale societies and of the district leagues which are members of the Coöperative League:

District Leagues

California Coöperative Council, 1615 West 9th Street, Los Angeles. Northern Division, Box 307, Berkeley, California

Central States Coöperative League, 3954 West 27th Street, Chicago, Illinois

Eastern States Coöperative League, 112 East 19th Street, New York

National Coöperative Women's Guild, Box 1000, Superior, Wisconsin

Northern States Coöperative League, Sexton Building, Minneapolis, Minnesota

Affiliated Coöperative Wholesales

Central Coöperative Wholesale, Superior, Wisconsin
Consumers' Coöperative Association, No. Kansas City, Missouri
Consumers' Coöperatives Associated, Amarillo, Texas
Consumers' Coöperative Services, 433 West 21st Street, New York
Coöperative Distributors, 30 Irving Place, New York
Eastern Coöperative Wholesale, 112 East 19th Street, New York
Eastern States Farmers' Exchange, Springfield, Massachusetts
Farm Bureau Mutual Automobile Insurance Company, Columbus, Ohio
Farm Bureau Services, Lansing, Michigan
Farmers' Union Central Exchange, St. Paul, Minnesota
Franklin Coöperative Creamery Association, Minneapolis, Minnesota
Grange Coöperative Wholesale, Seattle, Washington
Indiana Farm Bureau Coöperative Association, Indianapolis, Indiana
Midland Coöperative Wholesale, Minneapolis, Minnesota
Ohio Farm Bureau Service Company, Columbus, Ohio
Pacific Supply Coöperative, Walla Walla, Washington
Pennsylvania Farm Bureau Coöperative Association, Harrisburg, Pennsylvania
Recreation Coöperative, Inc., Delaware, Ohio
Workmen's Mutual Fire Insurance Society, 277 East 84th Street, New York

Readers desiring information on how to form coöperatives or any other matter concerning coöperative theory and practice should write to the office of the district league nearest their home town, or to the office of the national league.

All coöperative societies, whether local, regional or national, have printed matter describing how to organize and manage consumer societies, buying clubs, etc., which they gladly supply on request. The Bureau of Labor Statistics of the United States Department of Labor has published a bulletin describing the organization and management of coöperatives of all forms. This is Bulletin No. 598. Its title is *Organization and Management of Consumers' Coöperative Associations and Clubs* (*With Model By-Laws*). It may be secured for the price of ten cents by writing to the Superintendent of Documents, Washington, D. C., or from the Coöperative League.

Wherever practicable, the societies and leagues provide also expert personal advice and guidance. The first step in the organization of a new coöperative society should always be to avail oneself of these helps.

The same rule should be followed by those desiring to organize credit unions. They should write to the Credit Union National Association, Raiffeisen House, Madison, Wisconsin. This is the national organization of credit unions. It furnishes information and advice free of charge.

Its latest publication on credit unions is *Cuna Emerges, a Third Credit Union Book*. The author is Roy F. Bergengren, the executive secretary of the American credit union movement from the start. Chapter V deals with "Organization Procedure."

Cuna Emerges may be supplemented with *A Credit Union Primer* by Arthur H. Ham and Leonard G. Robinson, revised, 1930, by Rolf Nugent. This is a publication of the Russell Sage Foundation, New York. The chapter entitled "Questions and Answers" deals with the organization of credit unions.

APPENDIX III

SUPPLEMENTARY NOTE FROM MR. SIDNEY WEBB

In the course of the preparation of this book, I wrote to Sidney Webb for permission to quote from a letter of his to me the sentences printed on page 183 concerning the record of producers as self-managers.

Together with his permission, Mr. Webb was good enough to send a supplementary note which he begged might be added to the sentences quoted from his letter. Unfortunately, the note came too late for incorporation on page 183. The book was already in pages. But I am happy to add it as an appendix.

To me, it is a further confirmation of my analysis of consumer-producer relations. I am not so sanguine as Mr. Webb that the Russian government's "desire to increase the efficiency of the management will be any better satisfied by making the coöperative store a tail to the trades-union kite than by coöperative autonomy. The record, as the reader of this book must be aware, points the other way. But the government of Russia is dominated by the producer ideology, and what is involved in its policy here is the will to impose and maintain with the police power of totalitarian state, the primacy of the producer, and to subdue consumption to the service of production. On its record, the Soviet government can hardly be said to regard its citizens as consumers first. Its ruling passion has been, and continues to be, production; its personality image, the producer.

Mr. Webb's note follows:

Reading these words again, after our study of the social institutions of the U.S.S.R. (which we describe in our *Soviet Communism: A New Civilization?*), I feel only confirmation of the view stated several years ago. But it is only fair to add that, in contrast with all capitalist communities, the Soviet Union has enormously enlarged the sphere of Trade Unionism in every feature except that of management. It is interesting to see that the greater part of this enlargement of Trade Union activity has taken place in the sphere in which the Trade Union members are concerned not as producers but as consumers (such, for instance, as the provision of clubs, educational classes, dwellings, holiday homes, etc.). One of these developments of Trade Union function is particularly noteworthy in this connection. Those consumers' Coöperative Societies, which had been developed among the workers employed in many large factories, were presently (in 1930–2) definitely limited to such workers, and then (in 1934) completely transferred from the consumers' coöperative movement to the Trade Union Movement. Management and direction of these coöperative stores were thus taken away from the coöperative hierarchy of committees and handed over to the hierarchy of committees of the Trade Unions to which the members belonged. The motive for this change was a desire to increase the efficiency of the management. But it will be noted that this apparent contradiction of our thesis was, in reality, a confirmation of it. The committees of Trade Union members to which the coöperative store was transferred were not the producers of the commodities which they supplied to themselves. They were, it is true, producers, but producers of *other things* in their factory day. They now manage the coöperative store as representatives of themselves and their mates as consumers.

What we also learned in the U.S.S.R. was that Coöperative Productive Societies (self-governing partnerships of producers), which, we think, have seldom been able to make any considerable or durable progress in the capitalist countries, have, as cartels, within limits, proved very successful in the essentially collectivist environment of the Soviet Union: *where, however, they operate under the careful supervision and control of the Soviet Government, as representing the community of citizen consumers.*

SIDNEY WEBB

4 July, 1936

INDEX

(1)